The Hardball Times Baseball Annual 2012

Featuring contributions by THT's staff writers:

Lucas Apostoleris • Richard Barbieri • Brian Borawski

Brian Cartwright • Sam Hendrickson

Brandon Isleib • Chris Jaffe • Brad Johnson

Mat Kovach • Max Marchi • Jeff Moore

Harry Pavlidis • Dave Studenmund

Steve Treder • Tuck • David Wade • Josh Weinstock

With additional contributions by guest writers:

Rob Neyer • John Dewan • Craig Calcaterra

Matt Swartz • Michael Humphreys

Jack Marshall • David Golebiewski

James Holzhauer • Frank Jackson

Jon Daly • Adam Dorhauer

Produced by Dave Studenmund

**Edited by Joe Distelheim, Greg Simons
and Carolina Bolado Hale**

The Hardball Times Baseball Annual 2012

New articles daily at www.hardballtimes.com

Edited by Joe Distelheim, Greg Simons and Carolina Bolado Hale
Stats developed by FanGraphs and Dave Studenmund
Cover design by Tom Wright
Typesetting by Dave Studenmund

Published by: ACTA Sports
                  4848 North Clark Street
                  Chicago, IL 60640
                  1-800-397-2282
                  info@actasports.com
                  www.actasports.com

ISBN: 978-0-87946-474-5
ISSN: 1940-4484
Printed in the United States of America by McNaughton & Gunn, Inc.
Year: 13 12 11
Printing: 5 4 3 2 First

What's Inside

The 2011 Season

The American League East View................................. 11
by Lucas Apostoleris
The American League Central View 22
by Mat Kovach and Lucas Apostoleris
The American League West View............................... 32
by David Wade and Harry Pavlidis
The National League East View 41
by Brad Johnson and Harry Pavlidis
The National League Central View 51
by Harry Pavlidis
The National League West View 59
by Steve Treder and Josh Weinstock

Commentary

The Preseason in Frivolity 71
by Craig Calcaterra
In All Probability 74
by Dave Studenmund
Quantifying Excitement... 88
by Sam Hendrickson
The Braves, the BoSox, and
September Schadenfreude 93
by Steve Treder
GM in a Box: Theo Epstein 103
by Rob Neyer
Mike Stanton: Future Home Run King? 111
by David Golebiewski
The Annotated Year in Baseball History..................... 121
by Richard Barbieri
The Business of Baseball.. 127
by Brian Borawski
Ethics and Major League Baseball, 2011 136
by Jack Marshall
Diary of a Mad Sports Bettor 147
by James Holzhauer

History

Slow and Quick Hooks 159
by Chris Jaffe
Hank Thompson, Beyond the Trivia 169
by Frank Jackson
A Legacy of Mixed Feelings 179
by David Wade

Analysis

History's Greatest Hitters 193
by Adam Dorhauer
Down with Other People's Players 207
by Matt Swartz
People Will Most Definitely Come 221
by Max Marchi
Simple Fielding Runs Estimates 235
by Michael A. Humphreys
What Ground Balls Can Tell Us about Fly Balls 249
by Brian Cartwright
Separating the Pitching from the Fielding 255
by John Dewan

Statistics and Such

Quirky Baseball Stats 265
Glossary 299
Who Was That? 301

Welcome to Our Book

Hello, rabid baseball fan. You're in good company. This book is the work of a bunch of rabid baseball fans just like you, people who are obsessed about the National Pastime and love to think and write about it—every figurative angle and carom we can think of. The outlet we use is called The Hardball Times.

The Hardball Times started as a website in 2004 and we've grown into a vast media empire in the intervening years. No, not really, but we do publish books and we also sell a service on our site called **THT Forecasts**, which you'll love if you sometimes wonder how specific players will perform in the next couple of years. We don't just cover major leaguers in our forecasts, by the way. Our database includes virtually all minor leaguers as well as players from Japan and other far-off places. Come by and check it out at www.hardballtimes.com.

Let's talk about this book. This is the eighth edition of the *Hardball Times Annual* and we're very proud of every one. But we've changed the book format this year to make it more focused, readable and interesting. In the past, the Annual was bigger, 8 ½ by 11 inches, with lots of stats and graphs in the back. It had kept growing, too, from 300 pages in 2004 to 360 pages last year.

Every page was awesome, of course, but our readers started to tell us that it had gotten too big. They wanted something that would be easier to carry, read on the train … that sort of thing. We also know that, in this world of up-to-date, detailed baseball stats on the World Wide Web, iPhone and tablet, our voluminous stats weren't really that critical to our readers.

Yes, people buy the Hardball Times Annual for the articles. And articles are what we've still got. They're split into four sections.

First is a review of the 2011 season, broken out by division. There are two new features this year:

- A "PITCHf/x focus" for each division. These use the amazing PITCHf/x technology from Sportvision (the people who run the Gameday application on MLB Gameday) to pick apart pitch types, locations, swings and misses, etc. Our PITCHf/x experts have honed in on some of the more intriguing player developments in each division.

- Minor league system reviews by our minor league expert, Jeff Moore. You'll find these in the margins of each division review. In fact, we couldn't fit all of Jeff's outstanding writing in all of the margins, so we're making his entire text available for you to download from a special webpage. More about that in a minute.

Fun with Other Numbers

The Brewers, Rangers and Rays made for an intriguing playoff trio for an odd reason: they're the three teams never to have won at least 100 games over any 162-game stretch.

Not that they haven't come close. The Rays went 99-63 over several overlapping stretches from September 2009 to September 2010. The Rangers went 98-64 from June 29, 1977 to June 25, 1978 and again from Aug. 26, 1998 to Aug. 29, 1999. The Brewers had a 98-64 run as well, from mid-May 1978 to mid-May 1979. But each has a real chance of joining the other 27 franchises in having a 100-win stretch over a full season.

After July 24 this year, the Brewers were 42-17 (.711 percentage), so they'd need to start 2012 at 58-45 (.563) to get to 100 wins. The Rangers were 52-25 (.675) after July 3 and would need to start 48-37 (.564). The Rays are a harder case, as they didn't get hot until late. Still, they were 37-21 (.638) after July 27 and could ease up on that pace next year, getting to 100 wins off a 63-41 (.605) start. So the last three teams outside the triple-digit club can all play worse than their playoff versions and get in next year.

Commentary on the past season, including:

- Craig Calcaterra's "Year in Frivolity," which begins in spring training as an article and then continues for the year in the other article margins.
- A THT Annual tradition: GM in a Box, which is an in-depth look at a major league general manager. This year, Rob Neyer writes about someone who's been in the news lately, Theo Epstein.
- Diary of a Mad Sports Bettor, James Holzhauer's entertaining and enlightening reminiscence of his years betting on baseball.

History, such as a meditation on the life of Hank Thompson, one of the first black major leaguers.

Analysis, where our premier number crunchers investigate things such as:

- History's greatest hitters at their peak
- Which were the best fielding teams last year
- Whether teams know their own players best when they sign them as free agents or trade them away.

And, just because we couldn't help ourselves, there is a small section of statistics in the very back. These statistical tables comprise a unique statistical view of individual players by combining a few "value" stats and "story" stats.

We've also created a special webpage for you, where you can download extra articles and stats. The URL is http://www.hardballtimes.com/THT2012Annual/ (mind those capitals), the username is "tht12" and the password is "andrus".

All of our articles and stats are intended to accompany our "double play" book partner, the *Bill James Handbook 2011,* a complete statistical reference for the 2011 season. Be sure to check it out as well.

Unfortunately, we had to send our manuscript to the printer before the conclusion of the World Series, so you won't find anything here about postseason play. For postseason coverage, check out our webiste.

In addition to Jeff and Craig, Jon Daly and Brandon Isleib provided valuable fodder for the margins of each article, and they deserve some applause too. Also, you'll find several "toons" scattered throughout the book, contributed by our own Tuck! Yes, he puts an exclamation point at the end of his name.

The Hardball Times and, particularly this Annual, wouldn't exist without the support of a lot of people. David Appelman of FanGraphs (www.FanGraphs.com) supplies our stats, which are compiled by Baseball Info

Solutions. Sportvision and TruMedia Networks (http://www.baseballa-nalytics.org/) have also supplied stats and graphics for the Annual.

We have many friends on the Internet. Thank you all, and a special tip of the hat to Tom Tango, who has been a big supporter of THT for a long time. If you don't have his book, *The Book: Playing the Percentages in Baseball*, run out and get it right now.

Our publisher, ACTA Sports, has been supportive every step of the way. Our editors, Joe Distelheim, Greg Simons and Carolina Bolado Hale, worked diligently to edit all of the text you see in here. My thanks to each and everyone of you.

May first base rise up to meet you. May the wind be always at your back at bat. May the sun shine in the eyes of that outfielder trying to catch your pop fly.

May you enjoy our book.

Happy Baseball,
Dave Studenmund

Other factoids about 162-game stretches:

The best record is 127-32-2—an astounding .799—from the 1906-07 Cubs, achieved in six different overlapping stretches from June to June. The Yankees have the second-best record: 124-38 (.765) from May 30, 1927 to June 9, 1928.

Aside from the three discussed teams, the Padres, Blue Jays, Nationals, Marlins and Rockies lack 100 wins in any single season, but each team has a 162-game streak of at least 100 wins. The Padres were 101-61 from August to August in 1997-8, the Blue Jays went 101-61 from September to September in 1984-5, the strike-obscured Expos were 110-52 from Aug. 19, 1993 to May 3, 1995, the Marlins went 100-62 in the first Jack McKeon era (late May 2003 to late May 2004), and the Rockies have exactly one 100-62 streak: June 4, 2009 to June 1, 2010.

- Brandon Isleib

The 2011 Season

The American League East View

by Lucas Apostoleris

Play Against Other Divisions

Division	W	L	Win%
AL Central	104	82	.559
AL West	94	80	.540
NL East	14	16	.467
NL Central	33	21	.611
NL West	3	3	.500
Total	248	202	.551

Head-to-Head Records

Team	BAL	BOS	NYY	TBR	TOR	Total
BAL		8	5	9	6	28
BOS	10		12	6	10	38
NYY	13	6		9	11	39
TBR	9	12	9		12	42
TOR	12	8	7	6		33
Total	44	34	33	30	39	180

Read wins from left, losses from top

The recent success of
the Rays at the major
league level is due in
large part to the success
of their farm system
and player development.
While the major league
roster has raided the
farm system of its top
talent over the past year
or two, the organization
has restocked due to
back-to-back drafts with
multiple early picks. After
having six of the first 100
picks in 2010, the Rays
doubled up and had 12
of the first 100 in 2011,
infusing the farm system
with high-end talent,
the majority of whom
signed early and got
experience right away.

2012 is a make or break
year for...Tim Beckham

Beckham actually had
his best year as a professional in 2011, giving the
Rays hope that they didn't
crash and burn with their
No. 1 overall pick. Unfortunately, Beckham's best
career year produced only
a .271/.328/.408 line, with
42 walks to 120 strike-
outs. On the plus side,
his power potential finally
translated to something
on the field, and did so
even more in 111 Triple-A
at-bats. Beckham's resur-
gence, of sorts, in 2011
took him from bust to still
having potential, but he
will have to back it up in
2012, and will need to do
more than just match it.
He will have to continue
to improve if the Rays

We're used to seeing the AL East be a strong division due to the success of the Yankees and Red Sox. From 2003 to 2010, the two teams combined to reach the postseason 12 times. And 2008 introduced us to the rejuvenated, re-named Tampa Bay Rays, who surprised the baseball world by winning the AL championship after failing to reach .500 in any year since their 1998 entrance into the majors.

This year, after a magical comeback in which they gained nine games on the Red Sox in the final month of the season (the largest September comeback in major league history), the Rays claimed the Wild Card spot for themselves, winning second place behind the league-best Yankees and leaving the Red Sox with nothing.

The final month of the 2011 regular season was an exciting (and, for Boston, depressing) one. Considering the Rays were the ones to steal the headlines (the positive ones, that is), we'll begin our look at the AL East with the surprise club from the southeast.

Rebounding in Tampa

To get a feel for the Rays' story, it's important to flash back a year. In 2010, they won 96 times, besting the Yankees by one game for the AL East title as well as the American League's best record. After the Rays' first-round exit to the Texas Rangers, however, they had trouble on their hands. With their payroll ceiling, there was no chance that they could re-sign bullpen stalwarts Rafael Soriano and Joaquin Benoit, and they had to decide what to do about two key free agents, outfielder Carl Crawford and power-hitting first baseman Carlos Pena.

As it turned out, the Rays signed none of them. Benoit and Soriano signed three-year deals with the Tigers and Yankees respectively. Crawford signed with Boston for a hefty seven-year contract (more about him later on). Pena took a one-year deal with the Cubs. Also going to the Cubs was third starter Matt Garza, who was traded in December for three minor leaguers.

So, going into 2011 after losing all of these players, the Rays' chances looked questionable.

They lost eight of their first 10 games, but picked it up and had a share of the AL East lead for a week in the middle of May. Both the Yankees and Red Sox turned on the motors for the summer, leaving the Rays in third place, but still within striking distance for the next four months.

A big part of what kept them afloat was their starting rotation. James Shields, David Price, Jeff Niemann and Wade Davis had all been mainstays in 2010, and the first three appeared to make strides in 2011: Shields lowered his ERA by more than two runs, mostly due to getting some extra ground balls and allowing fewer home runs. Price shaved just less than one free pass per nine innings off of his 2010 total while picking up some more strikeouts. Niemann lowered his rate by about half a free pass per nine. Rookie Jeremy Hellickson joined the rotation and finished with an unspectacular strikeout/walk ratio under two, but ultimately had an ERA under three.

The Tampa bullpen was not as impressive as the rotation, but featured an effective late-end combo of 35-year-old acquisitions Joel Peralta and Kyle Farnsworth. Peralta primarily assumed setup duties. Farnsworth, notoriously wild, had what might have been his best season: While striking out eight per nine innings, he cut his walks to a career low (2.2, if you include hit by pitches and exclude intentional walks) and increased his groundball rate to more than 50 percent; his career average is around 40 percent. The two certainly did a nice job as the 2011 edition of Benoit and Soriano.

As for the offense, it held its own. Even in a down year, third baseman Evan Longoria was the star performer, hitting 31 home runs with an average/on-base/slugging triple slash of .244/.355/.495. First baseman Casey Kotchman, super-utility player Ben Zobrist and outfielder Matt Joyce also posted OPS marks at or above .800.

With their backs against the wall in their last series of the season, against the Yankees, the Rays mounted two late-inning comebacks in must-win situations. The most dramatic was their 14-inning victory on the final day of the season after being down 7-0 as late as the eighth inning. This game clinched the Wild Card for Tampa, as Boston blew a ninth-inning lead against Baltimore at the same time that the Rays walked off with their win.

The Rays might not have had the best-looking team on paper, but they made their runs count at the end of the season. They also reminded us that with a strong core of players and some small offseason pickups, player turnover isn't the end of the world.

In New York, Business as Usual

After losing in the 2010 ALCS to the Texas Rangers, the Yankees had some questions to address, primarily in their starting rotation. Three spots were locked up for CC Sabathia, A.J. Burnett, and Phil Hughes, all under team control and not going anywhere. This left two open spots, which the Yankees awarded in the last week of March to rookie Ivan Nova, who had spent some time with the team in 2010, and veteran Freddy Garcia, who was signed over the offseason.

However, after an April arm injury to Hughes that affected his velocity and landed him on the disabled list until July, the Yankees needed to find hope to get anything near what they expected out of a No. 1 overall pick.

Prospect Outlook: New York Yankees

The Yankees' farm system remains deep enough to supplement their free agent spending. They haven't produced a starting position player since Brett Gardner took over in the outfield, but should have another one coming in Jesus Montero. On the mound is where the real depth of the organization is, with Dellin Betances and Manny Banuelos projected as key cogs in the starting rotation, possibly as soon as next season.

Prospect Riser

Pat Venditte has gone from novelty to potentially useful player as a switch-pitcher. Venditte has produced at every level, but with just fringe stuff from both sides of the rubber. It was generally assumed he would struggle at the upper levels of the minors, despite his constant platoon advantage. He wasn't nearly as dominant in his first season in Double-A, but he was still effective and managed solid strikeout and walk numbers, finally suggesting that he may one day play a role in a major league bullpen.

one more starter. They turned to another veteran, Bartolo Colon, who missed all of 2010 and hadn't had much success since 2005. Intrigued by Colon's good velocity and command, the Yankees to put him in the bullpen to start the season. His three relief appearances were all behind Hughes, and on April 22, Colon made his way into the rotation. Over 164.1 regular season innings, he would compile a K/9 of 7.4 with a BB/9 of just 2.2, making him one of the league's most pleasant surprises.

The star of the staff was Sabathia, who had possibly his best season ever. In 237.1 innings, he posted a fielding independent pitching (FIP, an ERA estimator based on walk, home run, and strikeout inputs) score of 2.88, the lowest of his career. His actual ERA of 3.00 was second best to his 2008 season with Cleveland and Milwaukee. Burnett failed to fully recover from his disastrous 2010 campaign, but the rotation as a whole did a nice job, as Nova, Garcia and Colon all provided quality innings from the middle of the rotation.

The offense clicked as well, leading the Yankees to a team OPS of .788 that was third best in the major leagues. The MVP of the lineup was center fielder Curtis Granderson, whose revamped swing helped him hit 41 home runs from the left side. Also fulfilling the power quotient were second baseman Robinson Cano (29 homers) and Mark Teixeira (39 homers). Unsurprisingly, the Yankees led the majors in home runs with 222.

The Yankees were consistent, staying in first place for 86 games over the season and never falling more than three games behind. That's not to say the season was devoid of drama. Fans at Yankee Stadium on July 9 got to witness Derek Jeter's 3,000th hit (a home run off of David Price). Jeter became the first Yankee ever to reach the milestone.

In mid-September, Mariano Rivera reached three plateaus. On Sept. 14 in Seattle against the Mariners, he became only the second pitcher to record 600 saves. In Toronto, on the 17th, he tied Trevor Hoffman for first place on the all-time list. And in his next game, on the 19th, he passed Hoffman to become the major leagues' all-time saves leader with 602.

The Yankees team wasn't too flashy, but got the job done with some surprise veteran help and remained the class of the American League.

Failing to Live Up to Promise

After failing to reach the playoffs in 2010, the Red Sox were determined to improve their squad. Just before December's Winter Meetings, they agreed to a deal with the Padres that brought superstar first baseman Adrian Gonzalez to Boston in exchange for minor league talent. Less than a week later, they signed the Rays' Crawford for $142 million over seven years.

Things didn't exactly take off as planned, though. Much like the Rays, the Sox stumbled out of the gate, going 0-6 over their first six games and 2-10 over their first 12. They, too, rebounded, and they were over .500 for good on May 15. Things started to come together, and within two weeks they had reached first place for the first time. For the next four months, they would flip-flop with the Yankees for the best record in both the division and the league.

Once the Sox hit their stride, they were a dynamic force. A lot of this had to do with their offense, which at the end of the year led the major leagues in OPS at .810. Center fielder Jacoby Ellsbury set the tone as the leadoff hitter; his breakout season consisted of 32 home runs and a .321/.376/.552 overall slash line. Gonzalez (.957) and David Ortiz (.953) also contributed OPS marks over .900, making the Sox the only American League team with three regular players over .900 in OPS.

There was more tumult on the pitching side, however. Josh Beckett, rebounding nicely from his poor 2010 season, and Jon Lester formed a strong one-two punch at the top of the rotation, but beyond that was in question all year long. Out of spring training, it was expected to be Clay Buchholz, John Lackey and Daisuke Matsuzaka filling out the rest, but season-ending injuries to Buchholz's back and Matsuzaka's elbow cut their seasons in June and May, respectively.

Due to these injuries, the Sox had to insert Andrew Miller and Tim Wakefield into the rotation; neither had much success. On top of that, Lackey had a very tough go of it; his 6.41 ERA was the highest in Red Sox history for a full-time starting pitcher. The only part of the pitching staff that was a lock (for most of the year, that is) was the eighth-ninth inning combination of Daniel Bard and Jonathan Papelbon.

On Aug. 30, the Red Sox were flying high; they had 82 wins and were leading the AL East by two games going into a three-game series with the Yankees at Fenway. They wound up losing two out of three in that series, and by Sept. 2, their grip on first place was gone for good. From this point, the wheels began to fall off. Their pitching, already suspect, imploded from Aug. 30 to the end of the season, allowing 182 runs over 261.2 innings (or 6.26 runs per nine innings). This included some meltdowns from Bard and Papelbon: Bard gave up 14 runs and nine walks in his final 11 innings, and Papelbon blew two save opportunities over the last 10 days of the season—the most crucial part of Boston's year.

The pitching struggles allowed the Rays, who had been nine games back at the beginning of the month, to sneak back into the Wild Card

Prospect Outlook: Boston Red Sox

Despite trading away three of their top 10 prospects to land Adrian Gonzalez, the Red Sox still have as deep a farm system as any organization in baseball. This is due to their ability to restock year after year through the draft by taking chances on risky players and overpaying later in the draft. Anthony Ranaudo is a great example, as a player who was in the discussion for the top overall pick but dropped due to injury concerns his final year in college. The Red Sox nabbed him in the supplemental round and paid him top 10 money, a luxury few teams can afford.

Prospect Riser

After vision problems in 2010, Bryce Brentz saw the ball just fine this past season. Splitting time between both levels of A-ball, Brentz showed both average and power, blasting 30 home runs but also putting together a hit streak of over 30 games. The 22-year-old right fielder still needs to control the strike zone better, as was evidenced when he got to the Carolina League, but his power display this season makes him an intriguing prospect.

The Orioles' once-stacked farm system has been depleted due to the graduations of Zach Britton, Brian Matusz, Chris Tillman, Adam Jones, Matt Wieters and Jake Arrieta over the past three years. The restocking process hasn't gone as well as expected: The Orioles missed on their top draft pick in '09 before appearing to hit on Manny Machado in 2010, and, they hope, on Dylan Bundy in 2011. The Orioles have never spent money heavily in the international market (although they do appear to have found a gem in Jonathan Schoop), so they have to succeed in the draft.

Prospect Riser

Schoop has been bounced around the infield in deference to top prospect Manny Machado's presence at shortstop at the same levels, but it was Schoop, the 19-year-old infielder from Curacao, who was named the Orioles' minor league hitter of the year. Schoop played third base in Delmarva (alongside Machado), until Machado hurt his knee and Schoop slid over to his natural shortstop position. When both were promoted to Frederick, Schoop switched to the other side of second and manned the keystone position. All the while, Schoop hit a combined .290/.349/.432 in his first full season.

race. When it was all said and done on Sept. 28, the Red Sox had the biggest blown September lead in history, and they went home as the Rays marched on to the ALDS.

September's events completely changed the outlook for the Red Sox. Instead of heading to the postseason, the team had to deal with the departure of manager Terry Francona and then general manager Theo Epstein, who had combined to lead the team to two World Series championships over eight years.

Given their deep offensive talent, the Red Sox look to be contenders again in 2012, but in Crawford (a huge disappointment in his first Boston season with a .255/.289/.405 line), the pitching staff and the leadership situation, they have plenty of questions.

Salvaging through Spoiling?

The Orioles are not in great shape. They haven't finished at .500 or better since 1997, and the last time they won as many as 70 games was 2006. After taking over at midseason and leading the team to a 34-23 record in 2010, manager Buck Showalter was unable to build on his initial success, eventually losing 93 games in an extremely competitive division.

The offense was solid but unspectacular. They had six regulars—Mark Reynolds, J.J. Hardy, Adam Jones, Matt Wieters, Nick Markakis and Vladimir Guerrero—who were at or above league average, but not by a lot. With the middling offense and no clear superstars in the lineup, there wasn't much margin for error with their pitching and defense—and unfortunately for Baltimore, the pitching and defense were downright poor in 2011.

They were dead last in UZR and their .698 defensive efficiency (the percentage of balls in play turned into outs) was third worst. Their pitching low point was certainly second-year starter Brian Matusz, who failed to build on a strong rookie season and finished the year with a 10.69 ERA, setting a record for highest ERA by a pitcher with at least 10 starts. Defensively, Reynolds had plenty of issues, making 31 errors (26 at third base, five at first base).

An uneventful season dragged on for the Orioles, without much to get excited about. They completely fell apart during the summer months, going 20-45 from June 28 to Sept. 6. But even though they were mathematically eliminated from playoff contention by September, they were able to contribute to our playoff story. Coming off their horrible summer stretch, they finished the season on a 14-8 run, beginning with two extra-inning wins against the Yankees on Sept. 7-8. For the rest of the season, they:

- Won one of three at Toronto
- Won two of three vs. Tampa Bay
- Won two of three vs. Los Angeles
- Won three of four at Boston
- Won two of four at Detroit
- Won two of three vs. Boston

All those series, aside from the one against Toronto, were against teams headed to the postseason. Most notable was the Orioles' 5-2 September record against the Red Sox. They played a huge role in Boston's collapse, coming back from seventh-inning deficits three times. In a season hard-pressed for positives, the Orioles' say in the playoff race was where their impact was felt the most.

Featuring Joey Bats

As something of an anti-climactic end to our AL East story, we have the Toronto Blue Jays. They finished the year with an 81-81 record, and spent all but two days from May 18 onward in fourth place. Their offense overall wasn't anything special, but the middle of their order featured one of the most-feared hitters in the majors: the resurgent Jose Bautista.

Joey Bats' story has been told many times—after spending 2004-2008 as an unspectacular utility player, Bautista hit his stride with the Blue Jays at the end of 2009, when he and Jays hitting coach Dwayne Murphy revamped his swing to give him more power. The results were immediate: Bautista clubbed 10 home runs in September of 2010 and continued his tear the following year, leading the majors with 54 homers.

This past season showed that Bautista's breakout was not a fluke. Though he cooled off from his blazing start, in which he hit 20 homers before the end of May, Bautista still led the league in plenty of hitting categories: OPS (1.056), slugging percentage (.608), walks per plate appearance (20.2 percent), and home runs (43). As one of the best, if not the best, hitters in the majors, he became the focal point of the Jays line-up, which could produce only one other regular player with an on-base percentage above .335 (Yunel Escobar at .369).

In August, however, the Blue Jays got a look at top third-base prospect Brett Lawrie, who became an important part of their lineup for the last two months as he hit .293/.373/.580. He'll certainly play a big role in the Blue Jays' 2012 plans.

Prospect Outlook: Toronto Blue Jays

After years of going after big-time free agents in an attempt to keep up with the big spenders of the AL East, the Jays have revamped their organizational philosophy and worked toward rebuilding their farm system. Now their big money is going to international free agents like Cuban defector Adeiny Hechavarria and Venezuelan pitcher Adonis Cardona. They also restocked their organizational depth with trades, grabbing Brett Lawrie, Kyle Drabek and others.

2012 is a make or break year for...David Cooper

After back-to-back nondescript seasons, Cooper had a strange yet exciting 2011 season. His OPS, which had been hovering in the mid-.700s for his professional career, jumped to .974, thanks to a .364 batting average, more walks than strikeouts for the first time in his career, and 51 doubles. But now for the bad news: His batting average was inflated by a .380 BABIP, an unsustainably high number for any player, let alone a slow-footed first baseman. He hit just nine home runs, he produced these numbers in a hitting-friendly environment, and he struggled mightily in the majors. Cooper will get a chance to win a spot in Toronto next season, but he'll have to deal with less fortunate luck and prove he can sustain his strike zone control.

- Jeff Moore

Lefty Ricky Romero led the Blue Jays' pitching staff in his third big league season, maintaining an ERA under three over 225 innings. Brandon Morrow's ERA was 4.72, but on the bright side he led the American League in strikeout rate at 10.2 per nine innings.

The American League East was a fun division to watch—coming into the year, we could look forward to seeing 2010's two best AL teams and a retooled Red Sox team trying to make its way back into the race. But at the end of the year, it was the Rays who stole our hearts (well, maybe not for all of us) and pulled off one of the most exciting comebacks we've ever seen.

AL East PITCHf/x Insight

by Lucas Apostoleris

Though the Red Sox were eliminated from playoff contention in heart-breaking fashion on the final day of the regular season, there were still plenty of positives in their season. They led the majors in OPS, and their table-setter at the top of the order, Jacoby Ellsbury, was one of their key contributors.

Selected in the first round of the 2005 draft, Ellsbury showed good contact and discipline skills in the minor leagues, hitting .316 with an on-base percentage of .393 in his 259 games (including a smattering of 2010 rehab appearances). His elite speed made him No. 13 on *Baseball America's* Top 100 Prospects list in 2008.

He debuted in Boston in '07, playing an important role in the Red Sox postseason that ended in a World Series championship; his strong play in October guaranteed him a starting spot in the Red Sox outfield, and in 2008 and 2009 he was an everyday player. His 298 games over this period resulted in a triple slash line of .291/.346/.405 and a league-leading 120 stolen bases. In 2010, he suffered an April collision with third baseman Adrian Beltre and cracked four ribs. He played only 17 games that season, so Red Sox fans had no clue what to expect from Ellsbury when he returned in 2011.

What they got was a completely different and greatly improved player. Ellsbury hit for average, at .321, and reached base at a .376 clip, but he added an aspect to his game that had previously been virtually non-existent: power. Ellsbury clubbed 32 home runs in 2011, which is more than he had hit in his whole professional career up until last year.

His unusual power surge is similar to that of fellow AL East hitter Jose Bautista, who adjusted his swing with the Blue Jays' coaching staff at the end of the 2009 season and became a 40-plus home run hitter in 2010 and 2011. But with Ellsbury, there was no such swing overhaul. In a July interview with NESN, he attributed his success to being more aggressive in the strike zone. Whatever changed—whether it's mechanical, mental, physical or a combination of factors—Ellsbury was one of the best power hitters in the majors in 2011.

The chart on the next page shows Ellsbury's improvement in different areas of the strike zone. The lowest bar is for pitches low and out of Ellsbury's zone, the middle three bars are for lower third, middle third, and higher third, and the highest bar is for pitches high and out of his zone. The metric used here is slugging on contact, or the total number of bases

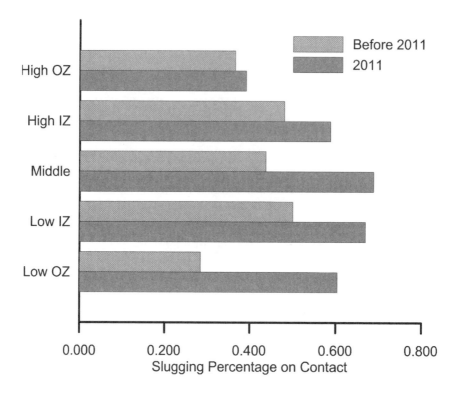

Legend: Before 2011, 2011

High OZ

High IZ

Middle

Low IZ

Low OZ

0.000   0.200   0.400   0.600   0.800

Slugging Percentage on Contact

per ball put in play; the league average slugging on contact in 2011 was .499. He's improved all around, but particularly on pitches below the bottom of the zone.

Using the same methodology but switching gears to horizontal plate locations, you can see in the graph on the next page that there's once again an overall improvement, but Ellsbury has become particularly adept at driving pitches that are away and off the plate.

Ellsbury's power surge is certainly intriguing. Whether he can keep it up is a different story—it remains to be seen if pitchers will start approaching him differently (for example, maybe by throwing more pitches up and in), and if Ellsbury will be able to adjust.

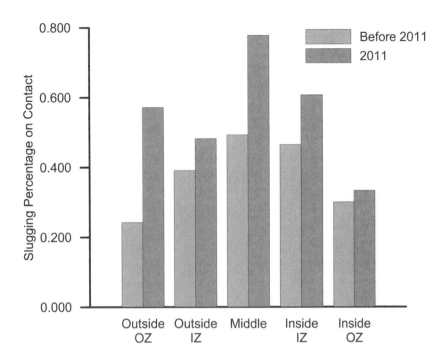

Special note on the strike zone:

The coordinates for the Ellsbury's strike zone are courtesy of former THT writer Mike Fast. Mike, now a writer for Baseball Prospectus, has been doing exhaustive research on the strike zone and was kind enough to share his findings on Ellsbury.

Resources: Statistics are from FanGraphs and Baseball Reference. PITCHf/x data originate from MLB Advanced Media and are courtesy of downloads from Joe Lefkowitz's site.

The American League Central View

by Mat Kovach

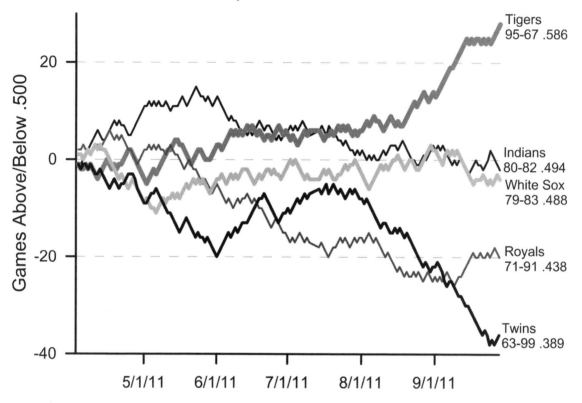

Play Against Other Divisions			
Division	W	L	Win%
AL East	82	104	.441
AL West	84	90	.483
NL East	2	4	.333
NL Central	19	14	.576
NL West	21	30	.412
Total	388	422	.479

Head-to-Head Records						
Team	CHW	CLE	DET	KCR	MIN	Total
CHW		11	5	7	9	32
CLE	7		6	12	11	36
DET	13	12		11	14	50
KCR	11	6	7		8	32
MIN	9	7	4	10		30
Total	40	36	22	40	42	180

Read wins from left, losses from top

Every team had its moment in the AL Central. The division featured a hot start by Cleveland and Kansas City, which were first and second in the standings for much of the spring. The Tigers clawed their way to the top of the standings in late June, though the Indians hung around until the middle of August. In late July fans were even teased with a four-way fight among the Tigers, Indians, White Sox and Twins.

The Tigers Took the Title

In mid-August, however, the Tigers moved away from the AL Central pack. The Tigers were the only team to finish with a positive run differential (787 runs scored and 711 allowed), but the big story in the division was one guy, Justin Verlander. Verlander pitched a no-hitter and topped the AL in wins, strikeouts and ERA. At about the mid-point of his 12-game winning streak, Verlander stopped fighting for just the AL Cy Young award and became a legitimate contender for the AL MVP award.

Lost in the Tigers' great year was the strength of their offense. While Verlander shined and midseason acquisition Doug Fister became the No. 2 starter, the pitching staff was 18th in the majors in ERA. The offense, on the other hand, was fourth in runs, OBP and slugging percentage, and third in batting average.

Victor Martinez and Miguel Cabrera were the Tigers' best-known bats, but others did their share. Shortstop Jhonny Peralta slimmed down a bit and revitalized his career with a solid year. Catcher Alex Avila shook off a bad 2010 to take over behind the plate while providing enough offense to join Peralta, Jose Valverde, Verlander and Cabrera at the All-Star game.

The Tigers were also helped by some effective midseason trades, picking up not only Fister, but also Delmon Young and Wilson Betemit. Fister boosted the starting rotation, while Young provided some late-season offense. Betemit helped fill an offensive hole at third base for the Tigers. While these in-season moves were generally off the radar and not the exciting trades that some teams made, the Tigers proved crafty in filling holes and giving themselves options.

The Tigers' bullpen was pretty effective, what with Joaquin Benoit's 29 holds and Jose Valverde's 49-49 record in saves. Of the six pitchers who appeared in 30 or more games, only Ryan Perry had a strikeout-per-nine inning ratio under 8.00. The Tigers had a bunch of outstanding offensive players, but fielding was an issue for them at times. Keeping the ball out of their hands was one for the best features of this bullpen.

Detroit relied on a rotation of Verlander, Max Scherzer, Rick Porcello, Brad Penny and Phil Coke. Coke's less-than-stellar performance got him moved back to the bullpen when Fister came over from Seattle. Brad

Prospect Outlook: Detroit Tigers

What the Tigers may lack in depth, they make up for in high-end talent. Jacob Turner will join the Tigers' stable of young pitchers in the majors at some point in 2012, and Drew Smyly and Andy Oliver won't be too far behind. At the plate, Nick Castellanos and Francisco Martinez give the Tigers a chance to replace some of their aging veteran hitters in a few years.

Prospect Riser

The Tigers liked what they had in Drew Smyly coming into the 2011 season, but had yet to see it in action. They saw it this past year, and have to be thrilled with the results. Smyly posted a 2.07 ERA, splitting time between High-A and Double-A. He actually got better against tougher competition, striking out over an extra batter and a half per nine innings in Double-A. The lefty could start the year back in Erie next season, but should make his way at least to Triple-A by the end of 2012.

Prospect Outlook: Cleveland Indians

The Indians' farm system has been significantly depleted by the combination of promotions to the majors (Lonnie Chisenhall and Jason Kipnis) and midseason trades (Alex White and Drew Pomeranz). Those are good reasons for the cupboard to be bare, since Chisenhall and Kipnis are contributors in Cleveland and White and Pomeranz returned Ubaldo Jimenez, but that leaves little on the way for the immediate future.

Prospect Riser

Tony Wolters did a nice job as a young player in the New York-Penn league in 2011, controlling the strike zone and hitting for average. The 19-year-old shortstop didn't display much power, but his is more of a speed game, and he showed that he embraces that quality on the field. He should be set for full-season ball next year and as long as he continues to hit around .300 he will prove to be a valuable player.

Penny ate up innings and provided some stability to the back end of the rotation.

The Tigers have some decisions to make during this offseason. They have a stable middle-of-the-order core of offensive players. While Austin Jackson does a good job of covering ground in center, the Tigers survive defensively by having pitchers who strike out batters. Valverde has a club option for next year. Carlos Guillen, Magglio Ordonez, Penny, Betemit and Ramon Santiago are free agents.

Surprisingly Good Early

The Indians had a wildly inconsistent year. They started with a 30-15 record, playing much better than they actually were. They spent the latter part of the year playing worse than they actually were.

The Indians managed to be an average offensive team, despite having a large number of players miss significant time to injury. Grady Sizemore played in only 71 games, Shin-Soo Choo 85, and Travis Hafner 94. This was an offense in which Shelly Duncan was the best right-handed batter. Youngsters Jason Kipnis and Lonnie Chisenhall were give the opportunity to play every day, but only Asdrubal Cabrera and Carlos Santana provided consistently excellent offense.

On the pitching side, the Indians were 23rd in ERA. While the bullpen was pretty successful, Cleveland had only two relievers who appeared in 30 or more games and had a K/9 ratio above 8.00. This inability to miss bats was part of the reason for inconsistency in the bullpen. Closer Chris Perez made the All-Star game, joining Cabrera, but as his outfielders (Choo, Michael Brantley, Sizemore) went down, he wasn't as effective.

The Indians' starting rotation featured Justin Masterson becoming a real workhore, logging 215 innings as a starter and keeping his ERA under 3.50, mainly because he gave up only 11 home runs. After that, Fausto Carmona was inconsistent in his 32 starts, but would show flashes of his 2007 self. If Josh Tomlin were left-handed, he would be talked about more often. But, and this became a theme for the Indians, he was sidelined by an injury.

To bolster its rotation, Cleveland made a midseason trade. In exchange for four pitchers, including their last two No. 1 draft picks, the Indians got Ubaldo Jimenez from the Rockies. Jimenez had an ERA of 5.10 for the Indians, flashing some brilliance, but was very inconsistent. The Indians feel that they now have a proven major league ace under a reasonable contract for the next few years. The move, by new Indians GM Chris Antonetti, is a gamble, but it boosted the Indians' rotation with a pitcher who has proven he can miss major league bats.

The rest of the Indians' rotation, like the offense, was hit hard with injuries. Mitch Talbot started in the rotation, battled injuries and spent the rest of the year in the minors. Carlos Carrasco pitched well at times, but he injured his elbow and is rehabbing from Tommy John surgery. Josh Tomlin was shut down because of elbow soreness.

The Tribe's other midseason pickup, Kosuke Fokudome, was really a move to fill a hole in the outfield. The Indians also picked up old friend Jim Thome, who in 22 games hit three home runs and had an OBP of .390.

The Indians have some of the pieces to make a strong team. Their biggest issue is right-handed hitting. Matt LaPorta has been a disappointment, reminding some people of Andy Marte. Travis Hafner, while productive when healthy, is rarely healthy.

Dunn and Friends

The White Sox have shipped manager Ozzie Guillen off to Florida after one of the most head-scratching seasons in a long time. On paper, the White Sox should have been pushing the Tigers for first, not fighting with the Indians for second place.

The big piece the White Sox acquired for 2011 was DH Adam Dunn. Bad move. He hit an appalling .159 with 11 home runs and 42 RBI. Other players they brought in, such as Jake Peavy, were better, but not nearly up to the value of their contract.

Despite some early-season woes, the bullpen performed very well. Jesse Crain, Chris Sale and Matt Thornton did a good job in front of closer Sergio Santos. In fact, all four relievers had K/9 ratios about 9.00 and HR/9 ratios of 1.00 or lower.

The starting rotation of Mark Buehrle, Gavin Floyd, John Danks, Phil Humber and Peavy was average. In the end, the pitching on this team gave up fewer runs than the Tigers.

The offense was just that—offensive. Alex Rios was given 570 plate appearances and reached base 26.5 percent of the time, spending most of the year hitting third through sixth in the batting order, as did Dunn, who was given 459 plate appearances and got on about 29 percent of the time.

The White Sox needed a change from Ozzie Guillen. Yes, he did win a World Series, but he won that Series with good pitching and getting a large number of runs via the home run. Home runs were down this year for the White Sox and too many issues in the lineup were not corrected. The White Sox did not score runs this year, and the blame for that has to lay directly at the feet of the person making the lineup.

Prospect Outlook: Chicago White Sox

The White Sox have never been afraid to trade prospects for proven talent, having done so to get Jake Peavy and Edwin Jackson over the past few years. Their past three top draft picks, Gordon Beckham, Jared Mitchell and Chris Sale in 2008 through 2010 respectively, have either jumped quickly to the majors (Beckham and Sale) or been dealt injuries (Mitchell). The result of all of this is a lack of high-end talent in the White Sox system.

2012 is a make or break season for...Jared Mitchell

Jared Mitchell was well on his way when a spring training injury derailed his entire 2010 season. After a year of rehab, 2011 was the first time Mitchell got back on the field, and it showed. His baseball skills, already raw from having shared time in college with his football responsibilities, looked rusty, and at times it looked like his explosiveness might not have come completely back from injury. Mitchell hit just .222 in a full season in the Carolina League, while striking out 183 times. He will need to start showing some progress in the right direction in 2012 before the White Sox start to look in other directions.

The Future is Coming

The Royals made it exciting in Kansas City at the beginning of the year, riding in second place behind the surprising Indians. Soon, their lack of pitching led to their demise. Despite scoring the second-most runs in the AL Central, they also allowed the second-most runs.

But the Royals were not meant to compete in 2011. This was a season to see if their numerous prospects could shed the prospect label and become major league players—with perhaps a few stars in the making.

The Royals added veterans Melky Cabrera and Jeff Franceour and mixed them in with Billy Butler, Alex Gordon and rookies Eric Hosmer and Mike Moustakas to form the foundation of a nice offensive unit. While only Hosmer looks to become a real star, there are enough positives with these other players to give the team an opportunity to build and bring other prospects up slowly.

One can't really view the Royals' bullpen as an issue (see the PITCHf/x sidebar for more information). The only real problem with the Royals' bullpen was their high walk rate. But, once again, the bullpen had good K/9 rates and the walks didn't hurt much.

In the rotation, Luke Hochevar had a respectable year, pitching 198 innings and posting an ERA of 4.68. Bruce Chen was the only Royals starter to have an ERA under 4, but he missed time due to injury. Danny Duff showed some good stuff, but his inconsistency made it difficult for the 22-year-old to get major league batters out. Felipe Paulino had the second-best ERA for a starter at 4.11, while Jeff Francis and Kyle Davis were simply warm bodies.

The Royals have to be in the market for starting pitching. With Chen and Francis being free agents, only Duff, Hochevar and Paulino have potential. Aaron Crow could move to the rotation, but the Royals lack a true ace. Their offense will mature and gain experience and an upgraded rotation would do much to bolster the Royals' future.

The Twins Fell Apart

Face it, the Twins stunk up the AL Central … but were in the discussion of winning the division for a few delusional weeks. The Twins' problems were of their own making. They knew that both Joe Mauer and Justin Morneau were coming off down seasons and had injury issues. But they had no backup plan. How many home runs did the Twins get from the catching position? FOUR. What batting average? .245.

The Twins displayed the same missteps with Morneau. Though he was coming off a concussion, they had no backup plan if he couldn't make it back. He didn't and while the Twins were able to get some production from first base, they did so at the expense of other positions.

Injuries were everywhere. Only three position players played in more than 100 games: Danny Valencia, Michael Cuddyer and Ben Revere. While Cuddyer had an excellent season, Valencia and Revere could not manage to have an OPS above .700. Tsuyoshi Nishioka, signed from Japan, broke his leg at the beginning of the year. When he came back, he showed little while playing second and shortstop… and even less at the plate.

The Twins' pitching was just as bad. Francisco Liriano did throw a no-hitter, but he hit the disabled list and finished with an ERA of 5.09 while walking five batters every nine innings. Liriano was consistently mentioned in possible trades at the start of the year but the Twins chose not to trade him. Scott Baker performed well, but an August stint on the disabled list derailed his season and he came back for only two short relief stints at the end of the year. Nick Blackburn and Brian Duensing walked too many people.

Carl Pavano would have to be considered the "ace" of the staff. While he didn't walk many people (1.6 per nine) he didn't strike out many batters either. He finished with a 4.30 ERA and made all 33 of his starts. At this point in his career, Pavano has proven to be a solid back-of-the-rotation innings-eater.

Except for Glen Perkins, the Twins bullpen struggled. Both Matt Capps and Joe Nathan, back after missing last year due to Tommy John surgery, had ERAs over 4. Only Nathan and Perkins were able to strike out more than six batters per nine innings.

The Twins are in trouble. They have an injury-prone ballclub with little depth on the bench or in the minors.

The AL Central is a melting pot of different philosophies in farily similar towns. The Tigers and White Sox look more toward fixing holes by using money that is available to them. The Royals are building a terrific offensive ball club but need to prove they can build a pitching staff. The Indians, a sabermetic-oriented team, seem to be going through a small change in philosophy as they transition GMs. The Twins, seemingly as old school as you can get in the league today, appear to be lost.

Prospect Outlook: Minnesota Twins

The Twins have been active in the international free agent market lately, spending big bucks on Miguel Sano to improve their organizational depth. As for helping the big league club, however, the Twins have little on the horizon. Their top talent is still far away, and the prospects who are close are not high-end players.

2012 is a make or break year for…Aaron Hicks

Aaron Hicks' career will be far from over if he has a bad 2012, but the shine will officially be off his prospect status. After two years in the Midwest League in 2009-10, the second significantly better than the first, Hicks advanced to the Florida State League in 2011. While scouts justifiably rave about his tools at both the plate and in center field, Hicks' production was not there. His power has not developed the way most thought it would; he hit just five home runs and slugged just .368. The good news is that he walks a ton and hit a career high in doubles. The bad news is that his only good offensive season came in a repeat of Low-A ball.

- Jeff Moore

AL Central PITCHf/x Insight

by Lucas Apostoleris

The Royals are the perfect example of a team that's in the "rebuilding" stage. They're not finding much success winning games right now, but their minor league system is dynamite—coming into the 2011 season, they had nine prospects in *Baseball America's* Top 100, becoming the first team ever to do that. Four of those prospects made an impact with the '11 club: first baseman Eric Hosmer, third baseman Mike Moustakas, left-handed starter Danny Duffy and right-handed reliever Aaron Crow.

Including Crow, the Royals have a multitude of young pitchers who spent time with the big league bullpen in 2011, setting up closer Joakim Soria. Using the PITCHf/x data released by MLB Advanced Media (which gives us data on various measures including pitch velocity, movement, release point, and plate location), we can look more closely at how some of these Kansas City pitchers went about their craft in 2011.

Let's start with Crow, the American League All-Star.

Aaron Crow

After failing to sign with the Nationals in 2008, Crow was drafted by the Royals in 2009 as the 12th overall pick in the country. He's a power guy, averaging above 94 mph with both a four-seam and two-seam fastball. The two-seam fastball is thrown with more movement and picked up some ground balls (rate of 55 percent) for Crow last year. To put hitters away, he showed a nasty slider in the mid-to-high 80s that generated a swinging strike on over 50 percent of swings (see table at the end of the article for more about whiff rates).

By the end of the year, he started to mix in a curve that ranged from the mid-70s to the low-80s, but the slider is still his primary out pitch. Crow will also throw a very rare change-up. Crow has an elite-relief repertoire, with the power two-seam/slider combination that makes up a large part of his total pitches. Control might be an issue, though: He'll need to cut down on his walks per nine rate of 4.2 to make the next step.

Greg Holland

Holland was arguably the most effective Royals reliever in 2011, posting an ERA under two with a K/BB of 4.4. He arrived from the minors in the middle of May, though his first introduction to the majors was a 15-game cameo at the end of the 2010 season.

Holland throws just about as fast as Crow and features a similar set of pitches: a fastball (a straight one; Holland's repertoire consists of mostly, if not all, four-seam fastballs), a hard slider (87 mph), a change-up that he holds with a split-finger grip (86), and a curve (78). Holland's slider was even better at missing bats than Crow's; it's a pitch that he threw almost 40 percent of the time in 2011, so hitters had plenty of opportunities to miss it.

Holland looks like the whole package so far—he gets strikeouts (over 11 per nine innings), limits walks (2.6 per nine), and gets a league-average number of ground balls, helping home run prevention (0.5 per nine). However, as a word of caution, throwing a lot of sliders can be difficult on a pitcher's arm, so that is certainly something to keep an eye on for Holland.

Tim Collins

Collins is left-handed, throws from an extreme over-the-top arm angle, and gets a lot of velocity compared to other southpaw pitchers. He's one of the smallest players in the league (5-foot-7), adding to his unusual look on the mound. He throws three pitches: a four-seam fastball (92 mph), a very straight change-up (82), and a big-breaking curveball (74). Once the effect of gravity is factored out, Collins' curveball breaks downward at an average of 12 inches*. Over all of the pitchers we've analyzed with four-plus years' worth of PITCHf/x data, that's the biggest break. For context: Barry Zito, who has a notoriously big curveball, generates 10.5 inches of vertical break.

Collins is the youngest of the relievers featured here; he turned 21 last August. He posted huge strikeout numbers, averaging 13 per nine innings in his two-year minor league career. That rate has dropped quite a bit in the majors, but his strikeout rate of 8.1 per nine is still a quality mark. However, control is a significant issue for Collins: His walk rate of 6.4 per nine was the third highest among all major league relievers with at least 50 innings, and his 1.25 K/BB ratio was third lowest.

(*These values are calculated using road data only. This is in order to strip out home park bias, as some PITCHf/x camera setups lead to bad data.)

Louis Coleman

Coleman's an interesting case. A 25-year-old drafted out of college in 2009, he's posted big strikeout numbers everywhere despite a fastball that often doesn't get out of the 80s. His main weapon is a high fastball that he throws from a low three-quarters motion that borders on sidearm. Hitters haven't been able to get a good read on it, resulting in a spectacular swing-

and-miss rate. He'll also throw a sweeping high-70s slider to both lefties and righties, and a rare change-up to lefties.

There's a lot to like about Coleman; he is a strikeout pitcher who frequently misses bats. Walks and homers will be a concern: His walk rate of three and a half per nine innings isn't as dangerous as Collins', but it's on the high side even for a reliever. Also, he picks up a ground ball only about 30 percent of the time, making him extremely homer-prone; his HR/9 rate was in the 10 highest among all relievers in 2011.

Nathan Adcock

Adcock, 22, is different from the other pitchers we've looked at so far; he's the Kansas City "swingman" and has pitched multiple innings out of the pen and as a starting pitcher. He's not a power pitcher; he's a finesse/ground-ball guy who usually tops out at 91-92 mph. His full repertoire consists of a two-seam fastball (90), straighter four-seam fastball (also 90), hard change-up without much off his heater (87), and breaking pitches that vary in speed from the high-70s to the mid-80s. Adcock doesn't have spectacular strikeout (5.5/9) or walk (4.6/9) rates out of the bullpen, so his 55 percent groundball rate gives him a bit of leeway.

Everett Teaford

Finally, we have lefty Everett Teaford, the veteran of the group. He's something of a late bloomer, as 2011 was his age 27 season. After fighting adversity throughout his minor league career, things started clicking for him at Double-A Arkansas, where a move to the bullpen coincided with an increase in velocity and strikeouts.

These days, he throws a fastball that averages 91, a cutter that's usually in the mid-to-high 80s, a tight curve around 80, and some mid-80s change-ups to righties. Sometimes he'll drop down to the side with his fastball, which loses about three miles per hour but adds some tail and sink. Teaford showed solid control in his debut season, posting a walks per nine rate of 2.9 out of the bullpen. He's not a strikeout guy (4.8 per nine), so keeping the ball over the plate will be important for him. The Royals see him, like Adcock, as a swing guy; he started three games in 2010 in addition to his 23 relief appearances.

(*NOTE: All "walk" totals exclude intentional walks and include hit-by-pitches.)

Royals Rookie Relievers

Swinging Strikes per Swing, Minimum 150 Swings Against

Pitcher	Pitch Type	Whiff%	League Average Whiff%
Aaron Crow	Sinker	11%	12%
Aaron Crow	Slider	51%	33%
Greg Holland	Fastball	13%	17%
Greg Holland	Slider	58%	33%
Tim Collins	Fastball	19%	19%
Louis Coleman	Fastball	30%	17%
Louis Coleman	Slider	32%	33%
Nathan Adcock	Sinker	11%	12%

Resources: Statistics are from FanGraphs and Baseball Reference. PITCHf/x data originate from MLB Advanced Media and are courtesy of downloads from Joe Lefkowitz's site.

The American League West View

by David Wade

Play Against Other Divisions			
Division	W	L	Win%
AL East	80	94	.460
AL Central	90	84	.517
NL East	21	24	.467
NL Central	4	2	.667
NL West	14	7	.667
Total	323	325	.498

Head-to-Head Records					
Team	LAA	OAK	SEA	TEX	Total
LAA		8	12	7	27
OAK	11		9	6	26
SEA	7	10		4	21
TEX	12	13	15		40
Total	30	31	36	17	114

Read wins from left, losses from top

Just a couple of years ago, the Texas Rangers were an organization that looked like it might never win a playoff series. They had been hindered since the late 1990s by huge contracts that didn't pan out, such as those given to Alex Rodriguez and Chan Ho Park. Their owner at the time, Tom Hicks, was running up a staggering amount of debt. The organization reached its nadir when the team changed hands, via a drawn-out process, in bankruptcy court in 2010. But amidst that turmoil, the players kept playing. They won a division title in 2010, their first since 1999. They also won their first playoff series and eventually made it to the World Series before they lost to the San Francisco Giants. These days, the team that was in bankruptcy court just last year is set to control the American League West for the next few seasons.

It was Texas' Year

Texas started the 2011 season with a 9-1 record, even though the bullpen had been shuffled around as a result of some injuries to start the year. They not only struggled with late-inning pitching problems, but soon had to deal with the loss of reigning American League MVP Josh Hamilton, he of the ill-advised slide into home against the Detroit Tigers on April 12 that resulted in a fractured arm. The mounting injuries and inevitable regression dragged the team down after its hot start, ever closer to a .500 record. Hamilton eventually came back a little earlier than most had expected, and the Rangers rode his bat—along with those of new faces Mike Napoli and Adrian Beltre, combined with the usual contributions of Nelson Cruz, Ian Kinsler, and Michael Young—to position themselves into what became a two-team divisional race with the Los Angeles Angels of Anaheim.

The Rangers only led the Angels by 3.5 games going into Labor Day, but they steadily pulled away late to clinch the division. They finished the season on a 16-5 run that included a pair of four-game winning streaks as well as a six-game flourish to end the year. All told, they ranked third in the American League in runs scored with an average of 5.28 tallies per game. They also finished in the top two in the AL in batting average and home runs. Quite simply, they pounded the baseball in a hitter's ballpark.

Texas pitched pretty well, too. C.J. Wilson, Matt Harrison and Alexi Ogando formed a core that helped the team post a respectable ERA of 3.79, which was better than average in the AL despite making half their appearances in that same hitter's ballpark. They helped themselves by limiting walks, as they were fourth best in the AL in that category. Management also shored up weaker areas on the staff. The Rangers were active at the trade deadline and brought in Koji Uehara and Mike Adams

Prospect Outlook: Texas Rangers

The Rangers' constant activity in the international market, coupled with extra draft picks the past few years, has kept their farm system restocked. Despite back-to-back World Series appearances, the Rangers have been able to replenish their minor league depth and provide their major league roster with constant reinforcement. The farm system remains one of the deepest in baseball.

Prospect Riser

Jurickson Profar was already a highly-regarded prospect when he signed as an international free agent, but even the Rangers couldn't have seen an .883 OPS coming from an 18-year-old in the South Atlantic League. Profar is a good defensive shortstop, but it was his bat that impressed the most: He walked more than he struck out while driving 57 extra-base hits. Profar looks like a star in the making.

to help fill the innings before closer Neftali Feliz. Ogando, a breakout starter, seemed to tire in the second half after he had passed his previous career high in innings pitched. Subsequently, manager Ron Washington decided he could afford to move Ogando to the bullpen for the playoffs, further strengthening his options for late innings with a pitcher that had the experience and stuff to make the transition. They were simply the deepest team in their division.

The A's Never Got Going

A 10-game losing streak that ran through the beginning of June crippled Oakland's season early on. General manager Billy Beane dismissed manager Bob Geren and brought in Bob Melvin to take over. Nonetheless, Melvin inherited the A's inept offense, and the club never really contended. The A's finished 12th in the American League in runs, batting average, home runs, and on-base percentage. There were a few bright spots, as Jemile Weeks and Scott Sizemore had nice results in their first extended action in the majors, and both should be expected to contribute next season. However, they are not the kind of players that can carry such an offensively-challenged team. The A's desperately need more hitters.

On the bright side, their pitching was third in the AL in ERA despite the losses of starters Dallas Braden and Brett Anderson to injuries. Guillermo Moscoso stepped in and pitched well, turning in a 3.38 ERA and 1.094 WHIP in 128 innings pitched. Although Trevor Cahill didn't pitch as well as he did in 2010—when he finished with a 2.97 ERA—he still logged 34 starts and won't turn 24 until March. Gio Gonzalez, on the other hand, did replicate the success he saw in 2010. The left hander followed up his 2010 ERA of 3.23 with a 3.12 mark this past season, and he struck out 197 batters in 202 innings. If Gonzalez can improve his control (he walked 4.1 batters per nine innings pitched), he could turn into a staff ace—and he's only 26. Oakland was able to get a lot of innings out of Brandon McCarthy this season, and perhaps the A's can nurse Rich Harden along next year as well, should he come back.

Setback in Seattle

As bad as Oakland's offense was in 2011, Seattle's was worse. In fact, as bad as Oakland's 10-game losing streak was, Seattle's 17-game skid that took up most of July was seriously worse. The Mariners finished last in the American League in runs, hits, batting average, and on-base percentage. The one advantage Seattle had on Oakland offensively is the experience gained by three promising young players. Dustin Ackley, Justin Smoak, and Michael Carp all got at least 300 plate appearances, and none is over 25 years old. They were Seattle's best hitters.

Seattle also has a couple of good young starters who had nice seasons. Michael Pineda looked like a Rookie of the Year candidate during the first half, and while he didn't keep the pace going for the whole year, he still finished with a 3.74 ERA and 1.099 WHIP. Felix Hernandez was not up to the standard he set in 2010, when he won the AL Cy Young Award, but still threw over 230 innings with a 3.47 ERA. He left little doubt that he will be a frontline starter again next season.

The Angels Gave it their Best Shot

The Angels, well, they nearly did it again. They've dominated the American League West since 2004, winning the division five times, and once again they put themselves in contention. The Angels are becoming sort of famous for their ability to outperform expectations. But trying to constantly excel despite posting pedestrian differences between runs scored and runs allowed year in and year out is difficult, especially if management makes bad decisions. Last offseason, the Angels traded Mike Napoli (and Juan Rivera) to Toronto for Vernon Wells. This season, Wells hit 25 home runs but had a pitiful .248 OBP. Conversely, Napoli— after Toronto flipped him to Texas— hit 30 home runs with an outstanding .414 OBP. To make matters worse, the Angels owe Wells almost $75 million.

Fortunately, there have been good decisions, as well. The Angels acquired Dan Haren during the 2010 season, and he rewarded his new team with a 3.17 ERA and 1.024 WHIP in his first full year in Orange County. Ervin Santana pitched as well as he had in three years, showing the form he displayed in 2008 when he was an All-Star. But there is no doubt that Jered Weaver is the crown jewel of the rotation. He holds a club-friendly five-year, $85 million contract that starts in 2012, a deal that many analysts have complimented. Weaver has a 2.70 ERA, 1.041 WHIP, and 431 strikeouts in 460 innings pitched over the last two seasons. Those terrific starters might have factored in a three-game final series against Texas, but by the time of the match-up, the Angels had fallen too far back to make the last weekend of the regular season matter.

Looking Ahead in the West

The Rangers, despite their tenuous financial standing just a year and a half ago, are now coming off two straight World Series appearances, and their attendance in 2011 was just over a million customers higher than it was in 2008. The money is coming in, and future commitments on

---

Prospect Outlook: Seattle Mariners

The Mariners have had some high draft picks in the past few years, selecting Dustin Ackley— who already looks like a star in the making in the major leagues—and taking Danny Hultzen second overall in the 2011 draft. Unfortunately, after Hultzen there's not a lot of high-end talent, and most of the prospects near the majors have significant flaws in their game.

2012 is a make or break season for...Carlos Triunfel

Once considered a top prospect, Triunfel has not developed as the Mariners had hoped, specifically with his plate discipline and power. He's played primarily shortstop despite most opinions saying that he will eventually move off the position, but the real issue is with Triunfel's bat. After almost 2,000 minor league plate appearances, Triunfel has hit just 21 homers and sports a career .690 OPS. Heading to Triple-A, this may be one of the last opportunities for Triunfel to prove his bat is for real.

Prospect Outlook: Los Angeles Angels of Anaheim

The story of the Angels farm system begins and ends with Mike Trout. Sure they have some other talent, but Trout will be the face of the Angels' future, and his success in the majors will determine their success in the AL West for the next decade. A true game changer, Trout should get his chance to be the Angels' everyday center fielder next season, and if his performance in the minors is any indication, he'll never look back.

Prospect Riser

C.J. Cron's debut season was cut short after he was drafted 17th overall in 2011, but in the 34 games he got to play before a season-ending injury Cron was an unstoppable offensive force. The first baseman took the Pioneer League by storm, blasting 13 homers while batting .308. He'll head straight to full-season ball in 2012, probably skipping to High-A ball, and should be a fast mover if he continues to hit.

- Jeff Moore

the payroll are relatively modest. Texas has committed a little over $45 million to Hamilton, Beltre, and Young for 2012. Other than Napoli, those three were the best hitters on the team this past season and should be able to perform about as well next year. With continued organizational stability, there's little reason to believe they won't be active in the free agent market this coming offseason.

On the other hand, Oakland executives continue to claim their hands are tied until they get resolution on the future of a new stadium. They would like to move the team to San Jose, but the San Francisco Giants are blocking that proposal because they don't want to lose market share. The A's want to move because they see a new home as about the only way to fix their revenue issues. The 2011 season marked the sixth straight year the A's have finished in the bottom three in attendance among AL teams. Lest we blame it all on their 474-497 record over that time period, keep in mind that their four-year run of playoff appearances from 2000-2003 resulted in attendance figures that only made it to the middle of the pack in the league. Josh Willingham was Oakland's best hitter in 2011, and his agent says the A's have told him their stadium situation means they can't negotiate a contract to retain him. The most realistic move for the A's may center on bringing back Hideki Matsui and his .251/.321/.375 line as designated hitter and middle-of-the-order presence. If that's all they can afford, then there does not appear to be much help outside the organization coming for their terrible offense.

The Mariners' outlook is a little brighter. They have $18 million committed to Ichiro Suzuki next season, but that will be the last year of his contract. They could be active this offseason and have a young core that's affordable and under team control for the next few seasons. Hernandez makes big money, but he's worth it. Chone Figgins is overpaid and on the books for the next couple of seasons, but that shouldn't present too much of a hurdle if the team decides to go after some big free agents. With a core of Ackley, Smoak and Carp providing much-needed punch in the lineup, the right infusion of free-agent talent could help this team tremendously. Oakland can only get so much better, but Seattle has the potential to make a big turnaround for next season and beyond.

The Angels are currently in the best position, talent-wise, to stay with the Rangers. But they also have some of the worst budgetary roadblocks for next year. Wells, Torii Hunter and Bobby Abreu combine for over $50 million in salary for 2012. While Abreu and Hunter come off the books after next season, Wells is there through 2014. There are better players they have money tied up in, like Weaver, Haren and Santana, with Weaver's representing the only long-term commitment of those three. If

Kendrys Morales can return to health, he could provide an internal solution to some of their offensive problems. The Angels often turn up as a potential landing spot for big-name free agents, but they shook up their front office at the end of the season, and much will depend on the direction the new general manager will want to go. They've displayed a willingness to spend in the past, so it may just come down to actually finding the right players.

With the competition in Oakland stuck in limbo, the Mariners looking to build on solid young players, and the Angels burdened with so many big contracts, Texas could have its way with the division—unless another team joins the fray. For now, there are only those three teams for the Rangers to contend with annually for the division title. That may change, as MLB has discussed options for realignment. Logic dictates the AL West should expand to five teams in order to even the number of teams in each league and each division. This would give the current West residents another team to outperform every year. However, it's a change that almost certainly won't happen in 2012, since regular-season schedules are already set for next year. Houston is the smart choice to move since the Astros are in the NL Central, the only division with six teams. With talks in beginning stages, realignment may not happen for a few years, providing a temporary period of stability in the division.

So in the short term, the Rangers appear to be favorites to remain at the top. Texas has a strong offense in a hitter-friendly ballpark, and the Rangers compete against three teams that, as currently constructed, simply cannot keep up with their run-scoring abilities. Texas may continue to improve this offseason, as well, while others try to rebuild, relocate or reorganize. The Rangers were reportedly big players in the Cliff Lee sweepstakes following 2010, and they wound up spending big on a five-year, $80 million deal to get Beltre. It is doubtful Beltre's .296/.331/.561 line in 2011 will do anything to deter the Rangers from continuing to reinvest in the successful run they have going right now.

AL West PITCHf/x Insight

by Harry Pavlidis

When the Rangers moved Alexi Ogando to the bullpen for the 2011 postseason, a few eyebrows may have been raised. He was, after all, named to the All-Star team in July based on his early season rotation success—success which continued until August, when things got rough for a while.

The move to the bullpen, even without the rough patch, made perfect sense. Ogando was part of a solid rotation, top to bottom, so picking two out of three back-end starters for the playoffs wasn't too big a risk.

Ogando also wielded what can be considered a reliever's repertoire. While he did mix in some two-seam fastballs in 2011, he remained a fastball/slider/change-up artist. And even the change-up wasn't a major component. So he had comfort getting hitters out with just a couple of pitches, something a relief pitcher needs to do. Very few bullpen guys throw four or five pitches; it's hard to keep them sharp.

Ogando is a converted outfielder who had thrown just 111 minor league innings to go with 41 big league innings through 2010. He had made only three starts as a professional, all in 2010 between Double- and Triple-A. Amazingly, he'd total 169 innings in the majors during the regular season (including some late-season relief work).

Three other young pitchers in the division made their big league rotation debuts, but they were already seasoned as starters. Guillermo Moscoso, Tyler Chatwood and Michael Pineda were regulars for the Athletics, Angels and Mariners, respectively. Pineda and Ogando displayed similar stuff in their debut seasons.

Despite having the least starting experience, Ogando, at 28, was the oldest of the foursome. This is due in part to his late start as a pitcher, but also because he became a pitcher after missing a year due to legal problems. Moscoso, one year his junior, had 81 starts before the A's put him in the loop. Even Pineda and Chatwood had around 70 starts as pros before this season, despite their youth. Pineda, 22 years old, had 71 starts while Chatwood, just 21, had 65 starts in the minors.

PITCHf/x Profiles

Chatwood delivers the ball from a high three-quarter slot, giving his bread-and-butter two-seam fastball tail as opposed to sink. This angle gives him a deep curveball, but it's not a big yakker nor a power curve—somewhere in between. Chatwood throws a few change-ups and the rare slider, too. Chatwood stands an even six feet tall, with a deep leg drive that makes him seem even shorter. He generates plenty of power, averaging over 93 mph with his two-seam fastball and nearly 94 with the four-seam.

Moving down the arm slot continuum, we next arrive at Ogando, who is a little above three quarters but below Chatwood. Ogando is primarily fastball and slider, but he did add a two-seam "sinker" and mixed in more change-ups as a starter than he had as a reliever. There were starts in which Ogando only threw heaters and sliders, though. Ogando is listed at 6-foot-4, one inch shorter than Pineda, and leverages his big frame to generate a fastball that averages above 95 mph.

Pineda is right around three quarters and with a similar set of pitches to Ogando. His two-seam fastball is quite rare (his arm slot varies a bit, so that makes finding specific types of pitches a bit trickier) and he's another occasional change-up thrower. Pineda may throw his fastball a fraction slower than Ogando, but his off-speed pitches are actually a couple of mph faster than his counterpart's.

Moscoso's arm slot is below three quarters and he varies his arm angle. He almost certainly throws both a two- and four-seam fastball, but the natural tail on the fastball, the variance in arm angle and dominance of the pitch make it difficult to tease out his "sinkers." We'll call the whole lot fastballs.

Moscoso throws a slurvy curve, possibly a knuckle-curve, and a change-up. He also started throwing his cutter after a few turns in the rotation, as noted by the blog Athletics Nation. An inch taller than Chatwood, Moscoso is the non-power arm of the bunch. His fastball averages less than 92 mph, his cutter is at slider speed (84), and his change-up at curveball speed (80).

Results

The similarities and differences in this group come out not just in stature and posture or arsenal and velocity, but also in the overall results. Moscoso, the apparent finesse pitcher, does not put the ball on the ground. Chatwood, coming over the top with a tailing fastball is the only groundball pitcher in the group. Pineda and Ogando are the bat-missers, Chatwood seemingly nibbles to contact, and Moscoso is either really good or really lucky, or in the right ballpark.

	Swing Rate	Swing and Miss Rate	Ball/ Called Strike	Groundball Rate	Slugging Percentage on Contact
Ogando	47%	21%	2.2	38%	.450
Pineda	49%	26%	2.0	38%	.479
Chatwood	41%	13%	2.3	47%	.510
Moscoso	49%	18%	2.1	26%	.384
AL West Total	**45%**	**20%**	**1.9**	**44%**	**.481**

Expectations

Ogando will likely put his reliever days in his past next year, with 200 innings as a starter not an unrealistic target. Pineda could separate himself from Ogando results-wise going into his age 23 season. Moscoso should come back to earth, as an extreme flyball pitcher is always vulnerable to a bad run of deep flies (unless he's Matt Cain). Chatwood's approach is dubious. He's always walked a lot of guys, and would be well served by developing his slider and attacking the zone more often.

Resources: Pitch classifications by the author in conjunction with Hardball Times and Complete Game Consulting. PITCHf/x data from MLBAM and Sportvision.

The National League East View

by Brad Johnson

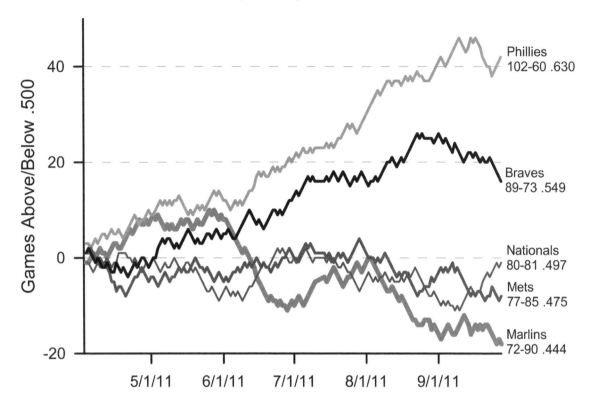

Play Against Other Divisions

Division	W	L	Win%
AL East	16	14	.533
AL Central	4	2	.667
AL West	24	21	.533
NL Central	108	92	.540
NL West	88	80	.524
Total	420	389	.519

Head-to-Head Records

Team	ATL	FLA	WSN	NYM	PHI	Total
ATL		12	9	9	6	36
FLA	6		11	9	6	32
WSN	9	7		10	10	36
NYM	9	9	8		7	33
PHI	12	12	8	11		43
Total	36	40	36	39	29	180

Read wins from left, losses from top

The Nats are making great strides with their farm system, and the improvement goes much further than having back-to-back first overall picks. Sure, the face of the farm system is Bryce Harper, and will be until he graduates to Washington, but it's hardly a one-man show. The Nats have gone above slot on many upper-round picks over the past few years, and took a haul away from the 2011 draft, nabbing four potential first-round picks (Anthony Rendon, Alex Meyer, Brian Goodwin and Matt Purke).

Under the Radar

It was easy to fly under the radar in Hagerstown the first part of the season with the Bryce Harper Show in town, and Robbie Ray did just that. A mid-round pick who got second-round money, Ray earned every penny in 2011, posting a 3.13 ERA in 20 starts with a 2.5 K/BB ratio.

2011 was an exciting year for the National League East. The division featured the best record in baseball, a historic collapse, breakout performances, and injuries aplenty.

The Washington Nationals Developed Some Stars

The Washington Nationals have been the ugly stepchild of the division since before they were Nationals. Despite relocating to a healthier media market, the franchise has not won more than 81 games since the 2003 Montreal Expos. After years of futility, the organization finished with an 80-81 record and is on the cusp of building a perennial contender. Much of that optimism stems from superstar prospects Stephen Strasburg and Bryce Harper.

In 2010, Strasburg burst onto the scene like a deity, earning praise for his superb performance before throwing a single major league pitch. After undergoing Tommy John surgery, Strasburg experienced a typical recovery and made his 2011 debut on Sept. 6.

Some pitchers struggle to command their pitches during the first season after recovery from Tommy John surgery, yet Strasburg appears to be back on top of his game. He threw 24 innings while allowing only 15 hits, five runs, and two walks along with 24 strikeouts. The Nationals intend to limit Strasburg's innings in 2012.

While Strasburg rehabbed, Harper mashed. He made short work of the lower minors and held his own against Double-A competition in his age-18 season. He put his five-tool skill set on display by swatting a combined 17 home runs, stealing 26 bases, and posting a .297/.392/.501 batting line. He did cool considerably in Double-A where he hit .256/.329/.395. He is headed to the Arizona Fall League for a second season.

The Nationals do not lack for other excellent players, many of whom bloomed in 2011.

Jordan Zimmermann returned from his own dance with Tommy John in late 2010. In 2011, he acquitted himself nicely as temporary staff ace. His 3.18 ERA in 161.1 innings was supported by 124 strikeouts and only 31 walks.

Michael Morse, 29, put together a monstrous season at the plate. He posted a .303/.360/.550 batting line with 31 home runs. He is a terrible defensive player, especially in the outfield where he gets bad jumps and takes circuitous routes.

Danny Espinosa and Wilson Ramos also cemented long-term roles with the club after posting strong performances. Espinosa batted .236/.323/.414 as the club's second baseman and could see time at shortstop in the future. Ramos hit a solid .267/.334/.445 and drew praise for his receiving skills.

2011 was not without worrying developments for the Nationals. In the first year of a seven-year, $126 million contract, Jayson Werth performed considerably below expectations. He posted a .232/.330/.389 batting line, by far his worst performance since 2005. Strikingly, the most noticeable changes from 2010 were a sharp reduction of power and a lower batting average on balls in play. The Nationals hope that Werth's performance was mostly poor luck and not a harbinger of things to come.

Altogether, the Nationals should be excited about the future. The club's weaknesses—the outfield, the rotation, and the bench—all appear to be fixable. Unsurprisingly, the club is expected to aggressively pursue an ace and an outfielder over the offseason.

The Philadelphia Phillies Crushed the Competition

The division stalwarts, the Philadelphia Phillies, lived up to expectations, steamrolling the competition. Their 102 wins led baseball and set a franchise record.

The 2011 Phillies led the league in attendance, with Citizens Bank Park operating at 104.1 percent of capacity. The fan support is a crucial element of the club's success. In the five years since squirming into the postseason in 2007, the Phillies have seen their payroll nearly double from about $90 million to roughly $173 million.

Much of the lineup has remained the same since 2007. Chase Utley, Ryan Howard, Jimmy Rollins, Shane Victorino and Carlos Ruiz have experienced all five seasons of the recent playoff run. Unsurprisingly, the lineup—once the team's strongest asset—is becoming a liability.

Age-related decline and injury are to blame. Utley missed April and most of May dealing with a degenerative knee problem. He had his worst offensive season since 2004, batting .259/.344/.425 in 454 plate appearances with only 11 home runs.

Howard failed to rebound from a down year in 2010, strengthening concerns that his power is permanently diminished. He batted .253/.346/.488 with 33 home runs. A ruptured Achilles tendon suffered in the last at-bat of the National League Division Series could further hamper his power.

Utley and Howard were not the only Phillies to post career-worst numbers. Placido Polanco, formerly a top pick for "Most Likely to Hit .300," hit .277, his worst average since 1999. Polanco has struggled with elbow problems over the past two seasons and also played the last month of the season with a sports hernia. Raul Ibanez rounds out the "Worst Season" club, batting .245/.289/.419—his worst numbers as a regular player.

Prospect Outlook: Philadelphia Phillies

In recent years, the Phillies' farm system has been like James Earl Jones' America and its army of steamrollers line from Field of Dreams—"it has been erased like a blackboard, rebuilt, and erased again." The Phillies continue to unload prospects for veterans at the trade deadline, this year trading Jarred Cosart, Jonathan Singleton and Domingo Santana to the Astros for Hunter Pence. But the Phillies have had enough success in the middle rounds of the draft in recent years to continually rebuild their farm system year after year.

Prospect Riser

Phillippe Aumont, who arrived in Philly in the original Cliff Lee deal, has had a roller coaster professional career, but it appears to be on an upswing at the moment. The Mariners had bounced Aumont back and forth between the starting rotation and the bullpen, before settling on a relief role for the 6-foot-7 Canadian, but the Phillies wanted to try him in the starting rotation again when they got him. After a lost season and a 5.68 ERA in 2010, the Phillies put Aumont back in the bullpen in 2011 and got the results they were hoping for—a 2.68 ERA between Double and Triple-A and better overall control.

Prospect Outlook: Atlanta Braves

The Braves farm system was depleted this season for all the right reasons. Mike Minor, Brandon Beachy, Craig Kimbrel and Freedie Freeman all exhausted their prospect eligibility, while Julio Teheran, Arodys Vizcaino and Randall Delgado all got a taste of the big leagues. Those experiences, coupled with the trading of Paul Clemens, Juan Abreu and Brett Oberholtzer to the Astros for Michael Bourn have eliminated seven of the team's top-30 prospects from the equation, with three more set to leave the list next year. It will be up to the development of the next wave of Braves prospects to replenish the team's always-deep farm system.

2012 is a make or break year for...Matt Lipka.

Lipka was the team's supplemental first-round pick in 2010 and had a good partial season after being drafted, setting himself up nicely for his first full pro season. The Braves raved about Lipka's advanced bat and questioned only whether he could stay at shortstop long-term. But in his first full season, Lipka showed no power (.304 SLG) and not enough plate discipline (.305 OBP) to offset his struggles at the plate. Even his speed and athleticism didn't translate as expected,

The Phillies did enjoy some breakout seasons. Shane Victorino should garner down ballot MVP consideration after batting .279/.355/.491 with 17 home runs. He also provided his usual stout defense.

John Mayberry Jr. had an excellent season, hitting .273/.341/.513 in 296 plate appearances while playing all three outfield positions and first base. He succeeded because he cut his strikeout rate considerably. If he can continue to strike out in fewer than 20 percent of his at-bats, he should be a useful regular.

The bread and butter of the 2011 Phillies was pitching. Pick a statistic and the Phillies rotation probably led the league. They pitched the most innings, won the most games, struck out the most batters, walked the fewest, posted the lowest ERA, and hurled the most complete games and shutouts. Advanced pitching statistics such as Fielding Independent Pitching (FIP) unanimously agree that the Phillies rotation was the best in baseball.

Roy Halladay led the staff and became the favorite to repeat as the National League's Cy Young Award winner. He posted a 2.35 ERA in 233.2 innings, striking out 220 batters while walking only 35.

Cliff Lee did his best to keep pace, tossing 232.2 innings of 2.40 ERA baseball. He struck out 238 batters and walked 42. In most seasons, that would garner Cy Young consideration, but Halladay and Clayton Kershaw were clearly better by a narrow margin.

Cole Hamels gets lost in the shuffle sometimes, but he improved yet again in 2011. He continued to master the cut fastball and posted a groundball rate over 50 percent for the first time in his career. He has always been prone to home runs, so the increased groundball rate is a welcome addition to his skill set. His 2.79 ERA in 216 innings would have led most rotations.

The rotation also received a boost from rookie Vance Worley. He posted a 3.01 ERA in 131.2 innings, earning himself a job in 2012 in the process.

Despite their early exit from the playoffs, expect the Phillies to remain active and aggressive this offseason to supplement their aging and injury-prone roster. Whether they retrench by re-signing fan favorites or explore more creative options, the Phillies will flex their financial might in an effort to stay atop the standings.

The Atlanta Braves Fell Apart

An awful September erased a strong season for the Atlanta Braves. Perhaps the worst part about missing the postseason by one game is the knowledge that there were so many opportunities to eke out just one more win.

The strength of the team was pitching. The staff combined for a 3.49 ERA which ranked fourth in the National League. In the rotation, the Braves combined veterans Tim Hudson, Jair Jurrjens, Tommy Hanson and Derek Lowe with an embarrassment of prospect riches in the forms of Brandon Beachy, Mike Minor, Julio Teheran and Randall Delgado. The Braves needed that depth since several starters suffered injuries.

Hanson sustained the most worrisome injury—shoulder soreness which ended his season early. He pitched well prior to injury, with a 3.60 ERA and 142 strikeouts in 130 innings. Hanson and the Braves will hope that an offseason of rest and rehab can prevent further complications.

Jurrjens and Beachy also struggled with injury. When healthy, both were effective. Jurrjens pitched to a 2.96 ERA in 152 innings. Beachy had an excellent rookie campaign that included a 3.68 ERA and 169 strikeouts in 141.2 innings.

The lone blemish to the rotation was veteran Derek Lowe, who threw 187 innings of 5.05 ERA baseball and lost 17 games. It's hard to blame the Braves for sticking with their veteran; advanced statistics such as FIP suggest he should have posted an ERA somewhere around 3.70.

The Braves featured an elite bullpen. Craig Kimbrel's performance included a rookie record of 46 saves to go with a 2.10 ERA and an incredible 127 strikeouts in 77 innings. He had every reason to win the NL Rookie of the Year award uncontested. Jonny Venters was similarly spectacular with a 1.84 ERA and 96 strikeouts in 85 innings.

Position players accounted for many of the Braves' woes. Jason Heyward was disappointing in his sophomore campaign, batting only .227/.319/.389 in 454 plate appearances while battling various minor injuries. He was expected to be a catalyst in the lineup but was ultimately moved to the bottom of the order.

Rookie Freddie Freeman rebounded from a poor start to post a solid .282/.346/.448 batting line with 21 home runs. Unfortunately, his season was bookended by two rough slumps including a September when he batted just .226/.306/.366.

Meanwhile, Dan Uggla had one of the most interesting seasons of 2011. Through the first half of the season, it appeared as though the Braves were doing themselves a serious disservice by sticking with him. He hit a meager .185/.257/.365. Then his bat came to life and he pounded a .296/.379/.569 line over the remainder of the season, rewarding the Braves' faith in him.

The team's biggest weakness all season was infield defense. Shortstop Alex Gonzalez had a solid defensive season, but Fathead cutouts of

as he stole 28 bases but was caught 14 times.

Lipka also saw significant time at second base, leading some to believe he'll vacate shortstop even sooner than expected. Lipka still has lots of developmental time left, and his ceiling remains high, but 2011 indicated that he may be further away than originally expected. If he doesn't hit early in 2012, Lipka risks falling behind other up-the-middle players on the Braves' organizational depth chart.

The Mets have been notorious during the Wilpon era for not going over slot in the MLB draft and thus, by default, not having remarkably productive drafts. Matt Harvey appears to be a hit from 2010, and the Mets have continued to spend big in the international markets, so there is some talent on the horizon, especially on the mound. They will have to do a better job of allowing that talent to progress, however, than they have with Fernando Martinez, who has gone from being a top prospect to a non-factor.

2012 is a make or break year for...Reese Havens

No one doubts Havens' abilities on the field—they just never get a chance to see them in action. Havens has appeared in just 213 games in the four seasons since being drafted, including just 61 this year. Due to his skill level and a lack of other top-tier prospects at his second base position, the Mets continue to keep Havens in their long-term plans, but another year with significant time missed due to injury could finally force the Mets to look another direction.

Chipper Jones, Uggla and Freeman would feature similar range in the field.

Altogether, the Braves are well positioned to contend in the NL East. They possess a deep roster with many excellent prospects to call upon. They are a team that should very reliably post roughly 90 wins over the next few seasons. Their biggest hurdle will be breaking through the 90-win plateau.

The New York Mets Flirted with .500

Entering 2011, the odds were stacked heavily against the Mets. Johan Santana was expected to be sidelined for roughly half the season, the Bernie Madoff hangover kept getting worse for the front office, and the roster was thin, injury prone, or otherwise untrustworthy. They made the best of it, falling just four wins short of .500.

The rotation was a cobbled together combination of veteran retreads and youngsters. Chris Young quickly hit the disabled list as he is wont to do, throwing only 24 innings over four starts. Santana experienced setback after setback and never threw a pitch.

Mike Pelfrey did his thing, striking out few and walking fewer. Despite seeing his ERA increase by over a point to 4.74, he pitched very similarly to his successful 2010 season. He did allow nearly twice as many home runs, leading to the higher ERA.

R.A. Dickey repeated his 2010 breakout, posting a 3.28 ERA. Jonathan Niese built upon his rookie campaign with a 4.40 ERA that understates how well he pitched. Dillon Gee also stepped up as an adequate swing man with a 4.43 ERA. Even Chris Capuano recaptured some of his former skills, posting a 4.52 ERA in 185 innings.

Despite welding a number of scraps and spare parts into something that resembled a rotation, the Mets still entered midseason as sellers. They ultimately parted with Francisco Rodriguez and Carlos Beltran.

Rodriguez had a fine season, pitching to a 2.64 ERA in 71.2 innings. He was dealt to the Brewers for a couple of minor league pitchers. Beltran had a strong season, hitting .300/.385/.525. The Mets were able to able to pick up exciting pitching prospect Zack Wheeler from the Giants in exchange for Beltran. He threw 115 innings of 3.52 ERA baseball at Single-A this season.

The club decided to hang on to Jose Reyes rather than trade him at the deadline. He hit a career-best .337/.384/.493 in 2011 on his way to free agency. Carl Crawford's seven-year, $142 million contract is thought to be Reyes' goal, although his long history of injuries could weaken his bargaining position. The Mets have the unenviable position of choosing between disappointing their fans or swallowing a potentially poisonous contract.

David Wright also survived the trade deadline. He is signed through 2012 with an option for 2013 that he can void if traded. Wright has not performed at a superstar level since 2008, batting only .254/.345/.427 in 2011.

The Mets discovered some interesting role players during the course of the 2011 season. Ike Davis had a quick start to his season, batting .302/.383/.543 with seven home runs in 149 plate appearances. An ankle injury erased the remainder of his season.

Daniel Murphy emerged as a valuable utility fielder, spending time at first, second, and third base while batting .320/.362/.427. Unfortunately, his season ended early with a torn MCL.

The injuries to Davis and Murphy opened more playing time for Lucas Duda, who shined during the final months of the season. He hit .292/.370/.482 with 10 home runs in 347 plate appearances.

Looking forward, the Mets are still potentially on the hook for $386 million in Madoff money. But even with the financial woes and uncertainty surrounding their on-field talent, the Mets reside in one of the largest media markets in sports and possess an extremely talented front office. They should be able to orchestrate a speedy recovery back to prominence.

The Florida Marlins Missed Their Best Players

The Florida Marlins—soon to be the Miami Marlins—will debut their new stadium in 2012. They finished a division-worst 72-90 in the club's final season with the Florida moniker. The Marlins featured a top-heavy roster heading into 2011 and injuries chopped the head right off the body.

Hanley Ramirez had a lost season, with career-worst numbers in all manner of statistics. He hit .243/.333/.379 in only 385 plate appearances. He missed the latter portion of the season with a sprained shoulder that could require surgery.

Staff ace Josh Johnson experienced shoulder soreness after only his ninth game and missed the remainder of the season. He was exceptional prior to injury, posting a 1.64 ERA. The Marlins were unable to replace Johnson, instead leaning on swingmen Brad Hand and Clay Hensley to cover the void. The pair combined to go 3-12 as part of the rotation.

Injuries were not the only problem with the club. Outfielder Logan Morrison filed a grievance after a punitive demotion in August. The front office felt the need to justify the demotion by claiming Morrison needed to work on improving his .247 batting average. However, weighted On

Prospect Outlook: Florida Marlins

The Marlins organization recently was a part of the discussion of which system had the best set of majors-ready position players, with Mike Stanton and Logan Morrison in the midst of the argument. With Gaby Sanchez, that trio should comprise the middle of the Marlins lineup as they break into their new stadium in 2012. Left behind in the organization are some bare cupboards. The Marlins have traditionally restocked their farm system through trades, but have held on to their big star Hanley Ramirez. While that's a good move for the organization, it's left the farm system up to the draft, where some recent first-round picks have been hit-and-miss.

2012 is a make or break season for... Matt Dominguez

Dominguez is supposed to be the Marlins' third baseman of the future, and the future was thought to be sometime during the 2011 season. Dominguez was in the running for the Marlins' Opening Day third base job, strictly because of his glove, but was sent back to Triple-A for a little more polishing at the plate. His season was interrupted when he was hit in the hand by a pitch, limiting him to just 95 games, but his results in his second go-round in Triple-A bore a striking resemblance to his first attempt (.743 OPS in 2011, .744 in 2010). Dominguez needs to grab the Marlins' major league hot corner spot this spring, but even still, he may only be an average hitter.

- Jeff Moore

Base Average (wOBA)—an advanced measure of offensive talent—suggests Morrison was the second-best hitter on the team. Ironically, Marlins hitters combined for a .247 batting average.

If that were not enough, closer Leo Nunez turned out not to be Leo Nunez. His real name is Juan Carlos Oviedo. Oviedo faked his identity in order to improve his standing in the international talent market.

The Marlins can take some positives away from the 2011 season. Mike Stanton improved on his rookie campaign, batting .262/.356/.537 with 34 home runs. His strikeout rate—27.6 percent—remains worrisome. He tied Miguel Olivo for the third-worst strikeout rate in the majors.

Emilio Bonifacio had his best season. He hit .296/.360/.393 in 641 plate appearances and stole 40 bases while spending some time at six positions. He still struck out in over 20 percent of his plate appearances, which is unusual for a slappy hitter like Bonifacio.

Anibal Sanchez continued to show mid-rotation stuff. He managed a 3.67 ERA while striking out over a batter per inning. His control and command have improved considerably since he returned from injury in 2009.

Javier Vazquez had the pitcher's version of Dan Uggla's season. He was terrible in the first half of the season with a 5.23 ERA. Had Johnson not been on the disabled list, he might have been cut. His velocity returned late in the first half of the season, and the results are clear as day: a 2.51 ERA in the second half of the season.

The Marlins are eagerly anticipating their new stadium. They triggered an unusual trade with the Chicago White Sox, dealing a couple of minor leaguers for manager Ozzie Guillen. Undoubtedly, Guillen is meant to entice quality free agents and inject excitement into the Miami fanbase with his fiery escapades.

The Marlins will hope that Guillen, healthy versions of Ramirez and Johnson, and free agent firepower can propel the club back above .500 in 2012.

NL East PITCHf/x Insight

by Harry Pavlidis

You can choose from a few, but two startling disappointments in the 2011 NL East were produced by a pair of big-name right fielders. Before the season began, Jayson Werth signed a big free agent contract to join the Nationals, only to put up the worst season of his career. Jason Heyward nearly won the Rookie of the Year in 2010, but the Braves right fielder found himself struggling at the plate and even spent time on the DL. Heyward eventually found himself sharing time in right field.

In his last three seasons as the Phillies right fielder, Werth put up a combined line of .279/.376/.513—good enough for a OPS+ of 132. Werth's best, and most recent, season saw his only actual above-130 OPS+, but the Nationals were likely expecting something at least approaching his three-year mark. Werth finished 2012 at 97, a below average mark. The .232/.330/.389 line is most marred by the putrid slugging rate.

Heyward's 2010 rookie season, as a 20-year-old, was right about the line the Nats were expecting from Werth—.277/.393/.456 for a 131 OPS+. Instead, Heyward dropped to .227/.319/.389 for an OPS+ of 95. Heyward's already disappointing power output in 2010 was bleaker in 2011, and his still decent walk rate (12 percent of plate appearances) was a bit lower as well (15 percent in 2010).

Werth saw a very slight drop in pitches for strikes as a Nat. From 55 percent to 54 in the "wide zone" and a balls-to-called-strike ratio that went from 1.9 to 1.7—he wasn't much of a pitch-taker as a Nat or a Phillie. This doesn't exactly fit the "exposed without the Phillies line-up" narrative.

Fastballs were actually more common for Werth in 2011—not by a grand amount, but heaters and sinkers made up 62 percent of his pitches seen, up from 57 percent the year before. The biggest change in his performance against fastballs was his slugging on contact (SLGCON). It dropped from .830 down to .563. He swung at fastballs just as as often, and actually whiffed a little less (17 percent, down from 21). Ground balls as a percent of batted balls shot up from 33 percent to 43 percent. That will take the bite out of the SLGCON, for sure.

Why so many ground balls? Werth had similar drops in SLGCON and spikes in groundball percentage against curves and changes, but not sliders. We can look at two things—fastball type (sinkers vs. heaters) and, for each pitch, location.

Werth actually saw, if anything, fewer sinkers in 2011 than in 2010... so far we haven't found a "pitched-to differently" explanation for Werth's struggles.

There were some minor differences in the location of pitches thrown to Werth in 2011, but not where you'd think he'd hit more ground balls. That would be down and away, but Werth actually saw a few more pitches up and in. Bottom line, Werth can't really blame the weaker lineup around him for his struggles, and nothing changed substantially in his opponents' approach.

Heyward was already a groundball hitter (56 percent in 2010, 54 percent in 2011), so there's no story there. His fly balls and line drives still left the park with the same impressive frequency (13 percent). But Heyward swung more, missed more, and didn't hit the ball as hard in 2011.

Heyward's trend was most evident against fastballs. On one hand, Heyward was not taking as many fastballs for strikes (down 8 points to 30 percent) but he was was whiffng more (15 percent to 19 percent) and lost about 100 points of SLGCON. So he swung more often, but he got less out of those swings.

On the bright side, Heyward improved his performance against sliders by swinging at more strikes. As with fastballs, he took fewer in the zone (44 percent to 31) but whiffed less (35 percent to 29) and lost nothing on contact, with nearly identical SLGCONS of .659 and .656. More swings, fewer whiffs, better contact.

Heyward's handling of change-ups declined. With roughly the same number of swings, he whiffed nearly 50 percent more (32 percent to 45 percent) and lost 240 points on his SLGCON, down to a meager .344. Ground balls were part of the problem here, moving from 65 percent to 75 percent. Heyward showed the same pattern with curveballs, but less severely so.

Considering his health issues and adjustment, it isn't hard to hope that Heyward's down year was an anomaly. His heavy ground ball tendencies will dampen his power production, but could actually lead to him getting on base more often over time.

At least Heyward is a young player, learning to adjust, and struggling with a shoulder injury. While both players will be under pressure to bounce back in 2012, the pressure and odds will be greater for the aging Mr. Werth.

Resources: Pitch classifications by the author in conjunction with Hardball Times and Complete Game Consulting. PITCHf/x data from MLBAM and Sportvision.

The National League Central View

by Harry Pavlidis

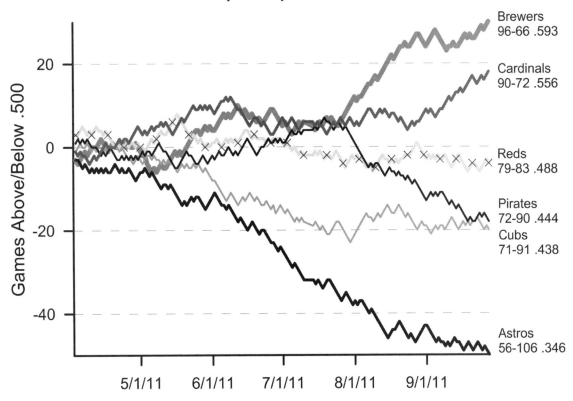

Play Against Other Divisions			
Division	W	L	Win%
AL East	21	33	.389
AL Central	14	19	.424
AL West	2	4	.333
NL East	92	108	.460
NL West	97	106	.478
Total	464	508	.477

Head-to-Head Records							
Team	CHC	CIN	HOU	MIL	PIT	STL	Total
CHC		7	8	6	8	5	34
CIN	11		9	8	5	9	42
HOU	7	6		3	7	5	28
MIL	10	8	12		12	9	51
PIT	8	10	11	3		7	39
STL	10	6	10	9	9		44
Total	46	37	50	29	41	35	238

Read wins from left, losses from top

The Brewers used virtually every available resource in their farm system to push their chips to the center of the table in 2011. They traded their best prospect, Brett Lawrie, to Toronto for Shawn Marcum, and sent a package of young players to Kansas City for Zack Greinke. That, coupled with a busted first-round pick in 2009 and failure to sign their top pick in 2010, puts the Brewers' farm system among the worst in the game.

Prospect Riser

When you look at the 5-foot 9 Caleb Gindl, "riser" isn't exactly what comes to mind, but Gindl has shown he can hit at every level, including an impressive .862 OPS in Triple-A last season. His stock may never sail too high because he's far from a stellar defensive player in the outfield (and because only two players in the last 50 years listed at 5-foot-9 or shorter have hit more than 30 home runs—Miguel Tejada and Kirby Puckett), but Gindl can hit and he should get the chance to prove it.

Like every other spring in recent memory, talk of the upcoming National League Central race included the always-competitive Cardinals. Set with three aces, St. Louis looked to be the division pacesetter once again. The typical Cardinal spring also includes some type of discovery. Tony La Russa and long-time pitching coach Dave Duncan always seem to find some revamped veteran or young kid with a newly perfected sinker, but that wasn't the big news this year.

This year, one of the biggest, if not the biggest, blows to a preseason contender was the late-February news about Adam Wainwright. That's when it was announced that the Cy Young contender and owner of one of best curveballs in baseball was in need of Tommy John surgery and would miss the entire season. Suddenly, Chris Carpenter and Jaime Garcia were in need of a third musketeer.

A strong front three has recently become the calling card of contending teams, and the Redbirds were down to two. Kyle Lohse and Jake Westbrook helped, but the revolving door at the back end of the rotation would spin its way into the bullpen even after the rotation was finally settled in a late-season trade.

The Brewers Set the Standard

The events that had created the three-strong starter standard for NL Central rotations came during the hot stove season. The Brewers set themselves up for a division title when they added Zack Greinke and Shaun Marcum to their rotation. Yovani Gallardo would now have some support (at the very least) and Randy Wolf and Chris Narveson were moved to the back of the rotation. This team was for real; their staff would no longer drag down their explosive offense.

Bolstering the rotation wasn't the only step the Brewers took. Defensive upgrades in center field and shortstop helped get the most out of their big pitching investment. Nyjer Morgan and Yuniesky Betancourt performed as expected by most measures, and Morgan also provided surprising value on offense. This was important, as the Brewers got very little (other than outs) out of Betancourt and third baseman Casey McGehee.

Milwaukee was able to overcome the lack of production at the hot corner as well as an injury to Rickie Weeks. Jerry Hairston Jr. was acquired to fill in for Weeks and did so admirably. Hairston, a third-generation ballplayer, stuck around when Weeks' ankle healed and eventually took over third base in the postseason.

The Brewers' offense featured two of the best run producers in baseball. While Ryan Braun and Prince Fielder don't exactly stack up well on defense, they are both elite offensive players who both rake and get on base.

Even with all that offense, the Brewers still scored fewer runs than the Reds and Cardinals. But only St. Louis topped Milwaukee in the NL once you consider park factors, according to Baseball Reference's OPS+ calculation.

The Resurgent Redbirds

The Cardinals' offensive leader, Albert Pujols, and Fielder both will hit the free agent market this winter, and the combined impact of the two star first basemen will shape most of the hot stove action for position players. Considering their attachment to Pujols, and despite the extension of Lance Berkman's deal, the Cardinals should be the leading contender to ink the prodigious run producer.

The Cardinals were very much involved in the traditional trading frenzy at the July 31 non-waiver deadline. It took three teams to get it done, but Edwin Jackson made his way to St. Louis from the south side of Chicago, while a bevy of relievers and Colby Rasmus went north of the border to Toronto. This was a critical move for the Cardinals to acquire that third top starting pitcher

Jackson did not fit the standard mold of a veteran Cardinal acquisition. Never a groundball pitcher, nor a pitch-to-contact guy, Jackson has more of a power set that you're likely to find in the bullpen. He's an often-impressive and usually-effective starter, nonetheless. Carpenter/Garcia/Jackson didn't have the same oomph as Greinke/Gallardo/Marcum, but they were good enough to chase down the faltering Braves and steal the Wild Card.

St. Louis entered September with no realistic hope of catching Milwaukee or Atlanta. But an 18-8 finish, combined with the Braves' 9-18 record, clinched a postseason spot for the Redbirds on the final day of the season and they rode that wave all the way to the World Series.

At the start of the year, the division was typically considered a three-team race, although the Cardinals were viewed as a straggler without Wainwright. But the Brewers and the Reds ended up part of an exciting four-team race that fizzled after it sizzled. August didn't hint at the exciting finish or the presence of two NL Central teams in the NLCS.

The Reds Couldn't Defend

The defending champion Reds found themselves foundering midseason, scoring runs but unable to prevent enough in return. Instead of being the second coming of the Big Red Machine, they worked on avoiding a trip to the second division.

Prospect Outlook: St. Louis Cardinals

After hitting on prep pitcher Shelby Miller, the Cardinals have stuck with polished college hitters in the draft over the past few years. The result has been Zack Cox and Kolten Wong, both of whom look like they will be contributors in St. Louis in the next year or two. The Cardinals have also been active on the international market, inking players like Carlos Martinez who project to have high-end talent.

Under the Radar

After starting the year in the Low-A Quad Cities starting rotation, Jordan Swagerty moved up to Palm Beach and soon went to the bullpen, where many predicted he would ultimately end up. The moves worked, as Swagerty posted a 1.82 ERA High-A ball this season and earned a promotion to Double-A. As a reliever, he could move quickly through the Cardinals farm system.

Prospect Outlook: Cincinnati Reds

The Jay Bruce, Johnny Cueto, Joey Votto wave of prospects from a few years back has led the Reds to a division title and given them the base for a strong team. But those graduations, coupled with the draft-to-majors jump of Mike Leake, have left the Reds' farm system without much in the way of top tier talent, especially on the mound. Intriguing prospect Billy Hamilton could end up being a game-changer, however, after posting a 100-steal season in 2011.

Prospect Riser

After three seasons of projections, Juan Duran finally produced the way the Reds expected. Of course, he's still just 19 and finally, at 6-foot-7, stopped growing and allowed his coordination to catch up. Once it did, he posted a .264/.329/.463 line in full-season ball as a teenager. He still needs to strike out less, but 2011 was a huge step in the right direction for the young outfielder.

Prospect Outlook: Chicago Cubs

The Cubs' farm system has been all over the map in recent years, missing with early first-round pick Josh Vitters and over-paying Jeff Samardzija, but hitting on center fielder of the future Brett Jackson, who could take over in the Windy City next season. In the draft, they have honored MLB's slot recommendations, but also remain involved in the international market, particularly in the Pacific Rim.

Prospect Riser

The Cubs paid outfielder Matt Szczur a lot of money to stop playing football, and it appears

The first memorable event for the 2011 Reds was one they'd rather forget. Mike Leake, who went from college to the Arizona Fall League to the Cincinnati rotation in 2010, was caught shoplifting. Jokes about the price of t-shirts followed, naturally, and Leake navigated his way through some minor legal troubles. It certainly was an odd way to start the year.

Despite his troubles and a brief stint in Triple-A, Leake improved on his rookie campaign and increased his workload. He could pull 200 innings in 2012, and he may be joined in the rotation by another young rising star, one who couldn't be more different in style.

As the weather turned warm, flame-throwing Cuban lefty Aroldis Chapman found himself in the minors. It took some time, but Chapman got comfortable working in relief and made his way back to the bigs after what was officially a rehab assignment. It paid off. In 13 innings before being placed on the disabled list, Chapman struck out 15 batters and walked 21. After returning, he worked 37 innings and walked "just" 20 batters. Oh, he also struck out 56 in those 37 frames. Those could be his last innings as a reliever.

With the season in the bag, Chapman is on his way to Arizona for some Instructional League work and then a month in Puerto Rico to convert to starting. Leake and Chapman could be the core of a formidable rotation, and two parts of a big three. A top trio for Cincy isn't out of the question, and the Reds seem to be heading toward 2012 with six realistic rotation candidates. Granted, that may have been their thinking going into 2011, too.

Bronson Arroyo will be back, but he will no longer be viewed as a front-end option. Johnny Cueto had an impressive season, working his way back from arm troubles into the league ERA race. Right now, Cueto is the best pitcher on the staff, but Leake and Chapman may not be far behind.

Even if Chapman doesn't fit the bill, Homer Bailey and Edinson Volquez both have the stuff and potential to be solid mid-rotation starters. Joey Votto and friends will likely continue to provide the offense they delivered in 2011. If the rotation improves substantially, watch out for the Reds.

Stuck in Neutral

The Cubs also had three featured starting pitchers. They shipped a bunch of prospects to Tampa for Matt Garza in the offseason to complement the steady but underrated Ryan Dempster and the apparently anger-managed Carlos Zambrano. Less angry, but not less emotional.

After some competition in Mesa, the Cubs settled on their fifth starter, Andrew Cashner. Cashner's first start in the big leagues was going very well on a cool Chicago day. Then he pointed to his shoulder, and the air went out of Wrigley Field. Cashner headed for an MRI and the disabled list, and the wind was sucked out of the Cubs' season when he was joined on the DL by fourth starter Randy Wells. The double announcement caused numerous double-takes. Wells was hurt? Who knew?

A converted catcher, Wells had some struggles in 2010 but had remained healthy. Looking to turn it around in 2011, he strained his forearm and left the Cubs suddenly short-handed. Too bad Carlos Silva couldn't handle being the sixth starter (or Iowa ace, as it were).

Cashner came back in September as a reliever and is set to remain in that role in the Arizona Fall League. Wells returned after a couple of weeks, but without his velocity or command. Even with some improvement in velocity through the summer, he still couldn't get guys out. Wells had a strong finish, perhaps over-attributed to a kick in the butt from Dempster.

It's not clear how much a little kick in the rear did for Wells, but it's pretty clear a long history of kicks did little for Big Z. In a memorably bad outing in Atlanta, Zambrano was ejected after throwing two pitches at Chipper Jones. He subsequently packed his things and left the park, reportedly texting some front office personnel about his retirement.

While GM Jim Hendry seemed happy to accept Zambrano's offer, it was not to be taken seriously. Nonetheless, quitting on the team led to 30 days on the restricted list. Not reactivated for the final two weeks, Zambrano's status remains unknown at this writing. It seems improbable that he'll suit up for the Cubs. Hendry, on the other hand, has clarity in terms of his role with the Cubs. He was fired in September and a new management team has taken over in Chicago.

Surprise in Pittsburgh

A club that started, and finished, without an impressive trio of starters created some of the most exciting stories of the summer. Stocked with young talent on offense and topped off with a dominating closer, the Pirates made headlines well into the season.

With a fastball touching 100 and a devastating slider, Joel Hanrahan worked the bottom of the zone for an impressive groundball rate (53 percent of balls in play) to go with his solid K rate (8.0 per 9). Hanrahan has typically posted double-digit K/9 rates, but a 10-percentage-point jump in ground balls and a career low in walk rate (by a long shot) more than offset the drop. While ground balls do mean more base hits, Hanrahan gave up just one home run all year.

Hanrahan's success was part of an exciting run for the Pirates. Scoring runs behind solid starting pitching, there was something special about

to be the right decision for both parties. In his first full season, Szczur displayed the power/speed combo the Cubs had hoped for, hitting 35 extra-base hits in 109 games between both A-ball levels and stealing 24 bases in 29 attempts.

Prospect Outlook: Pittsburgh Pirates

The consummate rebuilders, the Pittsburgh Pirates finally appear to have the talent on the horizon to actually make a difference. A few years in a row of major spending on amateur talent has been the difference, as Jameson Taillon and Gerrit Cole formulate a potential 1-2 punch atop the Pirates rotation as good as any in the game. The Pirates have also gone over slot in later round picks, infusing all levels of their system with upper-echelon talent.

Under the Radar

Kyle McPherson has been an afterthought in the Pirates' farm system, but his numbers this year won't allow that to happen much longer. After an impressive half-season in the Florida State League, where he posted a 2.89 ERA, McPherson graduated to Double-A and continued his success, posting a 3.02 ERA in 16 starts and increasing his strikeout ratio. McPherson could start 2012 back in Double-A and should reach Triple-A during the season.

Prospect Outlook: Houston Astros

A few years ago, the Astros not only had the worst farm system in baseball, but one of the worst of recent memory. The forfeiture of draft picks due to free agent signings was mostly to blame, along with their owner's unwillingness to go over slot for the picks they did have. The farm system has been turned around due to the housecleaning taking place at the major league level, and while it still ranks in the middle-of-the-pack at best, it now shows signs of producing major league talent.

Under the Radar

Paul Clemens joined the Astros midseason, coming over from the Braves in the Michael Bourn trade. Perhaps he'll get more recognition in the Astros' weak farm system, but he was overlooked in the deep Braves organization. Clemens doesn't wow anyone, but he does consistently produce, and has done so effectively as high as Double-A. He should get a full season of Triple-A under his belt next year.

- Jeff Moore

the ninth-inning vibe when their shutdown closer came in from the bullpen. The team felt like a winner.

You have to be of a certain age to remember when the Pirates were semi-regular contenders. An energy crackled in the Pirate fanbase that hadn't been seen in quite some time. As a matter of fact, many fans had never seen anything remotely like the enthusiasm that built up around PNC Park's inhabitants in mid-summer.

Alas, the dog days of summer were cruel. Quickly falling out of contention after a brief spell in first place, it was yet another losing season, as nearly two decades have now passed since the Bucs last cracked .500. One of the biggest problems for Pittsburgh was the quality of starting pitching. For more on that, check-out our PITCHf/x sidebar on the Bucs starters.

With Andrew McCutchen poised to be the next big thing and a solid supporting cast that includes Neil Walker and Jose Tabata, the Pirates could find themselves back in the running in 2012.

Just Awful

The Astros were simply bad. They had some recognizable names in their lineup (Carlos Lee, Hunter Pence and Michael Bourn) but were out of touch with even the lowly Cubs by the time the trading deadline loomed. When the dust settled and the calendar turned to August, the Astros were virtually unrecognizable.

Pence and Bourn left for the top two teams in the NL East, leaving El Caballo as the only name-brand player in the regular lineup. Even though Brett Myers was having a down year, the rotation had some quality in Wandy Rodriguez and Bud Norris. They didn't really help. With closer Brandon Lyon on the shelf, watching the Astros play was much like watching their Triple-A affiliate with Lee on a rehab assignment.

It got more confusing when everyday players Chris Johnson and Brett Wallace went from manning the corners in Houston to manning the same spots in Oklahoma City. Neither Johnson nor Wallace hit for any power in either location.

There isn't much help on the way, although Jordan Lyles (despite his struggles) is a promising young arm. Most rankings have the Houston farm system in the bottom five. The Astros look to have overtaken the Pirates in sustainable weakness and are likely to hold that undesirable distinction for some time.

NL Central PITCHf/x Sidebar

by Harry Pavlidis

So what happened in Pittsburgh? Solidly in contention in the middle of the season, things fell apart for the Pirates soon after. What impact did starting pitching have on the Jekyll/Hyde season? More specifically, did the rotation run out of steam?

During a late-season series against the Cubs, the Chicago radio and TV teams pointed out an increase in workload among Pittsburgh starters. I assume both crews were working from the same information, and neither took into consideration minor league innings. Still, 2011 did represent a heavier-than-normal burden for at least some of the Pirates rotation. This happened to coincide with a second-half drop in performance.

Innings and Starts

Only Paul Maholm could count a 200-inning season in his past, with Kevin Correia's 198 in 2009 being "good enough" to count, although Correia threw around 150 innings in 2010 and 2011. Even Maholm has pitched a few less innings each year since his 206.1 in 2008.

Neither would pitch in September.

Jeff Karstens had the best progression of work over the past few years, but managed just two September starts. James McDonald and Charlie Morton took four turns in the final month despite being the most likely candidates for fatigue.

Through June, each of the main five starters had at least four starts each. Only Karstens missed some starts in April (three). So, clearly, the main five starters carried the load, starting in April, ending sometime in August. The group totaled 25, 26, 27, 25 and 25 starts in each month, respectively.

Over those first five months, the "other five," led by Ross Ohlendorf and Brad Lincoln, contributed eight starts. September was upside down, with three of the main five contributing a total of just 10 starts while four other pitchers combined for 16.

Pitch Speed

Can we detect any hints at fatigue with PITCHf/x?

Correia gradually added velocity over the first few months, with his July cutter running as hot as his April fastball and sinker. Eventually, his cutter dropped to early season speed while the fastball/sinker leveled off. Everything was dropping in his last two starts. Correia was placed on the disabled list retroactive to Aug. 20 with an oblique strain.

Karstens added a cutter for a few starts in July, otherwise throwing just his sinker and fastball. Fastball velocity was fairly consistent for Karstens, with his sinker being a bit erratic. Overall, he was steady. The Pirates were cautious and shut him down halfway through September.

Maholm's velocity was also steady, although his cutter took an odd jump up toward his fastball and sinker speed for his final two August starts. Maholm was shut down two days earlier than Correia with a shoulder strain.

McDonald had the best fastball on the staff, but he actually started slower than Morton in April. McDonald steadily moved a bit faster with both his fastball and sinker. Morton, on the other hand, started strong but slowly lost steam before taking dip in late July. He flashed a good fastball here and there (even one day where he unleashed just a single four-seam heater), but he continued the slow leak with all three offerings after the big dip.

The somewhat surprising news out of Pittsburgh in October: Morton was undergoing hip surgery. He should be healthy for 2012, so perhaps a return to early-2011 velocity is in order even if he gets a late start on the season.

Average Four-Seam Fastball Speed, MPH						
	April	May	June	July	August	Sept.
Correia	90.2	91.4	91.8	92.4	91.7	
Karstens	89.5	90.0	90.1	90.1	90.5	90.8
Maholm	88.4	88.8	87.9	88.3	88.5	
McDonald	92.9	93.4	93.5	93.9	93.7	93.9
Morton	93.7	93.3	92.7	92.2	91.9	91.8

Karstens and McDonald finished well and, in Karstens' case, had their workload carefully managed. Both should be expected to at least open 2012 in good form. Morton presents a mild question mark, but Maholm is not expected back—free agency is calling, and the Bucs don't seem interested in picking up his option. Correia is expected back at the front of the rotation.

Resources: Pitch classifications by the author in conjunction with Hardball Times and Complete Game Consulting. PITCHf/x data from MLBAM and Sportvision.

The National League West View

by Steve Treder

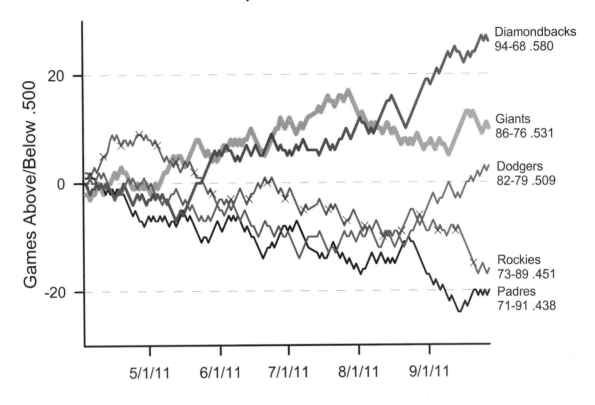

Play Against Other Divisions			
Division	W	L	Win%
AL East	3	3	.500
AL Central	30	21	.588
AL West	7	14	.333
NL East	80	88	.476
NL Central	106	97	.522
Total	406	403	.502

Head-to-Head Records						
Team	ARI	COL	LAD	SDP	SFG	Total
ARI		13	10	11	9	43
COL	5		9	9	5	28
LAD	8	9		13	9	39
SDP	7	9	5		6	27
SFG	9	13	9	12		43
Total	29	44	33	45	29	180

Read wins from left, losses from top

The Padres' farm system isn't nearly as devoid of talent as it should be, considering their horrendous record with first-round picks. Allan Dykstra in 2008 was hurt when he was drafted, so he came cheaper to the organization. He's now with the Mets. Donovan Tate in 2009 has been a disaster. And 2010 first-rounder Karsten Whitson has pitched incredibly well, only he's done it for the Florida Gators. He chose to go to college instead of signing. Despite it all, the Padres have a number of intriguing prospects, including Jedd Gyorko, Keyvius Sampson, and the trio they got from the Reds Sox for Adrian Gonzalez—Anthony Rizzo, Casey Kelly and Reymond Fuentes.

Prospect Riser

Taken in the fourth round of that 2009 draft was Keyvius Sampson, and Sampson has done nothing but get people out since. In his first full season, Sampson dominated the Midwest League, striking out 143 batters in 118 innings, going 12-3 in 24 starts and posting a 2.90 ERA. He'll battle the California League in 2012.

In recent seasons, the National League West has been a division on the rise. Recovering from a slump that bottomed out in 2005, in the four years from 2007 through 2010 the NL West produced five National League Championship Series contestants, two pennant winners, and a World Series champion.

The return to strongly competitive status wasn't driven nearly as much by burgeoning payrolls and high-profile free agent signings as it was by the development and blossoming of old-fashioned home-grown farm system products. Good young players have been gracing most of the five rosters in this division.

Whether they were in greater or lesser abundance in 2011, it seemed to be a year for breakout young stars in the NL West. Look no further than this year's division champ (a breakout young *team* if ever there was one): the Arizona Diamondbacks. Their No. 3 hitter was 23-year-old right fielder Justin Upton, a superb all-around performer who's getting better all the time (see Josh Weinstock's sidebar), and their starting rotation was anchored by not one but two suddenly-blossoming young aces in 26-year-old Ian Kennedy and 24-year-old Daniel Hudson.

But even amid circumstances of teams making disappointing showings—another distinct feature of this year's NL West—there were, if not breakout performances, at least impressive turns presented by young talent that should be acknowledged.

Even in Sorry San Diego

Bringing up the division rear, and in quite listless fashion for long periods of 2011, were the San Diego Padres. General manager Jed Hoyer fully anticipated a rebuilding year after trading away superstar first baseman Adrian Gonzalez in the offseason, but one doubts Hoyer expected the Padres—winners of 90 games who came within an eyelash of winning the division in 2010—to be this bad in 2011.

And it's fair to consider that in a way they really weren't. Among the many things going wrong for the Padres this year was the fact that they were unusually unlucky in the Pythagorean sweepstakes, underperforming their 79-83 run-differential record by a whopping eight games.

Yet Pythag isn't the record that the league actually, you know, counts, and besides, even 79-83 isn't a good record. The Padres struggled in 2011 pretty much all year long, never posting a winning record in any month following a 1-0 March. And what the Padres mostly struggled to do was to simply score runs, as their offense went through extended stretches of appalling feebleness.

The San Diego poster child for offensive struggle in 2011 was 21-year-old rookie first baseman Anthony Rizzo. The centerpiece of the package of young talent Hoyer extracted from the Boston Red Sox in exchange for Gonzalez, Rizzo wasn't supposed to play in the majors this year, at least not until September call-up time. But the interim first base platoon the Padres installed performed so poorly, and Rizzo hit up such a storm in Triple-A, that in June the organization decided, "What are we waiting for?" and promoted the long tall southpaw slugger to the big club, sticking him in the starting lineup.

Well, sometimes these things work out well. But sometimes they don't. Rizzo found National League pitching, and cool PetCo Park hitting conditions, a whole lot less accommodating than the toasty Pacific Coast League offerings he was pummeling away down in the hot Tucson desert. Rizzo hit .331/.404/.652 in Triple-A, but—get this—.141/.281/.242 in 153 plate appearances for San Diego.

Yet along with that debacle, and others, the Padres encountered some positive developments. When the crestfallen Rizzo was sent back to the minors in late July, the fellow who replaced him as the primary first baseman was a 27-year-old career minor leaguer named Jesus Guzman. The right-handed-batting Guzman was with his fourth organization, and had failed to stick in the majors because of shaky third base defense. But San Diego manager Bud Black just put the sweet-swinging infielder at first base (at this point, what did he have to lose?), and Guzman rewarded the manager by hitting a line-drive-rich .312 over the balance of the season. One door closing was another opening, and all that.

The most impressive young Padre was 24-year-old center fielder Cameron Maybin. Given his first chance as a full-time regular, Maybin didn't break out as a star, but he did prove to be a player worth watching: a graceful fielder with wondrous speed and a muscular presence in the batter's box who, though he isn't yet, hints that he might develop into a powerful hitter.

Soft Rockies

The division's other huge disappointment took place in Colorado, where the Rockies, expected by many to strongly contend, instead staggered in barely ahead of the Padres. Alas, no breakout star turns were forthcoming on Blake Street.

Yet there were angles from which to see the Colorado glass (of frost-brewed Coors Golden Banquet beer, no doubt) as half-full. In 2010, after all, the Rockies had produced the most dramatic breakout star of that

Prospect Outlook: Colorado Rockies

The Rockies have one of the most intriguing farm systems, with a stable of prospects that could completely hit, miss, or end up anywhere in between. Tyler Matzek is the poster boy of that description, but Christian Friedrich is another first round pick with great talent he has yet to harness.

Prospect Freefall

Tyler Matzek had nowhere to go but down after sitting atop most rankings of the Rockies' farm system, and that's exactly where he went. Matzek was horrendous early in the year, battling extreme wildness to the point of being removed from game action for a stint in the middle of the season. The Rockies had been working with Matzek's mechanics to improve his control, but the over-analysis backfired and Matzek couldn't throw a strike. He went back to his high school pitching coach and returned to form later in the year, and still could end up being a high-end pitcher. For now, however, he still walks too many batters and will have to make adjustments on his own; the Rockies are hesitant to correct him again.

Prospect Outlook:
San Francisco Giants

The Giants' farm system hasn't had depth in years, but it has produced top talent with high draft picks such as Tim Lincecum and Buster Posey. This year's trade-deadline move, sending Zach Wheeler to the Mets for Carlos Beltran, emptied the farm system of the Giants' next high-potential arm, leaving the organization without a real impact player anywhere near the majors. The closest thing may be Gary Brown, who likely won't be a regular in the majors until 2013.

Prospect Riser

Gary Brown was already a top prospect in the Giants' system and a former first-round pick, but no one could have predicted what he did in 2011. Brown hit .336/.407/.519, with 34 doubles, 13 triples and 14 home runs, while stealing 53 bases and playing center field. Those numbers have to be taken into the context of the California League, but regardless, Brown established himself as the Giants' best position prospect.

season in then-24-year-old outfielder Carlos Gonzalez. The 2011 season was thus a major test for Gonzalez: was he for real?

Though CarGo encountered some challenges with consistency in 2011, as well as with staying healthy, on balance he delivered a very fine performance. He does appear to be for real, and alongside 26-year-old shortstop Troy Tulowitzki, who delivered his third consecutive downright great season, the Rockies continue to feature two of the best young all-around talents in the game.

Another young Rocky who strongly consolidated his game in 2011 was 23-year-old right-handed starting pitcher Jhoulys Chacin. In his first full-year big league exposure, Chacin was sure and steady all year, delivering quality start after quality start.

Settling for Second in San Francisco

Though a disastrous August ruined their effort to repeat as division champs, the 2011 San Francisco Giants presented an interesting season on the breakout-star front. They didn't have one, exactly, but they featured several players worth examining in this light.

First of all, the Giants rather expected to have a breakout star. Based on his sensational minor league hitting, 23-year-old rookie Brandon Belt—in just his second professional season—was given the starting first base job for the defending World Champions to open the year. And when Belt launched a three-run homer in the season's second game, it looked as though that breakout might be at hand.

But, no. The Giants' commitment to Belt lasted a grand total of two weeks and 52 at-bats, at which point his batting average was .192 and the team sent him back to the minors. He would return—indeed, Belt would spend much of the year yo-yoing back and forth between Triple-A and the big club—but the rookie, colorfully nicknamed "The Baby Giraffe" for his towering-yet-gawky presence, was never given the opportunity to play regularly in the majors for more than a couple of weeks at a time, and he never got the kind of hot streak going that would force the issue.

It was a crazy, mixed-up year for Belt, a disappointing one for sure. But the kind of power he displayed in glimpses (nine home runs in 187 major league at-bats) suggests the breakout may be coming along at some point. By no means was Belt's struggle nearly as severe as Rizzo's in San Diego.

Another Giant had been a breakout star in 2009, then a major flop in 2010. Third baseman Pablo Sandoval shed about 40 pounds of excess weight in an intense workout program over the 2010-11 offseason, and the slimmer Panda delivered a tremendous performance that was marred only by missing six weeks with a broken hand after being hit by a pitch in late April. If it wasn't a breakout year, it was a stirring comeback from one of the game's more impressive young stars.

And the age of 33 may be far too old to be considered a breakout star, but that aside, the season presented by Ryan Vogelsong had "breakout" scrawled all over it. A complete bust in his extensive major league trial of many moons ago (Vogelsong put up a big fat 6.00 ERA in 280 innings for the Pirates in 2001-06), the right hander drifted all the way to Japan, where he pitched less than well for three years.

He returned to the 'States in 2010, toiling for parts of the season for two different Triple-A teams, compiling a record of 3-8 with a 4.81 ERA that didn't exactly suggest an imminent breakout. For no obvious reason, the Giants invited Vogelsong to spring training in 2011.

He pitched surprisingly well in the Cactus League, though not well enough to make the Opening Day staff. But Vogelsong was called up a couple of weeks into the season to replace an injured Barry Zito in the Giants' rotation and immediately began mowing batters down. Vogelsong threw hard and with fine control, and was calmly and consistently effective all year long. Where in the world has *this* pitcher been all these years?

Shining through the L.A. gloom

There was no shortage of problems plaguing the Los Angeles Dodgers in 2011. Start with one of the most corrupt and dysfunctional ownership situations in the history of baseball (and that history covers a whole lot of corrupt and dysfunctional ownership situations). Proceed to an Opening Day fan being beaten into a coma under no-security-to-be-found conditions in the Dodger Stadium parking lot. And add a thick layer of losing baseball being played before a largely-vacant Chavez Ravine grandstand for most of the season.

Yet amid the dystopian torpor, somehow two Dodgers found a way to perform brilliantly. Twenty-six-year-old center fielder Matt Kemp, after slogging through a 2010 season in which he was roundly criticized for putting forth less than his best effort, showed up in 2011 looking like someone with something to prove. From the get-go in 2011 Kemp was exquisite, confidently excelling in every phase of every inning despite his team spending most of the year drearily losing and the once-great L.A. fanbase alternating between being miserable, apathetic and absent.

Kemp did not miss a game all year. He led the league in runs scored, home runs, RBIs, and total bases (and for the sabermetrically inclined, he also led the league in OPS+ and WAR). He was second in the league

Prospect Outlook: Los Angeles Dodgers

The Dodgers have drafted a ton of pitchers over the past few years, but have failed to develop them successfully into starters at the big league level (with the exception of Clayton Kershaw). Chris Withrow, Ethan Martin and Aaron Miller were the Dodgers' top picks from 2007-2009 respectively, and none has developed into the rotation member the organization envisioned.

Under the Radar

The Dodgers have spent a lot of their first-round picks in recent years on pitchers, so it's easy for a second-round pick like Garrett Gould to get overlooked. Heck, he wasn't even the most notable pitcher on his own team last year (that would be 2010 first-rounder Zack Lee). But Gould won't be overlooked for long if he continues to post 2.40 ERAs and walk just 2.7 batters per nine innings. Gould will head to High-A ball next season and battle the elements of the California League.

Prospect Outlook: Arizona Diamondbacks

Once just Jarrod Parker and a gang of misfits, the Diamondbacks now have a stable of pitching prospects and envision a potential rotation similar to what the Giants have put together. With three of the top seven picks in the 2011 draft, the Diamondbacks took potentially the best college pitcher in Trevor Bauer, who should be in Arizona by 2012, and the prep pitcher with potentially the best fastball in Archie Bradley.

Prospect Riser

Tyler Skaggs was already highly regarded within the Diamondbacks' farm system but after his 2011 season he's going to get more national recognition. Skaggs was unfazed by the extreme hitter's environments of the California League, posting an impressive 3.22 ERA in his half-season there. Upon promotion to Double-A, Skaggs improved, posting a 2.50 ERA in 10 starts. For the season, Skaggs fanned 11.3 batters per nine innings and posted a K/BB ratio over four.

- Jeff Moore

in slugging and in stolen bases (think about that), third in the league in batting average, and fourth in the league in on-base percentage, all the while playing the sort of center field that may very well bag him a Gold Glove.

Twenty-three-year-old Clayton Kershaw had been among the more impressive young starting pitchers in baseball prior to 2011, but hadn't put it all together. Over the first half of 2011 he appeared to do so, compiling a 9-4 record for a team that was 10 games under .500, making his first All-Star team and even chipping in a scoreless inning toward the National League's victory in the Midsummer Classic.

But Kershaw was just getting warmed up. In his 14 second-half starts, the big southpaw was essentially unhittable, going 12-1 with an ERA of 1.31 and a WHIP of 0.89. In the month of September, Kershaw surrendered four walks against 36 strikeouts.

Between them, Kemp and Kershaw even managed to animate the deadwood that comprised most of the rest of the Dodger roster into a competitive ball club. At the end of July, the Dodgers were 48-59 and jockeying with the Padres for possession of last place. Over the rest of the season, L.A. went 34-20 and by the end the Dodgers were making the Giants sweat about hanging on to second.

Arriving in Arizona

The team that soared past the stumbling Giants to capture the division flag was expected by absolutely, positively no one to do so. Using the methodology we developed and presented in the 2009 Hardball Times Annual (when examining the phenomenally surprising performance of the spectacular breakout team of the 2008 season, the Tampa Bay Rays), the 2011 Diamondbacks' performance ranks as one of the 12 most out-of-the-blue in major league history.

This year's Snakes generally conform to the pattern we observed in that article as being typical of breakout teams: they're young, they rely upon run prevention (keyed especially by efficient fielding) more than run production, and most interestingly their manager is still new to the job (this was, after all, Arizona manager Kirk Gibson's first full year as a skipper at any level).

The success of the 2011 D-backs was keyed, no doubt, by the breakout stars Upton, Kennedy and Hudson. But the roster was dotted with cases of players who, while not breakout stars, came through with personal-best performances. Catcher Miguel Montero, 27 years old, has been a good player for several years, but never before as good as he was in 2011. Thirty-year-old third baseman Ryan Roberts was an end-of-the-roster marginality before emerging as a solid regular this year.

Crucial pitching depth was provided by erstwhile obscurities. Josh Collmenter, a soft-tossing 25-year-old rookie with an unorthodox delivery, earned his way into the starting rotation with some startling early-season work, and proceeded to hold his own. The Arizona bullpen included several low-cost youngsters producing fine results (David Hernandez, Joe Paterson and Bryan Shaw), as well as a scrap-heap project who emerged as a long-relief lifesaver in Micah Owings.

NL West PITCHf/x Sidebar

by Josh Weinstock

Selected No. 1 overall in the 2005 player draft and the brother of current major leaguer B.J. Upton, Justin Upton seemed destined for a special career. And he did not disappoint, dominating far more experienced players in the minor leagues and making his MLB debut before his 20th birthday. But his precocious talent also hurt him. Lacking the seasoning of most top prospects, he did not have the experience necessary to combat major league pitching. Chief among his struggles was his ability (or lack thereof) to make contact.

In 2008 he failed to make contact on 31 out of every 100 swings he took, a Mark Reynoldsian (over 800 strikeouts in the past four years) feat. What use were his 80-on-a-scale-of-80 power tool and lighting quick wrists if he could not get the bat on the ball?

The next year marked a sign of the promising career we all envisioned: At the age of 21, Upton cruised his way to a cool 132 wRC+ season. (Weighted Runs Created combines offensive statistics into one measure. Weighted Runs Created Plus—wRC+—measures how a player's wRC compares with league average. League average is 100 and every point above 100 is a percentage point above league average.) Despite a posting a similar BB/K figure as last year's, Upton used improved contact skills to put the ball in play more often. He walked or struck out in 33 percent of his plate appearances in 2009, compared to 42 percent in 2008. As his value at the plate is derived from his well-above-average batting average on balls in play and power, it's imperative that he puts the ball in play often.

Upton did not sustain the success of his breakout year in 2010. His wRC+ dropped to 110, despite his maintaining a very high BABIP. Key to his struggles was decreased power output and a decreased rate of putting the ball in play. Even though Upton actually improved his contact rate in 2010, he also became more passive, allowing pitchers to work him into deep counts to exploit his contact struggles. Bizarrely, Upton's increased patience at the plate seemed to hurt him more than help him, as his skill set relies on his ability to put the ball in play and to avoid deep counts.

In 2011, Upton made another plate discipline adjustment, but this time in the opposite direction. He began swinging at the highest rate since he made his debut, becoming far more aggressive at the plate.

This can be seen in the graph below:

Swing rates: 2010 vs. 2011

This graph indicates Justin Upton's 50 percent swing contours, meaning that all areas within the circles represent locations where Upton swung at least half the time, and all area outside the circles represent locations where he swung less than half of the time. The solid circle is for 2011, and the dotted circle is for 2010. The graph is also from the catcher's perspective, meaning that the left side of the graph corresponds to the inside of the plate for Upton. The dotted box represents an approximation of the actual called strike zone.

As you can see, Upton now attempts to cover much more of the strike zone, particularly in areas below and away from him. However, it's not that he has blindly started swinging more; he has been selective about where he has increased his swinging. For example, in 3-1 counts in 2011, he swung 75 percent of the time, a huge increase from 2010 where he swung just 49 percent of the time. We also see large change in 1-0 counts, where his swing rates jumped from 40 percent in 2010 to over 50 percent in 2011.

Also beneficial to his strikeout rate was his improved performance in dealing with 3-2 counts. Thanks to his increased aggressiveness, he was in fewer 3-2 counts in 2011 than 2010. And when he was in those counts he was better than before, showing improved contact ability: 84 percent contact on swings in 2011 compared to 76 percent in 2010. These adjustments allowed Upton to put 18.4 percent of all pitches in 2011 into play, trumping his 2010 rate of 14.7 percent.

Although he is an immensely talented player, we will need next year to decide if his rapacious style is here to stay. Despite the evolution of his approach, his contact skills are still poor, and pitchers may learn next year to combat his aggression at the plate.

Resources

- PITCHf/x data from MLBAM via Darrel Zimmerman's pbp2 database and scripts by Joseph Adler/Mike Fast/Darrel Zimmerman
- Justin Upton's FanGraphs player page
- Plate discipline numbers calculated by the author

Commentary

The Preseason in Frivolity

by Craig Calcaterra

This book is chock full of information about the 2011 baseball season. If you read even a portion of it and don't know who won, who lost and why this past year, there's no helping you.

But you can be forgiven if you forgot the year's ephemeral, trivial, embarrassing and pathetic events. That stuff doesn't stick in a fan's mind like who won the MVP. That's why I'm here. So, without further ado, I give you an overview of all things funny, sad, stupid and ignominious of the 2011 baseball season.

February

The Red Sox begin spring training following a most eventful winter in which they added Adrian Gonzalez and Carl Crawford to an already-potent lineup. A meeting is held at Major League Baseball headquarters and it is decided, after sharp debate, to continue to play the season even though, yeah, it pretty much is guaranteed to end with a Red Sox World Series title.

The Yankees' season begins with somewhat more controversy and rancor, with Hank Steinbrenner giving a press conference in which he blasts revenue sharing and the luxury tax, calling it "socialism." He said "communism, socialism, whatever you want to call it, is never the answer." Steinbrenner makes a great point about baseball owners relying on handouts. Would that they—as he and his brother Hal did—pull themselves up by their own bootstraps and make their mark on the world by their own merits, not on the work of others.

The Rays sign Johnny Damon and Manny Ramirez. At their introductory press conference, Manny Ramirez is asked about whether he is comfortable wearing his old number 24 jersey instead of his now-signature 99 jersey. Ramirez explains that it's OK because 24 is his American League number and 99 is his National League number. The assembled press decides that it is best not to inform Manny that he wore 99 for the White Sox in 2010 because it would probably only frighten and confuse him.

Jim Leyland assesses Miguel Cabrera's health: "Miguel Cabrera is in the best shape of his life. He's stronger than he's ever been. And he's quicker than he's ever been." This days after Cabrera was arrested after being found drunk in his car on the side of a road and, just prior to his arrest, taking a swig from a bottle of Scotch right in front of police officers. I'd make a joke at Leyland's expense here, but Cabrera did go on and hit .344/.448/.586, so maybe there's something to this Scotch training.

Michael Young, upset that the Rangers signed third baseman Adrian Beltre who, presumably, will take Young's playing time, asks for a trade. Then, when a trade doesn't happen, he arrives at training camp and refuses to talk to general manager Jon Daniels. Then, because the normal rules regarding pouting over one's playing time regardless of what it means for the team don't seem to apply to Michael Young, he is praised by sportswriters for his selflessness and "team-first" attitude later in the year. I know. I have no idea either.

Jose Canseco announces that he will soon be writing a third book. At one time the idea of "Jose Canseco: prolific author" may have seemed laughable, but given that Snooki, JWoww and The Situation have book deals, Canseco may as well be F. Scott Fitzgerald.

With the beginning of training camp, the period during which Albert Pujols is willing to negotiate a contract extension with the Cardinals also ends, with the sides far apart. The Cardinals are thought to be low-balling Pujols, secure in the knowledge that free agency's usual big spenders—the Yankees and the Red Sox—each have fine first basemen under long-term contracts. Pujols and his agents, however, are secure in the knowledge that the Cardinals just don't understand how the Yankees and the Red Sox do business.

March

WikiLeaks releases State Department documents in which an American diplomat calls Iranian president Mahmoud Ahmadinejad "the George Steinbrenner of Iran" as a result of his constant meddling with the coaching staff of the Iranian soccer team. Of course, given the man's reign of terror, such comparisons are really, really unfair to make. Wait, what? Of COURSE I mean Ahmadinejad's reign of terror. But I suppose I probably should have clarified.

Oakland Athletics outfielder Coco Crisp is arrested for drunk driving during spring training in Scottsdale, Ariz. When he is pulled over, a second car which had been following him also pulls over. It is later revealed that the second car contained Crisp's personal security detail, which he called his "secret service." The hilariousness of Crisp having his own secret service is outweighed by the inexplicableness of the man's security team allowing him to get behind the wheel of an automobile while intoxicated.

Cliff Lee gives a radio interview in which he says part of the reason he chose to sign with the Phillies instead of the Yankees was that "some of the Yankees guys were getting older." In other news, the Phillies had the oldest roster in all of baseball heading into the 2011 season.

The Extra 2%, a book by Jonah Keri about the hard-to-believe success of the Tampa Bay Rays is published. It's a shame for Keri that the book is coming out in a year in which, thanks to losing Carl Crawford and their entire bullpen, the Rays have absolutely no chance whatsoever to make the playoffs. I mean, just think what it would mean for sales if—once again—the Rays confounded the experts and went on an improbable playoff run!

The Rangers toy with the notion of moving Neftali Feliz to the starting rotation. Manager Ron Washington, however, is hesitant to make such a move unless the Rangers can find "an experienced closer" to replace Feliz in the bullpen. When told that Feliz had absolutely no experience as a closer when he saved 40 games in 2010, Washington said … wait, he said nothing, because no one in the baseball media has the guts to throw that kind of question right back at a manager when he says something silly like that.

Orioles utility man Jake Fox hits his seventh spring training home run. It's astounding stuff. It's one more spring training homer than Sean Rodriguez, Mike Napoli, Justin Upton, Aaron Hill, John Bowker and Delwyn Young had in 2010, and as you certainly remember, each of those guys went on to amazing, power-packed seasons that year.

Former Astros, Mets, Rockies, Braves and a few other teams' pitcher Mike Hampton announces his retirement. He sprains his vocal cords during the actual announcement, tears an elbow ligament signing the retirement paperwork, and then spontaneously combusts while walking to the parking lot. Even though his career is over, he's placed on the disabled list because, really, it's the only place he's found peace for the past decade.

Orioles manager Buck Showalter creates waves when he is quoted in *Men's Health* magazine ripping Theo Epstein and the Red Sox for having so many financial advantages at their disposal, saying "I'd like to see how smart Theo Epstein is with the Tampa Bay payroll." Epstein declines comment, but writes in his personal diary: "I can't wait for Sept. 28! Last day of the season! We play Buck and those stinkin' Orioles! We'll see who has the last laugh when we leave the field that day for our charter plane to take us home for the first round of the playoffs!"

Jose Canseco is sued when he tries to send his twin brother Ozzie Canseco to appear in his place at a celebrity boxing match before 400 paying customers at the Seminole Hard Rock Hotel & Casino in Florida. The legal case grinds to a halt, however, when lawyers are unable to decide whether anyone was actually harmed by not having to see the actual Jose Canseco in a celebrity boxing match.

**Follow Craig's Season in Frivolity in the
margins of the next six articles.**

In All Probability

by Dave Studenmund

In baseball, you can't take anything for granted. Teams with big leads can lose games. Batters on hot streaks can suddenly go cold. Even teams with a lock on the Wild Card slot can lose their grip.

This isn't as true in many other sports. In a basketball or football game, there comes a time when you know which team is going to win. Over the season, schedules are shorter, so titles are determined more quickly. It's easier to predict next year's NBA leading scorer than next year's major league batting leader.

Baseball is just more unpredictable than other sports. It doesn't have a timer, it has innings. Teams are never out of time, they just keep playing until they've run out of outs. This is why it's so dramatic. This is why it breaks your heart. This is why it's a game of probabilities.

There are no better examples in recent baseball history than four games played on the last day of the 2011 season. Tampa Bay and Boston were tied for the Wild Card in the American League; Atlanta and St. Louis were tied for the Wild Card in the National. They each played different opponents on the last day, and the potential outcomes ranged from two clearcut Wild Card winners and a day off to two playoff games the next day.

Let's look at each game through the lens of Win Probability (sometimes called Win Expectancy). Instead of tracking the score at each point of the game, we'll track the probability of each team winning that game. Win Probability is a relatively simple extension of the score, inning and base/out situation, expressed as the percent probability that the team in question is going to win the game.

Win Probability (or WP, to keep it simple) treats all teams and all players equally. Each team is given a 50 percent chance of winning in the beginning of the game, and the probabilities don't change based on who's at bat. It doesn't presuppose anything about the quality of the teams. It's a simple, straightforward way to measure the ins and outs of a game.

First up: St. Louis against the Astros. A WP game graph is on the next page.

The Cardinals put this game away quickly. Seven of their first eight hitters had hits (all singles with one double) and they scored five runs in the top of the first. By the end of the first, the Cardinals had an 85 percent probability of winning. Chris Carpenter took care of that extra 15 percent with nine

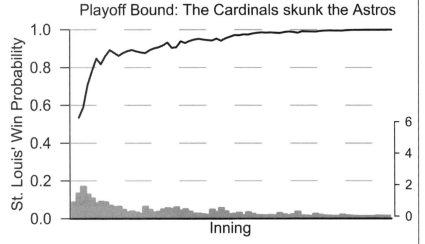

Playoff Bound: The Cardinals skunk the Astros

shutout innings and St. Louis finished with an 8-0 victory and assurance of at least a playoff game the next day.

Not much to see here. However, the action was intense in Atlanta, where the Braves played the Phillies (graph on the next page).

This game was a low-scoring affair for the first six innings. The Phillies and Braves both scored a run in the first, keeping the Win Probability relatively even. Then Atlanta added two runs in the third on a Dan Uggla homer. With a 3-1 lead, the Braves' Win Probability climbed over 80 percent as the game continued. Even a Philadelphia run in the seventh, which cut the score to 3-2, didn't drag their chances of a win below 80 percent.

By the top of the ninth, with closer Craig Kimbrel on the mound and a 3-2 lead, the Braves' Win Probability was 86 percent. However, Placido Polanco singled (WP dropped to 74 percent), Ben Francisco walked after an out (still 74 percent), Jimmy Rollins walked to load the bases (55 percent) and Chase Utley hit a sacrifice fly. The score was tied and both teams were essentially back to a 50 percent probability of winning.

See those gray bars in the next graph? Those measure a thing called "Leverage Index." Leverage Index (or LI) is an outgrowth of Win Probability as it measures the criticality of each moment of a game by assessing the potential variety of outcomes in each plate appearance. The more variable the potential impact on a team's probability of winning the game (in other words, the more critical it is), the higher the LI.

An average Leverage Index is 1.0. Not too critical, but not insignificant either. Just right.

Leverage Index helps fill in the game story. On the graph, you can see two moments when the game's LI jumped over 7.0 (Be sure to use the

The Yankees find themselves involved in a controversy when, on Opening Day, a team employee is spotted behind home plate, wearing a headset and relaying signals to Yankees hitters. When confronted with the evidence that the Yankees are perhaps realizing an unfair advantage as a result of this, general manager Brian Cashman says, "That's nonsense. Why would we do such a thing? Our $200 million plus payroll is all of the unfair advantage we require."

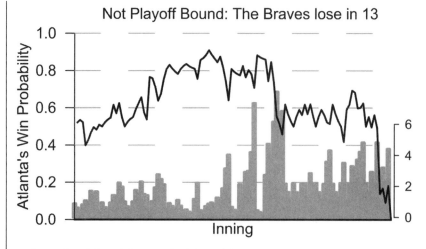

Not Playoff Bound: The Braves lose in 13

scale on the right of the graph). To put that in perspective, there were only 137 times that a game LI climbed over 7.0 over the course of the entire season for all teams. That encompasses nearly 200,000 plays and plate appearances, or less than 0.1 percent.

The first instance was in the top of the eighth. The Phillies were down 3-2, but they loaded the bases with two out. The Braves' WP was down somewhat, but the outcome of the duel between Raul Ibanez at the plate and Jonny Venters on the mound would have a huge impact on the game. Ibanez struck out and the game continued.

When Chase Utley came to the plate in the top of the ninth, with the Phillies still down a run, one out and the bases loaded, the LI jumped up to 8.1, which is very, very critical—the highest bar on that graph and the 58th most critical in-game moment of any game any time during the season. Utley's sacrifice fly was certainly a "clutch hit," even though it wasn't technically a hit.

As you can see, things stayed critical throughout the game's four extra innings. Neither team mounted much of a threat in innings 10 through 12, except for the bottom of the 12th. That's when the Braves had a runner on second with one out (WP of 68 percent and LI of 3.2) and runners on first and third with two out (WP of 62 percent and LI of 4.8) but couldn't capitalize on either situation.

The Phillies scored a run in the top of the 13th, however, on a walk, Utley single and RBI single by Hunter Pence. When Pence was at the plate (two out and runners on first and third), the LI was 4.8. After his single, the Braves' Win Probability dropped all the way to 14 percent; Pence's single accounted for a 35 percent drop. David Herndon closed out the bottom of the 13th for the Phils, and Atlanta was out of the postseason.

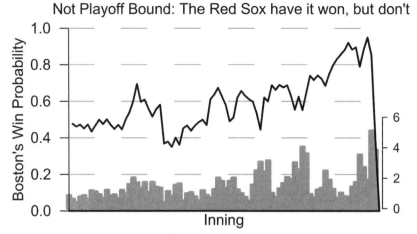

Not Playoff Bound: The Red Sox have it won, but don't

The Braves' game Win Probability dropped to zero, as did their chances of appearing in the World Series.

Let's turn to the American League Wild Card situation, where things were even more dramatic.

The Red Sox, who were playing the Orioles in Baltimore, took the first lead on a Dustin Pedroia single in the top of the third (70 percent Win Probability for the Sox) but Baltimore shortstop J.J. Hardy responded in the bottom of the third with a two-run home run and Boston's Win Probability dropped to 40 percent.

The Sox came back to score on a balk in the top of the fourth and then Pedroia hit a solo home run in the fifth to put Boston up 3-2—Win Probability up to 60 percent. The score stood at 3-2 until the bottom of the ninth, and you can see how Win Probability crept up as the game went on. Innings are time in baseball. By the ninth, the Red Sox had a 90 percent Win Probability.

Jonathan Papelbon struck out the first two Orioles and Boston's Win Probability was all the way up to 95 percent at this point. At least a Wild Card playoff game seemed at hand—perhaps sole possession of the Wild Card slot, depending on the outcome of the Tampa Bay/New York game.

The probabilities were good, but the outcomes did not favor the Red Sox this year. Chris Davis hit a double to right (WP down to 85 percent), Nolan Reimold smashed a ground rule double that drove in Davis (WP down to 40 percent) and then Robert Andino singled him home. Win Probability: zero.

Davis' double was worth 10 percent of Win Probability, but Reimold's was the really key hit. It changed the game's Win Probability by 46 percent. Andino's hit finished the job by adding another 40 percent to the

Manny Ramirez abruptly retires from baseball after it is revealed that he tested positive for performance-enhancing drugs during spring training. This being his second drug-related offense, his retirement preempts a mandatory 100-game suspension. Because it's Manny, no one is really sure if he's aware of what's happening to him, so it is decided that he be told that he is going to a farm up north where he will have more room to run around and will be much happier.

Chipper Jones records his 2,500th career hit, his 1,500th career RBI and his 500th career double during the month of April. When asked about it he said "I really like round numbers."

Tampa Bay Rays outfielder Sam Fuld roars out of the gate to post a 1.035 OPS as of April 18. His hard-charging outfield play combined with his sabermetrically-oriented mind makes him an instant sensation with brainy baseball fans. Brainy fans who are so smitten that they manage to forget everything they ever learned about small sample sizes and past performance serving as a reasonable indicator of future performance. Fuld's bobblehead does look quite fetching, however, on the mantle next to the brainy fans' Brian Bannister bobbleheads.

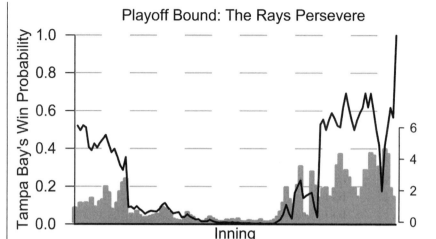

Playoff Bound: The Rays Persevere

total. In just three at-bats, the Orioles changed their own probability of winning the game from 5 per cent to 100 percent. These are the things that happen in baseball.

All eyes turned to Tampa Bay. This game had barely started, in front of 29,518 Tampa Bay fans, when the Yankees took a 5-0 lead in the second inning, thanks primarily to a grand slam home run by Mark Teixeira. Tampa's Win Probability was down to 10 percent in the second, and it would continue to decline—all the way to 0.3 percent (seriously)—as the Yankees padded their lead to 7-0 by the bottom of the eighth.

But probabilities are only that: probabilities. A single, double, hit-by-pitch, walk, another HBP, sacrifice fly and Evan Longoria home run later, the Rays had clawed back to trail by just one run. John Jaso singled and stole second, but the Rays couldn't capitalize and they finished the eighth down by a run. This was an incredible comeback, yet still the Rays' Win Probability was only 10 percent going into the bottom of the ninth.

Cory Wade was on the mound for the Yankees and he quickly recorded two outs, bringing Dan Johnson to bat. This wasn't even an auspicious at-bat by leverage standards, holding only a 1.55 LI. But Johnson turned Tampa's winning probability from 4 percent to 53 percent with one swing of the bat, a home run just down the right-field line. It was true baseball magic.

The drama didn't stop there. The Rays and Yankees went into extra innings. In the top of the 12th, the Yankees had runners on first and third with no outs; Tampa's WP was less than 20 percent. But the Rays got an out at the plate and Jake McGee retired the last two batters to keep them in the game. And then—more magic!—Longoria sealed a postseason appearance for Tampa with a home run in the bottom of the 12th. Final score: 8-7 Rays.

And so finished perhaps the greatest day in baseball history.

Okay, what do I mean by that? Well, having four critical games on the last day of the season, and then seeing three of those four games turn into heart-wrenching affairs, well, it just doesn't happen. I doubt it's ever happened to this degree before.

Think of it this way: we know that these **games** were dramatic; we've even quantified it through the use of WP and LI. But we also know that they occurred at a dramatic moment in the **season**. And we can quantify that, too.

Let's call on another set of probabilities: the probability of each team making the postseason as the regular season progresses. A number of sites on the Internet calculate each team's postseason probability during the year (try coolstandings.com or baseballprospectus.com), but we've added a wrinkle for the *Hardball Times Annual*: Championship Leverage Index.

Championship Leverage Index (CLI) was introduced a couple of years ago by Sky Andrecheck, and its purpose is simple: CLI measures the criticality of a game in the context of a pennant race, the same way LI measures the criticality of a plate appearance in a game.

A "neutral" game has a CLI of 1.0. Teams that fall out of the pennant race quickly, such as Houston in 2011, open the year at 1.0 and never have another game of even average criticality. Other teams build a big lead quickly—the Phillies for example—and never have a CLI above 1.5. When you have a big lead in your division, things just aren't so critical.

And then there are teams like Tampa Bay.

Derek Jeter starts the season with a dreadful 7-for-34 stretch. The most likely culprit: the revamped swing he and hitting coach Kevin Long worked on in the offseason. The second most likely culprit: Father Time. Because he's Derek Jeter, he has Long and Father Time killed. He doesn't even bother to make it look like an accident because, hey, he's Derek Jeter.

Tampa Bay's Championship Leverage Index

Josh Hamilton breaks a bone in his arm while sliding into home on a tag-up play from third base, landing on the disabled list. After the incident, Hamilton is asked why he bothered to try to score on the play. Hamilton says his third base coach told him to go. Hamilton then explains just how opposed he was to the idea of going and that he did so against his better judgment. The third base coach then joins Hamilton on the disabled list, suffering from multiple injuries as a result of being thrown under the bus.

Tampa's CLI was generally between 1.0 and 2.0 until August, when it appeared that the Rays were out of postseason contention and the Red Sox had wrapped things up. That changed in September and the Rays' CLI climbed all month long, to top out at 9.7 on the last day of the year.

Of course, all four contending teams had a CLI of 9.7 on the last day of the year, which means that their games were about 10 times more critical to making the postseason than a neutral game. Four times 10 equals 40 times more drama in one day.

Here's another way to think of it. When Utley hit his sacrifice fly to tie the Braves in the bottom of the ninth with one out, the Leverage Index of that moment was 8. Multiply that by 10 (the CLI) and you have a moment that was 80 times more critical to the Braves than a "neutral" game moment. That is heart-stopping drama.

Unfortunately, we don't have CLI for all previous years. But I think you'll be hard pressed to find a night in major league history with so many championship-critical moments, all within a few hours of each other.

————————————————

There are lots of other things you can do with game and season probabilities. It's fun to find the biggest plays of the year, measured by the change in Win Probability. This is called Win Probability Added, because it measures the difference in Win Probability before and after the play. Of course, lots of times the Win Probability goes down too, but the name "Win Probability Added" (or WPA) puts a positive spin on things.

For example, on June 21, the Nationals and Mariners were playing each other in an interleague game. The Nationals were losing, 5-3, with two out in the bottom of the ninth and runners on first and second. Washington had already scored two runs in the bottom of the ninth to make things close, but the Nationals' WP was still only 8 percent.

Wilson Ramos changed that with a swing of the bat, a three-run home run that won the game for the Nationals, 6-5. This created a WPA of 92 percent for Ramos and the Nationals (we tend to use this format for WPA: 0.92) but certainly a negative result for Mariners pitcher David Pauley.

According to WPA, that was the single biggest hit of the season.

Now, before you start complimenting Ramos on his clutch hitting, consider something that happened on Aug. 17. The Nationals were trailing the Reds, 2-0, going into the bottom of the ninth. Ryan Zimmerman led off with a home run, cutting the lead to 2-1, and the Nationals proceeded to load the bases against Francisco Cordero with only one out. Their WP was actually above 50 percent at that point and the LI of the situation was a sky-high 9.2.

Unfortunately, Ramos grounded into a double play, 4-6-3, and the game was over. The Reds won.

Actually, no one cost his team more with double plays than Ramos. Ramos grounded into 19 double plays (admittedly, a subset of all double plays) for a total WPA of -2.36, or about 0.12 per DP. Why did his double plays hurt the Nationals so much? Because he tended to hit them in high leverage situations: The average LI of all his GIDPs was 2.45.

Ramos was in rarefied company. The second- and third-most hurtful double play hitters were Albert Pujols (-2.35, average LI of 1.7) and David Ortiz (-2.13, average LI of 1.65).

On the defensive side, the biggest impact plays tend to be those just like Ramos': double plays in one-run games with one out and runners on base in the bottom of the ninth. The biggest non-DP play of the year occurred on May 5, when Nationals reliever Drew Storen struck out the Marlins' Wes Helms looking. This strikeout registered a WPA of 0.30, as the Marlins had runners on second and third and were down by a run with one out. The Leverage Index of that situation was 6.0.

We could review individual plays like this all day long. Let's go one better and group them together to see how individual players fared over the full season. For instance, we know that Leverage Index is indicative of how critical a situation is. Well, who delivered the most in critical situations?

One way of answering this is to isolate high-LI plate appearances. About 10 percent of all plate appearances have a Leverage Index of 2.0 or more, so we'll just look at those. Which batters performed best in those situations? We could calculate their batting average or slugging average or some such thing, but let's just add up their WPA in those situations.

The list is topped by some of the best hitters in baseball, with a surprise in the No. 10 spot.

The Barry Bonds trial takes place and ends with a not guilty verdict on most perjury counts, a hung jury on a final perjury count and a guilty verdict on one count of obstruction of justice. America breathes a sigh of relief as the nation's streets are finally safe again.

Player	Plays	WPA
Votto, Joey	80	3.53
Fielder, Prince	71	3.16
Abreu, Bobby	71	3.10
Berkman, Lance	69	2.96
Cabrera, Miguel	67	2.57
Hafner, Travis	47	2.48
Hamilton, Josh	41	2.34
Howard, Ryan	75	2.29
Damon, Johnny	65	2.27
Bautista, Jose	73	2.20
Morgan, Nyjer	44	2.18

I don't mean to overlook the terrific clutch performance of Joey Votto (who was intentionally walked in seven of those 80 high-LI situations, "unintentionally" walked in another nine, and also hit five home runs and seven doubles) and others (Bobby Abreu?), but what about Nyjer Morgan?

In 44 high-LI situations, the Brewers outfielder hit six singles, six doubles and a triple. He also walked three times, was hit by a pitch three times and hit a couple of sacrifice flies. The Brewers had a lot of things go right for them this year, but Morgan was an unexpected surprise, particularly in those clutch situations.

Okay, so let's put this all together. Who were the overall most productive hitters? Which ones led the majors in total WPA?

Name	WPA
Bautista, Jose	7.86
Fielder, Prince	7.52
Cabrera, Miguel	7.31
Votto, Joey	6.69
Kemp, Matt	6.43
Braun, Ryan	6.30
Ellsbury, Jacoby	5.66
Berkman, Lance	5.40
Howard, Ryan	5.14
Hamilton, Josh	4.60

First of all, let's recognize that total WPA is a reflection of a player's playing time, number of high-leverage opportunities and performance in those opportunities. There may be some significant differences between WPA rankings and standard baseball stats. Having said that, there are no big surprises here. These were the best hitters in baseball.

The fact that Prince Fielder is ranked above Triple Threat Matt Kemp, or teammate Ryan Braun, may surprise you. But take a look at the previous table—Prince Fielder posted the second highest contribution in high-LI situations. WPA rankings like this reward production and timing.

Let's flip this around and look at things from the other side of the diamond. Theoretically, WPA could be split between pitchers and fielders, but that is a very tricky thing to do. People have tried, but no one has yet found a way to legitimately separate the two. So all defensive WPA credits (and debits) accrue to pitchers. We won't discuss fielding today.

Here's a list of the top pitchers in WPA. I'm going to put starters and relievers on the same list even though that creates some problems. WPA effectively treats them differently, because the best relievers are often brought into games in only high-LI situations. So, if they're good, they'll register a high WPA in many fewer innings than starters typically accrue. In fact, relief pitchers sometimes top the leader board of top WPA pitchers in specific years.

Not this year, however.

Name	WPA	LI
Verlander, Justin	5.14	0.94
Clippard, Tyler	5.01	1.52
Weaver, Jered	4.63	0.99
Kennedy, Ian	4.57	1.07
Axford, John	4.29	1.87
Venters, Jonny	4.28	1.79
Robertson, David	4.26	1.68
Valverde, Jose	4.17	1.76
Beckett, Josh	3.89	1.01
Halladay, Roy	3.82	1.11

I added each pitcher's average Leverage Index to the table, so that you can more easily pick out the starters and relievers. Starters will usually have an LI around 1.0. Elite relievers will have an LI over 1.5.

CLI provides an easy way to present how "critical" each team's season was. You can almost think of it as a "Drama Index."

Below is a table of the total CLI of each American League team. The Rangers and Angels were in a tight race in the American League West for a while so they come out on top of this table.

The Red Sox, on the other hand, rank only fifth despite their late-season drama. This is because the middle of their summer was relatively quiet.

Team	CLI
TEX	212
LAA	211
TBR	192
DET	185
BOS	182
CLE	176
NYY	148
CHW	108
SEA	94
TOR	88
OAK	77
KCR	68
BAL	64
MIN	48

Here are the CLI totals for each National League team. The Cardinals and Braves, who fought for the Wild Card slot while also putting some pressure on their division leaders, are at the top.

The Giants, who made the NL West competitive for a while, are third.

The Astros had the least "dramatic" year of any major league team.

Team	CLI
STL	222
ATL	207
SFG	202
ARI	191
MIL	167
CIN	122
PHI	120
PIT	118
COL	105
FLA	95
NYM	80
WSN	72
LAD	67
SDP	51
CHC	51
HOU	31

- Dave Studenmund

Among the starters, Justin Verlander's big year is reinforced by the numbers. He led every pitcher in WPA, even the top relievers. However, his season wasn't "historic" in a WPA sense. His total of 5.14 is typical of pitching WPA leaders from previous years—even a bit on the low side. You can't pull a "Verlander for MVP" argument out of his WPA stats.

How about the No. 2 guy? The Nationals' Tyler Clippard didn't register a single save this year, but WPA says he was the best reliever in the majors. Clippard pitched in 72 games with an ERA of 1.83. He also pitched in very important situations—his average Leverage Index was 1.52, only slightly below that of a pure "closer," such as John Axford. Clippard also pitched more innings than the typical closer and he pitched extremely well in high-LI situations. For instance, batters hit only .087 against him when the LI was over 1.5.

To further illustrate the point, here's a list of "clutch" pitchers, those who performed best in high-LI situations (over 2.0). Jose Valverde, he of the 49 saves, is first, but Clippard is second. In fact, this list contains a number of non-closers, even a few starting pitchers.

Name	Plays	WPA
Valverde, Jose	122	4.28
Clippard, Tyler	91	3.90
Axford, John	128	3.44
Robertson, David	86	2.99
Sale, Chris	96	2.95
Putz, J.J.	106	2.91
Madson, Ryan	102	2.77
Venters, Jonny	118	2.72
Harang, Aaron	70	2.62
Jackson, Edwin	63	2.50

Who knew that Aaron Harang and Edwin Jackson performed as well, if not better than, their relief counterparts in high-LI situations?

The above table also highlights the importance of setup men. Many of us lament the advent of the modern-day closer, the flamethrower whose only role is to enter the game in the ninth inning with a save situation. However, since the closer role has become more confined to a single inning and type of situation, the role of setup men, such as Clippard, Robertson and Venters, has become nearly as important.

You can rank relievers by the Leverage Index when they first enter the game. This is a way of asking, "When the game is on the line, who do managers turn to most?" Here is a list of the top 10 in "initial" Leverage Index for relievers with at least 20 appearances. I've added saves so you can spot the closers and the setup men.

Name	Games	Team	LI	WPA	Saves
Walden, Jordan	62	LAA	2.108	0.005	32
Perez, Chris	64	CLE	2.079	-0.005	36
Rivera, Mariano	64	NYA	1.973	0.020	44
Putz, J.J.	60	ARI	1.910	0.007	45
Salas, Fernando	68	STL	1.880	-0.005	24
Wilson, Brian	57	SFG	1.861	-0.005	36
Bell, Heath	64	SD	1.833	-0.003	43
Wright, Wesley	21	HOU	1.824	0.007	0
Downs, Scott	60	LAA	1.823	0.000	1
Storen, Drew	73	WAS	1.775	0.006	43
Soria, Joakim	60	KC	1.774	0.004	28

Wesley Wright was Houston's LOOGY (Left-handed One Out GuY) in the last month of the season. He entered the game when a left-handed batter was up, and often left soon after. These were usually high-leverage situations, and he performed spectacularly well in those limited appearances.

Scott Downs was the Angels' LOOGY, though his role was a bit broader than Wright's. Still, you can see from this chart that another recently developed bullpen role—the LOOGY—also plays a critical role in a team's success.

One last thing. You know how some closers enter a game and immediately make things worse, only to (usually) get out a jam of their own making? You know how others closers seem to just close the door the minute they enter the game?

Well, I included the average WPA of each reliever's first appearance in the above table. Take a look and you'll see that no one was better than Mariano Rivera at immediately shutting things down. A few closers, however, tended to make things worse when they first entered. These included Chris Perez, Fernando Salas, Brian Wilson and Heath Bell. These "closers" had their fans reaching for the Tums before the inning was finished.

A lot of people have their own ideas about the Most Valuable Player award—some of them perhaps more enlightened than others—but I thought Joe Posnanski got it right when he said that there are basically two camps: those who believe the MVP should be the best player, regardless of which team he played on, and those who believe that the MVP should reflect the "narrative" of the season, in which the MVP should play for a contending team—preferably one going to the postseason.

One problem is that one of these camps has metrics; the other doesn't. You can use your own preferred stat—whether it's OPS or WAR—to choose which player was "best." But at least you have a metric.

On the other hand, everyone seems to have their own idea of what a good "narrative" is and no metric to refer to. In many years, the MVP vote seems to be a popularity vote among sportswriters for the year's best narrative.

You can probably tell where I'm going with this. WPA can help fill this gap. WPA is a quantification of the narrative of the game. When a batter hits a dramatic game-winning home run in the ninth, WPA captures that. When a starting pitcher pitches a shutout in a tight game, WPA reflects that.

And when you add a game's Championship Leverage to the equation, you can quantify a player's impact on the most important games of the year.

In that vein, here are the top 10 batters in "Championship LI WPA" (what a mouthful!). To calculate "CL_WPA," I took each batter's WPA in a game and multiplied it by the CLI of that game for his team. This puts an enormous emphasis on the last games of the season for the four Wild Card contenders, as you'll see:

Player	WPA	CL_WPA
Longoria, Evan	3.93	9.19
Ellsbury, Jacoby	5.66	7.93
Fielder, Prince	7.52	7.66
Berkman, Lance	5.40	7.17
Hamilton, Josh	4.60	6.96
Cabrera, Miguel	7.31	6.36
Pujols, Albert	4.34	6.10
Votto, Joey	6.69	5.79
Braun, Ryan	6.30	5.63
Upton, Justin	2.69	5.05

I've included each player's original WPA, so you can see what adding his CLI does to the results. That big game by Longoria on Sept. 28 vaulted him to the top of the charts. The rest of these batters all did well overall, but their teams also played in critical games and they performed particularly well in those games—and that's what makes this our list of MVP candidates.

Am I totally serious here? Do I think that Longoria should have been the American League MVP? No, not really. That would be putting too much emphasis on one game.

Am I being a little serious? Do I think Jacoby Ellsbury and Prince Fielder deserve MVP awards, based at least in part on this ranking?

Why yes, I do.

Resources: You can find WPA and LI statistics all year long at FanGraphs and Baseball Reference. All WPA and LI figures in this article have been graciously supplied by FanGraphs.

Quantifying Excitement

by Sam Hendrickson

What makes a game exciting? Well, impact on the pennant race, of course, but we've just spent an entire article talking about that. Setting aside the pennant race impact, there are a number of basic things that make a game exciting, just for the sake of the game's outcome. A close score, obviously, maybe some back-and-forth battles? Lots of "clutch" situations?

If you agree, then you would have particularly enjoyed a game played the day before all those crazy games that decided the outcome of the Wild Card race. According to our own highly scientific system, the most exciting game of the year was played on Sept. 27 between two non-contenders, the Reds and the Mets.

Before I break down what made this the most exciting game of the year, let's take a look at how our game excitement rating system (developed by THT's own Max Marchi) works.

Overview of the System

As I said, the game excitement rating system does not factor in the level of importance that a game has on a team's season. The Yankees-Rays contest on the final day of the season was an unbelievably exciting game, but much of that excitement came from the fact that a Rays victory would get them into the postseason. Since our system is blind to this fact, that game didn't come close to being the year's top game; it wasn't ranked low, but it was far from elite. We are trying to include game importance in the system for next season, but for now the system scores games in a vacuum.

Three distinct factors comprise a game's excitement rating, and each factor represents a characteristic of exciting games. The first factor represents the importance of the final plays of the game. Games with tense, decisive last innings are always exciting, and this factor serves to quantify that type of excitement.

The second factor helps quantify the excitement of rally games. If a team faces a very low win expectancy and goes on to win, then that game will likely score well on this factor.

The last factor quantifies the excitement of equilibrium games, or "back-and-forth" type games. Contests where a team's chance of winning constantly crosses the 50 percent line tend to score well on this factor, as do contests that are mostly played without one team having a high win expectancy. The final excitement score then weights these factors proportionally and combines them. Exciting games can either score highly on two or three factors or rely on the strength of one factor for their excitement.

These three factors were chosen through comments from our readers and factor analysis, a statistical process used to reduce the number of variables in a model while still maintaining the model's strength. The variables that make up each factor represent more specific characteristics of exciting games; however, many of them overlapped and were therefore unnecessary. So, the factor analysis served to eliminate these unimportant variables to make the model simpler yet equally effective.

Analysis of the Year's Most Exciting Game

With the excitement scoring system explained, let's see why the Sept. 27 Reds-Mets game was ranked the top game of the year.

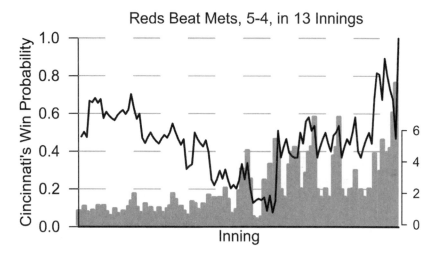

A quick game recap: The Mets took a 4-3 lead into the bottom of the ninth, although they never had more than a one-run lead at any point in the game. In the bottom of the ninth, the Reds' Juan Francisco swatted a double with two out and runners on first and second, tying the score and sending the game into extra innings.

The Reds and Mets mounted multiple scoring opportunities in extra innings, twice loading the bases but not scoring. The Reds finally broke through with a run in the 13th when Drew Stubbs pulled off a suicide squeeze with Francisco on third and one out (Francisco had just tripled). The Mets threatened in the bottom of the 13th, loading the bases with just one out, but Justin Turner lined into a double play to secure a 5-4 victory for the Reds.

That description was exciting enough, but let's break this game down in our system. To start, let's take a look at the first factor, endgame importance. This game scored a 1.17 on this particular factor. For some context, the average first factor score for 2011's top 20 most exciting games was 1.09 with a standard deviation of 0.22, and this game ranked ninth among those match-ups. So, by our calculations, this game had a little more endgame importance than the average exciting game. Keep in mind that the average for all games in the season would be even lower.

Looking at the leverage index graph, it is easy to see how this game scored well on endgame importance. Of the last six plays, three were extremely critical situations, and two more were not quite as critical but still much higher than average. Also, the Reds did not go above a 90 percent win expectancy ("cashing the game") until the very last play, which also contributed positively to the endgame importance score.

The second factor, or the rally factor, was the main contributor to this game's high score. The game scored a 2.49—second in the top 20 for this factor—while the mean for the top 20 was 1.32 with a standard deviation of 0.63. When the Mets' Manny Acosta struck out Yonder Alonso for the second out in the ninth inning, New York had a 92.3 percent chance of winning the game. The Reds then proceeded to tie the game two batters later and win in the 13th. While the rally wasn't the most impressive of the season, it scored fairly well due to the fact that it came with two outs in the ninth with only a runner on first.

This game didn't score as well on the equilibrium factor, as it ranked 13th on this factor out of the top 20 games with a score of 1.38 (the mean was 1.71 with a standard deviation of 0.72, but again, these averages are higher than the average for an ordinary game). During the first nine innings, there wasn't much equilibrium, as the Mets' win probability only dipped below 50 percent twice between the fourth and ninth innings. However, the back-and-forth nature of the extra innings boosted the equilibrium factor score to respectability, as the win probability crossed the 50 percent line nine times between the 10th inning and the game's conclusion.

The main reason this game ranked so highly in excitement was because the game scored respectably on all three factors. Only two other games in the top 20 scored at least a 2.00 on one factor and at least a 1.00 on the other two, and both of those games earned their 2.00s in the third factor, where the mean and standard deviation were both higher anyway. Many other games had higher scores than the Reds-Mets game in individual factors, but their lack of strength in the other factors set the Reds-Mets game apart from them.

Ranking the Game without Numbers

Since putting a number on level of excitement is obviously an inexact science, it may be useful to review the game's play-by-play with a human eye to help judge just how exciting this game was.

The top of the ninth has already been mentioned and was undoubtedly an exciting inning. In the bottom of the ninth, the Mets were able to get runners on second and third with two outs, but failed to capitalize—another tense situation that almost made the Reds' rally in the top of the ninth for naught.

There was more drama in the top of the 10th and the top of the 11th, as the Reds were able to load the bases with two outs in both innings but failed to push a run across the plate in either instance.

After the Reds broke through in the top of the 13th, the bottom of the inning featured the bulk of the game's drama. Needing a run, the Mets were able to get the bases loaded on four walks (one baserunner, Nick Evans, was caught stealing) with only one out, actually moving their win expectancy to 53.0 percent. However, Justin Turner then lined into that double play to end the game in the Reds' favor.

By any measure, this game was exciting and certainly warranted high scores. Whether it was the most exciting game of the year is completely up to the individual. Everyone will have games they prefer for various reasons, and labeling a game as "the most exciting" will always be met with well-reasoned debate. However, if this game had occurred in the World Series, or had the Rays won in this fashion to get to the postseason, it definitely would have been considered a classic. The game excitement ranking system is clearly doing a lot right.

Thoughts on the Game Ranking System

So, where do we go from here? This system will never be perfect for the reasons mentioned in the previous paragraph, but improvements can still be made to capture more aspects of excitement that the current system over-looks. For instance, as mentioned toward the beginning of the article, we are planning to add the importance of a game to a team's season to the system. Making this addition is crucial to the system, since it undoubtedly elevates the excitement of a game if the team needs to win to reach the postseason. Also, we could look for more variables (that make up the factors) to see if any other aspects of a game correlate highly with late-game importance, rallies or equilibrium. If any do, we could potentially strengthen each factor with their inclusion to make the factor more representative of all types of excitement.

There are more potential improvements out there, but many of them deal with matters that are related to the preference of the person, and this system aims to provide more of an objective average. Maybe next year we'll have the funds to strap baseball fans to chairs and measure their heart rates and endorphin levels as they watch games.

Special thanks to:

- FanGraphs for game data
- Max Marchi for creating the game excitement rating formula outlined here: http://www.hardballtimes.com/main/article/more-than-three-decades-of-exciting-games/

The Braves, the BoSox, and September Schadenfreude

by Steve Treder

You're driving down the freeway. Cruising easy. On pace to make your destination. But—oh, no. Brake lights up ahead. Big time. All lanes stopping, a serious jam. Just traffic, or…?

No, there, you can see it. Way up ahead, a half mile or so, maybe more: blinking and reflecting emergency vehicle lights. This isn't construction or something. This is an accident. Has to be.

Oh, hell. How long is this going to take? Nothing to do but wait and see.

You've seen worse. The far right lane—as you inch closer, you're able to get a clearer idea of what's going on up there—the far right lane seems to be squeezing through the least slowly. That must be because—yeah, that's what it is, you can start to see it now—it's because the crash was in the far left lane. At least that's where the wreckage appears to be.

Okay. Wait. Wait some more, then find a chance to—there we go!—merge into the middle lane and inch forward. You get closer to the frantically flashing crimson and blue beacons. Cautionary signals, warning observers to slow down, to be careful.

Of course, they are that. But they're more than that. Aren't they? Those eagerly blinking electronic sentries perform more than their official duties. Don't they? In addition to warning the observer, the light show also *invites* the observer. Like a strobing neon carnival barker, Vegas-style. Doesn't it?

"Here! Here! Look here! The good stuff is right here, this way!"

Don't try to fight it. You aren't fooling anybody, anyway. Everyone knows you want to look. Hell, everyone else is eagerly looking, too. Don't worry about it. Look!

As you slowly edge your car through the accident zone, your eyes are drawn, with irresistible force, to the most appalling and grisly images they can find. Broken glass and shards of shredded metal scattered across the roadway? Good. The crumpled remnant of a recently-mobile vehicle—what is that, a Toyota SUV?—sprawled helplessly and terribly sideways? Better. Omigod, look, there's the ambulance! There's the gurney, they're strapping someone in. A pathetic victim, in sheer agony, clinging to life.

The Year in Frivolity: May

Within days of one another, Braves starter Derek Lowe is arrested for a suspected DUI and Braves pitching coach Roger McDowell is suspended after making alleged homophobic remarks to fans at AT&T Park. Braves fans comfort themselves with the knowledge that clearly, this will be the worst thing that happens to the team all year.

It's a really good view you have. Better than one usually gets in these things. You can see it pretty well, until you then dutifully—and, admit it now, rather reluctantly—speed up and make your way clear of the emergency. There's suddenly room to accelerate and drive again.

That's fine, but, come on. That's boring. The hot stuff was just here, just now. Did you *see* the way that 4Runner was caved in on the side? Good lord, what the heck *happened*?

You looked. Of course you looked. And the issue is, you didn't choose to look. You didn't decide to look. You *had* to look. Your brain gave you no choice whatsoever but to look. You were compelled, not just to look, but to *see*, to *know*, to understand everything about this ghastly, horrific scene, that had absolutely nothing to do with you.

A terrible calamity is a more fascinating sight, a more riveting view, than the most gorgeous sunset or the most perfect seascape can ever hope to be. Disaster captivates and overrides our attention. We cannot get enough of the catastrophes that plague others. Can we?

It Feels Good

The German language, as it so often does, includes a single word that precisely and specifically describes this complex phenomenon: "schadenfreude," defined as "satisfaction or pleasure felt at someone else's misfortune." And this dynamic has rarely been in more vivid and prominent display than it was this past September, as the Atlanta Braves and the Boston Red Sox simultaneously presented slow-motion car wrecks for the nation's voyeuristic delight.

The down-to-the-wire action in the Wild Card races in both leagues was every bit as much a function of heroic, winning baseball being performed by the St. Louis Cardinals and the Tampa Bay Rays as it was the stumbling chokes suffered by the Braves and Red Sox. But the nation's media and fans, while granting a perfunctory nod of congratulation to the come-from-behind winners, didn't focus on that, at all. That wasn't the big story, by a long shot.

The story we all relished was instead the disastrous view from the losers' perspective. It was "The Collapses," as they were suddenly and universally dubbed, not just in the sports media, but everywhere. Heck, NPR covered it this way, played up the catastrophic angle. Everyone did, without hesitation. Within about 48 hours of the climactic events of that amazing final night of the 2011 regular season, stories had appeared everywhere, in the mainstream media as well as throughout the blogosphere, analyzing and dissecting in minute detail just how tremendous these Collapses had been.

For example, we were treated to—and, oh, yes, they were treats, delectable brain-candy to be ooh-and-aah-ingly savored—articles that presented long lists of the most notorious late-season collapses in the long history of the sport and assessments of where our latest contestants might fare within those dreadful sweepstakes. Who can resist lingering over a litany of such humiliated cases as the 1908 New York Giants (the "Merkle's Boner" team), the 1978 Boston Red Sox (casualties of the "Boston Massacre"), the 1969 Chicago Cubs (co-architects of that particular 17-game swing in the standings in that six-week period), or the 1951 Brooklyn Dodgers (whose odds against blowing their mid-August lead, Bobby Thomson be damned, were 384-to-1)?

We were promptly provided with the knowledge that only two teams in history (the 1995 California Angels and the 2007 New York Mets) ever achieved a higher mathematical likelihood than the 2011 Red Sox of reaching the postseason at any point in a season before failing to reach the postseason. The 2011 Red Sox, if you must know—and you must know, mustn't you!—reached a 99.78 percent chance of making the playoffs on the morning of Sept. 4. The 2011 Braves were very close behind them, in fourth place on the "greatest choke jobs" all-time list as counted by this metric, with a 98.99 percent chance as of Aug. 26. (Don't you love the two-figures-to-the-right-of-the-decimal-point precision?)

We also learned that the Red Sox's winning percentage of .250 from that highest-odds point through the end of the season ranks fourth-worst on the all-time list, behind only the 2005 Cleveland Indians, the 1964 Philadelphia Phillies, and the 2009 Detroit Tigers. The Braves' mark of .333 comes in at seventh-worst.

We were informed that in that fateful final 2011 regular-season Red Sox game, when the Baltimore Orioles were down to their last strike in the bottom of the ninth inning, Boston had only about a two percent chance of losing. We were further instructed that, in their own fateful final regular-season game, the Tampa Bay Rays had just a 0.3 percent chance of coming back when trailing 7-0 with two innings to play. The Rays then had about a two percent chance of winning in the bottom of the ninth, with pinch-hitter Dan Johnson (and his nifty .108 batting average) also down to his last strike.

Thus, the 2011 Boston and Atlanta teams were swiftly ushered into that unhappiest of elite salons, the Hall of Pathetic Screw-Ups. Most of its member teams and their ghastly stories are familiar to most any baseball fan with more than a casual interest in the sport's history. Baseball's cultural lore properly celebrates and honors the champions and super-

During an Orioles broadcast, Jim Palmer says that he thinks former teammate Mike Cuellar was denied the 1970 Cy Young Award due to racist voters. It was a particularly pernicious form of racism, apparently, which did not appear in 1969 when Cuellar shared the award with Denny McLain and returned to bite Cuellar the following season. In other news, Sam McDowell—who had a better year than Cuellar in 1970 and still didn't win—decides not to press his case that rampant anti-Pennsylvanian prejudice cost him votes.

As Frank McCourt's financial situation worsens, it is reported that the Dodgers may not meet May payroll. Several days later Andre Ethier's 30-game hitting streak ends when he is rendered too weak by malnutrition to effectively swing a bat.

stars of years gone by, as tales of dramatic victory will always be warmly retold. But tales of shocking defeat never grow stale, either—the more shockingly unlikely the defeat, the better—and if they aren't retold with warmth, they're certainly retold with relish, with vigor.

These episodes of epic failure, of blowing it on a grand scale, are endlessly intriguing. We humans just love to witness, recall, and ponder scenarios featuring other humans struggling, and erring, and losing.

And When it's Good, They Say it "Kills"

There's an old show business saying that neatly sums up the complex explanation of what it is that makes us laugh: "Comedy is tragedy that happens to somebody else."

We're all familiar with this essential truth. We couch-lounge, in languid evening repose, surfing channels in search of something silly and mindless and easy to enjoy. Wannabee famous chefs squaring off in some contrivance of a cook-off? Eh. D-list celebrities ballroom dancing for the favor of archly mugging judges? Eh. A meticulously-researched and brilliantly-edited documentary meaningfully illuminating a real and pressing situation facing our world today? Are you kidding?

That isn't what we want. Here it is, finally: Some re-run of some syndicated version of one of the many iterations of *America's Funniest Home Videos*. Oh, yeah. That's the stuff. Let's snuggle in here for a while. Because there's nothing funnier—come on, get over yourself, and admit it—there is *nothing* funnier than a video clip of some anonymous guy getting clobbered right in the unmentionables by a child's plastic baseball bat. There just isn't. You can't help yourself when you watch this stuff.

You've seen it all before, a thousand times. The grainy hand-held amateur footage. The predictable set-up of hapless Daddy helpfully instructing cute little four-year-old Junior on how to grip and swing that bulbous polypropylene bad boy. You know exactly what's going to happen. Dad won't sooner finish giving the little slugger the pep talk before that pint-sized rascal is cutting loose with a from-the-heels uppercut swing that would make Babe Ruth himself proud. And connecting with nothing but Father's foo-foo. It's flipping hysterical. You ROTFLMAO.

You can watch a thousand variations on this. Heck, you have watched ten thousand variations on this. It doesn't matter how stupid and shallow and banal the whole business might be. Whenever you see some poor soul getting his 'nads blasted by whatever manner of incoming missile, you just can't help but laugh yourself silly.

Of course, you've had your own 'nads blasted a few times, in real life. It happens to all of us (though rarely, alas, with the vividness displayed in a typical *America's Funniest Home Videos* segment). But when it happens to you, the last reaction you're going to display is laughter.

Because physical pain, well, *hurts*. It's quite insistent on that point. Pain is unpleasantness in the biggest way. It doesn't induce hilarity or enjoyment of any kind. It induces agony, and misery, and sometimes just for good measure, with its own mordant flair, it also induces nausea. When *you* feel this way, you aren't laughing at all.

Yet when we see another subjected to this sensation, so long as the incident involves enough photogenic perfection, it's comedic champagne. It's great theater. It's the best thing on TV.

Amazin'

This dynamic is pervasive in the world of sports, baseball prominently included. *The Bad News Bears* wasn't a tragedy, after all, it was a comedy. Watching someone, even a child, egregiously boot a grounder or misjudge a pop fly doesn't make us cry, it makes us laugh.

That most iconic of bad teams in the history of major league baseball, the 1962 New York Mets, with the record of 40-120, are one of the sport's most joyfully remembered ballclubs. No commentator or historian mentioning the '62 Mets does so without a distinct sense of amusement, and no fan discussing that team does so without a big and genuine smile.

They're just funny, those 1962 Mets. Almost nobody writing about them or talking about them focuses on a technical analysis, of, say, precisely why that club's fielding, pitching, and hitting were so substandard, or how, realistically, they might have been improved. Who cares about any of that complicated stuff when we're having such a good time? No, to engage in consideration of the 1962 Mets is just to have *fun*. Ineptitude is hilarious. Relax and enjoy it.

The comedic angles presented by the '62 Mets are so numerous that one scarcely knows where to begin. How about with their first baseman, Marv Throneberry (the name alone is comedy gold), who delivered more errors (17) than home runs (16)? "Marvelous Marv," the press quickly dubbed him, elevating the previously obscure utility player's status to that of punchline-in-chief. Likely no ballplayer in history had his name and image exploited as the go-to joke butt more than Throneberry. (For his part, Throneberry was sensible and secure enough not to put up much resistance; indeed he was able to monetize his still-bankable "lovable loser" persona by appearing in Miller Lite Beer advertisements on television in the 1980s.)

The manager of the 1962 Mets was 72-year-old Casey Stengel, at one time a brilliant tactician but by this point a tired and often bewildered

Orioles outfielder Luke Scott, who in the offseason made waves when he revealed that he did not believe that President Obama was a U.S. citizen, is asked for comment when the president produces his long-form birth certificate for public inspection. "Anybody can produce a document," Scott says, implying that he believes the birth certificate to be a forgery. Scott's belief about how easy it is to produce a document will be shaken in the winter of 2011-12 when no one tenders him a contract because he has a case of the flaming crazies.

old man who literally was apt to fall asleep on the dugout bench. The press, however, steadfastly avoided objective assessment of Stengel's competence and studiously ignored pursuing the obvious question of the degree to which his managerial performance might be a contributor to the team's horrific record. No, the press was too busy giggling itself silly over Stengel's creative mangling of the English language, never in finer form than in his days with the Mets. The Mets' story was all about humor, and nothing else.

Consider that the roster of the 1962 Mets included two pitchers named Bob Miller. Right away the comedic juices get flowing; two people in the same circumstance with the same name sounds like an ideal basis for, say, a Bob Newhart radio monologue bit from that period. The beat writers covering the '62 Mets were all over it, knocking themselves out coming up with outlandish anecdotes (whether apocryphal or not) surrounding the endless confusion created by the presence of the two Bob Millers. Long-running sitcoms have been built upon flimsier premises.

And the two-Bob-Millers shtick played perfectly with the funny-old-Casey shtick. They were made for each other. The storyline quickly became (again, apocryphal or not) that Stengel was hopelessly perplexed over which Bob Miller was which, and so he took to referring to one of the Bob Millers as "Nelson," which in turn served to confuse everyone else. Rim shot.

Finding humor in suffering and failure (indeed, seeing nothing but humor in suffering and failure) is the theme of another often-told misadventure in the '62 Mets saga. The best version of it ever read by yours truly was one presented by Roger Angell (natch), but there are various others. Anyway, the story basically goes as follows (bear in mind that, like all these '62 Mets tales, the truth underlying any of this might be, well, just a tad sketchy).

Richie Ashburn was playing center field for the 1962 Mets. The longtime star was deep into his athletic decline, 35 years old and in his final season, greatly slowed down and acutely feeling every ache and pain accumulated over his extensive career. The last thing Ashburn needed was to be exposing himself to further pain and injury.

However, early in the season, Ashburn would find himself jogging in for a pop fly in short center field, calling, "I got it," only to be bowled over by an out-charging shortstop, Elio Chacon, who would ignore Ashburn's calling for the ball. This happened time and again, either a dangerous collision or a near-miss.

"What the hell's going on?" Ashburn wondered.

Fellow outfielder Joe Christopher, who was also taking center field innings on that ballclub, helpfully took Ashburn aside. Christopher, who hailed from the Caribbean and spoke Spanish as well as English, explained that the Venezuelan infielder Chacon didn't speak any English. So Ashburn's calls of "I got it" were incoherent gibberish to Chacon.

The trick, Christopher elaborated, is that when you come in on those pop-ups when Chacon is coming out, you don't call, "I got it" in English. You say the same phrase, but in Spanish: "Yo la tengo."

"Yo la what?" Ashburn says.

"Yo la tengo. It means, 'I got it,'" Christopher says.

"Okay. Yo la tengo. Yo la tengo. I think I can do that," Ashburn says. "Thank you!"

One imagines Ashburn practicing before his hotel room mirror that night. "Yo la tengo! Yo la tengo!"

The next day, of course, Ashburn is in center field, and Chacon is at shortstop. Sure enough, high pop fly, short left-center field. Ashburn comes in. Chacon goes out. Ashburn remembers what to do.

"Yo la tengo!" Ashburn cries. "Yo la tengo!"

Chacon puts on the brakes, just as Christopher said he would. Chacon peels off and gives Ashburn plenty of room to comfortably settle under the fly ball.

At which point Ashburn gets clobbered, knocked sprawling by the Mets' hard-charging 200-pound-plus left fielder, Frank Thomas—who spoke no Spanish.

It's classic stuff. The reason the Ashburn "yo la tengo" yarn has been told and re-told so eagerly over the decades is not because it provokes a reaction of concern about Ashburn's health, nor even a reaction of disgust that a major league ballclub would operate on such a little-league level of communication and basic fundamentals.

No, the story is an evergreen hit because it provokes a reaction of *laughter*. To watch, even in one's mind's eye, a hapless outfielder being knocked every which way but loose, first by one teammate and then by another, is just plain funny. It's exactly the sort of thing that made *America's Funniest Home Videos* one of the monster hits in television history.

The Wickedly Fun Accounting

The flurry of statistical analyses we glimpsed above that swirled among the punditry in the days following the end of the 2011 regular season—the voluminous calculations of staggering improbabilities, and graphical illustrations of cliff-fallings—imparted the general lesson that,

Jorge Posada, insulted when manager Joe Girardi pencils him in ninth in the Yankees lineup for a game against the Red Sox, begs out of the game, citing a phantom injury. This leads to great controversy, and Girardi is enraged. At least until he remembers that, oh yeah, Posada not in the lineup at all is far better for the Yankees' chances than having him hit ninth would have been.

Tony La Russa gives Albert Pujols his first start at third base since 2002. La Russa could not be reached for comment as he was too busy setting the starting lineup for his fantasy team, cackling maniacally and muttering something about "eligibility."

Fred Wilpon is featured in an in-depth article in *The New Yorker*. Controversy is ignited when the Mets owner disparages Jose Reyes, David Wright and Carlos Beltran and when he calls the Mets "a shitty team." Well, there was no controversy about that last bit, but it is generally thought that saying it out loud was simply rubbing it in.

shocking (and thus thrilling) as they were to behold, it's probably the case that neither of The Collapses of 2011 was in itself the worst ever seen. It depends upon exactly how one wishes to measure these things, of course, but there are at least four teams that might be considered to have undergone worse collapses than either of this year's.

The first possibility is the 1964 Phillies, a ballclub indeed among the very greatest historic icons of this type. Most fans have heard the horrifying story. The Phillies were baseball's Cinderella team in September of '64, having been magically transformed from the lowliest of basement-dwellers to hold a six-and-a-half-game National League lead with 12 to play. Then the inconceivable occurred: Philadelphia lost its next 10 consecutive games to be eliminated from the race with two still to play. And the familiar accompanying storyline is that their collapse was at least partly caused by manager Gene Mauch, who repeatedly started his twin ace pitchers, Jim Bunning and Chris Short, on short rest, to repeatedly disastrous results.

Another candidate might be the 2005 Indians, whose tale of woe is far less known, perhaps because it was a Wild Card berth they blew, as opposed to direct participation in the World Series. But Cleveland's accomplishment was quite remarkable. Not only did they hold a one-game lead in the Wild Card standings with seven to go, they trailed their division by just a game-and-a-half, and so might well have gone ahead and won the AL Central with a strong final week.

What's the opposite of a strong final week? How about dropping six out of the seven games (with five of the losses by one run, and the sixth by two), including a three-game sweep at home over the final weekend, head-to-head against your rival for the division flag? That'll make you an October couch potato.

A stronger case might be made for the 2007 Mets, holders of a seven-game division lead with 17 left to play. The Mets began their descent by being swept in a three-game series at home against their closest pursuer—a time-honored method of converting a comfortable lead into an itchy sweater—and then proceeded to lose a couple more, such that almost the entire lead was blown with a week.

But the '07 Mets then rallied, winning three of four to get the lead back to two-and-a-half games with seven to play, the sudden crisis seemingly averted. But, no; the '07 Mets then lost six of the final seven, surrendering 50 runs in the process, securing themselves second place.

And ponder the case of the 1995 Angels. Things were heavenly for the Halos as they surveyed their nine-and-a-half-game division lead on Aug. 20. A humdinger of a slump ensued (as in 12 losses in their next

13 games), but the situation stabilized and still appeared well in hand on Sept. 12, with the lead at six and 17 yet to play. However, at this point the '95 Angels decided to lose their next nine in a row—achieving, indeed, their second nine-game losing streak within a month's time—and drop out of first place.

But the '95 Angels were ready for more. They pulled themselves together and managed to win the last five games of the regular season, grabbing a tie with the Seattle Mariners on the final day and forcing a one-game playoff. In that climactic contest, the Angels trailed 1-0 entering the bottom of the seventh, and then California pitcher Mark Langston presented one of the all-time magnificent meltdowns for our delectation on national TV. In the space of five plays, Langston threw to the wrong base on a sacrifice bunt, hit a batter with a pitch, and committed a hideous throwing error, translating two groundball hits into four runs and the ballgame. It was the Angels' 26th loss in their final 38 games.

Thus, this year's Atlanta and Boston teams were striving to match a daunting standard. The Braves held an eight-and-a-half-game lead in the NL Wild Card standings as of Aug. 26 but then went 10-19 the rest of the way. The Red Sox outdid that, fashioning a nine-game lead in the AL Wild Card race as of Sept. 3 (along with being just a half-a-game back in the division race), before proceeding to go 6-18 down the stretch. That's really, really bad, but perhaps not quite as bad as the performance of the 1995 Angels.

But Still

If neither of this year's contestants could quite grab the top spot individually, it's certainly true that no prior season in history has presented *two* simultaneous collapses of this magnitude. And both Atlanta and Boston earned plenty of style points while ascending their stairways to ignominy in 2011.

Take the Braves. ("Please!"…okay, sorry.) Bear in mind that when just one additional victory would have clinched a playoff, Atlanta lost seven one-run decisions in the month of September and won only three. Of those seven one-run losses, four involved blown late-inning leads, and four as well were extra-inning defeats. The season's final contest, the must-win showdown against the Phillies at home at Turner Field, was both. The Braves took a 3-1 lead into the seventh, but they allowed that advantage to be shaved, and then coughed up the tying run in the ninth. They surrendered the single run that would prove to be their killer in the top of the 13th. Meanwhile, over the final 10 innings of

Seattle *Times* columnist Steve Kelley writes that Mariners catcher Miguel Olivo "might be the team's most indispensable player." At the time, Olivo is batting .243 with a .659 OPS and ranks 25th among the 32 catchers in the game with at least 100 plate appearances. It is unclear if Kelley simply does not know what the word "indispensable" means or, rather, he has never been introduced to Felix Hernandez, Michael Pineda, Justin Smoak or Ichiro Suzuki.

that crucial game, Atlanta batters produced four singles, zero extra-base hits, and no runs.

As for the Red Sox, think about this: In four individual September games, Boston scored a total of 62 runs (an average of 15.5 per game), winning (ya think?) all four. But in their 23 other games in the month, the BoSox managed to score just 84 runs (an average of 3.65 per game) and thus tallied up a record of 3-20 in those contests. That's impressive. Blowing the season's final must-win game in bottom-of-the-ninth, two-outs, bases-empty fashion seems only appropriate for such a ballclub.

Thus, we bow in appreciation to the 2011 Atlanta Braves and Boston Red Sox, for combining forces to provide us with an unprecedented double dip of diabolical delight. Their failure, their agony, their humiliation were exquisite entertainment. We humbly hope to behold their like again.

So long as it's somebody else's favorite team.

GM in a Box: Theo Epstein

by Rob Neyer

Record and Background

Age: 38

Previous Organizations:

1995-2002: Padres—started in public relations, eventually became director of baseball operations

2002-2011: Red Sox—assistant general manager, 2002; general manager, 2002-2011

Years of service with the Chicago Cubs: 0

Cumulative Record: 839-619, .575 winning percentage

Playing Career: Epstein pitched for Brookline High School, two miles from Fenway Park.

Personnel and Philosophy

Any notable changes from the previous regime?

With the Red Sox, Epstein took over from Mike Port, who had the job for one season, on an interim basis, after John Henry and Tom Werner purchased the Red Sox in 2002 and fired Dan Duquette. Henry and Werner didn't officially take possession of the franchise until spring training in 2002, and Port made very few moves of significance during his tenure that season.

But someday when the historians write about the Theo Epstein Era in Boston, they will essentially ignore Port and focus on the difference between Epstein and Duquette. And in fairness, John Henry's ownership group was nothing like previous ownership.

Still, what characterized Duquette's tenure was a seeming inability to surround the team's big stars—Nomar Garciaparra and Pedro Martinez, in particular— with solid complementary players. In fairness, Duquette did put together some good teams, and the 2002 squad that won 93 games was largely his creation. Unfortunately, another thing that characterized his era was the signing of mediocre free agents at the cost of both performance and draft picks; from 2000 through 2002, the Red Sox owned exactly one first-round or supplemental first-round pick in the amateur draft (and that was used to select Phil Dumatrait, but that's definitely beyond the purview of this article).

Oakland Athletics manager Bob Geren is fired and replaced by Bob Melvin. At the press conference announcing the change, general manager Billy Beane says that he wanted the change to create as little disruption as possible, thus he only considered men named Bob as a replacement for Geren.

Florida Marlins manager Edwin Rodriguez resigns and is replaced by Jack McKeon. As The Hardball Times' own Chris Jaffe noted at the time, "McKeon was older than James Dean or Elizabeth Taylor. He's older than Mikhail Gorbachev or Ted Kennedy. He's older than Sam Cooke. He's older than Chuck Noll or Bill Walsh. He's older than Bud Selig and only 20 weeks younger than George Steinbrenner." Jaffe did not note, however, that McKeon is more lively and more mentally sharp than at least two of those people.

Epstein, on the other, has hoarded draft picks. The Red Sox have certainly signed their fair share of free agents, and surrendered draft picks as a consequence. But they've also been more than willing to let free agents get away, and collect the compensatory draft picks. In 2005, the Sox owned five of the first 47 picks; in 2006, four of the first 44; in 2011, four of the top 40.

Duquette also hadn't drafted particularly well, at least not in the first round. Somewhat amazingly, each of Epstein's first seven first-round picks wound up in the majors, which is all the more surprising considering that the highest pick in that group was the 17th choice in the 2003 draft (used on David Murphy, later traded in an ill-fated deal for Eric Gagne).

What characterizes his relationship with ownership? What type of people does he hire? Is he more collaborative or authoritative?

By all accounts, Epstein had an excellent relationship with Henry, who once said of Epstein, "I thought he was a magical person." When Epstein declined a new contract from the Red Sox after the 2005 season, it was largely Henry who convinced Epstein to return a few months later.

He did reportedly have some real issues with Red Sox CEO Larry Lucchino, which might well have contributed to Epstein's decision to leave the Red Sox the first time, and perhaps most recently as well.

Epstein has typically hired men like himself: young Ivy Leaguers who might have played some ball in college but might not have. His former underlings include Josh Byrnes, who served for a spell as GM of the Diamondbacks; Jed Hoyer, now running the Padres, and Ben Cherington, who at this writing is assumed to replace Epstein as Red Sox GM. Epstein has also worked, and by all accounts productively, with traditional baseball men like Bill Lajoie and Allard Baird. There's never been any doubt that Epstein was running the show—within the limits imposed by Lucchino, of course—but he's got a reputation for being collaborative and a fine boss.

What kinds of managers does he hire? How closely does he work with them?

Epstein inherited Grady Little, who had guided the Red Sox to 93 wins in 2002, his first season as manager. In Little's second season—and Epstein's first as GM—the Red Sox came within a pitch or two of reaching the World Series, but Little's stubborn refusal to remove Pedro Martinez from Game Seven of the American League Championship Series probably cost Boston the pennant and, ultimately, Little his job.

There's little doubt that Epstein was frustrated by Little's general lack of interest in scouting reports and suggestions from the baseball-operations staff, but the owner wasn't exactly a fan, either. As Henry later told journalist Seth Mnookin, "My feeling was that we were here to win a championship, and I thought that, sooner or later, he was really going to hurt us."

Which of course he did, in Game Seven against the Yankees. And shortly after the World Series, Little was gone.

That winter, Epstein hired Terry Francona to manage the Red Sox. Francona's record in four seasons as Phillies manager had been terrible. But as Mnookin reports, "Francona seemed to intuit the need to combine a deft interpersonal approach with the utilization of as much information as he could possibly get his hands on."

That was information which Epstein, of course, would be only too happy to provide his manager. At this writing, Francona's a free agent and Cubs manager Mike Quade's status is highly questionable. One can assume that if Epstein doesn't actually hire Terry Francona to manage the Cubs, he'll find someone quite like Francona.

Player Development

How does he approach the amateur draft? Does he prefer major league-ready players or projects? Tools or performance? High schools or college? Pitchers or hitters?

Shortly after taking the reins, Epstein gave perhaps his most famous quote, saying he wanted to turn the Red Sox into a "$100-million player-development machine."

The 2003 edition of *Baseball America Prospect Handbook* ranked the Red Sox farm system 27th in the majors, with this comment: "End of the Duquette regime means this ranking could finally turn around."

Just three years later, the Red Sox had vaulted to seventh in *Baseball America's* ranking and generally maintained that status until last spring, following the trade for Adrian Gonzalez that sent three prospects to San Diego.

The Red Sox owned 23 first-round and supplemental first-round picks during Epstein's tenure, and used only eight of them on high school players. But, like a lot of sabermetrically inclined organizations, the Red Sox have been more willing to draft high schoolers in recent years. Not including the supplemental round, the Sox have owned seven first-round picks in the last six amateur drafts, and four of them were used to select high school players. Historically, high school catchers have been bad bets,

Washington Nationals manager Jim Riggleman resigns and is replaced by Davey Johnson. It is widely suspected that the threat of his resignation was a bluff designed to force management to offer Riggleman a contract extension. General manager Mike Rizzo is placed on the 15-day disabled list after straining his vocal cords while vigorously calling the bluff.

Cardinals outfielder Matt Holliday helps the team break out of a seven-game losing streak. The secret: he wore uniform pants which belonged to Cardinals legend and coach emeritus Red Schoendienst. Reached for comment, the 88-year-old Schoendienst said that, at his age, he was happy for anyone to get in his pants.

but last summer the Red Sox used one of their two first-round picks on one. While the scouting directors share responsibility for the draft, it's probably safe to say that Epstein has been flexible in this area.

Does he tend to rush players to the majors or let them marinate?

Epstein has generally elevated his hitters no later than they have obviously deserved, with three future stars—Kevin Youkilis, Dustin Pedroia and Jacoby Ellsbury—graduating to starting slots right on schedule.

The same has generally been true of the pitchers, with the caveat that the Red Sox, like most high-payroll teams, are habitually impatient with young pitchers, especially young starting pitchers. In Epstein's entire time as GM, only two pitchers have (a) graduated from the Red Sox farm system and (b) started more than 15 games for the Red Sox. Of course, those pitchers are Jon Lester and Clay Buchholz, and only Lester has been an unqualified success. One truly impressive starting pitcher doesn't seem like a lot from an outstanding player-development machine.

And the Red Sox's inability to develop young starting pitchers—aside from those they've traded—really hurt them in 2011, when the only young farm product to start for the Sox was mid-range prospect Kyle Weiland … and he was awful in five starts.

Roster Construction

Is he especially fond of certain types of players? Does he like proven players or youngsters? Offensive players or glove men? Power pitchers or finesse guys?

Early on, Epstein picked the low-hanging fruit: on-base guys with low batting averages but maybe some power. First there was Todd Walker, then Mark Bellhorn. But those guys wouldn't be around forever, and they weren't. In *Feeding the Monster*, Seth Mnookin wrote, "Within the Red Sox, there was considerable anxiety about *Moneyball's* publication even before it was released … If (author Michael) Lewis disclosed the extent to which baseball players were improperly valued, one of the most potent tools the Red Sox had in their arsenal would, they feared, be neutralized."

It eventually was, but by no means completely. The Red Sox just had to dig deeper.

When they gave J.D. Drew $70 million for five years, they presumably believed that his apparently chronic injury issues made him improperly valued, and thus worth $70 million; as things turned out, the condition really was chronic.

When they traded for Coco Crisp, they presumably saw something in their proprietary defensive metrics that made them think his fielding in center field would more than outweigh his just-passable hitting.

It's obviously gotten more difficult to find improperly valued players, which has led to the Red Sox populating their roster with players whose skills are hardly mysterious: Adrian Gonzalez, Carl Crawford and John Lackey were stars and the Red Sox paid star prices to get them.

Epstein probably doesn't prefer offensive players over glove men, or vice versa. He seems to follow the Bill James dictum: Everything counts. If a player's glove and bat and baserunning and hustle are 20 runs better than average, exactly how he gets there is mostly irrelevant.

The same goes for pitchers, though perhaps to a lesser degree since power pitchers typically are less subject to the vagaries of luck, and they also age better. It's hard to imagine Theo Epstein signing (for example) Barry Zito to a long-term mega-contract, considering Zito's lack of power when he signed with the Giants.

Does he allocate resources primarily on impact players or role players? How does he flesh out his bullpen and bench? Does he often work the waiver wire, sign minor-league free agents, or make Rule 5 picks?

Epstein's been blessed with great resources, so hasn't often been forced to scrimp with impact players or role players; theoretically, anyway, one thing that the organization's wealth permits is the accrual of great depth, and the Red Sox have entered some seasons with six or seven viable starting pitchers.

Because the Red Sox are usually near the top of the standings, Epstein's ability to work the waiver wire or make solid Rule 5 picks has been limited. Most famously, he did sign minor-league free agent David Ortiz shortly after taking over as GM. More recently, the Sox signed minor-league free agent Andrew Miller as a sort of project, which hasn't worked out nearly so well.

When will he release players? On whom has he given up? To whom has he given a shot? Does he cut bait early or late?

During Epstein's tenure with the Red Sox, there was always a tension between him and CEO Lucchino, with Epstein always more willing (or eager) to let superstars leave the franchise.

When Nomar Garciaparra's situation became untenable during the 2004 season, it was Epstein who pushed for a change and Lucchino who wanted to figure out a way to keep Garciaparra with the Red Sox.

Frank McCourt, desperate to maintain control of the Dodgers as they work their way through bankruptcy, obtains a loan for $150 million with which to run the team. The terms of the loan are exceedingly unfavorable, charging in excess of 10 percent interest and imposing stiff fees and penalties on McCourt personally in the event of default. McCourt had no choice, however, given that this particular lender was the only one who called him back after he filled out the online form at Moneytree.com.

When Pedro Martinez explored free agency after the 2004 season, it was Lucchino who headed the ultimately unsuccessful effort to retain him; Epstein saw a pitcher with a frayed shoulder who wouldn't be worth whatever it would cost to sign. And he couldn't have been more right.

Most famously, Epstein gave a shot to David Ortiz, though it's always worth mentioning that Ortiz was behind Jeremy Giambi on the depth chart for roughly three months; if Giambi had ever hit, Ortiz might never have gotten a real chance to play.

Is he active or passive? An optimist or a problem solver? Does he want to win now or wait out the success cycle?

These days, few baseball executives are passive; they're not allowed to be passive. But Epstein is perhaps more active than most, exemplified by Boston's unsuccessful pursuit of Alex Rodriguez and the successful pursuits of Daisuke Matsuzaka and Curt Schilling, both of which required a great deal of preparation and negotiation.

Epstein reportedly discussed, within the organization, the potential need to fail in one season to build for future seasons. But in the event, that just wasn't an option. Once the Red Sox won 95 games in his first season as GM and the World Series in his second, failure simply wasn't an option; the goal every season was 95 wins and another World Championship.

Trades and Free Agents

Does he favor players acquired via trade, development, or free agency? Is he an active trader? Doe he tend to move talent or horde it? With whom does he trade and when? Will he make deals with other teams during the season? How does he approach the trading deadline?

It's not clear that Epstein prefers one mode of acquisition more than any other; with their resources, the Red Sox usually had the prospects to make any trade or the money to sign any free agent. Like most GMs, Epstein would presumably prefer to develop his own stars, if only because they're a lot cheaper that way. He certainly has not hoarded talent, trading a big package of prospects to acquire Josh Beckett and another for Adrian Gonzalez.

Epstein and the Red Sox have generally been active at the trading deadline, which is the case with nearly every contending team but especially the rich ones. But Lucchino has long believed that a contending team should make a deal at the deadline, if only to show the players that the front office is doing everything it can to win, too. We'll see if Epstein has taken that philosophy to heart when he's out from under Lucchino's thumb.

Are there teams or general managers with whom he trades frequently?

Not really. While you might expect Epstein to trade more often with like-minded souls—Jed Hoyer and Josh Byrnes, for example—that hasn't really happened, with the exception of the deal that sent Gonzalez to the Red Sox and a passel of prospects to the Padres. Epstein also made a few deals with the Indians and Mark Shapiro over the years. But perhaps it's more difficult to make trades with general managers who see the game basically the same way you see it.

Contracts

Does he prefer long-term deals or short? Does he backload his contracts very often? Does he lock up players early in their careers or he is more likely to practice brinksmanship? Does he like to avoid arbitration?

Through the first few years of Epstein's tenure with the Red Sox, organizational policy was four years maximum on contracts. In 2007, though, the Red Sox went six years (and $52 million) for Matsuzaka and five years (and $70 million) for Drew. Considering the additional $51 million the Red Sox paid the Seibu Lions for the rights to sign Dice-K, ultimately neither of those deals were good for the franchise. But the Rubicon had been crossed with Drew and Matsuzaka, and recently the Sox have behaved like any other rich franchise, ladling out a five-year deal to Lackey and seven-year deals to Gonzalez and Crawford.

Obviously, the early returns on Lackey and Crawford have not been good; if that doesn't change, it would make four out of five contracts gone awry, which would obviously vindicate the discarded policy. One might surmise that Epstein would love to revisit the policy in Chicago—especially considering the burden of Alfonso Soriano's eight-year deal, which runs through 2014—but contracts longer than four years are probably just the cost of doing business if you're running a high-revenue club like the Cubs or Red Sox.

Red Sox contracts have generally been backloaded very little, or (more often) not at all.

The Red Sox were never involved in an actual arbitration hearing during Epstein's tenure as general manager. The organization was frequently willing to non-tender players not deemed essential, and this led

Tony La Russa joins Connie Mack as the only manager in baseball history to have managed over 5,000 games. While, according to the record books, La Russa is still some 2,700 games behind Mack, experts agree that La Russa's had roughly the equivalent of 8,000 games managed when adjusted for over-managing.

to the collection of a great number of draft picks when the players signed elsewhere as free agents.

The Red Sox have not signed any of their young players to Evan Longoria-style contracts, but in 2009 the Sox did buy out Kevin Youkilis', Jon Lester's and Dustin Pedroia's arbitration years with four-, five- and six-year deals. On the other hand, the Sox never showed any real interested in locking up Jonathan Papelbon, as Epstein has professed skepticism about long-term contracts given to relief pitchers. (His skepticism might have been reinforced by Keith Foulke, who signed a three-year contract with the Red Sox after the 2003 season and was excellent in 2004 but posted a 5.10 ERA and lost his job as closer during the next two seasons.)

Anything unique about his negotiating tactics? Is he vocal? Does he prefer to work behind the scenes or through the media?

True to his nature, Theo Epstein brings to bear all the information he can bring. When trying to convince Schilling to join the Red Sox, Epstein asked Bill James to prepare an essay suggesting that Fenway Park would be perfectly well-suited for Schilling's talents. He also had people check into Schilling's and his wife's charitable pursuits, and made the case that Boston would present innumerable opportunities for that sort of work.

Epstein has generally been reluctant to drag negotiations into the press, but that's not because he's shy; he presumably doesn't believe that using the press will help him get what he wants in negotiations. Epstein cooperated with Seth Mnookin, the author of *Feeding the Monster*. And he's offered perfectly fine quotes to writers for national magazines. It's also widely believed that Epstein was for years one of Peter Gammons' best sources within the organization.

Bonus

What is his strongest point as GM?

Epstein's greatest strength is probably his ability to solicit and process a great deal of information and opinion from the people around him, reach a conclusion upon a course of action, and move decisively in that direction. All within a fairly short period of time.

What would he be doing if he weren't in baseball?

If he hadn't gotten a job in baseball, today Theo Epstein would be running some billionaire's charitable foundation.

Due to a rock concert scheduled for June 29 at Sun Life Stadium, the Marlins are forced to move their scheduled home games for June 24–26 against the Seattle Mariners to Safeco Field. While it seems odd that one evening's concert should displace an entire series and require the use of the ballpark for several days, it must be remembered that Hotblack Desiato and Disaster Area's shows are quite elaborate, what with the space ship crashing into the sun to create a solar flare and all. Oh, wait—sorry. It wasn't Hotblack Desiato, It was U2 that required all that time and space. Methinks they've moved on somewhat from a red guitar, three chords and the truth.

- Craig Calcaterra

Mike Stanton: Future Home Run King?

by David Golebiewski

On Sept. 19, 2011, Mike Stanton stepped into the batter's box at Sun Life Stadium to face Atlanta's Mike Minor. The 6-foot-5, 240-pound Stanton, just barely old enough to sip on hops and barley, belted a first-pitch fastball 10 rows deep into the upper deck, which, luckily for those looking to avoid a trip to the ER, was closed off to fans earlier in the season.

Stanton lingered at the plate after making contact, mouth open and eyebrows raised, as if wondering, "Did I really just do that?"

"That," Marlins play-by-play announcer Rich Waltz bellowed, "was a Ring of Honor shot!"

Waltz was referring to the names of retired Miami Dolphins greats that line the stadium's second tier. But he just as easily could have been talking about where Stanton's shots—he hit a 461-foot rocket off Minor later in the game—placed him among the game's all-time great young sluggers.

With 34 home runs, Stanton went yard more often during his age-21 season than all but three players in the history of the game. Just being in the majors at 21 shows that a player is way ahead of the development curve, as most players that age are either chasing a trip to Omaha for the College World Series or racking up Greyhound rewards points in A-Ball. But being that young and ranking as one of the game's premier power bats? That's a good indication that a hitter could be headed for the ring of honor known as Cooperstown. On the next page, take a look at the company Stanton keeps among age-21 sluggers.

For those of you keeping score at home, there are 10 Hall of Famers, plus two future first-ballot Hall of Famers in Pujols and Cabrera, on the list. While the list is packed with legendary hitters, we also see a few guys for whom young slugging didn't portend lots of plaques and press. We'll return to this list later, examining the career paths of age-21 power hitters to see what the future may hold for Stanton. But next, let's pop the hood on Stanton's historic season.

On July 27, John Lackey beats Bruce Chen and the Royals, putting the Red Sox up in the AL East by three games. A Major League Baseball informant confirms that the plan by which the Red Sox were to throw games in order to preserve a veneer of competitive balance is over, and the unstoppable Boston Red Sox are now free to play to their abilities and trounce the rest of the division. Red Sox manager Terry Francona says, to no one in particular, that it is now "time to witness the firepower of this fully-armed and operational baseball juggernaut!"

Most HR Hit During Age-21 Season

Player	Year	HR
1. Eddie Mathews	1953	47
2. Albert Pujols	2001	37
3. Hal Trosky	1934	35
4. Mike Stanton	**2011**	**34**
T-5. Miguel Cabrera	2004	33
T-5. Jose Canseco	1986	33
T-5. Bob Horner	1979	33
T-5. Jimmie Foxx	1929	33
9. Andruw Jones	1998	31
10. Ruben Sierra	1987	30
T-11. Frank Robinson	1957	29
T-11. Joe DiMaggio	1936	29
T-13. Cal Ripken	1982	28
T-13. Tony Conigliaro	1966	28
T-15. Juan Gonzalez	1991	27
T-15. Eddie Murray	1977	27
T-15. Orlando Cepeda	1959	27
T-15. Al Kaline	1956	27
T-15. Hank Aaron	1955	27
T-20. Justin Upton	2009	26
T-20. Darryl Strawberry	1983	26
T-20. Johnny Bench	1969	26
T-20. Ken Keltner	1938	26

Source: Baseball Reference.com

Breaking Down Stanton's Slugging

With run-scoring down yet again in 2011, Stanton hit his shots in a less homer-happy environment (0.94 home runs per game for each team) than other recent players like Upton (1.04 in 2009), Cabrera and Pujols (1.12 in 2004 and 2001, respectively). Sun Life Stadium wasn't a launching pad, ranking 18th in ESPN's home run park factor. Divisional games on the road were no picnic either, with Citizens Bank Park (16th in HR park factor), Turner Field (17th) and Citi Field (28th) also ranking in the bottom half. Despite these obstacles, Stanton crushed pitches of all velocity and movement.

Trumedia Networks and Sportvision keep track of a batter's performance against both "hard" pitches (fastballs, sinkers, cutters and splitters) and "soft" pitches (curveballs, sliders and change-ups). Against hard

Stanton's Slugging Percentage on Contact vs. "Hard" Stuff

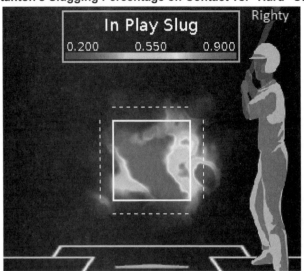

On that very same day—July 27—the Tampa Bay Rays lose to the Oakland Athletics 13-4, falling 11.5 games behind the Red Sox. Joe Maddon issues the Rays' formal surrender to Boston and forfeits the rest of their games. "Look, they signed our best player last winter," Maddon says. "What chance have we got?"

pitches, Stanton slugged .567. That ranked in the 92nd percentile among major league hitters.

Above is a heat map of Stanton's in-play slugging percentage against hard pitches by pitch location, compared to the league average heat map below. The more dark grey you see, the better. Stanton has a thick grey stripe that cuts across the middle of the strike zone.

Average Slugging Percentage on Contact vs. "Hard" Stuff

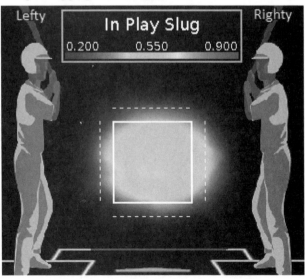

Hall of Fame manager
Dick Williams dies. Due
to a bureaucratic mix-up
he is mistakenly sent to
hell instead of heaven.
Before the situation can
be remedied, however,
Williams, as befitting his
reputation, leads hell's
long-losing baseball
team to victory over
the forces of heaven,
but then gets into a
personal feud with Satan
himself and eventually
tenders his resignation.

Lest you think Stanton was a one-dimensional, Pedro Cerrano-esque hitter, he slugged .491 against soft pitches. That ranked in the 94th percentile among big league batters. Unless a pitcher located his soft stuff low and away, Stanton annihilated it:

Stanton's Slugging Percentage on Contact vs. "Soft" Stuff

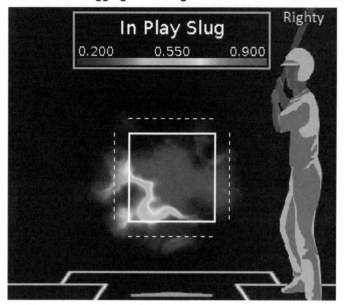

Average Slugging Percentage on Contact vs. "Soft" Stuff

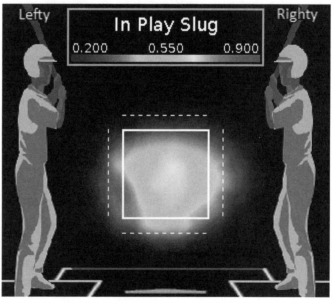

Twenty of Stanton's home runs came against hard pitches, and 14 against soft ones.

Stanton's power-hitting prowess reached mythical levels even before he made his major league debut. He obliterated a pitch at Double-A Montgomery in May of 2010 that sailed over the center field scoreboard and landed an estimated 500-550 feet from home plate. Around that same time, Mississippi manager Phil Wellman said to the Florida *Times Union*, "[Stanton] looks like a 15-year-old playing on an 8-year-old's Little League team." Given how far Stanton's homers traveled in 2011, it often looked like he was taking swings in a Little League park.

Stanton didn't hit any cheapies. His homers rocketed off the bat and landed (they did eventually land, right?) in parts of the bleachers that mere mortals could only dream of reaching. Hit Tracker Online shows that Stanton's home runs came off the bat at an average speed of 107.4 miles per hour, four miles per hour above the major league average. Factoring out the influence of wind, temperature and altitude, Stanton's shots traveled an average distance of 415 feet. The big league average? A mere 394 feet. And no NL hitter topped Stanton's 15 "No Doubt" homers, which are clouts that clear the fence by at least 20 vertical feet and land at least 50 feet past the fence. Who needs a space shuttle program when you've got Mike Stanton?

What History Says about Stanton's Slugging

The young sluggers on the age 21 HR list at the beginning of the article went on to post some prolific home run totals. Five joined the 500 home run club (Hank Aaron, Frank Robinson, Jimmie Foxx, Eddie Mathews, Eddie Murray). Albert Pujols is poised to do so within the next two seasons, and Miguel Cabrera is a good bet to eventually reach that mark as well. Four others aside from Pujols topped 400 homers (Jose Canseco, Juan Gonzalez, Cal Ripken and still-active Andruw Jones), and four more went deep over 350 times (Al Kaline, Johnny Bench, Orlando Cepeda and Joe DiMaggio).

But, more impressively, these guys are anything but all-or-nothing batters. The average career OPS+ of our young sluggers is 135, and the median OPS+ is 132. They not only hit for power, but also got on base and provided all-around value at the plate. Stanton is holding his own so far, posting a 132 OPS+ during his first two years in the majors.

On average, our young sluggers showed marked improvement in their strike-zone control in subsequent seasons. At age 21, they had a collective 0.53 walk-to-strikeout ratio. At 22, they bumped that BB/K ratio up to 0.66, and at 23, it was 0.76. Whether it's pitchers tiptoeing around the

Derek Jeter gets his 3,000th career hit. A home run, no less, caught by a Yankees fan named Christian Lopez. While experts agree that the ball would be worth hundreds of thousands of dollars if sold at an auction, Lopez gives it back to Jeter in exchange for some merchandise and tickets to Yankees games for the rest of the season. When reached for comment, Mr. Lopez says "Derek Jeter may have a gigantic mansion, a scorching hot actress for a girlfriend, five World Series rings, hundreds of millions of dollars in the bank, and the adoration of millions and millions of people, but I really felt it necessary that he have this ball."

The All-Star Game is played in Phoenix. Once starters, reserves and replacements for those who have backed out or are injured are counted, there are some 66 players who can claim to be an All-Star in 2011. To save time before the game, the PA announcer decides that it would be quicker to announce those players who *are not* All-Stars.

zone, respecting the hitters' prodigious power, or batters learning to lay off junk pitches and make more contact, these guys quickly learned how to walk more and punch out less.

It remains to be seen how Stanton's plate approach will evolve, but he took more free passes and whiffed less in 2011, increasing his BB/K ratio from 0.28 during his rookie year to 0.42. Ironically, the age-21 hitter that Stanton most resembles is Cabrera. Back in 2004 with the Marlins, Miggy hit 33 home runs and had a 0.46 BB/K ratio. He has since cut his strike-out rate drastically while averaging 20-plus intentional walks per season. I don't know if Stanton can pare his strikeout total that much, but big-time power has its perks—pitchers don't want to mess with you.

Stanton's boost in walks (from 8.6 percent to 11.6 percent) and decline in strikeouts (31.1 percent to 27.6 percent) was due to a combination of pitchers showing caution and Stanton tweaking his two-strike approach. According to Trumedia data, Stanton's rate of pitches seen within the strike zone fell from 44 percent to 42 percent, a figure similar to those of Adrian Gonzalez and Cabrera and one of the 10 lowest among qualified hitters. With two strikes, Stanton was more aggressive (he swung at 60 percent of two-strike offerings, up from 58 percent) and missed less often (36 percent of the time that he swung, down from 38 percent).

Stanton's improved BB/K ratio is a great sign that he's headed for sustained stardom instead of a career path akin to that of Ruben Sierra, one of the cautionary tales on the young sluggers list. Sierra was hardly a total bust—he finished with over 300 career home runs, made four All-Star teams and finished as the runner-up in the 1989 MVP race—but his production fell off in his mid-20s and he turned into a journeyman in his 30s, finishing with a 105 OPS+ that is by far the lowest among the young sluggers. Sierra never walked much, routinely posting OBPs in the low .300s that dragged down his offensive value. Homers are important, but so is reaching base by other means.

Aside from poor plate discipline, the other pitfall Stanton needs to avoid is injury. Hal Trosky, an Indians first baseman in the 1930s, routinely ranked among the game's best home run hitters but saw his career derailed by migraine headaches in his late 20s. Bob Horner's bulky, beat-up body made him a defensive liability at third base. He played a year in Japan after collusion left him without a real big league offer in 1987, and he retired at age 30 due to injury. Darryl Strawberry dealt with injury, among other issues, during his career, and Juan Gonzalez couldn't stay on the field in his early 30s.

And then there's the tragic tale of Boston's Tony Conigliaro, a local boy who became the youngest home run champion in American League history. On Aug. 18, 1967, Tony C. was hit by a Jack Hamilton fastball under his left eye, ruining his vision and shattering his cheekbone. He attempted two comebacks but was out of baseball by age 30.

So far, Stanton's Hulk-like physique hasn't been bothered by more than an eye infection and a tweaked hamstring. But Conigliaro's case goes to show that no matter how much we analyze and prognosticate, baseball is a capricious game.

The Quest for 500, 763

Could Stanton one day join the likes of Aaron, Robinson, Foxx, Mathews and Murray among the game's all-time great home run hitters? There's a pretty good chance if you ask Oliver, a projection system developed by Brian Cartwright that is featured on The Hardball Times' website. Oliver envisions Stanton becoming the pre-eminent slugger in baseball, averaging just under 48 home runs per season from 2012-2017. If Stanton meets that forecast, he'll have a staggering 341 career homers through his age-27 season. That would be more than The Kid, The Machine, The Mick and Hammerin' Hank. In fact, only Alex Rodriguez hit more home runs through that age in the history of the game:

Player	Years	HR
1. Alex Rodriguez	1994-2003	345
2. *Mike Stanton Projected*	2010-2017	341
3. Jimmie Foxx	1925-1935	302
4. Eddie Mathews	1952-1959	299
5. Ken Griffey Jr.	1989-1997	294
6. Albert Pujols	2001-2007	282
7. Mickey Mantle	1951-1959	280
8. Mel Ott	1926-1936	275
9. Frank Robinson	1956-1963	262
10. Juan Gonzalez	1989-1997	256
11. Hank Aaron	1954-1961	253
12. Andruw Jones	1996-2004	250
13. Miguel Cabrera	2003-2010	247
14. Johnny Bench	1967-1975	240
15. Adam Dunn	2001-2007	238

Source: Baseball Reference.com

Former THT writer David Gassko developed a tool that predicts a hitter's chances of reaching certain career milestones based on his

The Pirates begin the day on July 16 tied for first place in the National League Central. While the team's fortunes went south soon after and the Pirates finished yet another season below .500, Pirates fans look back fondly on those 10 days or so when it looked like the Buccos could contend. Not unlike the way you look back on that big road trip to Canada you and the guys in your dorm planned when you were drunk that night but never got around to taking.

stats from the past three seasons (weighing the most recent season more heavily), his career totals to that point and his age. Based on Stanton's work so far (56 career home runs through age 21), Gassko's tool gives the Marlin a 46 percent chance of reaching 500 home runs and a 25 percent chance of one day becoming the all-time HR champ by hitting his 763rd homer (though A-Rod or Pujols could have something to say about that total).

Out of curiosity, I plugged Stanton's Oliver projections into the tool to find how his chances changed if he indeed finished his age-27 season with 341 career jacks. Under those conditions, Gassko's tool shows Stanton with a 75 percent chance of joining the 500 HR club and an 18 percent chance of usurping Barry Bonds as history's greatest home run hitter. A three-quarters' chance of going deep at least 500 times and nearly a one-in-five shot of becoming the most prolific homer hitter ever. Prettay, prettay, prettay good.

While I don't have nearly as powerful a crystal ball as Oliver or Gassko, I do have one prediction. At some point in spring training, new Marlins manager Ozzie Guillen will watch Stanton take BP, turn to the guy next to him and say, "can you #$&*n' believe there were rumors about trading him for me?"

Stanton's Competition for Best Young Slugger

We've established that Stanton has enjoyed one of the best starts to a career of any young power hitter in history, and that Oliver would propose marriage to him if computer/human unions weren't so taboo. But is it possible that some other hot shot could challenge Stanton for the title of best young slugger in baseball?

I'm loosely defining "young slugger" as any hitter who played pro ball in 2011 at age 23 or younger. Within those parameters, three names stick out: Justin Upton, Jesus Montero and Bryce Harper.

Upton, who himself appeared on the list of age-21 sluggers, has cracked 91 career home runs through his age-23 season. Oliver predicts that the first overall pick in the '05 draft will settle in as a perennial 25-30 homer guy, though I think that might sell him short. Upton's forecast might be hurt by a relatively poor 2010 during which he suffered through a shoulder injury, and Chase Field favors power hitters.

Montero didn't have a huge power year at Triple-A Scranton/Wilkes-Barre, but 18 home runs and a near-.470 slugging percentage from a 21-year-old is very impressive. Oliver thinks that Montero could hit around 25 homers annually over the next few seasons, peaking with around 30 shots per year.

And then, of course, there's Harper. At just 18 years old, Harper dominated in the minors to the tune of a .297/.392/.501 line and 17 home runs between Low-A Hagerstown and Double-A Harrisburg. To fully appreciate how special that kind of performance is, consider that the average age of South Atlantic League hitters in 2011 was 21.4, and 24.2 in the Eastern League. Can you imagine the numbers Harper would have posted if, instead of getting his GED and becoming eligible for the 2010 draft, he had played high school ball this year? Yeesh.

Oliver projects that Harper could hit 15 home runs as a teenager in the majors next season. Only five teenagers have hit double-digit dingers in major league history: Conigliaro (24 in 1964), Mel Ott (18 in 1928), Ken Griffey Jr. (16 in 1989), Mickey Mantle (13 in 1951) and Ed Kranepool (10 in 1964). We might not get to see Harper hit bombs and blow kisses in April 2012, but he figures to be a strong divisional nemesis to Stanton and has a 20-25 HR projection for 2014, when he'll be 21. A word of advice to fans thinking about buying Marlins/Nats bleacher seats in future years: duck.

Other guys who could enter the conversation are Jason Heyward, Freddie Freeman, Mike Moustakas and Eric Hosmer, though Oliver sees low-20s homer totals for those guys in future seasons.

All manner of trades are made at the trading deadline. One that wasn't made: Rich Harden from the Athletics to the Red Sox, who backed out of the deal once they reviewed Harden's medical records. "We're a sure-thing playoff team," Theo Epstein tells reporters, "the last thing we need is an injured pitcher to derail our irresistible march to a world title. So we're going to trade for Erik Bedard instead."

The HR Wild Card: The New Stadium

Gone are the days of the Marlins playing home games amid a sea of empty orange seats at Sun Life Stadium. The newly-dubbed Miami Marlins will move into a new retractable-roof ballpark in 2012. We don't yet know how the new park will play, but here are the expected dimensions of the Marlins' new digs compared to Sun Life Stadium:

Part of Park	Miami Ballpark	Sun Life Stadium
Left Field	340 feet	330 feet
Left-Center	384 feet	360 feet
Center Field	416 feet	404 feet
Right-Center	392 feet	385 feet
Right Field	335 feet	345 feet

Source: Marlins.com

There are other factors that could influence how hitter or pitcher-friendly the park is, such as temperature, altitude, wind and the height of the outfield fences. Sun Life, for instance, featured a "Teal Monster" in left field that was 26.5 feet tall and had eight-foot fences elsewhere in the park. The "Bermuda Triangle" in center will be a feature in the new ballpark, though it will be 420 feet instead of 434 feet. We don't yet know the height of the fences in the new park, however.

During his first two seasons, Stanton has been a pull hitter. Thirty-six of his homers have been hit to left field, 13 to center field and seven have gone the opposite way. At first blush, it doesn't seem like the new park, with deeper dimensions to left, left-center and straightaway center, will do Stanton many favors. But again, that's speculative.

One thing Stanton has going for him is that Hit Tracker Online indicates the vast majority of his homers would clear any fence. Of his 56 home runs, 33 would have gone out of every major league stadium. Twelve would have left between 25-29 stadiums, three would have gone out of 20-24 parks, and one would have exited 15-19 venues. Only seven homers would have left less than half of major league ballparks.

Conclusion

Mike Stanton just bashed his way into an elite group of young power hitters, the great majority of whom went on to enjoy many All-Star seasons or even Cooperstown-worthy careers. The former three-sport star, who easily could be playing tight end in the NFL or power forward in the NBA, has put himself on a path that could one day place him among the game's all-time power-hitting luminaries. Pitchers are approaching him cautiously and Stanton is adapting his two-strike approach to punch out less often, resulting in improved walk and strikeout rates that make him a quality all-around hitter instead of a one-trick pony.

He'll have to stay healthy and will face stiff competition from the likes of Upton, Montero and Harper, but Stanton currently wears the crown as baseball's best young power hitter. One day, he could join an even more exclusive ring of honor.

The Annotated Year in Baseball History

by Richard Barbieri

On The Hardball Times website, I look back every week at events from that week in history. When I write those columns, I have the whole of history to look back on. Here, we reflect on the past year and find news, big or small, that connects to the past in one way or another. Some of these events you probably remember; others might not even have registered. Read on.

November 2010: *Mariano Rivera Turns 41:*

Besides being remarkable for Rivera's continued dominance as he ages—no reliever has ever had a better season at that age—this also got Rivera into the 40/40 club. And no, it isn't that 40/40 club, the one with the likes of Jose Canseco and Alfonso Soriano as members. Rather, this would be those pitchers who earned 40 saves at age 40 or older.

Perhaps not surprisingly, Rivera is the only member of the club. In fact, only Trevor Hoffman, Dennis Eckersley and Doug Jones join Rivera as pitchers who recorded 30 or more saves at 40 or older. If Rivera can do it again in 2012, he will stand alone as the only pitcher to have three seasons of 30 or more saves at 40 or older.

It seems likely, however, that Rivera will ultimately fall short of the all-time record for saves recorded by a pitcher in his 40s, since that title belongs to Hoyt Wilhelm who—pitching until he was 49—recorded 129 saves.

December 2010: *Adam Dunn Signs with White Sox:*

In many ways, this seemed like a good move for both parties. The White Sox would give Dunn, a Washington National in 2010, a $56 million contract and allow him to play his natural position: designated hitter. The White Sox, who finished six games behind the Twins, would be adding a potent slugger to a lineup whose regular designated hitters had a collective .247 average and .728 OPS in 2010.

Of course, the move was an utter disaster all around. Dunn put up one of the worst seasons ever by a regular player, while the White Sox finished well below .500.

In addition to his misery this season, the White Sox' other struggles doomed Dunn to yet another year without a playoff appearance. He now has more than 1,500 major league games with Cincinnati, Arizona, Washington and Chicago without seeing any postseason action. Barring a remarkable turnaround by the White Sox next season, Dunn seems likely to become—as of that moment—the 38th player to reach 1,700 games without a postseason appearance.

January 2011: *Red Sox Cancel Plans to Modify Fenway Park*

Or, more accurately, Red Sox modify plans to modify Fenway Park. As they have during many offseasons of John Henry's ownership, the Sox made changes to the nearly 100-year old ballpark, including the installation of new scoreboards around the park. (Needless to say, the hand-operated scoreboard inside the Green Monster remained unchanged.)

But the bigger plans were ones that didn't happen, specifically ones that would have moved the right-field bullpen fences in by between six and nine feet to allow for bigger, more modern bullpens. The plans were cancelled after various historic preservation groups which have some control over Fenway Park objected.

Talk of moving walls is quite in fashion this year, especially in New York, where talk of making CitiField more hitter-friendly (and, to a lesser extent, the new Yankee Stadium less hitter-friendly) has been heard ever since the parks opened. Both the Tigers and White Sox have changed their home parks recently—in both cases making them more conducive to offense.

Whether the Red Sox try again to modify Fenway's bullpen remains to be seen, but there's no doubt ballpark modification will continue to be one element of baseball's only constant: change.

February 2011: *Gino Cimoli Dies*

Cimoli had the misfortune to pass away the day after former Pirates manager Chuck Tanner died, so his death was largely overshadowed. And it is true that in the history of baseball Tanner—who managed four teams for more than 2,700 games and won the 1979 World Series with the "We Are Family" Pirates—was a larger figure than Cimoli.

Cimoli is important too, though, even if his career is more trivia than accomplishmenta. It was Gino Cimoli who on April 15, 1958 led off for the Dodgers against Ruben Gomez of the Giants. What makes this newsworthy is that Cimoli was leading off for the Los Angeles Dodgers and Gomez was pitching for the San Francisco Giants. This made Cimoli the first batter to bat in a major league game on the West Coast. Cimoli struck out and the Giants would go on to win 8-0.

This was rather appropriate as Cimoli himself was a Californian, born in San Francisco in 1929 and continuing to live there for most of his life. It is fitting that Cimoli lived long enough to see the Giants—for so long the West Coast's "other" team—win a World Series.

March 2011: *Kendrys Morales Announces Name Change*

This was a good season for name changes in baseball, another one of its oldest, if rarely seen, traditions. The notion of a player known by one name changing to another dates at least as far back as 1917. That was the year Herman "Germany" Schaefer announced he was to be known as "Liberty" Schaefer, lest anyone think a Chicago-born professional baseball player with vaudeville aspirations was secretly aligned with the Kaiser.

While baseball has seen names change now and then since Schaefer (Albert, *née* Joey, Belle being a prominent example), this past season had two notable name switches, bookending the season. The first was in spring training when Morales—known heretofore as Kendry—announced that his actual name was Kendry**s** and he would like to be known as such in the future.

At the end of the year, there was a name change under less willing circumstances after Marlins closer Leo Núñez left the team in the last week of the season. It was revealed that this was because he had been playing—since he first signed a professional contract in 2000—under an assumed name. The real name, apparently, is Juan Carlos Oviedo. It remains to be seen what effect this will have on the career of Núñez/Oviedo.

April 2011: *John Lackey Has Worst Game of Season*

Unfortunately for Lackey, his worst game of the season has lots of competition. It could be this game, on April 2 at Fenway when he went fewer than four innings while giving up nine runs, 10 hits and two home runs. Or it could be July 4, when he gave up seven runs on nine hits in two and a third innings. Or a number of others. But by game score, this was Lackey's worst effort of the year, so it is the symbolic choice for Lackey's induction in the all-bust starting rotation.

So far, the Red Sox have paid Lackey more than $33 million and been rewarded with 375 innings of pitching with a 5.26 ERA, nearly a run and a half higher than his career figure with the Angels. And the Red Sox are still on the hook for more than $45 million for Lackey for the next three years.

Lackey is not even the only current AL East pitcher with a claim to the all-bust starting rotation. For the second straight year, A.J. Burnett was

Alex Rodriguez is in hot water once again when multiple tabloid outlets report that A-Rod played "in an underground, illegal poker game where cocaine was openly used." MLB states that it will investigate the matter, but it won't begin to do so for several days because, "Frankly, we're shocked that someone like Alex Rodriguez would exercise bad judgment. Really. Rodriguez? I mean, who could have predicted that he'd get into the kind of trouble that gets splashed all over the tabloids."

Following a poor start against the Atlanta Braves in which he was ejected, Cubs starter Carlos Zambrano cleans out his locker, leaves the ballpark and tells team-mates that he plans to retire. Cubs management announces it will investigate the matter, but it won't begin to do so for several days because, "Frankly, we're shocked that someone like Carlos Zambrano would exercise bad judgment! Really. Zambrano? I mean, who could have predicted that he'd react angrily to a bad game and behave in such a way that makes him seem like a selfish guy who quits on his team?"

Chipper Jones records his 4,500th total base, his 1,000th extra-base hit and his 450th home run. When asked about it he said, "I really like round numbers. So much so that one month of milestones seemed too odd and asymmetrical for me."

dreadful for the Yankees, and has only his debut 2009 season with New York (13-9, 4.04) to keep his contract from ranking with Carl Pavano and Kenny Rogers in all-time Yankese pitching disasters.

May 2011: *Diamondbacks Defeat Dodgers*

In the long-run, this was a relatively insignificant game. Unlike some of their postseason brethren, the Diamondbacks cruised to their division title, clinching the NL West on Sept. 24. The Dodgers, meanwhile, would be as many as 14 games under .500 before rallying to finish a distant third in the NL West.

But what makes it notable is just not the 1-0 score, but rather that Arizona needed just one hit to do it. Stephen Drew led off the second inning with a double, moved to third on a botched pickoff throw and scored on a Melvin Mora sacrifice fly. Dodgers pitcher Chad Billingsley would not allow a hit the rest of the way, but suffered the hard-luck loss as Josh Collmenter and the Diamondbacks 'pen combined to allow just four hits while throwing a shutout.

A team has won a game while recording only one hit just 44 times since 1919, which makes it appreciably more rare than, for example, a no-hitter. (Teams have won five games since 1919 with **no** hits, most recently in 2008.) Obviously, this is something of a fluke accomplishment at best— the combination of strong pitching and inept offense—so it is deservedly not awarded the same recognition, but a baseball rarity should not go wholly unnoticed.

June 2011: *CitiField Holds Soccer Game*

This game saw Ecuador and Greece play to 1-1 tie, to the scorn of soccer-haters everywhere and the muted appreciation of soccer fans. Even as multipurpose stadiums fall out of favor—next year only the A's and Blue Jays will play in a facility that hosts another sport full-time— alternative uses for baseball stadiums are more popular than ever.

In 2011, in addition to the Mets hosting soccer, three teams—the Yankees, Rays and Giants—saw their home stadium converted to football for a bowl game. In recent memory, two major league baseball stadiums have hosted the NHL Winter Classic, with Citizens Bank Park scheduled to hold the 2012 event. When you consider the Raiders sharing the Coliseum in Oakland with the A's, basketball is the only major sport that will not play a game in a major league venue this year. (Of course, the NBA may not play many games in the 2011-12 season at all.)

And all these other sports do not even consider the other uses for stadiums; for example, six of the eight 2011 dates on Paul McCartney's

"On the Run" tour were in major league stadiums. Perhaps most notoriously, a date on U2's 360° Tour in Miami forced the Marlins to play three of their "home" games in Seattle's Safeco Field.

July 2011: *Francisco Rodriguez Records His Final Save*

Following the 2008 season, it would have seemed an incredible suggestion that after the 2011 season Francisco Rodriguez would have fewer career saves than Jason Isringhausen. It is true that at that point Rodriguez had 208 career saves compared to Isringhausen's 293. But K-Rod was also coming off a season of 62 saves—a single-season record—and was just completing his age 26 season. Isringhausen was nearly a decade older and recorded just 12 saves and a 5.70 ERA in a year that ended in early August due to arm trouble.

And yet since then, things have gone largely downhill for Rodriguez. Though he recorded 35 saves in 2009, he managed just 48 combined in 2010 and 2011, the former year shortened by an arrest for assault and the latter seeing him traded to Milwaukee and shifted to a set-up role.

With Rivera now holding the all-time record at 603, and showing no meaningful signs of slowing down, Rodriguez' chances of someday breaking that record have gone down hugely in just three years. If K-Rod is to someday hold the title of all-time saves leader, it will take a strong bounce-back season in 2012.

August 2011: *Dan Uggla's Hitting Streak Ends*

I have always found the hype that surrounds hitting streaks a little overdone. I find hitting streaks inherently overrated—they seem closer to trivia than actual accomplishment—but the attention seems unwarranted mostly because it seems highly improbable anyone will come close to Joe DiMaggio's record of 61 straight games.

Since the Yankee Clipper set his mark in 1941, only Pete Rose has come within a dozen games. In fact, Rose is the only player since '41 to hit in more in 40 or more straight games. Jimmy Rollins came close—reaching 38 games spread across two seasons—but no one has seriously challenged DiMaggio.

It seems likely that DiMaggio's hit streak is entering the realm of records that may never be broken, like Nolan Ryan's strikeouts or Rose's hit total. Of course, none approach the insurmountable level of Cy Young's 511 wins—barring a rule change, no one is touching that—but I am confident that I will never be writing about a new consecutive-game hit record.

Luis Castillo, who was a Yankees batboy from 1998 to 2005, comes out with a new book called *Clubhouse Confidential*. In it he details all manner of sordid and embarrassing tales from inside the New York Yankees clubhouse. None of them are quite as embarrassing, however, as being a batboy for seven years.

ESPN reports that four current players have said that they've witnessed Blue Jays hitters being relayed signs from the center-field stands at Rogers Centre. At the time of the report, the Jays were 28-27 at Rogers Centre and 30-30 on the road, so apparently the scheme only involves unimportant signs.

September 2011: *Major League Baseball Plays 200,000th Game*

How you end up at 200,000 games depends on how you count. What leagues should be considered major league? Do you count playoff games or just regular season games? And so on. But based on Major League's Baseball's count, the big game was in Houston, where the Astros hosted the Rockies.

It is generally accepted that game No. 1 took place in 1876, but everything after that is pretty much estimation, especially when you consider that start times are not precisely recorded. Arguably the most notable game in baseball history—Jackie Robinson's debut—was game 77,130 while the Yankees hosting the Orioles in July of 1964 was number 100,000.

At the moment, MLB plays roughly 4,900 games a year, which means we can all look forward to game number 300,000 in roughly 2031. I hope I'll still be here to write about it.

October 2011: *Terry Francona Leaves Red Sox*

First, some straight historical perspective: The last time a two-time World Series-winning manager left the Red Sox was after the 1916 season, when Bill "Rough" Carrigan left the team. Carrigan and Francona also remain the only two managers in Red Sox history to win two titles.

This was a big year for World Series-winning managers leaving their teams. Jack McKeon had left the Marlins once before after winning a World Series—and his decision to not return in 2012 to manage at age 81 was hardly a surprise. McKeon will be replaced by yet another man leaving a town where he had championship success: Ozzie Guillen. After eight years in Chicago with some very good years—the White Sox' first World Series championship since Liberty Schaefer was still around—and some not so good, Guillen was released from his contract.

With the retirement of Bobby Cox last year, only five current managers—Bruce Bochy, Joe Girardi, Charlie Manuel, Tony La Russa and Mike Scioscia—remain in charge of clubs where they have brought a title through 2010.

The Business of Baseball

by Brian Borawski

It was a year of selective turmoil. Most teams went about their business in an ordinary manner, with the players and the games taking the headlines. Attendance generally held its own in a tough economic environment. But a select few teams just seemed to make other off-field news every day.

The Dodgers in Turmoil

In late November, 2010 Los Angeles Dodgers owners Frank and Jamie McCourt were officially divorced. Speaking from experience, while not all the headaches are resolved at that point, you should definitely be looking at calmer waters down the road. This couldn't have been further from the truth in the McCourts' divorce. Because of conflicting copies of a post-nuptial agreement between Frank and Jamie, there was a question as to whether Frank owned the team outright or whether he and Jamie should be considered co-owners. In early December 2010, the judge in the case threw out the post-nuptial agreement and awarded ownership of the team to both McCourts.

That was the first pitch of a 2011 in Los Angeles that saw financial and legal wrangling wrest attention from a mediocre Dodgers team that had a mediocre season.

Frank McCourt fired the attorneys who wrote the post-nuptial agreement, and in early January met with Major League Baseball executives to talk about his plans for the team. He pleaded his case for three days, but from how things turned out, the baseball officials must not have liked what they heard. Later that month, news leaked that the Fox media conglomerate had lent Frank McCourt money to cover some of the expenses for the Dodgers and that Fox had a leg up in getting the teams' television rights.

By late February, it looked like McCourt might finally have found his lifeline. The television deal with Fox began to come to fruition, with a deal that included included a $200 million loan from Fox to the Dodgers with extra years of television rights as collateral. But MLB stepped in. It didn't like the precedent the deal was setting.

In late April, all hell broke loose. Major League Baseball used its "best interest of baseball" power, and took over operations of the team and appointed former Texas Rangers president J. Thomas Schieffer to run the Dodgers.

It was MLB's first big step toward attempting to force McCourt out of his ownership position. He fired back, saying he was unjustifiably singled out and that the league had a predetermined agenda to take his team away. McCourt also said that his pending television deal with Fox would allow him to get back on his feet.

By May, though, while McCourt had gone the legal route to try to get his television deal pushed through regardless of MLB's objections, money had dried up and McCourt needed to make payroll. While the details still aren't clear, he managed to buy himself some time, paying his employees without help from Fox.

Mid-June turned out to be a major turning point for the team. The McCourts agreed that Frank would buy Jamie's stake for $100 million. The catch was the approval of the television agreement; there was no other way for Frank to drum up that amount of money. The following week, MLB vetoed the television deal and forced Frank McCourt's hand. On June 27, he put the team under bankruptcy protection.

The next month, Major League Baseball won its first big court victory. The bankruptcy judge said that rather than going with outside financing, the Dodgers must use financing provided by MLB during the course of the bankruptcy, since MLB offered better terms. The downside for the Dodgers and McCourt was that the decision gave MLB an even greater stake in the proceedings. The bankruptcy judge did temper the victory by saying that the loan would be provided independent from the league's oversight of the team. The judge also said that if MLB doesn't follow through, the team could use outside financing.

The wrangling goes on. MLB filed a petition to try to force McCourt to sell the team. McCourt is lobbying the judge to allow the Fox television contract to be signed saying that once it is, the team will be able to pay off all of its debt. By the time you read this, there could be some resolution, but I'm not holding my breath. There still are plenty of court dates to get through.

Trustees and Ponzi Schemes

In her 2009 book on the Bernie Madoff scandal, *Too Good to Be True*, Erin Arvedlund predicted that New York Mets owners Fred Wilpon and Saul Katz would be forced to sell the team because of the losses they incurred investing with Madoff. Nearly two years later, Wilpon and Katz still own the team, but their problem isn't the losses they incurred in Madoff investments. It's that they didn't lose enough.

In late January 2011, Irving H. Picard, the trustee for the victims in the Bernie Madoff scandal, sued Wilpon and Katz saying that they were financially sophisticated enough to know that Madoff was running a Ponzi scheme and that they were at least loosely involved because they walked away unscathed. He wanted a billion dollars. Shortly thereafter, the owners announced that they were going to sell a minority stake in the team to raise money to fight their legal battle and still pay the Mets' bills.

In February, the public learned that Madoff was more intimately involved in Wilpon's finances than had been known, and that at times it appeared as if Madoff had been acting as a personal banker for the Mets. Also that month, it was revealed that the Mets had received $25 million in loans from the league the previous fall to deal with a cash shortfall.

This was around the same time that real estate mogul Donald Trump expressed some interest in buying a stake in the team. In May, though, the Mets announced that they'd be selling a 33 percent stake in the team to hedge fund manager David Einhorn. With a sales price of $200 million, Einhorn also received a one dollar option to increase his stake to 60 percent if Wilpon and Katz didn't pay back the $200 million in three years. It seemed like a win/win for Einhorn because he'd either receive a third of the team for a three-year, interest free loan or he'd get 60 percent of the team for $200 million.

In August, Wilpon and Katz took their first hit in court. A three judge panel determined that Wilpon and Katz benefited from the Madoff scheme to the tune of $300 million. At issue was when Wilpon and Katz would have to turn over the money but the judge decided to push to September the decision as to whether Wilpon and Katz would have to pony up another $700 million.

In September it was announced that the sale to Einhorn had fallen through. Einhorn wanted to be preapproved as a majority owner and that raised some feathers. Einhorn also apparently wanted more involvement in the team then what's normally afforded to a minority partner. The Mets then announced that they'd be looking at several smaller investors of about $20 million each but to date, there have been no further developments on that front.

Later in September, Wilpon and Katz scored a major victory. The judge overhearing their case determined that the most the two owners would have to pay would be $386 million and that the number could end up being less than that. The judge threw out nine of the 11 counts from the suit and at this point, it appears that Picard is planning an appeal. For now though, it looks like the damage is going to be way less then what many thought was on the horizon for the Mets and their owners.

The *New York Post* reports that the agents for Phillies rookie outfielder John Mayberry Jr. have been trying to get him a date with Antoinette Nikprelaj, an actress and model who played a mermaid in "Pirates of the Caribbean." Turns out that Nikprelaj is married and has a daughter. Mayberry's agents earn their commission, however, when they point out that Mayberry is a platoon player and is perfectly fine with having access to her half the time.

In the Heart of Texas

And then there was Texas. On the southern side of the state, the Houston Astros were put up for sale. On the other side of Texas, the Rangers had their own ownership upheaval.

Astros owner Drayton McLane announced in 2010 that he'd sell the team, primarily for estate planning reasons. Then, in April 2011, McLane said he hoped to sell the team by the end of the summer and that the frontrunner for the team was Jim Crane, who owned the Houston based Crane Capital Group. Crane almost bought the Astros in 2008 and he was on the short end of the stick when both the Texas Rangers and Chicago Cubs were sold.

A month later, it appeared that Crane finally had his team. He was announced as the buyer, for $680 million. Then the sale hit the proverbial bump in the road. News started circulating that one of Crane's businesses was charged with profiteering during the Iraq War. While this wasn't the official reason, it appeared enough for MLB to postpone a vote on the sale. There was also speculation that Crane would resist an Astros move to the American League as part of a realignment.

Well into the fall, nothing had been settled. Crane's agreement with McLane was to expire at the end of November.

Meanwhile, in Dallas, Chuck Greenberg, a key part of a group that purchased the team with Nolan Ryan just the year before, was pushed out of his role as president of the team. Apparently he was stepping on toes and was more involved than expected in on-field matters. He and Ryan began to butt heads. One of them had to go and that was Greenberg. He still owns a piece of the team, but he was always a minority shareholder and largely a figurehead in the ownership battle that ensued when Tom Hicks put the team up for auction in 2010.

In one other piece of ownership news, oil trader Ray Bartoszek, one of the odd men out when the Mets decided to go with Einhorn in their minority stake sale, purchased a minority interest in the Yankees. His share of the team wasn't announced, but he joined about 30 others as limited partners in the team.

Attendance: Good News and Bad

Major league teams sold 73.1 million tickets in 2011. Whether that's good or bad is all in how you spin it.

On the good side, it was better then 2010's 73 million by 0.5 percent and it's also the fifth highest attendance mark ever. On the bad side, it was well south of the record hit in 2007, when attendance was 79.5 million.

Jeremy Affeldt is lost for the remainder of the season after sustaining nerve damage in his right hand as a result of a cut he received while trying to separate frozen hamburger patties.
In other news, Affeldt makes $4.5 million a year and lives in a city that contains multiple In-N-Out Burger locations. The Giants strongly consider designating Affeldt for assignment on the grounds of having no damn sense or taste.

For the first time ever, the Philadelphia Phillies led baseball with a franchise record 3.68 million tickets sold and a per-game average of 45,441. The Phillies sold out every home game, bringing their consecutive sellout run to 204 games. Right behind the Phillies and leading in the American League were the perennial attendance contenders, the New York Yankees, with 3.65 million fans and a 45,107 per-game average.

Three teams besides the Phillies set franchise attendance records. The Milwaukee Brewers made some noise during the offseason when they traded for Zack Greinke and Shawn Marcum, then made a successful playoff run in the National League Central. The San Francisco Giants finished third overall in attendance on the heels of their World Series win last year. Also drawing more fans than ever were the Giants' World Series opponent, the Texas Rangers.

Other attendance highlights:

- The Boston Red Sox, despite their historic collapse in the final month of the season, sold 3.05 million tickets in 2011. That's the second-most ever, and they extended their consecutive sellout streak to 712 games.

- The Los Angeles Angels of Anaheim went over the three million mark for the ninth straight season. Only the Yankees have a similar streak.

- The Cleveland Indians saw the largest increase in attendance, almost half a million.

- Nine teams went over the three million mark in 2011, which matches the 2010 total. Twenty teams topped two million, also the same as last year.

- Embroiled in their ownership battle and fielding a team that was going nowhere, the Los Angeles Dodgers saw an attendance decline of more than 600,000, their lowest mark since 2000.

- The Oakland Athletics took over last place in attendance with 1.48 million tickets sold. Second to last, with the lowest attendance for a playoff team, were the Tampa Bay Rays.

- For the second year in a row, the Yankees were first in road attendance with 33,228 tickets sold per game. The worst draw on the road were the Angels (26,125 per game).

In some ways, MLB dodged a bullet in 2011; with the economy appearing to be turning south right at the end of the season, next year looks more challenging. Teams that did well in 2011 and the postseason

Tim Wakefield finally gets his 200th career win after seven unsuccessful attempts to do so. "I knew I'd get it eventually," Wakefield says, "I mean, we have such a big lead in the Wild Card race that it's OK to keep sending me out here even though I don't have anything left in the tank. So we lost a couple as I pursued my milestone. It's all good."

could see increased attendance, but my guess is most will see a moderate decline. Of course Major League Baseball has other ways to make money. For example, further developing its MLB.TV product might help baseball weather the financial storm.

A Major Year in the Minors

Since 2008, when major league attendance began to turn down, minor league baseball—affordable and family-friendly—has been able to hold its audience. This past season wasn't an exception. Overall attendance was down to 41.3 million tickets sold in 2011 from 41.4 million in 2010, but average attendance was up a notch because of all the crazy weather. The per-game average in 2011 was 4,029 compared to 2010's 3,992.

As has been the case the past several years, nine of the top 10 teams in attendance were Triple-A teams. For the second straight year, the Lehigh Valley IronPigs led minor league baseball with an average attendance of 9,248 tickets sold per game. The Louisville Bats (8,715) and Columbus Clippers (8,704) were second and third.

The lone outlier was the Dayton Dragons of the Midwest League. This Single-A team finished sixth in overall attendance with 8,288 tickets sold per game and on July 23, 2011, did something no other professional sports team has done: The Dragons sold out their 815th consecutive game. That surpasses the record of the Portland Trailblazers of the National Basketball Association.

With 2011 being an odd numbered year, you shouldn't see any movement among minor league teams and their big league affiliates. A couple of teams are playing elsewhere, though. The Scranton/Wilkes-Barre Yankees are having major renovations done to their home ballpark so they're hitting the road. They'll be playing at six different venues in 2012 while their home, PNC Park, gets its facelift. The Double-A Carolina Mudcats will be moving to Pensacola, Fla., while the Kinston Indians become the new Mudcats and will be playing in the Carolina League.

Places to Play

No new ballparks opened in 2011. The Minnesota Twins enjoyed the second year in their new stadium and while they were able to sell enough tickets to put them fourth overall in attendance, we'll see if they can keep that up with the poor product they put on the field this past season. Meanwhile, the Florida Marlins continued work on their new ballpark, which is set to open in 2012. Of course, those are the done deals. What makes for more interesting stories are the places where stadiums aren't getting done.

The Oakland Athletics have been looking for a new home for a while now. A commission formed to examine the A's stadium situation has been doing its due diligence for two and a half years now and there's no end in sight. The Athletics want to move to San Jose and San Jose appears to want them, but this is a potential land mine because the city of San Jose is smack dab in San Francisco Giants territory.

The Giants have said they won't allow the move into their territory. Many thought that this stance would change when Giants CEO Bill Neukom announced his retirement, but his replacement, Larry Baer, says nothing has changed. Meanwhile, the A's have said that all spending decisions are on hold until the stadium issue is resolved. This came to light when outfield Josh Willingham expressed an interest in signing a contract extension and was told a deal wasn't happening because there was no resolution on a new stadium.

The Tampa Bay Rays also cranked up the rhetoric on their new stadium. Despite a terrific September run and a spot in the playoffs, the Rays finished second to last in attendance. The Rays have a lease with the city of St. Petersburg until 2027 and the bonds that were used to pay for the stadium don't expire until 2016. To date, St. Petersburg has not allowed the Rays to look for a new home. Another option is that the team or even the league could buy out the contract with the city so the Rays could move. It doesn't look like this will be settled soon.

Spring Training: Looking West

For the second year in a row, it looks like every team is standing pat on spring training homes, but there's still news.

As we were about to go to press, the Chicago Cubs finalized a deal that will keep them in Mesa, Ariz. for the foreseeable future. Mesa and the Cubs agreed to a 30-year lease on a new $99 million complex. The Mesa City Council expects to break ground no later than the summer of 2012 and be ready for spring training, 2014.

Another hot spot is Phoeniz, the spring training home for both the Milwaukee Brewers and Oakland Athletics. The city was hoping to sign lease extensions for both teams, but neither deal got done. The Brewers are the more immediate flight risk because they have the option to leave after the 2012 season. The Oakland lease expires in 2014.

Things should remain quiet on the spring training front for some time, but 2016 is a pivotal year. Five teams from the Grapefruit League have expressed an interest in moving to Arizona, and 2016 is when the leases for those teams begin to expire, with the Houston Astros coming up first.

The Atlanta Braves and Boston Red Sox continue to see their Wild Card leads shrink. "'Tis but a scratch," say Fredi Gonzalez and Terry Francona.

The Cardinals and the Rays continue to gain ground. "I've had worse," say Gonzalez and Francona.

The Sox and Braves continue to lose games in both blowouts and in heartbreakers. "Have at you!" say Gonzalez and Francona. "It's just a flesh wound! I'm invincible!"

Peace Reigns on the Labor Front

Conspicuous by its absence in baseball news (at least until now) is that the collective bargaining agreement between the players' union and the league is set to expire near the end of this year. I think in this case, no news is good news. While I expect some cosmetic changes, I don't see any major changes and you'd hope it'd be business as usual. In fact there's even a chance that the two sides have agreed in principle to a new agreement and have waited until the end of 2011 to make the announcement.

Unlike football, which almost had a work stoppage, and basketball, which doesn't look like it's going to have a full season, baseball seems to be getting things right, at least relatively speaking. Baseball played its 200,000th game this year, and while I think 2012 is going to be tough year for a lot of teams with the economy heading south, baseball is still going strong in a lot of ways. Let's just hope the people in charge have the foresight to keep things going like they have the past few years.

2011 Attendance Statistics

	Team	Home Attendance	Road Average	Home/Road Average
1	Philadelphia	3,680,718	33,000	39,220
2	NY Yankees	3,653,680	33,228	39,167
3	San Francisco	3,387,303	32,757	37,287
4	Minnesota	3,168,107	28,949	34,031
5	LA Angels	3,166,321	26,125	32,608
6	St. Louis	3,093,954	30,439	34,318
7	Milwaukee	3,071,373	30,657	34,356
8	Boston	3,054,001	31,999	34,851
9	Chicago Cubs	3,017,966	32,797	35,028
10	Texas	2,946,949	28,674	32,552
11	LA Dodgers	2,935,139	32,584	34,421
12	Colorado	2,909,777	30,299	33,128
13	Detroit	2,642,045	27,629	30,123
14	NY Mets	2,378,549	33,079	31,603
15	Atlanta	2,372,940	31,029	30,539
16	Cincinnati	2,213,498	33,120	30,205
17	San Diego	2,143,018	32,929	29,693
18	Arizona	2,105,432	30,175	28,084
19	Houston	2,067,016	28,588	27,053
20	Washington	1,940,478	29,484	27,224
21	Chicago White Sox	2,001,117	29,256	26,980
22	Pittsburgh	1,940,429	30,905	27,580
23	Seattle	1,896,321	27,873	25,642
24	Cleveland	1,840,835	30,671	26,698
25	Toronto	1,818,103	27,656	25,051
26	Baltimore	1,755,461	27,819	24,899
27	Kansas City	1,724,450	29,257	25,273
28	Florida	1,520,562	30,834	24,920
29	Tampa Bay	1,529,188	28,353	23,616
30	Oakland	1,476,792	30,476	24,354

Ethics and Major League Baseball, 2011

by Jack Marshall

Ethics and sport are strange bedfellows, but they are stuck with each other. This is especially true for baseball. Major League Baseball's image and culture has always been tied closely to traditional American values like individualism, character, accountability, sportsmanship; its players are supposed to be family friendly, and not threats to corrupt impressionable Little Leaguers. Of all the major sports, baseball has traditionally been the least tolerant of personal misconduct, and as a consequence, has had less of it to tolerate.

Still, baseball's ethics and society's ethics are not completely congruent. Each has distinct cultures, and like all cultures, they are constantly adjusting and refining what should be permitted as right and rejected as wrong in that culture.

In a previous Annual, I examined how baseball's determination of what constituted cheating was affected by (1) *historical factors,* such as how that conduct had traditionally been regarded through the years; (2) *structural distinctions,* such as what the rules specifically permitted or didn't explicitly forbid; and (3) *societal standards,* such as whether baseball could maintain the respect of its fan base while allowing certain conduct. All these factors combined go to the issue of integrity, which for any sport is a matter of survival.

There were three serious allegations of cheating in the 2011 season, all involving teams using their control over their home parks to handicap visiting teams. The Blue Jays were accused of having an employee in the stands stealing opposing teams' signs and relaying them to batters. In Milwaukee, the Brewers had to deny allegations that the team was manipulating the stadium lighting to make it darker around home plate when Brewers opponents were batting. In Colorado, Major League Baseball enacted stringent controls over the baseball humidor used by the Rockies to deaden balls enough to compensate for the high altitude, in response to new rumblings that different procedures were used on the balls the Rockies batters got to hit.

All of these were integrity issues. Baseball cannot permit fans to think that games are rigged by home teams giving themselves the benefit of spies, livelier balls or blinded batters.

I'm an ethicist by profession, and my job is to try to help determine, in various professions, what is right and ethical, what is wrong and unethical, whether standards are evolving, and whether they are evolving in a productive direction. Sometimes small incidents can signal an important or ominous shift. Sometimes I am completely wrong, but that's all right; another one of my jobs is to stimulate useful discussion, even if it consists of proving I'm confused.

As usual, there were too many ethical issues and controversies during the 2011 season to cover, but here are some that I think are worth thinking about:

Honesty: The Twins Celebrate Cheating

Major league baseball's traditional mixture of sportsmanship and expediency was on display early in spring training, when the Minnesota Twins announced that the team would commemorate the 20th anniversary of its dramatic 1991 World Series victory over the Atlanta Braves with a bobblehead specially designed for the occasion. It depicted the infamous, and pivotal, play in Game Two when Braves outfielder Ron Gant singled and rounded first safely, only to be tagged out on the throw because the Twins' jumbo first baseman, Kent Hrbek, illegally wrapped his arm around Gant's leg and lifted him off the base as he applied the tag. Since first base umpire Drew Coble completely missed Hrbek's manhandling, he called Gant out to end the inning. The Twins went on to win the game by one run, and triumphed in one of the most closely contested World Series of all time, four games to three.

What Hrbek did to Gant was a fairly egregious example of in-game cheating. For the Twins to glorify it in this manner established the concept of unethical promotional give-aways; I don't think I've encountered one before. To me, it constituted unsportsmanlike gloating at the Braves, as if the Mets had decided to celebrate their 1986 Championship with a bobblehead of Bill Buckner. That's a small complaint, however. My bigger one is the warped baseball values the bobblehead conveyed. The Twins, an organization I always think of as embodying the idea that baseball should be played the right way, took an official position that a Twins player cheating in the World Series was something to revel in, because the Twins benefited and he got away with it thanks to poor umpiring.

People get furious with me when I assert this, but I'll do it again: Baseball still, in spite of everything, holds on to its America, apple pie and motherhood status. It is unwise and unseemly for any sport, but especially this sport, to send messages that cheating is cute or acceptable if it works.

In August of 2008, the Hardball Times ran an online survey asking baseball fans to rank a large number of ethical situations, from least ethical to most ethical.

The following is a select list of some of those situations, starting with those ranked least ethical.

Kill the Ump

In a minor league game in 1899, one player took enormous exception to a call made by umpire Samuel White. The player took a swing, with his bat, at White's head. He connected. The umpire was killed. Violent attacks on umpires were frequent in the early era of baseball.

Segregation

No blacks were allowed to play in the organized major leagues of baseball from 1887 until Jackie Robinson put on a Dodgers uniform in 1947.

The Fix

According to baseball author Cait Murphy, the first recorded baseball bet took place in 1858, and the first fixed game in 1865. Then there was the case of the Louisville Grays.

In 1877, the Grays were doing fine, when suddenly their play turned sour, and the talented team ended up finishing out of first place. It later came out that some team members had secretly worked with a gambling syndicate out of New York to throw the games. Four Louisville players were thrown out of baseball for good. There are scores of other examples of fixed games from baseball's early era. Salaries were much lower in those days, and every dollar made a difference to most of the players.

Early Racism

The man widely thought to be the first black major league player was Moses Fleetwood Walker. The son of a physician and an erudite man himself, Walker had been a Latin and Greek scholar at Oberlin College before turning to pro ball in the 1870s. A catcher, Walker was routinely smashed into and otherwise physically abused by players on other teams.

One time, the Chicago White Stockings, led by Cap Anson, threatened to refuse to take the field if Walker played. A sportswriter termed him "the coon catcher." Other black players of that era regularly heard taunts like "Kill the nig#@*r!" In 1887, the owners gathered in Buffalo, and reached an informal agreement to keep blacks out of organized baseball.

Crooked Higham

There are many examples in which attempts were made to bribe umps to affect the outcome of games. This was particularly true in the early years of baseball. Salaries for both umpires and players were often barely enough to live on. Most players had second jobs in the offseason

If someone wants to issue an "Ends justify the means bobblehead," let Wall Street do it.

Fairness: The Jeff Bagwell Ethics Follies

The Twins' enthusiasm for cheating notwithstanding, when the Hall of Fame voting came around leading into the new year, baseball writers not only took a hard line against cheating, but decided to punish anyone who reminded them of the kind of player who *might* have engaged in cheating, specifically that particularly odious form known as PED use.

The victim of this strange logic was Jeff Bagwell, who played first base for the Houston Astros from 1991 to 2005 while compiling lifetime batting statistics that obviously warrant election to the Major League Baseball Hall of Fame. He was a dominant offensive player in the National League who did not become especially famous because he stayed with one, not very prominent, not very popular, not very good team for his whole career. He was not elected to the Hall in 2011, however, in part because Bagwell played during the so-called steroid era, when Mark McGwire, Barry Bonds, Sammy Sosa and others chemically mutated themselves into ball-crushing behemoths using illegal and banned substances.

(Another reason Bagwell was shunned was because some baseball writers inexplicably believe that even a fully qualified player shouldn't be elected in his first year, but that's another story.)

Those players *were* cheaters, and harmed the game of baseball and the integrity of the sport. They should be denied admission to the Hall of Fame on that basis alone, whatever their unenhanced talents may have been, how long they used drugs, or why. The standards for Hall enshrinement are very clear on this point:

> *"Voting shall be based upon the player's record, playing ability, integrity, sportsmanship, character, and contributions to the team(s) on which the player played."*

Integrity, sportsmanship, and character are not consistent with cheating. Those who don't like those criteria—I do, but I'm not objective where ethics are concerned—should work to change them. Football's Hall of Fame has no such character requirements; it is not necessarily a prerequisite for honoring career achievements. But as long as baseball's Hall does, the writers and fans who argue that steroid use shouldn't matter are ignoring the official qualifications.

The limitation, however, has nothing to do with Jeff Bagwell, because there is no evidence that he used steroids or any other banned substance.

What apparently kept him off many writers' ballots was suspicion, based on five dubious factors:

1. He started out slim, and became huge during his prime, a pattern which other steroid users exhibited.

2. He lifted weights like a bodybuilder, and bodybuilders often use steroids.

3. He played during an era in which many of the sluggers who put up equivalent power numbers were later shown to have used PEDs.

4. Late in his career, when there was increased emphasis on drug-testing and anti-steroid enforcement, Bagwell became noticeably lighter, suggesting to some that he had abandoned illegal substances to avoid being caught.

5. His body finally broke down, as many steroid users' bodies do.

That's not enough to rob an outstanding athlete of his well-earned status and recognition. Bagwell never tested positive for banned drugs. His name was not mentioned in the Mitchell Report, Major League Baseball's admittedly incomplete and flawed study of PED abuse by players during Bagwell's era. No player or former player, including Designated Vengeful Snitch Jose Canseco, ever accused him of using steroids.

He lifted weights like a bodybuilder, but weight training, separately from weight training with steroids, was and is an accepted method of improving strength and athletic performance. He lost weight later in his career, but aging players have chosen to slim down to compensate for diminishing mobility and ailing joints for decades. His body indeed broke down, but that happens to drug cheats and clean players alike.

The decision to keep Bagwell out of the Hall was unfair and incompetent. The use of banned substances by so many of Bagwell's colleagues is no excuse for punishing other outstanding performers from his era. This is what Bonds, McGwire, Clemens et. al. have done to the deserving players who played by the rules.

Many Hall of Fame voters are taking what they call a "wait and see" approach, fearful that they will anoint Bagwell or another player only to have it subsequently revealed that he was indeed a steroid cheat. That is also unfair when there is no pending controversy to be decided. My recommendation would be to pass a rule that allows the BBWAA to throw cheats out of the Hall of Fame when and if new evidence comes out, whenever it comes out. Then, at least, a player will be excluded based on facts rather than guilt by association.

just to try to make ends meet. At least one umpire took the bribe; in 1882, umpire Dick Higham was thrown out of baseball for fixing games.

Black Sox

The most publicized of the many game-throwing teams was the Chicago White Sox of 1919. Eight of these players were banned permanently from baseball for their alleged roles in conspiring with gamblers to "fix" the 1919 World Series. Books have been written about this complex and unhappy episode. Every player was acquitted in a court of law of any wrongdoing. It was unclear how involved each of the eight was.

Bloody Assault

The terrible rioting in the Watts area of Los Angeles in August of 1965 set the stage for an ugly incident in baseball. It took place in Los Angeles, in a game between the Giants and the Dodgers, and involved perhaps the two best pitchers in the National League that year, Sandy Koufax and Juan Marichal.

First, the Giants' Marichal knocked down Dodgers speedster Maury Wills with a threatening, inside pitch. As luck would have it, Marichal came to bat in the very next inning. Koufax kicked and delivered low. Dodgers catcher John Roseboro dug the inside fastball out of the dirt. When Roseboro flung the ball back to Koufax, the ball nicked the nose of Marichal, who went ballistic.

Marichal smashed Roseboro over the head three times in quick succession with his bat before being tackled by the home plate umpire. Roseboro left in a bloody mess. Black-and-white photographs of the assault are gruesome. Marichal was suspended for nine days and fined $1,750. There are other examples of assaults with bats. There have also been reported incidents of assaults with a catcher's mask.

Father-Son Fighting

Here's how the Associated Press described the action when a father and son, both shirtless and out of control, decided to attack a first-base coach during a game in September, 2002:

With his eyes on home plate and his back to the seats, Tom Gamboa never saw them coming. One second, the Kansas City coach was standing near first base. The next he was slammed to the ground, a bare-chested father and his teenage son pummeling him. "I felt like a football team had hit me from behind. Next thing I knew, I am on the ground trying to defend myself," Gamboa said. "It just happened so fast." In a scene athletes have feared for years, Gamboa was attacked without warning by two fans who came out of the seats.

The Royals rushed to his aid and the 54-year-old Gamboa escaped with a few cuts and a bruised cheek. He walked off the field to a standing

Competence and Diligence Breakdown: July 2, 2011, Mariners v. Padres

For a genuine failure of competence, nothing quite compares to the July 2 game between the Mariners and the San Diego Padres. With one out in the fifth, San Diego's Cameron Maybin walked when umpire Phil Cuzzi called a pitch high and sent him trotting to first base. Maybin eventually scored the only run of the game, allowing the Padres to defeat the Mariners, 1-0.

The problem? *The pitcher never threw ball four!* A video review of the at-bat by official scorer Dan Peterson confirmed the count should have been 3-2 when the umpire called the base on balls. Cuzzi, who like all umpires carried a pitch counter, saw that the scoreboard showed a three-ball count before the pitch was thrown, although his counter showed only two. He decided that the scoreboard was right.

Astoundingly, no argument was made by anyone on the field or off of it. The Seattle manager, coaches and players didn't notice. The other umpires said nothing, apparently asleep on their feet. The official scorer didn't flag the mistake. The scoreboard operator, who started the whole mess, kept quiet. Maybin, of course, accepted the gift, and took the base he didn't deserve.

This is a failure of competence and diligence on a grand scale. The game is supposed to be major league baseball. The umpires are supposed to be professionals. The managers, coaches and players are supposed to be paying attention. If Bud Selig and the baseball power structure weren't at least as inattentive as everyone at the park that night, they should have insisted that there was some accountability, that fans and players alike were reassured that this was unacceptable and would not occur again.

Nothing happened. Perhaps the feeling was that it was best to ignore it and deal with the matter behind closed doors. Maybe the umpires were fined or reprimanded; maybe everyone on the Mariners got a tongue-lashing from the brass for being asleep at the switch. I sure hope so. If there is one attitude professionals in any field must never display, *it is not giving a damn*. In other professions, this kind of slovenly inattention gets people killed.

Integrity, Fairness and Gil Meche

Not all of the ethics stories in 2011 were negative ones. Kansas City Royals pitcher Gil Meche, for example, gave us an exemplary exhibition of selflessness and generosity during spring training. All he needed to do to collect the $12 million guaranteed under his contract was to show up at camp, do his best to pitch—which his ailing right arm would no longer permit him to do—and cash checks all season long. Instead, Meche decided to retire, ending his contract and forfeiting the money.

"When I signed my contract, my main goal was to earn it," Meche explained. "Once I started to realize I wasn't earning my money, I felt bad. I was making a crazy amount of money for not even pitching. Honestly, I didn't feel like I deserved it. I didn't want to have those feelings again."

Nobody on the cash-strapped team that Meche saved $12 million, including executives and ownership, would have thought less of him if he had done what every almost every other professional athlete has done when his mega-million contract lasted a year or so more than his ability to earn it. Teams sign free agents to long-term contracts accepting the likelihood that the money paid for the last, often declining or injury-reduced years is a necessary price to pay to sign the player at all. The Royals were resigned to watching the 2011 season be a lost one for Meche, and paying for it. It was Meche who couldn't stand the idea of being paid so much for doing so little. I suppose an argument could be made that Meche had an ethical obligation not to create a precedent that would make other players look bad. I'm sure Kansas City, however, is glad he did.

Equity: The Lessons of the Star Fallacy

While Meche quit to be fair to his team and its fans, there were other quitters in 2011 who betrayed their teams and demonstrated severe ethics deficits in the process. Carlos Zambrano walked out on his team, the Cubs, mid-game, claiming that he was through with pitching. Manager Jim Riggelman quit the Washington Nationals midseason, in a bizarre tantrum over being "disrespected" by not getting an extension on his contract while the Nationals were on a rare winning streak.

Neither quitter approached the unethical thoroughness of Manny Ramirez. In April, Ramirez abruptly quit his new team, the Tampa Bay Rays, and left without so much as an explanation or good-bye. He had learned that he had tested positive for a banned substance for the second time, thus mandating a 100-game suspension. In perfect harmony with his virtually character-free conduct throughout his career, Ramirez just shrugged and walked away, quitting baseball on the spot and leaving the Rays without a designated hitter rather than serving out his punishment.

The ethics failing of interest here is not Manny's, because Ramirez's conduct was predictable. The failing was a collective one on the part of all the teams in Manny's career that had an opportunity to embrace the ethical value of equity, consistency and responsibility, and instead adopted the management ethics mistake known as "the star fallacy." That means

ovation from the crowd at Comiskey Park, where the Royals beat the Chicago White Sox 2-1. A folded-up pocket knife was found on the ground near the scene, and White Sox outfielder Aaron Rowand said he saw it slip out of one of the fans' pockets.

Umbrella Spears

By the early 1900s, there was already great animosity between the Brooklyn squad and the Giants. Then the Brooklyn fans got into the act. When the Giants visited, Brooklyn supporters would climb up to the top of the apartment buildings near the park, and make spears from the metal spokes of their umbrellas. Then they would heave these self-made spears at the Giants outfielders.

Hating Aaron

The use of nasty racial slurs has long been part of baseball's history. Such racial animosity reached a fever pitch in 1973 and 1974 when Hank Aaron, a black man, closed in on Babe Ruth's career record for home runs. Aaron was sent some 930,000 pieces of mail, much of it racist in nature, in 1973 alone. Among these missives were letters that included comments like "You may beat Ruth's record but there will always be only one Babe. You will be just another black f#*k down from the trees."

Dark Skin

During World War II, many players entered military service, and owners had to be creative to fill out their rosters. Take the case of Tommy de la Cruz, from Marianao, Cuba, who won nine games for the Cincinnati Reds in 1944. Unfortunately for de la Cruz, his skin pigment was dark. The powers-that-be in Major League Baseball at the time finally decided that his skin was too dark to suit them. In short order, he was dropped from the Reds team and that was the end of de la Cruz's major league career.

Spike to Injure

In the 1890s, Tommy Tucker, first baseman for Boston Beaneaters, tried to spike every base runner that went by, in a deliberate attempt to cause injury. Many, many others throughout baseball history, including notably the legendary Ty Cobb, have engaged in similar behavior.

Take the case of Dick Bartell, a scrappy, mean little shortstop whose 18-year career ended in 1941. Bartell had a well-earned reputation of trying to spike opposing players' hands around second base. One man whose hands Bartell stomped on was Harry Walker, who stood a full 6 feet 2 inches tall. Recalled Bartell, "I was kinda' sorry 'cause the groundskeeper had just sharpened my spikes that day but, boy, he never came close to me again."

Some were less obvious. Said speedster Maury Wills, "I think I spiked more guys than Ty Cobb. I did it

a high-level performer is allowed to break organization rules and defy an organization's culture in direct proportion to his perceived value.

A supremely talented baseball player who went through life with the discipline and selfishness of a six-year-old, Ramirez was regarded early on as such a valuable commodity that he was required to suffer few consequences for conduct that got less gifted players fined, benched, or released. This was unfair to other players, and dangerous to team morale, and it was unfair, ultimately, to Ramirez himself.

He eventually became uncontrollable, giving a professional effort only when he felt like it, sulking when he was admonished, faking injuries, and even losing a game on purpose, just out of spite. Those who stood up for him or trusted him were inevitably disappointed and betrayed—friends, teammates, managers, owners, and, of course, his fans.

Manny Ramirez never believed in rules, and he never accepted responsibility. Why would he? Everyone let him do whatever he wanted for most of his career, on the ethically bankrupt theory that expectations of good conduct should be on a sliding scale—the better a player was, the worse he was allowed to treat everyone. This almost always paves the road to disaster.

Later in the year, when Ramirez was arrested and charged with battering his wife, I realized that this, too, was a natural and predictable byproduct of the star fallacy. Making Manny Ramirez accept early on that being brilliant at one's craft does not entitle you to exemptions from responsibilities to employers, colleagues and society might have made him a better teammate, player and human being. Manny's accountable, but the Indians, Red Sox and Dodgers helped to make him what he became.

Integrity: The Unwritten Rule

On July 31, Detroit Tigers pitcher Justin Verlander was six outs from joining Bob Feller, Sandy Koufax and Nolan Ryan as the only pitchers since 1900 with three or more no-hitters in their careers, and Johnny Vander Meer as the only other pitcher to throw two no-hitters in the same season. But the Angels' Erick Aybar tried to end the historic bid with a bunt single leading off the eighth. He got it, too, except that the home town scorer attempted to preserve Verlander's no-hitter by charging an error instead. (Unethical. But I digress.)

Bunting for a hit in the late innings of a potential no-hitter is considered by many—especially pitchers with a chance at no-hitters— to be a violation of baseball's "unwritten rules," which is to say they think it's unethical. Why? Well, a no-hitter is usually the result of a pitcher pitching unusually well, and thus is a measure of his excellence on a special day. (It is also, to some extent, luck.) Almost any pitch can be bunted, however; whether a bunt is a hit or not has little to do with the pitcher and more to do with the skill of the batter and the competence of the player who fields the bunt.

The argument is that any no-hitter could be spoiled by a lucky bunt, and that a pitcher in the midst of a historic display of excellence deserves some measure of collegial and professional respect, even from adversaries. The Golden Rule is supposed to be in play. Try to get a hit, by all means, but try to get a clean, genuine hit, not a cheapie. A pitcher's equivalent to a hitter bunting to wreck a no-hitter would be intentionally walking a player in his last at-bat during a consecutive game hitting streak, or when he needed to complete a "cycle"—a feat about as common as a no-hitter.

Predictably, Verlander, who didn't get his no-hitter anyway, thought Aybar was unethical to bunt, calling the move "bush league." For his part, Aybar said he was just trying to help his team win, and in fact his bunt did open the way for the Angels to score two runs. He needn't have justified his conduct, for he did exactly the right and ethical thing.

The objective in baseball is to win the game, not help players get records and reach milestones. Integrity demands that players facing a no-hitter do whatever they can to score runs, which means getting on base. If a bunt looks like it is the best way to do that, then so be it.

Some have suggested that the ethics might be different if the game was a rout. But the ethical considerations are exactly the same, regardless of the score. Baseball either has integrity or it doesn't, and a player helping the opposition pitcher succeed is by definition a breach of integrity. This is a zero sum situation: A pitcher's success is the opposing team's failure.

The Golden Rule: Buster Posey's Injury

In May, Florida Marlins outfielder Scott Cousins, trying to score on a close play at the plate, slammed into Giants catcher and 2010 Rookie of the Year Buster Posey. The collision grievously injured Posey's leg, knocking him out for the season.

Seeing his team's chances of repeating as World Champions vanishing, Giants general manager Brian Sabean lashed out at Cousins in the press, suggesting that the player had been "malicious." Giants fans took their cues from the GM, and some began sending death threats to Cousins, who was only doing his job. Posey, who could have defused the situation by taking responsibility for the accident (he was, after all, blocking the plate with his leg), gave a statement that didn't address the issue of Cousins' innocence at all. Then Hall of Fame catcher Johnny Bench weighed

in a way that appeared accidental. It wasn't."

Head Smash

During a 1921 pre-season game, feisty Tigers outfielder Ty Cobb got into a fight with umpire Billy Evans. It was a nasty scene. Cobb won the fight. He did so by continually smashing the umpire's head into the cement floor under the stands. Cobb split open Evans' eyebrow and cheek. Said Cobb, "I fight only one way, and that is to kill."

The thrashing would have continued except a burly groundskeeper broke it up. Evans survived to arbitrate another day. Such fisticuffs were not unusual for many of baseball's early years. There are hundreds of similar examples of brutal and bloody fights in baseball.

Rose the Gambler

In February of 1989, baseball hired attorney John Dowd to investigate whether Pete Rose, baseball's all-time hits leader, bet on baseball. Rose strongly and loudly denied doing so. Nonetheless, Dowd compiled overwhelming evidence that not only had Rose bet on baseball, he had also bet on his own team when he had managed the Reds.

In August of 1989, Rose was given a lifetime suspension from baseball, but admitted to no wrongdoing. He was given permission to reapply after one year but cannot enter the Hall of Fame, even today, unless and until he is readmitted. Rose later admitted that he is a compulsive gambler, and in 1990, pled guilty to failing to pay taxes on income earned during autograph sessions at baseball card shows. Rose, now a convicted felon, served five months in prison.

In 2004, in what was considered a none-too-subtle attempt to win admission to the Hall of Fame, Rose released a bizarre autobiography in which he finally admitted he had bet on baseball games but refused to apologize for his actions. Rose angered many by releasing the controversial book during the very same week in which the 2004 Baseball Hall of Fame members were officially being inducted into the hallowed shrine. The man known as "Charlie Hustle" is still not in the Hall of Fame today.

Noose

Efforts to intimidate umpires were commonplace in 19th century baseball. Both the fans and the players got into the game. There was one reported case in which a group of fans were clearly unhappy with the umpire's calls during a game. After the contest, the unruly fans took it upon themselves to stand outside the umpire's locker room, waiting for him to emerge. They took no pains to hide the fact that they had a noose. Eventually, the police had to be called.

Palmeiro's finger wag

Rafael Palmeiro was called to testify, under

in by blaming Posey for his injury, explaining that the catcher had used poor technique.

Eventually tempers cooled and there were apologies all around. Posey's injury, however, still sparked loud calls from many in the game and some outside it for new rules banning such collisions. This sentiment from Giants manager Bruce Bochy was, I believe, the result of bias and self-interest: he had never expressed this opinion before his own star catcher was injured, and I suspect if Cousins had been a Giant and Posey a Marlin, Bochy would not have adopted this view at all.

Joe Torre, the MLB executive in charge of such matters (and a former catcher), dismissed the idea of a prohibition, but if another star catcher is hurt in a violent collision, the movement for change will be more persistent. The unusual proliferation of advocacy for banning contact at the plate, as in football's fair catch rule, indicates that a significant shift in ethical values may be underway.

In 1974, Boston Red Sox catcher Carlton Fisk, also young, also a recent Rookie of the Year (1972) sustained a similar season-ending injury in a collision with Cleveland Indians outfielder Leron Lee. There were no calls to change the rules. Like Posey, Fisk had been blocking the plate with his leg, as catchers had in such plays for many decades. The universal reaction was that Fisk's injury was part of the game.

I think the ethical culture of sport is changing, in baseball, in sports, and in society. Once, the idea of men hurting each other in competition was accepted without question: Boxing was one of the top three sports in the country. Now there is less tolerance for violence that results in actual injury, and as a result, watching violent physical contact in a spectator sport has become an ethical dilemma, where a value—respect for an individual's health and welfare— is in conflict with non-ethical considerations like winning and entertainment value.

We know more about athletes now; we know their families and personalities. We also are kept up to date on their post-career lives more than ever, and when we learn of former players suffering premature dementia, as in football and hockey, those exciting, violent collisions don't seem like so much fun any more. The more spectators see human beings, rather than generic competitors, as the victims of injuries, the more unacceptable the injuries become.

Players too are beginning to apply a Golden Rule standard, because they understand the huge amounts of money a serious injury can cost a player, and many are reluctant to risk inflicting such a catastrophic result on another even to win a game. Many players simply won't barrel into a player like Cousins did, especially the superstars.

All of sports may be facing a prolonged ethical debate about balancing the costs of entertainment with their effects on the lives, careers, income and health of athletes. The Buster Posey collision may prove to be a tipping point for new ethical standards that could change the intensity with which baseball is played, and with that, its integrity as well.

Accountability: Terry Francona's Moral Luck

The tenure of Terry Francona, beyond question the most successful manager in the century-plus history of the Boston Red Sox, ended as a consequence of his squad's historic September collapse that robbed it of the playoff spot that had seemed guaranteed a month before. Everyone, including Boston general manager Theo Epstein and Boston's famously vicious press corps, agreed that Francona was not at fault for the team's meltdown, yet he lost his job.

The starting point for most ethical analysis in such mysteries is the clarifying question: *"What's going on here?"* The answer has two parts: One is a classic ethical principle of leadership and organization management, and the other is a perplexing ethical phenomenon.

Being at fault is not the same as being accountable. A leader is always accountable for disasters and misfortune under his or her authority; fault is secondary. If an employee causes a disaster, the leader allowed the employee to be in a position to do so. If an unexpected event throws the leader's brilliant plans into disarray, he or she is accountable for not adopting a different plan.

Organizational disasters, whether it is Abu Ghraib, the aftermath of Hurricane Katrina, or Pearl Harbor, cannot and must not be attributed to factors beyond the leadership's control, nor should they occur without real consequences attaching to those in charge. Without the certainty of accountability, leaders will be tempted to occupy precious time constructing ways to shift blame and punishment to others, and this leads, inevitably, to weaker and less trustworthy leaders. Worse still, it causes the constituencies of leaders to lose faith and trust in the organizations they lead.

Sports can be a valuable simulation of society and life in general, and the plight of a team that fails when it should have succeeded poses a valid ethics example for businesses, movements and nations. Unless team leaders are held accountable, fans of the team will conclude that success or failure just doesn't matter to the ownership very much, and if it doesn't matter to the team itself, why should fans care? I could identify five players whose poor play and miserable performance under pressure were infinitely more responsible for the Red Sox crash than anything Terry

oath, about steroid use in major league baseball, in front of the U.S. House of Representatives on March 17, 2005. He was subpoenaed after former teammate Jose Canseco wrote in his controversial book, "Juiced," that Palmeiro was among the many ballplayers who had used illegal steroids to try to gain an edge on the baseball field.

During his appearance before Congress, Palmeiro was unequivocal in stating that Canseco had it all wrong. Said Palmeiro in his now-famous testimony, "I have never intentionally used steroids. Never. Ever. Period." As he read his statement, Palmeiro wagged his finger at the congressmen for emphasis.

Just months later, Palmeiro was suspended by Baseball Commissioner Bud Selig for failing a drug test administered by Major League Baseball. It later came out that Palmeiro had tested positive for an illegal steroid. So much for his finger wagging. In July of 2005, Palmeiro had become just the fourth baseball player in history to collect 3,000 hits and 500 home runs; The other three are Willie Mays, Hank Aaron and Eddie Murray. The 2005 campaign would be his last season.

Mirrors

Flamboyant owner Bill Veeck was always looking for a home field advantage. During the late 1930s, he used one particularly dirty trick. Fans who came to his park were able to buy tiny, hand-held mirrors. The idea was they were supposed to try to reflect the sun directly into the eyes of the opposing team's batters. This was hardly a new concept in the 1930s. Four decades earlier, it was reported that fans would bring their own mirrors to the park and try to use them to distract the visiting team.

Crooked Cox

Of course, Pete Rose took much abuse, and reasonably so, for betting on his own team when he managed the Reds. He was summarily thrown out of baseball. But Rose's act was hardly original to baseball. In 1943, William D. Cox, the owner of the Phillies, was thrown out of baseball for life for not only betting on games, but, like Rose, betting on his own team. Cox said at the time that he did not know there was a rule against betting on his own team.

This exercise was coordinated by Carleton College visiting professor Willy Stern, who also wrote the capsule summaries. You can read more about this exercise at:

http://www.hardball-times.com/thtstats/other/ethics_set.php

- Dave Studenmund

Francona did as manager, but both practically and symbolically, making a single player the scapegoat is both ineffective and unfair *(Red Sox fans: See Buckner, Bill)*. The manager is the obvious and proper target, both because he is the face of the team, and also because his punishment makes the necessary point with the least damage to the organization.

Francona's fate resulted from *moral luck*, the annoying but unavoidable phenomenon that causes conduct to be judged as right or wrong based on events that have little to do with the conduct itself. Two identical drivers, both intoxicated, take the same route home. One reaches his destination safely, and the other would have, if a child on a bicycle hadn't suddenly and fatally veered into his path. The driver's intoxication may or may not have stopped him from braking on time, but it doesn't matter: That driver will be a pariah in the community, and will probably be sent to jail….and he will deserve it. The only difference between him and his neighbor is moral luck, and yet that luck causes us to regard his act as worse, because he is accountable for the horrible consequences.

Had Terry Francona done everything exactly the same way, except that on that epic Wednesday night that ended the season, the Rays' Dan Johnson, hitting .108 as he came to the plate with his team down a run with two outs in the ninth, had swung and missed at the two-strike pitch to end the game, rather than hitting the ball into the right field stands to send the game into extra innings….and Red Sox closer Jonathan Papelbon, needing one more strike to get his team the victory it needed to live another day, hadn't given up three straight hits to the Orioles, turning a ninth-inning lead into a loss for the first and only time in the Boston season, Francona would be manager of the Red Sox today.

It may be more fun watching baseball without being troubled by ethical issues, but they arise nonetheless, and, over time, relentlessly shape not only conduct in the game, but ethical standards off the field as well.

Diary of a Mad Sports Bettor

by James Holzhauer

In 2006, I took a hiatus from my job search to try my hand at betting on baseball for a living. Five years later, I retired at age 26. These are my stories.

I graduated from college in 2005. At that time I was dabbling in sports betting to pay the bills while I interviewed to become an actuary. Those interviews were full of banalities, topped by the world's most asinine question: "Where do you see yourself in five years?" I don't remember my exact response, but I certainly didn't explain that Tampa Bay would go from worst to first, shocking the world and setting me up financially for life. (At that time, I suspect that discussing the Devil Rays as a potential contender might not have been the best way to make myself look hireable.) I received zero job offers, but I did appreciate the irony of insurance companies not hiring someone because he seemed uncertain about the future.

Where do I see myself in 2016, five years from now? I can only guess, just as I can only guess who will win this year's World Series, AL Cy Young, or Ford Frick Award. Forecasts—for life or for baseball—are just an educated stab in the dark, and we should stop pretending this isn't the case.

I first started betting baseball seriously during the World Baseball Classic in March 2006. Many people would opt not to gamble on games featuring players they've never heard of; as a cocky 21-year old, I had no such misgivings.

Placing winning sports bets often hinges on an information advantage. The problem is that most publicly available information is already factored into the betting odds.

Consider the example of home-field advantage. The home team in baseball wins about 54 percent of the time; if bookies were not aware of this fact, you or I could make a fortune just blindly betting on every home team. Because the sports betting market adjusts the odds to reflect the home-field advantage, this information alone will not give anyone an edge. (If, however, I have reason to suspect that a specific team has a greater or lesser home-field advantage than 54 percent, and the betting odds don't reflect this outlier, that could be used as part of a profitable approach to gambling.)

If you walk into a sports book and eavesdrop on bettors explaining the logic behind their picks, they often say things like "Lincecum is on a roll" or

Bookies offer an option called futures wagering, where the bettor backs a certain team to win its division, the League Championship Series or the World Series. We can't predict the future, but we can guess more accurately than the bookie. High-stakes gamblers tend to stay away from futures because they have low maximum bets and require complex math, but those who are savvy with statistics and simulations can make a killing on them.

"The A's have no offense." Everyone knows these things already! Widely known information is of little or no value in sports betting.

Inside information is a different animal. There's a classic episode of *The Simpsons* where the degenerate Moe comes to the Simpsons' house before young Bart and Lisa face off in a pee-wee hockey game:

> *"How are the little kids doing? I mean, really, how are they doing? Any disabling injuries, something, say, that the gambling community might not yet know about? (grabs Bart's leg) Come here, let me see those knees."*

Moe didn't get what he was looking for, but the trainer for a major league team knows when his staff ace is more fatigued than usual or when his star first baseman is about to get a day off. This information, unknown to the public, would be of tremendous value to someone looking to place a large bet against that team. One hopes that no current trainers are committing the baseball equivalent of insider trading.

I felt I could have a legitimate information advantage in betting the World Baseball Classic. The bookies don't pay as much attention to lightly bet events because it's more important for them to focus on accurately handicapping NFL or NBA games, where many more bets are coming in. Hours of thought go into setting the point spread for an NFL game, but a bookie isn't going to waste time looking up Michihiro Ogasawara's wOBA; it's far more efficient for him to just make a guess at the correct game odds and limit his risk by not accepting large bets. (This is why small bettors can get their biggest edges on futures bets, which high rollers typically ignore.) I studied the WBC teams intently, determined to know far more about them than the bookies did.

Clay Davenport translated each team's statistics so they could be compared against each other, and his methodology seemed mathematically sound. Comparing the translations to the bookies' odds, it seemed clear that the smart bets were on the underdogs to topple the favored Americans and Dominicans. Canada was a 9-1 underdog in its game against the USA: my $1,000 bet collected $9,000 in profit when the Canadians pulled off the upset. Other bets I cashed included Mexico to win its initial pool (12-1) and Japan to win the tournament (30-1). I ended up making 50 cents of profit for every dollar I bet on the WBC, an encouraging start to my baseball betting career.

The World Baseball Classic gave me both the money and the confidence I needed to approach gambling seriously for the 2006 major league season. I programmed a spreadsheet to simulate the season thousands of times, and loaded it with projections from PECOTA, ZiPS and CHONE. The results recommended a number of wagers, but three stood out above the rest.

The first was a bet on who would lead the majors in home runs in 2006. Bookies typically set these odds by listing last year's top homer hitters as this year's favorites. With Barry Bonds and Sammy Sosa fading fast, there was no clear top slugger in the majors. The Phillies offered a good candidate: a new first baseman who had destroyed pitchers in Triple-A, slugged 22 dingers in half a season in the bigs in 2005, and was projected by PECOTA to lead the majors with 46 homers in '06—no one else was forecast for more than 41.

Because he was unproven and hit "only" 22 homers the year before, the sportsbooks didn't even list Ryan Howard as a candidate to win the home run crown until I wrote an email to the bookie requesting that he be added as an option. Howard, of course, smashed 58 homers en route to an MVP award. Unbelievably, a bet on Howard that year paid 40-1 odds: a $250 max bet cashed for a $10,000 profit.

The second and third recommended bets resided in the AL Central. In 2005 the White Sox had won 99 games and the World Series, while the Indians had looked like potentially the best team in baseball before choking away a playoff spot in the season's final week. Naturally they were listed as the two big favorites to win the division and advance in the playoffs, but the projected standings showed the Twins and Tigers only slightly behind Cleveland and actually *ahead of* Chicago. Joe Mauer, Justin Morneau and Francisco Liriano seemed poised to become household names for the Twins in 2006, while the Tigers had Curtis Granderson and Justin Verlander as their aces in the hole.

Fixated on the 2005 standings, the bookies listed the Twins as 7-1 underdogs to win the division, and the Tigers at an astonishing 30-1. After leading the Twins by 12 games at one point, Detroit lost the division crown to Minnesota in one of the worst late-season collapses ever, but both teams left the White Sox and Indians in the dust. The Tigers won the Wild Card and rebounded to take the AL pennant, which paid a whopping 60-1: a $1,000 max bet paid out sixty grand in profit. Had they won the World Series (Vegas made them a 2-1 favorite over the Cardinals before the first pitch) that would have paid 150-1.

The most important advice I can give regarding futures betting is that bookies tend to underestimate the frequency of low-probability events. Surprise playoff teams like the 2011 Diamondbacks aren't nearly as uncommon as we think: The 2002 Angels, 2003 Marlins, 2005 White Sox, 2006 Tigers, 2007 Rockies, 2008 Rays and 2010 Giants each entered those seasons regarded as 83-win or worse teams. All seven advanced to the World Series, and four won it all.

If you decide to bet futures, focus on a few undervalued longshot teams. You might catch this year's lightning in a bottle.

Before the start of every season, many pundits come out with their projected standings. If today's best prediction model forecasts 95 wins for the 2012 Yankees, how accurate will that forecast be?

The Yankees will deal with injuries, breakouts, collapses, trades, midge attacks and the vagaries of random chance. All of these cloud our forecast: My estimate is that they will win exactly 95 games just 4.4 percent of the time. That's a one-in-23 shot, which means that if we project the full major league standings, we will nail the W-L record of only one team in 23, or about one team per season.

What if we relax our standards of accuracy? I estimate that the Yankees have a 45.9 percent chance of winning 90-100 games. Our "95-win" Yankees will actually finish below .500 more frequently (one time in 18) than they will go 95-67. They also have a one-in-18 shot of winning 110 or more games. I believe that given the current limits on our ability to predict the future, this is the best we can do: miss the target by 15 or more wins in either direction "only" one time out of nine.

The White Sox entered 2007 with essentially the same personnel that had averaged 94.5 wins the previous two seasons. Many fans saw no reason that they wouldn't be competitive again, but Nate Silver's computer disagreed. Silver's PECOTA projections suggested a 72-90 finish for the South Siders, a sudden and steep dropoff. PECOTA saw an old line-up that would likely regress heavily; the 2006 team had benefited from unexpectedly big seasons from Paul Konerko, Jim Thome, Joe Crede and Jermaine Dye.

The *Chicago Tribune* featured an article, "Computer Crashes White Sox," which quoted GM Kenny Williams bashing the forecasting methods: "Don't you get tired of being wrong or is it you figure one of these days you're going to be right?" Konerko sarcastically laughed off the forecast: "Well, we're screwed now."

Bettors, meanwhile, saw an opportunity. Each year, sportsbooks post Over/Under odds on season wins for every team. If a team has an Over/Under of 80.5 wins, those betting on the Over need the team to win 81 or more times that season to cash their bets. If they win 80 or fewer games, the Under bettors collect. When many more people bet the Over than bet the Under, the bookie will move the line upward to 81, 81.5, or maybe even 82 or 82.5.

This serves two purposes: it entices more people to bet the Under and balance the books; and it limits the amount that can be won by wiseguys betting on the Over. (Even if a professional likes the Over on 80.5 wins, he understands that the team will win exactly 81 or 82 games nearly 9 percent of the time—a huge difference—so he will stop betting once the line moves too far.)

Sportsbooks released an Over/Under of 89.5 wins for the 2007 White Sox, essentially flipping PECOTA's 72-90 forecast. This number was eventually bet down to 86 wins. That difference, 3.5 wins, is an unusually large move, indicating heavily unbalanced action on the Under—clearly some people believed in the computer forecast. In the end, the old offensive core tanked just as PECOTA predicted and the White Sox finished precisely 72-90. Score one for the computer.

———————————————

The 2007 World Series pitted the Rockies, who had won 21 of their last 22 games, against the Red Sox, who were the far superior team on paper. Would Colorado's magical run continue or end in heartbreak?

The media often portray sabermetricians as heartless robots for not believing in the predictive power of clutch hitters or hot streaks. Clearly there were many believers in the Rockies: Based purely on the numbers, Boston should have been about a 75 percent favorite in the Series; but the actual odds had them as only a 67.5 percent favorite. This level of disparity is rare in a heavily bet market, and it was a golden opportunity for me to speculate that the streak wouldn't continue. To me, betting on the Red Sox was like buying a stock for 10 percent less than its value.

Colorado looked outclassed right from the start, losing 13-1 in Game One. The Red Sox swept the Rockies, ignoring Alex Rodriguez's attempt to steal the spotlight by opting out of his contract during the clinching game.

When I was 13, I told my dad that there should be a stock exchange for sports teams, which would allow me to turn my obsession with statistics into a profitable venture. It turns out that the markets for sports betting and stocks are very similar: in each case, you have a large population of speculators gambling that they can outsmart a weakly efficient market.

If investors are rushing to buy Google stock, the price of a share will go up. If bettors are rushing to back the Yankees against the Red Sox in tonight's game, the betting odds will change, effectively increasing the price of a bet on the Yankees. Just as buyers and sellers determine the market price of a stock, bettors determine the market odds on a contest. Your bookie has no more control over the odds for a Yankees-Red Sox game than your broker has over the price of a share of Google; he's just there to execute your trade and take a commission.

The big difference—legality aside—is that a typical person can expect to make money investing in stocks and lose money betting on sports. But there are exceptions: the Tampa Bay Rays outperformed the Dow Jones pretty handily in 2008.

The 2008 Rays were quite the conundrum. The previous season, they had finished with the worst record in the league at 66-96 despite above-average production from their hitters and starting pitchers; all of this good work was undone by a historically bad bullpen and a historically bad defense. These are two aspects of team performance that tend to regress heavily toward the mean the next year, but the Rays took no chances: They underwent a complete bullpen makeover and made several moves to shore up the glovework.

The 2007 squad featured the iron gloves of Delmon Young, Brendan Harris, Ty Wigginton and B.J. Upton; the former three were shipped out of town and Upton was shipped out of the infield. On paper Tampa Bay actually came into 2008 with an above-average defense, as hard as that was to believe.

The World Series winner in any given year is usually not the best team in baseball. It's become popular to suggest that once the playoffs start, everyone has about a 1-in-8 shot of taking the trophy, and we might as well determine the winner via a series of coin flips.

This is a total oversimplification. In a typical year, the best team in baseball has a 25-30 percent chance of winning three playoff series. That's not as Calvinist as the NBA playoffs, but it's still a meritocracy of sorts. A truly great team will be a big favorite to prevail over a lesser squad; the "problem" is that major league baseball playoff teams are rarely so badly mismatched.

The Rays also featured an impressive young lineup with no real holes and three players (Carl Crawford, B.J. Upton, Carlos Pena) who had put up star-level performances in 2007. Top prospect Evan Longoria looked ready to star in The Show.

The rotation was anchored by the solid trio of Scott Kazmir, James Shields and Matt Garza. If the bullpen held together, there looked to be no reason the Rays couldn't win 90 games—after never winning more than 70 in their franchise history. In fact, PECOTA projected them to do just that, offering a 90-72 forecast. This drew the attention of a feature story, "Leap Year," in *Sports Illustrated*. Most readers laughed it off as another case of a computer ignoring the obvious.

This was a perfect storm for sports bettors. Here we had a perpetual last-place team that was bound for a huge improvement due to regression and smart player management. Unlike, say, the 2010 Miami Heat, the Rays made moves that flew under the radar and only a few sabermetrically inclined people took notice. The best betting values occur when a team has gotten significantly better or worse without attracting mainstream attention.

The 2008 Rays Over/Under opened at 68.5 wins. Betting opened before PECOTA and other forecasts became public, but the wiseguys were ready ahead of time. Within a few hours, enough money been bet on the Over to move the line to 71 wins. A day later it was 72.5, then 74 the next day. Eventually the line settled at 76.5 wins—an unprecedented eight-win move. It was as if the Rays had traded Cliff Floyd for Albert Pujols.

Of course, it all came together for Tampa Bay that year. The pitchers' BABIP went from a league-worst .331 in 2007 to a league-best .277 in 2008, a remarkable defensive turnaround. Despite an increase in xFIP from the year before, the starters posted a combined ERA of 3.95 versus a 5.20 mark in 2007. The Rays' bullpen ERA, an eye-popping 6.16 in 2007, came all the way down to 3.55, fifth best in the majors. Longoria burst out of the gate to anchor a lineup featuring nine regulars with 1.9 WAR or better.

Tampa Bay went 97-65, capturing the AL East crown and shattering even the loftiest of preseason expectations.

With so little mainstream media attention paid to the Rays in the preseason, it was no surprise that the bookies didn't give them much respect in the futures markets either. If the bookie feels a team has no chance whatsoever, he might simply make up odds that seem high enough to entice people to throw away some dollars on a prayer. The Rays were 50-1 longshots to win their division. After all, even if they overachieved, how could lowly Tampa Bay ever hope to topple the mighty Red Sox and Yankees? A maximum bet of $1,000 cashed for a cool fifty grand. They were 125-1 underdogs to win the ALCS; the books took a maximum of only $500 on this, but that was enough to win $62,500. A bet on the Rays to win the World Series would have paid 300-1…and they opened the Series as 7-5 favorites over the Phillies.

It's fun to check your favorite team's live in-game win probability at FanGraphs, but its models assume each game begins as a 50-50 contest. How can we use the Vegas betting line to determine the *a priori* chances that a team will win tonight?

You may have looked at the odds in the sports section of your local newspaper and seen something that looks like this:

Phi   Halladay -130

Atl   Hanson +120

What these numbers mean is that bettors who want to take the Phillies must *risk* $1.30 for every dollar they hope to win, while Braves backers will *win* $1.20 for every dollar they risk. So, you could bet $13 on Philadelphia to win back $10, or $20 on Atlanta to win back $24, and so on.

The difference between the lines on each team is like the bid-ask spread on a stock: if we believe that the market is efficient, the odds must be set so that neither Atlanta bettors nor Philly bettors can make a quick profit. In gambling terms, this means that bets on both teams do not offer a favorable expected value (EV).

To calculate the EV of a bet, multiply the probability of winning by the amount that can potentially be won. For example, many states have a pick-3 lottery where you must correctly guess three ping-pong balls with values between 0 and 9 inclusive. If you match all three, you win $500. What is the EV of a lottery ticket?

We essentially need to match a three-digit combination from 000 to 999. There are one thousand such combinations, so the one you pick has a 1/1,000 chance of winning. Multiplying this probability by $500, we get an EV of 50 cents. The state will happily sell you a ticket for a dollar, knowing it is worth only half that much. If it instead sold tickets for 40 cents or raised the jackpot to more than $1,000 (thus giving each ticket an EV of more than $1) the lottery would effectively be giving money away.

Back to our baseball example: A Braves bettor can risk $100 and get back $220—$120 in profit plus his initial $100—if they win. The bookie

MLB is often praised for its competitive balance because nine different franchises won the World Series from 2001-2010. During that decade, the Spurs and Lakers combined for seven NBA titles, while the Patriots won three Super Bowls in a four-year span. Baseball looks pretty good in this comparison, but this isn't a good way to measure systemic imbalance.

Baseball produces fewer championship dynasties for two reasons. First, its playoff structure gives little advantage to the best teams: five or seven games aren't nearly enough to distinguish a 95-win team from a 90-win team. Furthermore, home-field advantage is practically meaningless in a best-of-seven series—the home team would win only 51 percent of playoff series if the teams were otherwise evenly matched.

Second, baseball teams are less reliant on the impact of a single franchise player. The Cavaliers collapsed after losing LeBron James and the Colts collapsed without Peyton Manning; the Cardinals lost Adam Wainwright for the season and advanced to the World Series anyway.

Acquiring and developing Tom Brady or Kobe Bryant isn't a built-in advantage, but the Yankees' budget is. Baseball isn't any fairer; it's just a harder sport to dominate.

wants to set the odds so the EV of this bet is less than $100; otherwise he would be selling you something for less than it's worth, like a foolish lottery operator offering a pick-3 ticket for 40 cents. The EV is calculated by multiplying Atlanta's chances of winning by the $220 we receive when the Braves do triumph:

$$EV = A\% * 220$$

If the EV of our ticket is exactly $100, we have a bet that will break even in the long run. This break-even case occurs when Atlanta's chances of winning are 45.5 percent:

$$A\% * 220 = 100$$
$$A\% = 100/220 = 45.5\%$$

If Atlanta's chances of winning are greater than 45.5 percent, they make for a profitable bet. So, assuming an efficient market, Atlanta's win probability must be less than this.

Similarly, a Phillies bettor can risk $130 and get back $230 if they win. The bookie wants the EV of a bet on the Phillies to be less than $130. Now a break-even winning percentage is 56.5 percent:

$$EV = P\% * 130$$
$$P\% = 130/230 = 56.5\%$$

If Philly's chances of winning are greater than 56.5 percent, this bet is profitable, so in an efficient market Philadelphia will win less frequently than this. Note that the sum of our two break-even win rates is 102 percent. This implies that with equal betting action on both teams, the bookie will pay out $100 for every $102 he takes in; he keeps the rest as his commission. The break-even percentages must always add up to more than 100 percent or the bookie would be giving money away.

If Philadelphia wins less than 56.5 percent of the time, it means Atlanta wins more than 43.5 percent of the time. We have now pegged Atlanta's chances of winning at somewhere between 43.5 percent and 45.5 percent, a pretty good estimate.

Today there are some online sportsbooks with minimal spreads between the odds on each team. For example, we might see Philadelphia -125 / Atlanta +124. Assuming an efficient market, we have pretty much pinpointed the Braves' chances of winning at between 44.4 percent and 44.6 percent. Indeed, studies of gambling odds show that teams with these betting lines will win at almost exactly the frequency we calculate using this method.

Of course the sports betting market is not perfectly efficient—I couldn't have made a living if it was—but it's close enough that we can be reasonably confident the Phillies are about a 5-4 favorite to win this game.

In *Popular Crime*, Bill James describes how he used to anger his teachers by writing funny notes to his friends and tinkering with sports statistics during class. Later, he became the first accessible author of baseball analyses, precisely because he learned how to write from humorous notes instead of essay prompts. If Bill James didn't have such an endearing writing style, he would still be toiling in obscurity and sabermetrics may never have gotten off the ground.

I changed my focus of study five times in college. My degree is in mathematics, but if you ask me what I majored in, the most honest answer would be either fantasy baseball or Internet poker. Math was always my favorite subject in school, but my friends convinced me that a math degree wouldn't get me a desk job. This prophecy turned out to be both accurate and irrelevant.

The most important lesson the past five years have taught me: To be happy, make your own way in life. Study the things you're truly passionate about, in the classroom and in your free time. If you search hard enough, you'll find a way to make a living from it.

(Unless you're majoring in English; then you're actually screwed.)

There's no magic formula to build a team for the playoffs, but one component that will improve a squad's postseason performance is rarely mentioned: a terrible fifth starting pitcher. You hear all about the increased reliance on closers and staff aces in the play-offs, but no player sees his role change more in October than the fifth starter, who almost never throws an important pitch in the postseason. The 2009 Yankees appreciated sending CC Sabathia to the mound, but not as much as they appreciated getting Sergio Mitre off of it.

If two playoff teams look roughly equal, the one with the worse fifth starter is likely the better bet. Call it the Zito Theory.

- James Holzhauer

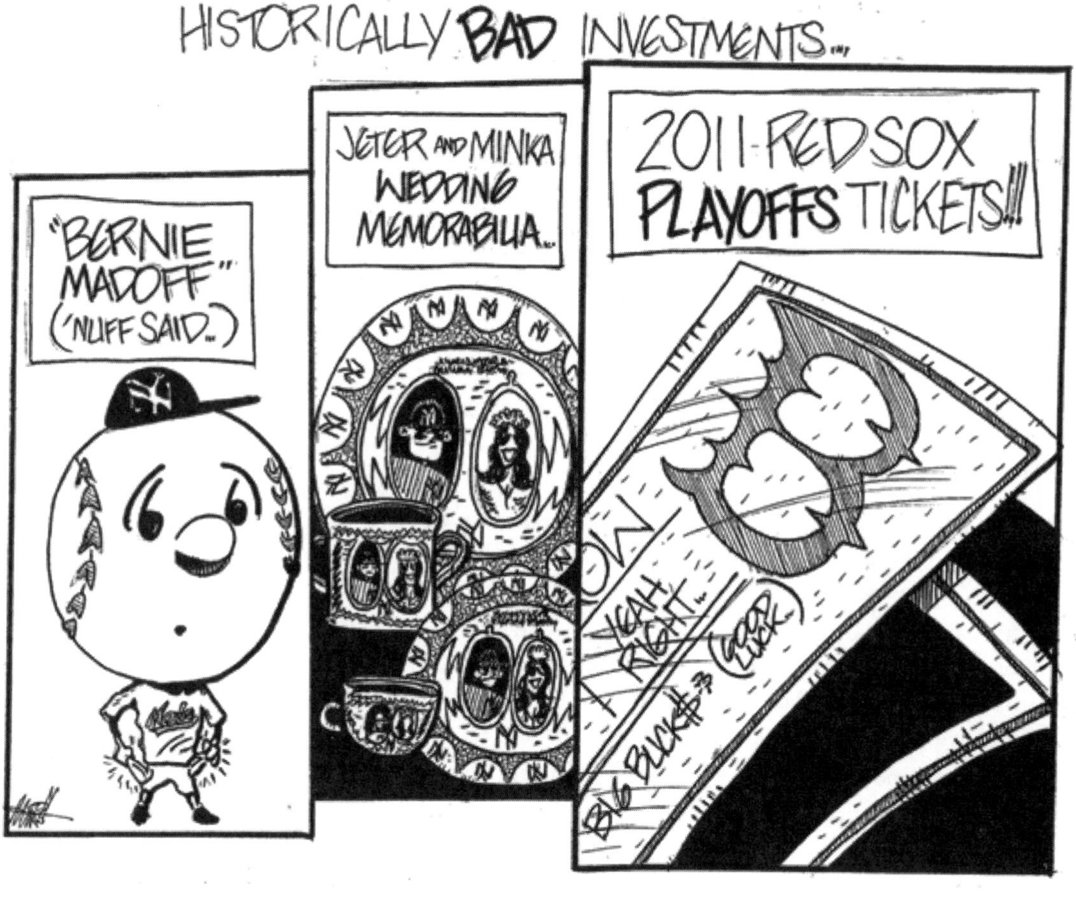
HISTORICALLY BAD INVESTMENTS...
"BERNIE MADOFF" ('NUFF SAID..)
JETER AND MINKA WEDDING MEMORABILIA...
2011-RED SOX PLAYOFFS TICKETS!!!
YEAH RIGHT..
(GOOD LUCK)

History

Slow and Quick Hooks

by Chris Jaffe

Vic Raschi must have known what was going to happen when he saw a familiar figure walk up the dugout steps in the first inning on May 29, 1953.

Raschi was one of the top starting pitchers for the New York Yankees, world champions for four years running, but that didn't matter. All that mattered was that he was having a rocky start to today's game, and Raschi had been a Yankee long enough to know what that meant.

Sure enough, Casey Stengel made his way from the dugout toward the pitcher's mound. So far on the day, Raschi had allowed five hits while only recording two outs against the sad sack Philadelphia A's, and Stengel wasn't the sort of manager to stand for that.

Never mind that it was still just the first inning. Never mind that the pitcher was due up. For that matter, never mind that Raschi was one of New York's ace pitchers, with a record of 58-34 over the previous four seasons. What Stengel did mind was this: Raschi didn't have it, and that meant he had to come out of the game, and sooner rather than later so the team wouldn't ruin its hopes for a victory.

This could not have surprised Raschi. Just four days earlier, he had witnessed Stengel remove Ewell Blackwell in the first inning after facing exactly four batters. Three days before Blackwell's blink-and-you-missed-it start, Stengel pulled veteran ace Allie Reynolds after one frame.

Giving three guys the early hook in barely a week was a bit unusual for Stengel, but not terribly so. He would do it nine times total in 1953 while leading the team to its fifth consecutive world championship—and that's how he treated a staff he liked. With lesser teams in Boston in the 1940s, he'd pull a starter after one inning or fewer 13 or 14 times a season.

The way managers handle their pitchers has changed a lot since the time of Stengel. People are aware of this, but they only understand half of it. Nowadays, it's all too obvious for people to note that teams don't let their starters go as deep into games as they used to. The complete game has become a rarity.

While that's true, it's only half the story. Sure, modern day managers have a quicker hook than guys like Stengel, but paradoxically they also have a slower hook. Once upon a time teams were a lot more willing to pull their starter at the very beginning of a game.

Hooks Miscellania

Hooks used to be very quick once upon a time. In 1948, 4.9 percent of all starters were pulled after one inning or less of work. That's the highest total in any season— barely. In 1950, managers yanked 4.5 percent of their starters after one inning. In contrast, in 2010, only 0.6 percent of starters lasted such a short time. And that's just the tip of the iceberg.

Managers in 1948 also pulled 4.9 percent of their starters in the second inning, and 6.6 percent in the third. In all, one-sixth of all starters didn't last 10 outs. Similar rates happened throughout the 1950s. In contrast, in 2010, managers pulled just 0.6 percent of starters in the first inning, and 19 out of 20 times a starter got the 10th out.

Look at Stengel. In his 3,766 games managed, he let the starter go the distance 1,382 times—over a third of the time. No one is close to that nowadays. Yeah, but he's also a guy who pulled his starter in the first inning 183 times, nearly five percent of all the games he managed. And Stengel was by no means an aberration for his day. In contrast, in the 21st century fewer than one percent of starters get pulled before recording the game's fourth out.

Choose any year in history, and there are always managers with slower hooks than their peers, while other skippers have comparatively quicker hooks. What managers do is always influenced by two things—their own personal inclinations and the era in which they manage. If Stengel managed nowadays, there's no way his pitchers would toss 1,300-some complete games, nor would they get yanked in the first inning so often.

Currently, the trend is toward standardization: Have a pitcher go as long as he can, but don't let his pitch count go too high. But if Terry Francona or Mike Scioscia had managed a half-century ago, they would have had more extremely quick or slow hooks, like Stengel did.

That said, while eras matter, managers matter as well. Guys may have been willing to yank their starting pitchers a lot earlier in Stengel's day, but that doesn't mean they all did it at the same rate. Similarly, while current managers have a more standardized way of handling starters, some tend to leave their starters in a little longer or pull them a little earlier than their peers.

Understanding which managers have a longer hook and which ones have a shorter hook is vital to learning about their approach to the game. It's one of the most obvious and important elements of how the skipper handles the game and his pitching staff. But to really understand which managers have a slow or quick hook with their starting pitchers, you need to compare them to their peers.

While eras change, and what constitutes a quick or slow hook shifts with them, regardless of whatever era it is, some managers generally have a quicker hook than others, and some have a slower one. And knowing which skippers have a quick or slow hook matters.

The best way to determine which managers have a long or short leash on their starting pitchers is a method developed by (of course) Bill James. In his annual *Bill James Handbook*, there is a section on managers that includes stats called Quick Hooks and Slow Hooks.

The logic behind James' Quick and Slow Hooks is simple. There are two elements that determine if a pitcher will get yanked from a game: How long he's been in and how well he is doing. The Quick/Slow Hook stats account for both elements. The stat works as follows: Take a pitcher's runs allowed, multiple it by ten, and then add that to pitches thrown. Thus, you combine the pitcher's quality and quantity of performance to see how much leeway the manager gave him.

What is a Quick or a Slow Hook? Simple. The 25 percent of starts with the lowest numbers are Quick Hooks, and the quarter of performances with the highest numbers are Slow Hooks. The middle half is neither. Ultimately, a perfectly average modern-day manager should score 40-41 Quick Hooks and as many Slow Hooks in a season. The notion of a quicker/slower hook is a bit general rather than exact, and this stat gives you a general sense of where each manger stands, and it does so by comparing him against his peers at his specific moment in history.

Thus, you should be able to look at any era in baseball history with this approach and evaluate which managers have quicker and slower hooks. Well, any era for which you have runs and pitches thrown info. And therein lies a huge catch. We only have the latter stat for all starts going back to the 1990s. So there's no way to look at previous periods, right?

Well, there's a way around this, thanks to a pitch count estimator popularized by the online sabermetrician Tom Tango. It's: (3.3*Total Batters Faced)+(1.5*Strikeouts)+(2.2*Walks). It gives you a rough idea how many pitches someone actually threw.

Is it perfect? No. Obviously, actual numbers would be ideal, but this works. Think for a second. There are two kinds of stats—ones that are designed to be exact and precise, and others that give you a general lay of the land. Quick/Slow Hooks are firmly in the latter category. Therefore, why not use a pitch count estimator for the years where exact pitches thrown aren't known? The estimator isn't exact, but it does help you get the general lay of the land, and that's all we're aiming for here.

So let's get on with it. Who had the quickest and slowest hooks ever? Well, thanks to the wonder and glory that is Retrosheet—and Baseball Reference.com's powerful Play Index tool—I have on file every single starting performance from 1919-2010 sorted by year, pitch count estimated (for the years I need an estimator), and sorted as Quick Hook/ Slow Hook.

Which managers have the quickest or slowest hooks ever? Let's look at the longest-lasting managers—guys who lasted at least 10 seasons as a team's primary manager. That gives us 63 managers from 1919-2010—and they're the important ones worth looking at in those years. I'll order them by percentage of games managed in which they had a Quick Hook.

The numbers below aren't perfect because of the pitch count estimator, but the general sense is more important than the precise figures.

For almost all baseball history, the most common inning for a starting pitcher to last pitch in was the ninth. It doesn't mean that most starters made it to the ninth, but that more pitched in the ninth than had been yanked in any other specific frame. In 1981, that came to an end. For the first time ever, the seventh inning surpassed the ninth. In that strike-shortened year, 565 pitchers lasted 19-21 outs, and 517 starters recorded outs 25-27. The seventh remained the top frame until 2001, when the sixth inning nudged past it, 1,315 starts to 1,312. The sixth remains the most likely frame to end a pitcher's night. In 2010, ten times as many starters had 16-18 outs as had 25-27 outs.

John McGraw was always willing to use his bullpen. From 1903-09, his Giants recorded 102 saves (retroactively determined, of course), almost twice as many as the next-highest NL team. Strangely, once they adopted Doc Crandall as the game's first relief specialist, their save totals declined. McGraw didn't use Crandall as a fireman to protect the big leads but as a slop man to handle the low-leverage innings. From 1917 onward, McGraw began trusting his bullpens with big leads again, resulting in eight straight seasons leading the NL in saves.

Bill Rigney was one of the first great apostates of the complete game. In 1961, his Angels starters completed 25 games, a new record low for a major league team. That record low lasted one year, when Rigney's team completed only 23 games. A few years later, they completed 19 games in a season. Rigney had some decent rotations, so he didn't need to pull his starters so often—his hook was just quick.

Let's start with the 10 guys whom the ratio says had the quickest hooks:

Manager	%	Q.H.	All Games
Jimy Williams	37.3%	635	1,701
Felipe Alou	32.4%	666	2,055
Bill Rigney	31.2%	798	2,561
Frank Robinson	31.1%	697	2,241
John McGraw	30.1%	578	1,918
Jack McKeon	29.8%	581	1,952
Joe Torre	29.4%	1,272	4,329
Bobby Cox	29.3%	1,322	4,508
Alvin Dark	29.1%	567	1,950
Leo Durocher	28.9%	1,027	3,555

(Totals don't include 2011 for McKeon or anything before 1919 for McGraw.)

Jimy Williams is No. 1—that makes sense. Back when pitch counts came in vogue a decade ago, he was always given lots of accolades for being gentle with his starters. For that matter, so was Felipe Alou, and there he is as the runner up. What is amazing is the gap between Williams and Alou, 4.9 percent. That's equal to the gap between second-place Alou and Burt Shotton —in *eighteenth place!*

Not too surprisingly, Williams also has the smallest percentage of Slow Hooks of anyone, 14.6 percent. He just beats out Bill Terry at 15.6 percent, which is a bit of a surprise because Terry isn't on the above list. True, but Terry just misses it at 28.8 percent of games with a Quick Hook. (As it turns out, 55.6 percent of the games Terry managed had neither a Quick Hook nor a Slow Hook, and that's the highest percentage for any manager.)

The most interesting name on the list above is also its most prestigious member—John McGraw. Since the data only go back to 1919, this only covers a minority of McGraw's 30-plus year career, but that makes the results more impressive. As a general rule of thumb, the longer managers last and the older they get, the less likely they are to score as a leading Quick Hook.

Sparky Anderson, for example, had one of the fastest hooks in the game when he began managing. They even nicknamed him Captain Hook. But then he kept managing, and the league caught up to him and then passed him.

McGraw, though, was almost always a strong believer in the bullpen. He used Doc Crandall as baseball's first relief specialist, and his teams frequently finished first in saves (though baseball didn't have that stat until well after his death). If we had his entire career, McGraw might rank even higher.

Leo Durocher makes the list based on how he managed early in his career. Durocher managed in New York City from 1939-55 and had 813 Quick Hooks (versus only 469 Slow Hooks) in 2,481 games, a 32.7 percent rate, higher than anyone but Jimy Williams. Then, after over a decade on the sidelines, he returned to managing and had 214 Quick Hooks in just 1,258 games; barely half as many as he would've had under his old rate. This just shows how impressive McGraw's late career score is.

Ron Gardenhire may have pushed Durocher off the top ten by the time you read this. Through nine years, he's at about the same level as Durocher; depending on how the 2011 Twins score, Gardenhire could crash the leaderboard.

Actually, one other manager should be mentioned. Roger Craig was the primary manager of a team for only nine years, and thus just misses qualifying, but if Gardenhire gets brought up, we need to discuss Craig. In 1,475 games managed, his teams had 510 Quick Hooks—34.6 percent. Had he managed just a few months more, he'd be a shoo-in for second place on this list and help bridge the gap between Jimy Williams and the rest of humanity.

Oh, yeah, Casey Stengel doesn't miss this list by too much. In all, 28.2 percent of his games featured a Quick Hook. In news that would not surprise Vic Raschi, Stengel had one of the quicker hooks of his era. But because era matters, while Stengel was more likely to pull a starter earlier than any current skipper, when placed in context he's nothing too historic.

OK, what about the other half? Which managers by this method had the slowest hook?

Let's flip this around a bit: who had the most evenly-used hook? If a quarter of all starts are supposed to be Quick Hooks, and another quarter Slow Hooks, who came closest to matching that?

Over his career, it was Sparky Anderson. He used a Quick Hook 24.9 percent of the time and a slow hook 25.0 percent of the time. That's over his full career. In the 1970s, he had 260 Quick Hooks and 267 Slow Hooks, but later on his numbers shifted. The second-most even career stats belong to Tommy Lasorda, and in his case there's no big transformative career arc He interspersed his Quick Hook seasons and Slow Hook campaigns throughout his career. For example, in 1987 Quick Hooks led, 58-33, but the next year Slow Hooks dominated, 62-32.

Manager	Percentage	S. H.	All Games
Billy Martin	33.6%	762	2,267
Bucky Harris	31.5%	1,387	4,410
Johnny Oates	31.4%	485	1,544
Jimmy Dykes	31.4%	929	2,962
Cito Gaston	30.9%	535	1,731
Terry Francona	30.8%	548	1,782
Red Schoendienst	29.8%	595	1,999
Mike Hargrove	29.8%	703	2,363
Connie Mack	29.4%	1,403	4,776
Joe McCarthy	29.1%	1,014	3,487

From 1919-2010, teams have a .514 record in games with Quick Hooks, a .405 record with Slow Hooks, and .541 in their other games. But it hasn't always been the same in all eras. From 1919-47, there was no big trend: teams were .440 with Quick Hooks, .443 with Slow, and .559 otherwise. The Slow Hook Era was 1948-72, when the Slow Hook had a better winning record every year except once (1952). Results: .408 mark with Quick Hooks, .502 with Slow, and .544 otherwise for that quarter-century. Things flipped entirely in 1973; beginning that season, the Quick Hook has provided a better record each year without fail. Through 2010, teams are .593 with a Quick Hook, .345 with a Slow Hook, and .531 otherwise.

(Again, career numbers incomplete for anyone managing in 2011 or before 1919).

Gee, Billy Martin finished first? That isn't very surprising. He's infamous for his handling of the 1980 A's staff. That team not only topped the league in complete games, but they had more than any squad since the 1941 White Sox (managed by Jimmy Dykes, who is also on the list). In Detroit, Martin had Mickey Lolich throw over 370 innings with a league-leading 29 complete games. Three years later in Texas, Fergie Jenkins led the league with 29 CG for Martin. When Martin had a pitcher he trusted, he pushed him as relentlessly as possible.

That said, if you were to look at the bottom ten for Quick Hooks, Martin would not be on it. Sure, he let guys stay in all the time, but he would occasionally yank someone early if need be. As a result, Martin had only 42.9 percent of his games fall in-between the Quick/Slow Hook borders, quite a bit below the normal 50 percent. In fact, Martin had the smallest percentage of games by any manager land between the hook categories.

Jimmy Dykes has the fewest Quick Hooks, as just 17.9 percent of his games had one. Dykes really liked to lean on his starters. Pitching for Dykes in 1942, Ted Lyons became the only pitcher in the live ball era to qualify for the ERA title while completing all of his starts. In nearly a decade's work, Lyons completed almost four-fifths of his starts for Dykes.

The most unexpected name on the list is Bucky Harris. As a young player-manager in the 1920s, Bucky Harris helped create the relief ace when he used Firpo Marberry as a fireman in clutch situations late in the game. Others had used relief pitchers before, but never had a relief specialist been so central to a team as Marberry with the mid-1920s Senators. You'd think a manager at the forefront of the bullpen revolution wouldn't have such a big score here.

Aye, but here's the real oddity—after Harris experienced tremendous success with Marberry in the fireman's role, he stopped using any relief ace after a few years. He made Marberry a starter and had no one fill the old bullpen role. It's the damnedest thing. Over 20 years later, Harris used another ace reliever with Joe Page on the 1947 Yankees, but in between, Harris wasn't interested. Go figure.

That's for careers. What's the most Quick or Slow Hooks a manager ever had in a single season? Here are the results for Quick Hooks (on the next page).

Team	Year	%	Q.H.	G	Manager
BOS	2000	51.2	83	162	Jimy Williams
MON	1994	49.1	56	114	Felipe Alou
MON	1993	49.1	78	163	Felipe Alou
CWS	1968	47.9	75	162	Eddie Stanky, Les Moss, and Al Lopez
BOX	1999	46.3	75	162	Jimy Williams
OAK	1975	45.1	73	162	Alvin Dark
BRK	1940	44.9	70	156	Leo Durocher
PIT	2002	44.1	71	161	Lloyd McClendon
MON	1996	43.8	71	162	Felipe Alou
NYM	1981	43.8	46	105	Joe Torre

Before looking over the numbers, I need to quickly confess a little secret. Even though I used the same formula as Bill James, my numbers may not perfectly line up with his for the period he has numbers. When doing the [(RA*10)+Pitches] formula, the numbers don't nicely add up to breaks at the exact 25 percent markers, and I just put it as best as I could. It's not a huge concern, as again the point is to get a general lay of the land, not exact precision.

At any rate, it's impressive to see Williams once topped 50 percent. Keep in mind, this stat is designed to account for only a quarter of all starts. Plus, Williams has back-to-back years in the top five, a nice achievement. Alou has two seasons in the top three, though one of those was in a strike-shortened year, and it's always a little easier to score really high in a rate stat with a smaller sample size. Still, he's the only guy on here three times.

Williams' performance is part of a larger trend—six of the top ten seasons come from 1993-2002. Yes, it's when the two great kings of Quick Hooks managed—Williams and Alou. However, aside from them, Quick Hook scores tend to be a bit more extreme around the turn of the millennium. That's around the time when pitch counts first start gurgling up. The ones who paid more attention to it were more likely to yank a starter earlier than their peers, even when he hadn't allowed many runs.

It was an interesting time. Some managers would let a starter toss 140 pitches without blinking, and others would never let a guy last 120 pitches. Previously, virtually no managers would pay that much attention to pitch counts, and since then no one will let a guy last that long. Thus the turn-of-the-millennium era dominates because that was the great transition of pitch counts, one of the two key stats in determining Quick Hooks.

Sparky Anderson and Leo Durocher both shifted from Quick to Slow Hooks as they got older. What about some other long-lasting managers?

Prior to coming to the Yankees, Joe Torre had twice as many Quick Hooks as Slow Hooks. From 1996 onward, it was evenly split. Similarly, Gene Mauch, Earl Weaver and Bucky Harris all scored as quicker hooks in their first four or five years but shifted to slow hooks.

Ralph Houk, Walter Alston, and Bill McKechnie were both Quick Hook-inclined for a decade before shifting to Slow Hooks. Dusty Baker was a Quick Hook until pitch counts came into vogue, at which point he suddenly became one of the game's slowest hooks.

If the Anderson/Durocher pattern is common, have any managers flipped from Slow to Quick Hooks? Tony LaRussa did the rare reverse flip. In his AL years, he generally had more Slow Hooks, but since coming to St. Louis, he's had a Quick Hook. Rather fittingly, LaRussa's old protégé, Jim Leyland, has undergone the same reverse trajectory.

Leo Durocher's 1940 Dodgers dominate their decade like no other. Aside from their 70 Quick Hooks, the second highest total of the decade was 60, by Leo Durocher's 1942 Dodgers. Then come three teams at 59, including Durocher's 1941 Dodgers. The other two teams were Braves teams run by Casey Stengel.

Looking at decades not represented in the list above, tops in the 1920s was Connie Mack's 1926 A's. They had 60 Quick Hooks in 150 games, 40 percent in all. In the 1930s, Walter Johnson's 1931 Senators lead with 68 Quick Hooks in 156 games. That's second only to the 1940 Dodgers for highest percentage of Quick Hooks for a team in a 154-game season.

In the 1950s, the top mark belongs to Charlie Dressen's 1952 Dodgers with 61 Quick Hooks. Following that up were Dressen's 1953 Dodgers with 60. Dressen actually leads all managers here in one category: In 5.4 percent of the games he managed, Dressen yanked a starter in the first inning. Even Stengel can't compete with that.

The best total from a non-strike year in the 1980s is a tie between Roger Craig and Roger Craig. His 1988 and 1989 Giants each had 70 Quick Hooks in 162 games. Interestingly, both Craig and 1930s single-season leader Walter Johnson are among the few pitchers to become managers. I don't know if Craig paid strict attention to pitch counts, but he was very engaged in the pitching process. He always looked at mechanics and would personally call all the pitches from the dugout.

The smallest percentage of Quick Hooks in a season belongs to Cito Gaston's 1995 Blue Jays, with 13 in 144 games. Then again, they played in a strike-shortened year. In a full season, Kevin Kennedy's 1996 Red Sox are tied with Sparky Anderson's 1988 Tigers, each of whom had 15 in 162 games. Clearly, Anderson was no longer the Captain Hook of his youth. Or rather, the baseball world of the late 1980s was no longer the same as it was in the early 1970s.

Let's flip it around once more. Who has the most single-season Slow Hooks?

Team	Year	%	S.H.	G	Manager
OAK	1981	54.1	59	109	Billy Martin
OAK	1980	53.7	87	162	Billy Martin
BOS	1996	50.6	82	162	Kevin Kennedy
STB	1943	49.7	76	153	Luke Sewell
TOR	1995	48.6	70	144	Cito Gaston
STB	1938	48.1	75	156	Gabby Street
TEX	1988	47.2	76	161	Bobby Valentine

Team	Year	%	S.H.	G	Manager
BOS	1985	46.6	76	163	John McNamara
BOS	1984	46.3	75	162	Ralph Houk
CIN	1942	46.1	71	154	Bill McKechnie

Billy Martin blows everyone away, and it's not close. Those A's teams are famous, or should I say infamous, for how hard Martin worked them. A great young corps of pitchers—Rick Langford, Mike Norris, Steve McCatty, and Matt Keough—all blew their arms out. Those A's teams were so overworked that it led to a league-wide reduction in complete games in response, and complete games have been declining ever since.

In one stretch from 1980-81, team ace Langford completed 36 of 39 starts. Among his three non-completions was a time he went nine innings in an extra-inning contest and another in which he went 8.2 innings in a nine-inning game.

In fourth place, Luke Sewell had a very odd season with the 1943 Browns. Despite the huge number of Slow Hooks, the team had a normal number or Quick Hooks—36 in 153 games. The team had 26.8 percent of its starts fall between the Quick/Slow Hook boundaries, far below the quota level of 50 percent.

In fact, it's by far the smallest percentage of games any team had between hooks. Second smallest was 31.8 percent, by Bill McKechnie's 1942 Reds (who are also listed above in tenth place on the Slow Hooks leaderboard). The most starts falling between Quick and Slow Hooks belongs to the 1993 Astros managed by Art Howe, at 64.8 percent.

Looking at the decades not represented above, Tris Speaker's 1924 Indians top the 1920s with 60 Slow hooks in 153 games (narrowly edging Wilbert Robinson's 1923 Dodgers with 60 in 155 games).

In the 1950s, the top team was the 1956 Tigers, managed by Bucky Harris in his 29th and final season as skipper. They had 58 Slow Hooks in 155 games. The decade's runner up with 57 in 155 contests was the 1950 Senators, also managed by Harris.

In the 1960s, the 1966 Cubs led with 62 Slow Hooks in 162 games. Their manager was Leo Durocher, making his return to the dugout after an 11-year layoff. Clearly, times had changed since Durocher was the quickest hook in the land back in Brooklyn. Managers like Durocher and Anderson really help us appreciate how impressive it was for John McGraw to have such a Quick Hook in his final seasons as a manager.

In the 1970s, Roy Harsfield led with the 1977 inaugural Blue Jays: 72 Slow Hooks in 161 games. That narrowly edges Gene Mauch's 1971 Expos

Lou Piniella might have the strangest career trajectory of any long-lasting manager. He began his career with the Yankees and Reds as a Quick Hook. So far, so normal—most mangers do that. In Seattle, he changed to a slower hook. Again, nothing new here—most managers do that. But then he switched back to the quick in 2000, around the time pitch counts came into vogue, and stayed one of the quicker hooks until retiring. Managers normally change from quick to slow, and a few go the opposite route. But I don't know of anyone who did both—except for Piniella.

- Chris Jaffe

and Darrell Johnson's 1974 Red Sox, who each also had 72 Slow Hooks, but both in 162 games.

In the 21st century, the king is Ozzie Guillen, whose 2004 White Sox had 71 Slow Hooks in 162 games. The runner-up in modern times is also a Guillen squad, the 2006 White Sox with 68 Slow Hooks.

At the other end, the 1939 Cardinals had only 11 Slow Hooks in 155 games, the lowest single-season percentage by any club. Manager Ray Blades was a rookie skipper, and the team fired him early in 1940. That 1939 Cardinals team narrowly edges Pie Traynor's 1938 Pirates, who had 11 Slow Hooks in 152 games. That club famously blew a seven-game lead in the final weeks of the season.

Hank Thompson, Beyond the Trivia

by Frank Jackson

If you're a baseball trivia buff, you've got to love Hank Thompson. While he had a decent major league career (which is to say a few good years, a few mediocre years, and a few forgettable years), mostly with the New York Giants, it is for a number of firsts that he is largely remembered.

The fates decreed that Larry Doby of the Cleveland Indians would be the first black man to play in the American League on July 5, 1947—but he only beat Hank Thompson by 13 days. Thompson collected more than a few consolation prizes, however.

For example, Thompson was not only the first black man to take the field for the St. Louis Browns, he was also the first black player to have a black teammate (Willard "Will" Brown joined the Browns at the same time as Thompson). On July 20, when Brown and Thompson both played in a Browns-Red Sox contest, that was the first time a major league team had two black players in the lineup. When the Browns faced the Indians on Aug. 9, the appearance of Thompson and Larry Doby in the game marked the first time black players were on opposing teams in major league baseball.

In 1949, when Thompson joined the New York Giants, he (and Monte Irvin) were the first black players for that franchise. At the same time, Thompson became the first black player to play for two teams (and in both leagues). When Thompson faced Dodger pitcher Don Newcombe that year, it marked the first time a black batter had faced a black pitcher in a major league game. When he, Monte Irvin and Willie Mays loaded the bases on June 3, 1951, it was the first time three black men were all on base at the same time in a major league game. And the first time an all-black outfield appeared in a major league game (during the 1951 World Series), Hank Thompson was among the three men on duty.

More recently, when former St. Louis teammate Willard Brown was voted into the Hall of Fame, Thompson became the answer to yet one more trivia question: of the first four black players in major league baseball, Thompson was the only one who was *not* in the Hall of Fame.

Now there's no disgrace in not being enshrined in Cooperstown. Plenty of outstanding ballplayers never got the call, as we are reminded every year when ballots are cast for the honor. Certainly, Thompson was not lacking in

Mariano Rivera saved Enrique Wilson's life. He blew Game Seven of the 2001 World Series but made his best save ever.

Wilson, a utility infielder with the Yankees that year, was scheduled to fly home to the Dominican Republic on American Airlines Flight 587. But Arizona defeated the Yankees, so there was no victory parade. Wilson changed his travel plans and took an earlier flight home. Flight 587 crashed into the Belle Harbor neighborhood of Queens on Nov. 12, 2001. In a cruel twist of fate, one of the passengers had survived the attacks on the Twin Towers two months prior.

Rivera told Wilson "I am glad we lost the World Series because it means that I still have a friend."

Chris Dial saved Alex Rodriguez's life. Dial is a big baseball fan; has been a Mets fan since 1973. He developed a way of converting a fielder's zone rating, or how often he fields balls in certain areas of the ball field, into runs saved for his team. Dial is also a chemist and inventor. He invented the Soft Ground Arrestor System. This is bubbly concrete placed at the end of a runway to slow down a plane that is going too fast. Think of it as a runaway truck ramp for airplanes.

talent, but was it enough to land him in Cooperstown? Arguably, he had one advantage over the other three players (Jackie Robinson, Larry Doby, and Willard Brown), as he made his big league debut at a younger age and had the potential for a longer career. Like Doby, who was 23 when he debuted, but unlike Robinson and Brown, he came of age when the major leagues were actively seeking black players. Though he had fought in World War II and had played in the Negro Leagues, he was only 21 when he came up with the Browns and only 23 when he came up for good with the New York Giants, one of major league baseball's storied teams. So what kept him from realizing his potential? Perhaps the answer lies in yet another trivia question:

Who was the only professional ballplayer who ever shot and killed a man the day before he reported to spring training?

Hank Thompson, of course. It was the only time he killed a man, but it was not his only brush with the law. To be sure, the circumstances under which he grew up were less than ideal, but other forces were at work within him which proved far more destructive.

Born in Oklahoma (most sources list Oklahoma City, but Thompson said Muskogee) on Dec. 8, 1925, Henry Curtis Thompson grew up in a broken home in Dallas. He was arrested twice, once for theft (at age 11 he was accused of stealing jewelry from a parked car) and once for truancy. The former charge proved false, not so the second. Numerous prolonged absences from school are hard to rationalize—indeed, they went on his permanent record—and with his mother's consent, he was sent to reform school in Gatesville, about 40 miles west of Waco.

As a teenager (though that term probably wasn't used in the late 1930s and early 1940s when Thompson was in his teens), his main interest in life appeared to be playing baseball. Once he discovered that the reform school offered "the first organized baseball team I'd ever seen," his good behavior was assured. But after his release from reform school at age 15, another abiding interest cropped up: Thompson discovered the joy of drinking cheap wine. At the time, he was playing baseball for a local black team and pitching batting practice for the Dallas Steers of the Texas League.

In 1943 he joined the famed Kansas City Monarchs of Negro League baseball. The Monarchs, like other professional baseball players, were subject to the military draft, so fielding a team had become more troublesome. Thompson, who was only 17 years old, was not yet subject to the draft so he was a safe addition to the roster. Here he got into the habit of getting a good beer buzz after the day's labors were over.

All in all, it must have been a heady experience. While most boys his age were high school kids or working stiffs, he was not only drawing a paycheck for playing baseball, he was a teammate of such legendary Negro League veterans as Satchel Paige, Buck O'Neil, Willard Brown, and Connie Johnson.

But after Thompson's rookie season, he turned 18. Now it was Thompson's turn to be drafted into the Army. With the 1695th Combat Engineers, he was sent to Europe in 1944, where he was a machine gunner in the Battle of the Bulge.

Having graduated to hard whiskey (resulting in some fighting and stockade time) while in the Army, he was discharged as a sergeant on June 20, 1946, and went back to the Kansas City Monarchs, where he helped them win a pennant. Between the Negro Leagues, winter ball in Cuba, and barnstorming tours, Thompson was not only earning decent money but honing his skills and showcasing his talent. People began to take notice. Bob Feller, who played against Thompson and a team of Negro League All-Stars in a lucrative barnstorming tour after the 1946 season, opined that Thompson was the best player on the team.

In mid-1947, the St. Louis Browns purchased his contract from the Monarchs. The Browns were entrenched in last place, 27.5 games out of first place, and it was assumed bringing up former Monarchs Thompson and Willard Brown was a publicity stunt. Having noticed that baseball fans were turning out in droves to see Jackie Robinson and the Dodgers play the Cardinals in St. Louis, the Browns were anxious to find a way to boost attendance for their games. Clearly, something had to be done. The Browns played one game before a "crowd" of 478 at Sportsman's Park. That might be understandable for a meaningless game in late September on a drizzly, unseasonably chilly evening—but not on July 14.

The *St. Louis Gazette-Democrat* called the Browns' roster moves "an eyebrow-lifting experiment." The Browns, who had not gotten around to desegregating their grandstand till the season before, were suddenly leading the majors in black players with *two*. The Dodgers and the Indians each had one. The other thirteen teams had none. This tended to obscure the fact that the two men the Browns had signed were at opposite ends of their careers.

Willard Brown, Thompson's cohort, had long been an offensive juggernaut in the Negro Leagues. He started with the Monarchs in 1935 and racked up seven home run titles and a .355 batting average but, depending on one's source, he was anywhere from 32 to 36 years old when he joined the Browns. He never felt welcome on the Browns (outfielder Paul Lehner actually turned in his uniform when informed two black players

On Friday the 13th of October 2006, Rodriguez and several others were on a private jet that made a hard landing at Bob Hope Airport in Burbank, Calif. The arrestor system stopped the plane.

Other sports stars haven't had this luck with plane crashes; including some in pinstripes, as we shall soon see. Roberto Clemente might be the most famous one; flying a mission of mercy from Puerto Rico that never made it to Managua, Nicaragua. There was also Knute Rockne and Rocky Marciano. Team planes have crashed. There was Manchester United in 1958, the University of Evansville basketball team in 1977. There was a Uruguayan rugby team that crashed in the Andes and the survivors ate the dead. The movie *Alive* was about this incident.

But a more macabre story is that of Len Koenecke. Koenecke was a fairly decent outfielder in the 1930s. He didn't really get a chance to play regularly until he was 27. He was a big drinker and that may have had something to do with his late start. His drinking problem was so bad that he got kicked off of the Dodgers and sent home. Keep in mind this was when drinking in baseball was rampant. A few years earlier, Hack Wilson set the record for runs blottoed in while he was half in the bag.

Koenecke had a few before his flight home and he stormed the cockpit. The pilot and copilot fought him off, but he kept coming. Finally, one of them grabbed a fire extinguisher and gave Koenecke one fierce blow and killed him.

In 1999, Payne Stewart's runaway plane was followed in real time by CNN and MSNBC. Peter Finch must have been rolling in his grave laughing. Stewart was supposed to fly from Florida to Texas, but the plane he was a passenger in lost cabin pressure and kept flying until it ran out of fuel and crashed into a Dakota field.

Alan Kulwicki and Davey Allison survived the 200 mph ballet of the speedway, but both perished in aviation accidents. Allison was piloting a helicopter. Billy Southworth Jr. may have made the majors if it weren't for World War II. He was International League player of the year once. Southworth became a bomber pilot and flew the requisite number of missions before rotating stateside. Alas, he crashed taking off on a routine mission from LaGuardia.

were joining the team) and he considered their talent level (their final 1947 record was 59-95) far below that of the Monarchs. His motivation was also hampered by the deep salary cut (from $9,000 to $5,000 per year) he took when he moved from the Monarchs to the Browns. He really wanted to stay with the Monarchs but his coaches and teammates prodded him to go to the major leagues and show what he could do. At any rate, he hit just .179 in 21 games before being released. He was not through with baseball, however, as he continued to play in winter leagues, the Negro American League, and the minor leagues until 1957.

But if Willard Brown was past his peak in 1947, Hank Thompson was just getting started. On July 18, he played his first major league game at age 21. It was an inauspicious debut, a 16-2 loss to the Philadelphia A's in which Thompson went hitless in four times at bat. Things improved somewhat after that, but Thompson didn't set the league on fire. Playing mostly as a second baseman, he hit .256 in 78 at-bats during his rookie year. The crowds the Browns were hoping for, however, never materialized—at least not in St. Louis. In other American League cities, Browns games did show an uptick in attendance.

After 36 games, Thompson and Brown were released by the Browns on Aug. 23 because they "failed to reach major-league standards." At least, that was the official word from General Manager Bill DeWitt. According to their contracts, however, DeWitt would have owed the Monarchs additional funds if the two men remained on the roster any longer. Since the anticipated crowds never materialized and neither player had set the league on fire, it made no financial sense to exercise the option clause.

While Thompson's rookie season was hardly stellar, it was far from a disaster. Since the Browns' team batting average was a paltry .239, Thompson was far from being the anchor man in the offense. The Browns could have kept him or could have sent him to the minors for more seasoning. If so, he might have avoided what happened the following spring.

After his release from the Browns, Thompson re-joined the Kansas City Monarchs. In the spring of 1948, he was on his way to the Monarchs' training camp in San Antonio. He stopped to visit his sister Margaret and her husband in Dallas on April 3, and while visiting a beer garden late that evening, he encountered James S. Crow, a former sandlot player who apparently resented the idea that this kid Thompson he used to play with was now a hotshot professional ballplayer. "Hello, Mr. Money-man," sneered Crow, who had a reputation as a mean drunk. Accosting Thompson with a knife, he snarled "I'm gonna get you." He probably assumed that Thompson was unarmed, but a number of the Kansas City Monarchs considered a pistol to be a standard accessory for the well-dressed ballplayer, so Thompson himself had taken to carrying a .32 automatic. When Crow advanced on him with the knife, Thompson instantly flashed back to an incident in which he had seen Crow disembowel another man. Thompson knew Crow meant business so he shot him—three times according to Thompson, six times according to a terse write-up that appeared on page six of the April 5, 1948 issue of *The Dallas Morning News*. At the time Thompson was only halfway through his first bottle of beer, so his reaction was not clouded by alcohol.

The next morning, after learning that Buddy Crow had died, Thompson turned himself in to the police and was charged with murder. He pled not guilty, posted bond, and went on to San Antonio to join the Monarchs. As he succinctly put it, "I killed a man and the next day I was playing ball like nothing had happened." Ironically, though he was charged with murder, it made more "sense" than the lesser crimes he was charged with later in his career, since he was only defending himself. No one died during any of his subsequent brushes with the law, but the crimes were truly senseless.

The shooting haunted Thompson for the rest of his life, but on the field he was undeterred. He batted .375 for the Monarchs in 1948 with a .633 slugging percentage.

Thompson was not an imposing figure at the plate, standing just 5'9" and weighing 175 pounds (Thompson listed himself at 5'8½" and 168 pounds), but he packed a surprising amount of power. In a winter league game in Cuba, he once was awarded $2,000 for hitting a home run into the distant center field bleachers. Pitcher Connie Johnson stated, "He could hit that ball as far as anybody—Doby and all of 'em. He was a home run hitter and one of the best."

In 1949, the New York Giants purchased him from the Monarchs and gave him a $2,500 signing bonus. While playing at the Giants' Jersey City, N.J. farm club, he marred Maria Quesada, a girl he had met while playing ball in Cuba. Four weeks later, on July 5, he and Monte Irvin were called up from Jersey City, and Thompson made his National League debut four days later. His association with the Giants also helped bring about a resolution of the Buddy Crow imbroglio in Dallas (from "murder" to "justifiable homicide") the following year. Maybe Crow hadn't dodged a bullet, but Thompson sure had.

For the most part, Thompson's stay with the Giants worked out well. Starting out as a second baseman, he finally settled in as a third baseman but occasionally returned to second base and also played the outfield

Southworth and Allison were second-generation sports figures. Allison's father was a NASCAR legend and Southworth's dad was a Hall of Fame manager. But there are also plenty of brother combos from Hank and Tommie Aaron to Peyton and Eli Manning. There are even a few twins. Tiki and Ronde Barber were both in the NFL. (And Tiki wants back in.) Bob and Mike Bryan rule doubles tennis. There's Ozzie and Jose Canseco. The New Britain Rock Cats once had a manager/pitching coach duo of Stan and Stu Cliburn. (This makes sense. They are a Minnesota Twins affiliated farm team.) Jim Thorpe had a twin brother who died young. Ryan Howard has a twin brother Cory. At one point Cory Lidle was his teammate with the Phillies. Lidle had a twin brother named Kevin.

Lidle crashed a plane into a New York City high-rise two days before Alex Rodriguez's near crash. The stock market was open at the time. Fears that this was a terrorist attack sent the Dow tumbling briefly. His brother Kevin was a ballplayer too. He played in the twilight world of independent league ball. One year he was on the Somerset Patriots. A teammate of his was a Florida kid named Jeff Anderson. Anderson's father, Jerry, was a pilot himself. Back in 1979, the Anderson family lived in Canton, Ohio and Jerry was a passenger in a Cessna Citation when it crashed and burned while practicing take offs and landings. The pilot was another baseball player. His name was Thurman Munson.

- Jon Daly

when necessary. He played for the Giants from 1949 to 1956 with his best years in 1950 (.289, 20 homers, 91 RBIs), 1953 (.302, 24 homers, 74 RBIs) and 1954 (.263, 26 homers, 86 RBIs).

He played in two World Series (1951 and 1954), and though other Giants received more glory for those two pennants, Thompson's contributions were hardly inconsequential.

While Bobby Thomson still gets the lion's share of credit for propelling the Giants to the 1951 pennant with his famous shot-heard-around-the-world (the New York press often referred to Bobby Thomson and Hank Thompson as the Thom-Thom twins) that propelled the Giants past the Dodgers in the 1951 playoffs, Hank Thompson's contributions are often overlooked. Though he had been injured for most of the season, Thompson returned for August and September and hit all eight of his home runs during the stretch drive. Without his bat in the lineup, the Giants might not have been in position to tie the Dodgers at the end of the season and bring about the playoff games, and hence Bobby Thomson's home run.

In 1954, Willie Mays' legendary catch is probably the first thing that comes to mind when the World Series is recalled. Dusty Rhodes' two pinch-hit home runs (the only ones hit by the Giants in the Series) also loom large. Hank Thompson's contribution (four hits in eleven at-bats, seven walks, six runs scored) is often overlooked, even though it was a key part of the Giants' four-game sweep.

Even if Thompson's accomplishments were sometimes overshadowed, it would seem that he had all that was necessary for the good life. He was young, he was making good money, he was starring in America's pastime in America's biggest city, and he had already played in two World Series by the time he was 28 years old. What could go wrong?

Like a lot of ballplayers, Thompson was enamored of the good life, and adult beverages were definitely a big part of it. In this respect, one might say he was in a league all by himself. Typically, Thompson would unwind after a game with a couple of drinks before dinner (he preferred Scotch). This probably wasn't his undoing; rather, it was the postprandial fifth (or more) he consumed nightly. This rate of consumption took its toll, and he was basically washed up by 1956. "It was awful," noted Thompson. "I couldn't move around third base. Balls were going by me that I should have had. I was disgracing baseball and I still kept boozing it up." The Giants optioned him to their Minneapolis Millers farm club in 1957. After hitting only .240 at the Triple-A level, Thompson decided it was time to call it a career. He was only 31 years old when he retired on July 27, 1957. There can be little doubt that his alcohol consumption had precipitated the premature erosion of his skills. While it not only cut short his career, it might have held him back from greater accomplishments when he was one of the Giants regulars. Whatever his struggles with the bottle, they did not seem to affect his relationships with his teammates. Apparently, he was well liked by the other Giants. Though third base was his best position, he was willing to play wherever they needed him, and if his teammates received more acclaim than he did, it didn't seem to matter to him. One might say he was Dr. Jekyll in a baseball uniform and Mr. Hyde in street clothes.

The Dr. Jekyll facet was eliminated when Thompson retired. No longer able to play the game he had loved all his life and no longer making the big bucks, Thompson took a severe one-two punch to the ego. Though he had earned approximately $250,000 as a professional ballplayer, his savings ran out in January 1958. Not surprisingly, his life spiraled downward. Drifting from job to job, working as a bartender or cab driver, he found domestic tranquility eluded him. His wife divorced him in 1959.

Despite his unpleasant memories of the Buddy Crow incident, he started packing again (this time a .25-caliber model) in 1960. In February, 1961, he was drowning his sorrows and spontaneously decided he would try to hold up a bar in New York. To say that the caper was ill-planned would be a gross understatement. Bill's Place, the bar he chose to rob, was a watering hole he had patronized regularly. "Do you know who I am?" he asked the bartender, who responded in the negative. "Good, this is a stickup. Put the money on the bar." He was arrested one half-block from the bar. The take was a mere $37. Luckily, Giants President Horace Stoneham (who was now based in San Francisco, where the Giants had moved in 1958) and Baseball Commissioner Ford Frick went to bat for him and he was released on probation.

Later Stoneham got him a job at the Giants' winter instructional league in October 1961. Hooking up with an old girlfriend in California in 1962, they both found work in Los Angeles. When his girlfriend went to Houston to visit her sick mother, he followed her, intending to accompany her back to California. But after a spat with her, he made a decision that changed his life—and not for the better, at least not right away. On July 13, 1963, while staying at the Midtown Hotel in Houston, he decided to hold up a nearby liquor store. This time around, the take was better. He got $270 and a bottle of Scotch. But no one spoke up for him after he was arrested and the court was not in a magnanimous mood. After all, Thompson had a pretty long rap sheet. All in all, he had been arrested seven times. The Houston judge decided mercy was not an option, so Thompson was sentenced to ten years.

Historical Sidebar: Pour Low the Foundation, Masons

Munson was a rival of Carlton Fisk. They were both catchers who came of age around the same time. Fisk was tall and patrician. Munson was the dumpy plebe.

Keith Olbermann has a blog on mlb.com. In August of 2010 he made a post about Fisk and J.D. Salinger (who died earlier that year.)

Autographs, documents, confirmation of personal interaction with the late and famously reclusive author of The Catcher In The Rye (J.D. Salinger) are rare, to say the least. But this one describes, to his World War 2 Division Commander, meeting a teenaged Carlton Fisk when he came to put in the foundation for Salinger's home in Cornish, New Hampshire. I have no way of verifying the story (the inquiries to Fisk are out, but I only saw this thing tonight) but it offers verisimilitude: born in Maine, Fisk grew up in Charlestown, N.H., about 20 miles away from the site of the concrete in question.

Back in The Sixties, Salinger had a foundation poured. He claimed that one of the young men pouring it was Carlton Fisk. In W.P. Kinsella's *Shoeless Joe*, Ray Kinsella kidnaps Salinger and takes him to a game at Fenway Park. Near as I can tell, the game took place in either '78 or '79. Mike Torrez pitches for Boston against the Twins while Don Zimmer manages. Among the Twins are Roy Smalley, Bombo Rivera and Ken Landreaux.

If Thompson was one of those people who has to touch bottom before he can turn himself around, then Oct. 8, 1963, the day he started serving his sentence at the Texas Department of Corrections in Huntsville, was his personal nadir.

In a 1965 *SPORT* magazine starkly titled, "How I Wrecked My Life—How I Hope to Save It," he laid out how he got himself into such a mess. And he emphasized that he had done it to himself. There was no finger-pointing at anybody else. "Don't ask me to blame society, or the fact that I'm a Negro in a white world, or the fact I have a grade-school education, or the fact I was washed up as a major-leaguer when I was 31 years old." Though he received some physical abuse from his father (also a heavy drinker), he asserted, "I've never been mistreated in jail, either in reform school or county jail or city jail or the Texas state penitentiary."

The stay in prison was a much-needed reality check. From Oct. 29, 1963 to Feb. 13, 1964, he toiled at a work farm at the Eastham Unit at Huntsville. He kept his nose clean and was transferred to the Ferguson Unit, where he was a baseball coach and gym teacher for first offenders under age 21 and was given "trusty" status. He responded well to Alcoholics Anonymous group therapy sessions and was paroled after four years.

After getting out of Huntsville, Thompson went to Fresno to visit his mother, who was a missionary in the Church of God and Christ. And so it would seem that everything was now in place for Thompson to redeem himself. Indeed, he found work with the city as a playground director and often used his life as an object lesson. "I try to help the youngsters by pointing to my life," he said. "I tell them how easily and quickly a man can fall from the limelight and get into trouble if he isn't careful. I tell them how easy it is to go the other way." And he didn't mean hitting to the opposite field.

It would be nice to report that a chastened Thompson lived a long, fulfilling, productive life. But it was not to be. It was obvious he was a changed man, but he didn't have long to enjoy it. After two years of post-Huntsville grace, he suffered a cardiovascular event (some sources say a stroke, others a heart attack) at his mother's house and never regained consciousness. He died on Sep. 30, 1969 at the age of 43 and was buried in the Odd Fellows Cemetery in Fresno. That summer, he had made his last appearance in a Giants uniform when he played in an old-timer's game in San Francisco.

Today it might have ended differently. Therapeutic and/or legal intervention might have kicked in before the boozing had taken its toll. Typically, we read stories of troubled youths who, when given a chance to make good through athletic talent or some other gift, straighten out their lives. Hank Thompson didn't do that—at least not off the field. He was in the right place at the right time. He was a talented youngster who came of age at the moment when the major leagues were actively looking for black players. By the time he finally realized he was his own worst enemy, the battle was all but lost. Yet he realized his wounds were largely self-inflicted. "I'd say 99 percent of my trouble came right out of a bottle," he admitted. That may be AA-speak to a certain degree, but that doesn't invalidate the statement.

While Thompson is still best remembered for all the "firsts" in which he participated, there was yet one more, albeit unrecognized at the time. That historic at-bat in 1949 when Thompson faced Don Newcombe (who would go on to win the Rookie of the Year award), the first confrontation between a black pitcher and hitter, could also be remembered as the first pitcher-batter confrontation between two black alcoholics. Newcombe provides an intriguing foil for Thompson.

Like Thompson, Newcombe admitted his career on the diamond was curtailed by alcohol. His life, however, has been long and productive—and he's still involved in baseball. Since 1968, he has worked for the Dodgers as Director of Community Relations. Drawing on his own experiences with the bottle, he has counseled and lectured on alcoholism and substance abuse. Even though he was one of the first players the Dodgers traded after they moved to Los Angeles, he is a renowned baseball ambassador in the City of Angels.

Things didn't work out so well for Hank Thompson. Even though he has been gone for more than 40 years, he can still offer advice from beyond the grave. Let the following, originally published in the *SPORT* magazine article, serve as his epitaph:

> *Get advice about money, how to save it, how to invest it.*
> *Live a clean life.*
> *Stay away from those goodtime people who pretend to be your friends.*
> *Stay away from liquor.*
> *Stay healthy.*
> *Baseball is the cleanest sport we have, so treat it decent.*

And while on that trip, Kinsella stops at another game where Thurman Munson was playing (Munson died in '79.) I could not find a game that matched Kinsella's description perfectly. However, if that story of the baseball road trip were true, then it's quite possible that Fisk was Torrez's battery mate. I wonder if Salinger leaned over to Kinsella at some point and said, "You know, that young man once poured my foundation." If I were Salinger, I would've name-dropped Fisk in a heartbeat.

- Jon Daly

Sources

Gutman, Dan. *Baseball Babylon: From the Black Sox to Pete Rose, the Real Stories Behind the Scandals That Rocked the Game.* New York: Penguin, 1992.

Holman, John. *The Complete Book of Baseball's Negro Leagues: The Other Half of Baseball History.* Fern Park, FL: Hastings House, 2001.

Marazzi, Rich and Len Fiorito, ed. *Baseball Players of the 1950's.* Jefferson, NC: McFarland & Co., 2004.

Markham, William. *Baseball's Pivotal Era: 1945-1951.* Lexington, KY: University Press of Kentucky, 1999.

Moffi, Larry and Jonathan Kronstadt. *Crossing the Line: Black Major Leaguers 1947-1959.* Lincoln, NE: University of Nebraska Press, 2006.

Prager, Joshua. *The Echoing Green: The Untold Story of Bobby Thomson, Ralph Branca and the Shot Heard Round the World.* New York, NY: Pantheon Books, 2006.

Thompson, Hank with Arnold Hano. "How I Wrecked My Life—How I Hope to Save It," *SPORT* magazine, December, 1965.

Wilson, Walt. "Willard Brown, a Forgotten Ballplayer," *The National Pastime: a Review of Baseball History,"* No. 24, 2004, Society for American Baseball Research

Dallas Morning News, April 5, 1948.

A Legacy of Mixed Feelings

by David Wade

The designated hitter has had an enormous impact on baseball. In January of 1973, *The New York Times* called the American League's decision to allow a DH for the upcoming three seasons "the most basic change in the rules since 1903." Since then, several of the game's best players have extended their careers as DH in their later years. We've also seen players with questionable defensive skills make a career out of becoming professional hitters.

But the decision stunned baseball fans at the time, especially many who felt the decision was made without enough consideration. Fans remain divided on the issue, with the majority of those who identify themselves as American League fans supporting the rule and those who follow the National League opposing. Overall, polls usually indicate that most would like to see the rule abolished, but absent of that option, at least want to see Major League Baseball come to a consensus and use it in both leagues or in neither.

Regardless of dissenting opinion, ranging from fans to club owners, during its inception baseball's top officials tried to somehow spin a united front. They maintained that if the experiment, as it was known in its first incarnation, proved successful, then both leagues would eventually adopt it. In 1973, Commissioner Bowie Kuhn said that if the DH indeed were a proven benefit, "...then I hope the National follows suit." Despite Kuhn's expectation, the National League never has. It's easy to see why, given that American League teams, as committed as they were to increasing offense in the late '60s and early '70s, were not a united force even when they created the rule.

Following the 1972 season, Kuhn felt he had to break an impasse between the two leagues he presided over. He had hoped the two would find agreement, but really, he knew they wouldn't. The Commissioner and club executives also were dealing with labor issues, and were trying to broker a new deal with players to replace the one that had expired at the end of 1972. Since players had rejected an earlier proposal from owners, a possible lockout weighed heavily on the commissioner's mind.

For those reasons, he called for two representatives from each club to gather once again, after their regularly scheduled Winter Meetings had ended. Despite the ongoing labor dispute, the proposal to add the Desig-

First Designated Hitters for Each Team:

BAL	Terry Crowley
BOS	Orlando Cepeda
CLE	John Ellis
CHW	Mike Andrews
DET	Gates Brown
KC	Ed Kirkpatrick
LAA	Tommy McCraw
MIL	Ollie Brown
MIN	Tony Oliva
NYY	Ron Blomberg
OAK	Billy North
SEA	Dave Collins
TBA	Paul Sorrento
TEX	Rico Carty
TOR	Otto Velez

nated Pinch Hitter Rule was the dominant theme of the special meeting. American League owners and general managers had been persistent in their desire for passage of the new rule, while their National League counterparts were firm in their opposition. The two groups finally hashed it out on Jan. 11, 1973, over the course of seven hours, at the Sheraton-O'Hare Motor Hotel near Chicago.

A compromise had been sought just a month before, in the more inviting climate of Hawaii, during the Winter Meetings. But, that relaxed, tropical setting didn't facilitate the tense, often harsh disagreement between executives from the leagues. In Hawaii, baseball's Rules Committee refused to mandate an-across-the-majors modification. American League officials, feeling their needs were not addressed, came away frustrated and even more determined to implement the rule. They pushed Kuhn to allow them to use the DH in their league, and in Chicago the commissioner did just that. He decided to allow the American League to adopt the controversial rule on a three-year trial basis. He also allowed the National League to carry on as it had before, without the drastic change.

The idea of a designated hitter wasn't new; it actually went all the way back to the late 1800s, when the game was still in its infancy. John Thorn, MLB's official historian, relays the following:

> *William Chase Temple, owner of the Pittsburgh Pirates, was the first to come up with the idea of the designated hitter, back in 1891. His idea was for the DH to replace the pitcher in the batting order throughout the game. James W. Spalding, Albert's brother, alternatively suggested that the pitcher's spot in the order be skipped, so that only eight men would bat. The NL actually voted on Temple's proposal in 1892, declining to adopt it by the narrow margin of 7-5.*

Baseball's Rules Committee voted down a similar proposal in 1929, and throughout the years, baseball icons such as Philadelphia A's manager/owner Connie Mack and longtime National League President John Heydler promoted the idea. Support of the rule centered on the lackluster efforts often seen from pitchers at the plate. Most early proponents of a designated hitter, or of James Spalding's idea of skipping the pitcher's spot in the batting order, felt that pitchers' at-bats were simply boring. Some may have believed that pitchers' notorious hitting struggles, as a group, took away from the beauty of the game. The view was shared by *New York Times* writer Wells Twombly, who, after its implementation, welcomed the Designated Hitter and noted that a major benefit would be that "…the pitcher will be spared the agony of having to look like a palsied ape at home plate—a triumph for art and culture if there ever was one."

While some in the game, even some pitchers, shared that opinion at some level for decades, many felt pitchers had to bat to be complete players. Opponents of the rule feared such a dramatic modification to the makeup of baseball could become a perilous precedent, and eventually result in separate groups of players on offense and defense, as in football. Some players and managers also feared that pitchers might be more inclined to pitch high and tight, knowing there could be no retribution against them if they didn't have to take a turn at bat later in the game. Those opposed to the rule feared that unchecked aggression could lead to rampant head-hunting.

Despite those possibilities, calls for designated pinch hitters came with renewed vigor as pitching dominated baseball in the 1960s. The pleas by several owners and executives for drastic rule changes were in response to lower batting averages in the 1960s and early 1970s. Pitchers were enjoying unprecedented success during that period, posting historically low ERAs. Many cite Carl Yastrzemki's American League batting title in 1968, which he won with a .301 average, as the landmark stimulus in the movement to increase scoring in baseball. Never had a league leader had a batting average that low.

It was the peak of frustration for those in favor of better hitting in the game, and New York Yankees general manager Lee MacPhail would prove prophetic when he said, during spring training of 1968, "The pitching and defense have become too overpowering and I think there is a real possibility that some sort of major rule change will come about in the next couple of years."

Eager to reduce the advantage held by pitchers, executives debated several changes before the 1969 season. One called for increasing the 60-foot, six-inch pitching distance from the mound to home. Another proposal, one that eventually passed, centered on lowering the maximum elevation of the mound in relation to home plate to 10 inches. The previous maximum was 15 inches, and some suspected that many teams went even beyond that height.

Also new for 1969, MLB instructed umpires to reduce the height of the strike zone. They brought the bottom limit of the zone up from the bottom of the batter's knee to the top, and they lowered the top of the zone from the top of the shoulders to the armpits. Of course, ideas for a designated pinch hitter were also bandied about, to force the pitcher to work harder to get through the opponent's batting order.

American League executives, in particular, feared that their teams were not as exciting as those in the National League. While AL concerns were rising around the time of the "year of the pitcher" in '68, they went

From a 1973 *Sports Illustrated* article:

"The most important factual document pertaining to the DPH is kept in a desk drawer in the office of Carl Steinfeldt, the 32-year-old general manager of the Rochester Red Wings of the International League, which experimented with a DPH rule during the 1969 season. On the last three days of the season 5,000 questionnaires were given out to spectators at Rochester. The fans were asked to return them at their own expense, and 3,322 were completed. The verdict was 59% in favor of the DPH, 31% against and 10% on the fence. By Presidential election standards, that is landslide popularity."

From the *New York Times:*

On June 11, 1988 Rick Rhoden became the first and only pitcher to start a game as the designated hitter. Rhoden had been the losing pitcher in the previous game, but he started as the No. 7 batter in the lineup in the Yankees' 8-6 victory. He grounded to third against Jeff Ballard in the third inning in his first turn at bat. In his second time up, he drove in a run with a sacrifice fly to right field that tied the game at 3-3. Jose Cruz pinch-hit for him in the fifth.

Manager Billy Martin explained the unusual lineup move tersely. He said he had raised the possibility of doing something like this in spring training, and that injuries to his lineup left him with limited options.

When asked if he didn't think several of his left-handed hitters such as Claudell Washington, Mike Pagliarulo and Cruz wouldn't fare better against the left-handed Ballard, Martin responded:

"If they would or could hit this guy, they'd be the designated hitter and not Rhoden. This pitcher throws curves and slow curves. The book says they can't hit this guy."

through the roof in 1972, when the National League scored 824 more runs than AL teams did. While that was an unusually large gap, the National League had also held an advantage over the American League in league batting average for nine straight years going into '72.

The gap in attendance between the two leagues was even more dramatic. American League teams' attendance figures had been lower than those of their National League counterparts every year since 1956. What was already an unsettling trend became a huge concern for AL owners when the gap grew to historic proportions, with the National League advantage reported to be 30 million customers from '63-'72.

In addition to reducing the strike zone and the mound height, executives in the American League strongly supported the Baseball Rules Committee when, in early 1969, they approved experimental usage of designated hitters in four minor leagues (the International, Eastern, Texas, and New York-Penn) and allowed major league teams to try it during spring training games. American League owners felt the correlation between lower batting averages and lower attendance was strong enough to warrant drastic change; they cast their lot with those willing to push for rules to boost scoring.

On Nov. 28, 1972, Kuhn reiterated his desire to address proposals to increase hitting, telling the Rules Committee during the Winter Meetings in Hawaii that he was "seriously concerned." The committee, however, would suggest only that the highest minor leagues experiment with the designated hitter. Not satisfied, three days later the American League "unanimously called for" the DH at the major league level.

The Committee voted down that proposal 7-2 initially, then, evidently after more haranguing from the AL, struck it down with a final tally of 5-3, with one abstention.

Meanwhile, the National League strongly opposed the rule beyond the trials approved for the minor leagues. The two sides also disagreed on Kuhn's proposal for interleague play—a much more limited version than we see today. Kuhn and American League owners still pushed for interleague games and the designated hitter after the rebuff in Hawaii, and the likelihood for passage of the latter rose when some American League executives shifted their focus from a major league-wide rule change to the adoption of the designated hitter in their league only.

After Kuhn called for the special meeting in Chicago, American League President Joe Cronin identified some AL proponents of the DH. He said the New York Yankees and Milwaukee Brewers, led by their respective presidents, Michael Burke and Allan H. (Bud) Selig, were "prime backers" for the DH.

Those two certainly fit the criteria of owners concerned about attendance and scoring. The Yankees were coming off the first year since 1945 in which they failed to draw a million fans for the season. The Brewers had scored only 493 runs in '72, and had finished last among the six teams in the American League East. Worse, they also finished last among all American League teams in attendance, drawing just over 600,000 patrons. Minnesota Twins owner Calvin Griffith also aligned with those advocating change, and said he was going to push hard for the designated hitter rule in Chicago. In 1972, Griffith's Twins had drawn only 797,901 fans, sharply down from 1,483,547 in 1967. Attendance wasn't the only thing down in Minnesota: In 1969, the Twins had scored 790 runs, followed by 744 in 1970. But in '72 they scored only 537.

Cleveland Indians owner Nick Mileti not only backed the designated hitter, but said he would vote for interleague play and a designated runner rule as well. In '72, his team had scored only 472 runs and finished second to last in the American League in attendance, with just 626,354.

Despite the public support of those owners, and the alleged unanimous backing of all of them a month before in Hawaii, about a week after the Chicago meeting, American League President Joe Cronin revealed the actual AL vote for the DH was only 8-4. Cronin did not say which teams had voted against.

MLB historian John Thorn confirms that there is no official record of which teams voted against the proposal on that day, or why they would change their vote. We might safely assume that the Yankees, Brewers, Twins and Indians, whose owners publicly reiterated their support shortly before the vote, were among the eight teams in favor at the Chicago meeting. It is a bit more tenuous, but we might also assume, based on their comments after passage of the rule and the sorry shape of their respective offenses in the preceding year, that the Angels and Rangers voted for the DH in January as well.

A *Sports Illustrated* article a couple of weeks after the vote noted that the California Angels stood to benefit from the new rule. They quoted general manager Harry Dalton as saying, post meeting, that "Speaking from a selfish point of view, I like the rule." Dalton's Angels were fifth in the American League in hits in 1972, but dead last in runs because they hated to walk (they were last in the AL in walks and 10th out of 12 teams in on-base percentage). Dalton saw the DH as a way to put a better hitter in the middle of the batting order.

Following the '73 season, AL owners were pleased with results they saw from the designated hitter rule and hoped to drop the "experimen-

DH Fun Facts:

In his last nine seasons, Harold Baines played just two games in the field.

On June 17, 2007, Frank Thomas hit his 244th home run as a DH, breaking the record previously held by Edgar Martínez.

Mike Piazza's 10 homers as a DH is an NL record.

In 1986 Danny Heep became the first player in a World Series to be a designated hitter (DH) with the initials "D.H."

Three players have won the MVP award in years they played at least 20 percent of their games as DH, but no player has won it playing over 40 percent of his games as DH. Boston's Jim Rice played 49 of his 163 games as a DH in 1978. The next season California Angels league MVP Don Baylor played 65 of 162 games at DH, and in 1996 Texas' Juan Gonzalez played 32 of 134 games at DH.

A special MVP footnote belongs to David Ortiz, who finished in the top five in MVP voting five consecutive years while primarily serving as Boston's DH. He never won the MVP, however.

Ten Best DH Seasons

Player	Year	OPS
Edgar Martinez	1995	1.107
Travis Hafner	2006	1.097
David Ortiz	2007	1.066
Frank Thomas	2000	1.061
Edgar Martinez	1996	1.059
Rafael Palmeiro	1999	1.050
David Ortiz	2006	1.049
Jim Thome	2006	1.014
Edgar Martinez	1997	1.009
Travis Hafner	2005	1.003
Edgar Martinez	2000	1.002

(Players qualified for batting title and played at least 70 percent of games at DH)

Source: Baseball Reference

tal" label. At that time, Texas Rangers owner Bob Short claimed he was also one of the bigger supporters of the DH. In 1972, the Rangers had been last in the American League in nearly every significant offensive category except steals. They scored a meager 461 runs. In their first year in a new city, with high hopes of improving the attendance woes they suffered in Washington D.C., they drew only 662,974 fans.

So, after unanimously backing the rule in December when the Rules Committee shot it down, and with some owners going on record as backing the rule at the special meeting, which four American League owners would have voted against their league adopting the designated hitter on the day it finally passed?

One clue may lie in a straw poll Cronin had taken among American League owners. In between the two meetings in Hawaii and Chicago, Cronin indicated that nine teams were still in favor of the DH. He didn't say that any of the 12 franchises noted their disapproval in the poll, but it's interesting to note that ownership from the Detroit Tigers, Boston Red Sox, and Chicago White Sox didn't vote. Incidentally, those three teams were the only clubs in the American League that had drawn over a million fans in 1972.

Furthermore, all three ranked in the top five in runs in the American League that year. They might be good candidates to as possible "nay" votes for the rule's adoption, because they presumably had the least to gain, assuming they also believed the DH would boost scoring, and subsequently attendance and finances. If nothing else, a look at those three teams may demonstrate why a franchise would oppose an AL-only version of the rule.

Days after the vote in Chicago, Detroit owner John Fetzer actually described himself as a leading proponent of the rule. He said he believed it was, "...a weakness of the game to have pitchers batting." But, he also said that his general manager, Jim Campbell, opposed the rule. A *Sports Illustrated* article published a couple of weeks later revealed that Campbell was against the designated hitter being used only in the AL. Detroit manager Billy Martin also spoke out against the rule's use in just one league. Organizationally, Detroit favored implementation of the rule, but had second thoughts when it was not going to be adopted across all of major league baseball.

It's even possible that Detroit, despite favoring the rule in general, could have voted against it in Chicago, since the Tigers were coming off a year in which they nearly made the World Series and led the American League in attendance. They certainly wouldn't have had as much to gain if they believed the DH would increase attendance. On the other hand,

Detroit had Al Kaline, Gates Brown and Norm Cash, who each seemed to be a good fit for the new position.

For another of the three teams that missed the straw poll, the case for a "nay" vote is much clearer.

Before the Chicago meeting, papers reported that Boston Red Sox GM Dick O'Connell had heard that Minnesota's owner, Calvin Griffith, was in favor of the DH. O'Connell said he believed some owners were going to use their roster construction as a factor in deciding how to vote.

"Maybe such a change would be to the advantage of some teams now," O'Connell said. "Tony Oliva can't play every day for Griffith, and I'd like to have him as a designated pinch hitter, too."

Just after the rule passed, *The Daily Sentinel* reported that Boston was in fact one of the teams that opposed it because the Red Sox did not believe that anyone on their roster would be suitable in the role. The Red Sox immediately signed Orlando Cepeda, who was still a good hitter, but was coming off knee surgery. Many saw that signing solely as a reaction to the rule's passage.

In 1972, the Red Sox had been the dominant offensive team in the American League without the designated hitter rule. They ranked either first or second in runs, hits, doubles, triples, homers, total bases, and on-base percentage. They were the only team in the league that averaged over four runs a game (4.13). Given their success, both on the field and in the stands the year before, it's easy to see why their general manager would rather have kept the game the same.

Unlike the Red Sox, if the White Sox were one of the four teams that voted against the rule, they kept their ballot close to their chest.

A couple of days before the vote, the *Chicago Tribune* quoted the South Siders' counterpart, Cubs GM John Holland, as saying he liked the idea of a designated hitter because he felt it could bring excitement to the game. The paper also said Cubs front office officials, apparently not as reluctant to adopt the rule as other National League executives, had identified players on their team they felt would be good fits if their league ever played with the rule.

But, when the subject turned to Chicago's American League team, the paper reported that White Sox owner John Allyn was, "…not as outspoken about the merits of the designated pinch hitter…"

It's difficult to make a strong case that the Sox voted against the rule, but it's just as hard to find any evidence that they supported it. They were the only team in the AL West that finished within shouting distance of the A's in '72, and as noted earlier, they drew over a million fans that

Ten Worst DH Seasons

Player	Year	OPS
Alvin Davis	1991	.635
Dave Parker	1991	.653
Mitchell Page	1979	.657
Dave Kingman	1986	.686
Hank Aaron	1975	.687
Hideki Matsui	2011	.696
Alex Johnson	1973	.698
Lee May	1978	.700
Tommy Davis	1974	.702
Reggie Jackson	1984	.706

(Players qualified for batting title and played at least 70% of games at DH)

Source: Baseball Reference

season. The White Sox also signed Dick Allen, who was coming off a 37 home run season, to what was reported to be the richest contract in baseball at the time, just after the rule passed. White Sox general manager Stu Holcomb spoke of his hopes for Allen in the future and said , "...the designated pinch-hitter rule, if nothing else, will make him invaluable for a long time." They didn't seem like a team desperate for the designated hitter, but once it passed they quickly signed a player they thought might fill the position into the mid-'70s.

The search for another "nay" vote turns to an owner many considered unpredictable throughout the years for many reasons. Oakland A's owner Charles Finley had backed any proposals that might increase excitement in the game, as he was always in search of a boost in attendance. He supported interleague games and proposed a designated runner rule.

Of course, he backed the designated hitter as well. Some even consider Finley one of the founding fathers of the DH. Executives ranging from Selig to Griffith have listed him as a zealous proponent of the rule. "Charlie Finley was vehement that he wanted both the designated hitter and the designated runner," Griffith once noted.

But Finley, rabid supporter of the DH, may have actually voted against it in Chicago. Steven Riess wrote, in his *Encyclopedia of Major League Baseball Clubs*, that Finley voted against the DH because he was upset that the designated runner idea had been taken off the table. Finley may have also been frustrated that he had cut the injured Orlando Cepeda when the rule was shot down in December, only to see it brought back to life the next month when his best player to fill the role was gone.

Years later, Selig said Finley was a leading proponent of the DH, but also said that "He wanted both a designated hitter and designated runner." Could it be that Finley, stung by releasing Cepeda because he assumed a no-vote, and faced with the rejection of another pet project like the DR, voted down a rule he agreed with in principle just to spite those who would not accept his other proposals? It wouldn't have been the first time he did something like that.

Room for speculation likely exists because MLB, hoping to portray a unified stance, didn't want the voting record made available. Acting National League President, Charles S. (Chub) Feeney, noted later that those four nay votes in Chicago, when combined with his league's staunch refusal to adopt the rule from the beginning, meant that the American League was moving forward on this radical change when a majority of teams actually opposed it.

Of course, Feeney divulged that only at a time when he was pressed to explain why his league did not accept the rule. He also covered his bases, so to speak. After the vote, Feeney explained his and the league's decision to not take on the DH experiment by saying, "We like the game the way it is." But, he also said, "If it does work out, we wouldn't be hesitant to adopt it." That left the door open for a future trial if it proved successful, and perhaps toed the company line a bit.

He proved to be wrong on his league's acceptance of the rule at some point. The American League considered the DH a smashing success, and so voted to make it permanent following the 1973 season. But the closest the National League ever came to adopting the rule likely was in 1980, when it lost a tight vote at the summer meetings in Detroit. Although some at the time, like St. Louis Cardinals general manager Larry Claiborne, expected the rule to pass soon after that, it hasn't happened.

The vote may have been closer still, as one of the three teams (Houston, Pittsburgh and Philadelphia) that abstained almost voted yes.

Phillies executive Bill Giles said many in his organization were pushing for the NL to adopt the DH because it would put Keith Moreland and Greg Luzinsk in the lineup together. Phillies President Ruly Carpenter was against adopting the rule in principle, but instructed Giles to vote for it if he thought that was best for the Phils' roster in the coming season. Giles, afraid that the rule, even if voted in, would not take effect for the next season, could not pull the trigger and abstained. Pittsburgh executives, according to Giles, were going to vote whichever way he did, so they abstained as well. The vote ended up 5-4 against.

Even if the actual records of American League votes aren't clear from the Chicago meeting, the reasons a few of the teams changed their mind are. Roster construction was a factor when the voting strategy shifted to passing the rule in the American League only. General managers had to decide if the benefits outweighed the drawback of fighting for a playoff spot against teams better suited to start a DH. Owners of clubs that held an advantage over their daily competition due to better gate receipts had to wonder if the new rule would help their competitors more than it would help them. Nevertheless, the rule did pass, and the game changed for every team in the American League.

Run scoring in the AL improved 23 percent in the first year of the designated hitter rule. The American League outscored the National League in runs per game that year, and in 1975 started a streak of outscoring them that is still going strong following the 2011 season.

Another turnaround was the difference in league batting averages. In the first year of the DH, the American League not only ended the NL's nine-year run of topping them in average, but also started their own streak of outhitting the NL that also is still going through 2011.

According to research by the "Baseball Economist," JC Bradbury, the presence of a DH in the American League raises the likelihood of a batter being hit by a pitch by 11 to 17 percent. Why? Because of the law of demand.

For pitchers who don't have to bat, the "price" of hitting a batter is lower—the other team can't retaliate directly against them, only their teammates.

As economists like to say, when price goes down, demand goes up. And so has the rate of hitting batters in the American League since the introduction of the designated hitter.

Rob Neyer's All-Star DH's for Each Team:

BAL	Harold Baines
BOS	Jim Rice
CLE	Andre Thornton
CHW	Greg Luzinski
DET	Rusty Staub
KC	Hal McRae
LAA	Don Baylor
MIL	Paul Molitor
MIN	Chili Davis
NYY	Don Baylor
OAK	Geronimo Berroa
SEA	Edgar Martinez
TBA	Jose Canseco
TEX	Larry Parrish
TOR	Paul Molitor

From Rob Neyer's Big Book of Baseball Lineups, 2003

Some of the DHs Rob would probably consider putting on the list now are David Ortiz (Boston), Jim Thome (White Sox) and Travis Hafner (Cleveland).

Two of the closest years in averages between the two leagues were '75 and '76, when, many believe, the talent in the National League was superior. In 1976, the two leagues were nearly identical, with an AL slash line of .256/.320/.361 versus the NL's .255/.320/.361, despite the fact that the AL had the benefit in batting average from their DHs while NL pitchers batted.

Some estimates after passage of the rule showed that the designated hitters' contributions could account for as much as nine points in league-wide batting average. The typical advantage for the American League, since 1980, has been about seven points in batting average.

Nevertheless, the American League's attendance continued to fall far behind the NL's from 1973-1975, by an average of 26 percent fewer fans per season. The American League would narrow the gap by the end of the decade, while still remaining behind by at least 10 percent per year.

Attempts to correlate even the moderate improvement in attendance with the DH rule run into several problems. As Steve Treder pointed out in the 2004 edition of the *Hardball Times Baseball Annual*, owners who attributed the struggles of the American League to lower run-scoring were missing the bigger picture. There were many more differences in the two leagues in the '50s and '60s than their respective hitting. For one, the NL was quicker to integrate black players into the league, giving its teams a chance to find great players the AL might have ignored.

The National League's greater employment of minorities meant a deeper talent pool in which to find good players. As Treder pointed out, in 1960 there were more than twice as many black players in the NL as there were in the AL. By 1970, American League acceptance of minority players improved, but the margin was still nearly 25 percent in favor of the NL. Out of that larger number of players to draw from, the NL produced stars like Willie Mays, Hank Aaron, Frank Robinson and Bob Gibson.

There was also the addition of attractive ballparks and markets in the National League. By 1972, 10 of the 12 National League teams played in new stadiums. The NL was also first to stake claim to franchises in California and picked other attractive markets like Atlanta and Houston. Good markets led to higher attendance, which in turn led to more revenue, which the NL used to attract better players.

Many other confounding variables abound. While there's temptation to attribute the American League's eventual improvement in attendance to the DH, that rise wasn't really very profound in the immediate years after the DH came into existence. Factors such as competitive pennant races in the AL, a late-'70s return to dominance by the Yankees, and an arguably improved talent level likely had some effect on gate receipts. But even with those factors, added to the fact that they consistently outscored and outhit the National League, AL teams' attendance did not reach NL levels until the DH had already been around for nearly a decade.

Baseball had almost always been, with a few notable exceptions, dominated by conservative men, especially when it came to changes to the game's rules. But, two-thirds of the way through modern baseball's first century, some of baseball's higher-ups were interested, amidst the malaise attributed to suppressed hitting, in any idea that could increase attendance. The process of implementing to the DH rule that started in earnest following the 1972 season was not smooth. Some who favored the rule initially changed their minds when the commissioner amended the proposal to apply only to the American League.

Many executives have disagreed since. Following the 1995 season, a straw poll among American League owners and executives showed that franchises were split 7-7 on their support of the designated hitter. One executive, Wendy Selig-Prieb of the Brewers, opposed the rule even though her father had supported it so strongly over 20 years earlier. The players union, obviously wanting to protect their members who make a good living because of the rule, will likely continue to oppose abolishing the DH. There's likely no going back now.

One could argue that those in favor were proven right and that their acceptance of the designated hitter helped increase the popularity of the product in their league. However, a more compelling argument could be made that since the American League remained far behind in attendance in the years immediately following the new rule, the far-from-unanimous decision in 1973 continues to be a divisive issue in baseball.

Hitting may have seemed to the commissioner and to most AL executives the primary reason the National League was more popular, but while it may have played a role, its significance was not as great as they had assumed. The designated hitter exists because some American League executives mistakenly thought better hitting was the solution to all their problems.

Ron Blomberg, the very first DH, in 2003:

"I screwed up the game of baseball. Baseball needed a jolt of offense for attendance, so they decided on the DH. I never thought it would last this long." (From the *Journal News*)

Analysis

History's Greatest Hitters

by Adam Dorhauer

My grandpa once told me that Joe DiMaggio was the best player he ever saw. It was in the middle of a three-generation discussion about baseball history at my uncle's wedding reception. Someone or other was arguing about Mike Schmidt vs. Eddie Mathews, or some such thing, when he leaned over to me and said it.

"Joe DiMaggio." He smiled and nodded as he spoke the name.

I nodded back, though his answer caught me a bit off guard. The man had spent his childhood summers watching Stan Musial at Sportsman's Park (albeit as a Browns fan for the first half of Musial's career), and I know there was not another person at the table who would have put Joltin' Joe ahead of Stan the Man. Yet it was the dapper center fielder in the away greys who had captivated him most, more even than Musial. More even than Ted Williams, or, later on, than Mickey Mantle, Willie Mays, or Barry Bonds.

DiMaggio's career, I was aware, did not stack up to my standards for the game's upper echelon. Sensational though it was, he took the plate fewer times than Kirby Puckett and retired at age 36. His career WAR, even considering the three years he missed to the war, falls well short of the game's top marks. Musial himself was no Mays or Bonds, but he was at the level where someone who grew up idolizing him could understandably elevate him to that class. So Stan Musial I could have understood. Ted Williams? Sure. But not Joe DiMaggio.

There are many ways to approach the question of the best players in major league baseball history, however. One can talk about total production, rate production, production above average, production above replacement, career production, seasonal production, peak production, and enhanced protein production, using slash lines, linear weights, base runs, defensive metrics, and, of course, the good ol' eye test (but not RBIs).

Often when we talk about the best players in baseball history, we carry an implicit focus on career production. Even when we give extra consideration to a player's peak, the idea remains that the ones who do it the longest get the nod. After all, few would put Hank Greenberg and Hank Aaron in the same class as hitters, even if Greenberg, at his best, might have equaled Aaron in skill.

Many, however, are uncomfortable with the term "best" being synonymous with "highest career production." Call it the Koufax-Sutton problem, if you will. (This is, of course, a loaded way to refer to the dichotomy, given Koufax' legacy; substitute Darryl Strawberry or Ralph Kiner or whomever for Koufax, and maybe Eddie Murray for Sutton, and you might be better off). While Sutton may have amassed more pitching production over his career, he was never at any singular moment as good a pitcher as Koufax had once been.

It is at the Koufax end of the spectrum where one stops asking about career production and begins wondering instead which players achieved the highest level of talent at some point in their careers. These are the players you go to the ballpark just to see play, not because of whatever legacy they have carved or will carve for themselves in their careers, but because in that moment, they are better at what they do than anyone else has ever been. That was Joe DiMaggio to my grandfather.

What do the numbers say about this type of "best?" While career production is relatively straightforward to quantify (via WAR, wins above average, etc.), quantifying instantaneous talent is a bit more difficult. We can never know precisely how good a player is at any particular moment, nor precisely how his talent changes over time. We can, however, use the available data to estimate as best we can what a player's talent level is.

In order to estimate a player's talent level in a given season, we first need to understand the relationship between his observed stats and his underlying talent level. Obviously, a player's stats are heavily influenced by his talent level, but the two are not the same thing.

If Albert Pujols goes one-for-four with a homer in one game and then two-for-three with a walk the next, it does not mean that he suddenly got better at getting on base or worse at hitting for power. His stats for each game are distinct from his talent level on that day; rather, we infer from his performance in other games that Pujols is a highly-skilled hitter regardless of how he does in any individual game and accept that there is a lot of random variation in his day-to-day performance.

The longer you observe a player, the more his stats will reflect his underlying talent, but even over full seasons, a player's stats remain a mixture of his talent level and the random variation of his performance. The key to estimating his talent level is to determine how much random variation is associated with his performance and to separate the random variation from the influence of his underlying talent level.

In order to do this, we can learn from projection systems, which estimate player talent levels to project future performance. The most openly described such system, Marcel, outlines two important factors in interpreting player stats to infer talent: Incorporating multiple years of data and regression to the mean.

Specifically, Marcel looks at the past three years of data, weights the more recent seasons more heavily, and regresses that data toward the league mean to provide an estimate of a player's talent level at the present. Additionally, it includes an age adjustment to account for predictable changes in talent from year to year (namely, that players approaching or entering their prime are expected to improve while those beyond their prime are expected to decline).

Estimating talent levels for previous seasons works pretty much the same way, except that by focusing on past seasons instead of the coming one, we have access to data from both before and after the target year. For this model, I am using data from up to a five-year period (the target year, plus the two years before and after, when available). The target year is weighted most heavily, while the first and last years in the window are weighted the least. The exact weights given each year were determined using a multiple regression process similar to that described in Matt Crawford's article, "Estimating True Talent in Past Years," published on FanGraphs.com.

We can also get more accurate results by dividing each player's stats into various components and projecting his talent in each component separately. For example, a hitter's walk and strikeout rates over a given sample are more reflective of his talent than his batting average on balls in play, so we would want to regress those by different amounts rather than lumping them together and then projecting the hitter's overall performance all at once.

I divided each player's observed stats into seven distinct component rates. The first five rates, starting with HBP per PA, progressively remove the previous stat from the denominator in order to remove the direct dependencies of rates on each other (an idea from Voros McCracken's seminal work on DIPS). The final two deal with dividing hits between singles, doubles, and triples in order to reconstruct a complete stat line. The rates are:

- HBP per PA (excluding SH and intentional walks, when available)
- Non-intentional walks per PA-HBP
- Strikeouts per PA-HBP-BB
- Home runs per PA-HBP-BB-K (HR per contact PA)
- Hits per PA-HBP-BB-K-HR (BABIP)
- Extra-base hits per hit (excluding home runs)
- Triples per extra-base hit (again, excluding home runs)

Footnote:

About these Component Rates: Using PA as the denominator for all five rates, i.e. HBP/PA, BB/PA, K/PA, HR/PA, and H/PA, would require the sum of all rates (plus other outs per PA) to equal one, so when one rate decreases, another necessarily has to increase. Using progressive denominators removes this restriction so that changes in one rate don't necessitate offsetting changes in the other rates, which leaves us with a simpler model to consider.

- Adam Dorhauer

Footnote:

I don't have strikeout data for hitters from 1900-1912, so for those years, strikeout rate and BABIP are combined into one hit rate that regresses somewhere between the individual hit and K rates. The average regression constant for dead-ball era BABIP is 476; for 1900-1912, the average regression constant for the combined hit rate is 319.

- Adam Dorhauer

Each of these components was interpreted separately with unique park factors, aging curves, yearly weights, and regression components in order to estimate the player's talent in each of the seven rates.

Of these, a hitter's strikeout rate was the most closely linked to his underlying talent, with only about 40-50 at-bats required before the random variation in the observed rates becomes smaller than variation in talent between hitters. The practical implication of this is that once you have 40-50 AB, the talent level implied by a hitter's strikeout rate will be roughly halfway between his observed rate and the league average strikeout rate.

For example, if a league average hitter strikes out 20 percent of the time, and you observe a group of hitters each striking out 10 percent of the time over their first 40-50 AB, that same group of hitters, on average, is likely to continue to strike out about 15 percent of the time (halfway between what you observed and what you'd expect from an average hitter).

That 40-50 AB figure represents the regression constant, which is the amount of league-average performance you need to add to the hitter's observed rate to estimate his talent level. If you have 40-50 observed AB, then the league-average strikeout rate gets the same weight as the player's observed strikeout rate. If you have 500 observed AB, then the observed rate gets about ten times as much weight as the league average. Obviously, the more at-bats you observe from each hitter, the closer the implied talent level will be to whatever his observed rate is.

The other six rates had varying degrees of relationships to the hitter's underlying skill in that component. The numbers of opportunities required for each rate to reflect as much individual talent as random variation are listed in the following table. Since this value has varied over time for some stats, I have listed the average value over the past decade as well as the average value for the live- (1920-present) and dead-ball (1900-1919) eras as a whole.

Regression Constants

	Denominator	2001-2010	Live Ball	Dead Ball
HBP	PA	252	502	323
BB	PA-HBP	93	89	94
K	PA-HBP-BB	47	55	91*
HR	contact PAs	78	77	363
H	balls in play	754	681	375*
xBH	hits	174	208	108
3B	xBH	26	73	72

Note that the denominators for each rate get progressively more exclusive, so that, for example, 174 xBH opportunities take significantly longer to observe than 252 HBP opportunities. Hits per ball in play takes the longest to reflect a given level of talent; it takes about 25 percent longer for the observed BABIP to reflect the same amount of talent as xBH per hit, which is the next least linked to talent over a given amount of time or number of PA.

These figures are used to regress each player's observed stats to estimate his talent level. The next step (or previous step; it doesn't really matter what order you do it in) is to figure out exactly what numbers we are regressing for each player. This is less straightforward than it might seem; we not only have to figure out how much to weight the observations from adjacent years, we also have to translate those rates to the target year. This involves establishing park and age adjustments for each rate, and then adjusting the rate to the league average of the target year (using the Odds Ratio method).

Component Rate Peak Ages

	Peak Age
HBP	-*
BB	35
K	32
HR	28
H	23
xBH	25
3B	-*

* HBP/PA and triples per extra-base hit did not peak at all, instead decreasing every year.

Finally, once we have each player's five-year stats translated to the target year and properly regressed, we combine the rates to produce a full batting line and apply linear weights to value each player's line in terms of runs. (Linear weight values were derived based on the level of run-scoring for each season using the process published in Tom Tango's blog post "wOBA Year-by-Year Calculations" on InsideTheBook.com). We then normalize that run value to the league average by dividing by the run contributions of an average hitter (pitchers excluded) from the same league and season. This gives us a final rating on the same scale as wRC+ and OPS+.

The Results

Any stat posted by a baseball player is a glimpse into his true talent. To better estimate his true talent, you should regress that glimpse toward the mean to make sure you're giving proper weight to what you don't know.

As Tom Tango has put it: "Every observation is a sample of something true. Every observation is accompanied with good luck or bad luck. The further you are from the population mean, the more likely luck was involved. And if you did better than the mean, it was more likely it was good luck than bad luck. In order to strip out as much of the luck as you can, you regress the observation toward the population mean. This gives us our best estimate to the true mean, with a certain level of uncertainty."

So how do you determine how much someone's statistics regress towards the mean? The following math has been borrowed freely from Phil Birnbaum's blog, using team winning percentage as an example:

First, figure out the standard deviation of team performance. In major league baseball, for all teams playing at least 160 games up until 2009, that figure is 0.070 (about 11.34 wins per 162 games).

So who does the model say were the best hitters, relative to their league, of all time? Here are the top 10 (the rest of the top 100 are listed at the end of the article):

Rank	Year	Player	wRC+
1	2003	Barry Bonds	222
2	1921	Babe Ruth	215
3	1923	Rogers Hornsby	204
4	1946	Ted Williams	203
5	1929	Lou Gehrig	193
6	1914	Ty Cobb	189
7	1957	Mickey Mantle	188
8	1914	Tris Speaker	184
9	1998	Mark McGwire	183
10	1994	Frank Thomas	179

As one might expect, Bonds and Ruth top the list, followed by Hornsby and Williams. The list is not without its surprises, however. Dick Allen shows up at No. 17, the highest for an eligible non-McGwire non-Hall of Famer. (By the way, the Frank Thomas in the top 10 is not the one who hit Allen with a bat. I'm sure there was confusion about which Frank Thomas that was). Willie Stargell makes the top 15, and recent sluggers Jason Giambi and Gary Sheffield make the top 25 ahead of some of their more heralded contemporaries.

Of course, we should expect this sort of list to contain some surprise names that don't mesh with more career-centric player rankings. Baseball can be a volatile game where injuries, aging, and myriad other circumstances can derail even the most promising of careers. It stands to reason that not all of those who reached the highest levels at their peaks made it through long, productive careers.

One such player is Charlie Keller, ranking in the top 50 alongside such names as George Brett and Mike Schmidt, and not too far off from Frank Robinson and Hank Aaron.

Keller was an outfielder for the Yankees in the 1940s who, at age 26, was among the game's best hitters. He had just completed his fourth consecutive 100-walk season, and over the three years from 1941 to 1943, he led the majors in walks and home runs and trailed only Ted Williams in wRC+. In 1943, he trailed only Rudy York in home runs and only Stan Musial in wOBA, and he led in walks.

Keller missed most of the next two seasons to the war. He returned and had another big season in 1946, but he ruptured a disc in his back and was limited to part-time duty by age 30. He hung on a few more years as a bench player but finished his career with just 4,604 PA. He's basically an even more abbreviated version of Ralph Kiner (the notoriously short-careered slugger who makes the list at No. 27). Though his legacy has been mostly lost to the annals of baseball history, for a short time, Keller truly was an elite hitter.

We also see well-known players who tend to fall much lower in career ratings—such as Chuck Klein, Hack Wilson, and George Sisler—showing much better from this perspective. Other famously good but ill-sustained hitters who rated well include Johnny Mize (22nd), Al Simmons (32nd), Albert Belle (44th), Darryl Strawberry (72nd), Roger Maris (75th), Jose Canseco (81st), and Ken Williams (82nd).

At No. 34, we have the underappreciated Arky Vaughan (it took the better part of four decades after his retirement before Vaughan was elected to the Hall of Fame by the Veterans Committee). One of the truly spectacular shortstops in baseball history, Vaughan ranks ahead of even Alex Rodriguez and Honus Wagner, as well as ahead of DHs extraordinaire Edgar Martinez and David Ortiz. Basically, take a player who is great solely because of his ability to hit, add solid shortstop defense to his resume, and you've got Arky Vaughan.

On that note, it is important to keep in mind that these numbers are solely measures of hitting talent. Vaughan's defensive ability, including his position at shortstop, is not a factor in his ranking. Nor is Rickey Henderson's baserunning considered in his 153 wRC+ peak (No. 77 on the list). As such, this is just a subset of the necessary considerations for rating a player's overall abilities.

Even restricting consideration to hitting talent, there are limitations to these rankings. There are no adjustments for era other than normalizing to the league average. Treat these figures as you would OPS+ or wRC+ with regard to the effects of segregation, expansion, international talent, population growth, AL-NL disparity, etc., and add whatever additional adjustments you feel are warranted by those factors.

These are also not measures of actual production (though they are sorted by how well each player's talent level translates to run production, as opposed to more abstract interpretations of "most talented" such as "best pure hitter" or other such terms fans sometimes apply), nor are the peak seasons necessarily indicative of each player's "best" season. Many

Second, figure out the theoretical standard deviation of "luck" over a season, using the binomial approximation to normal. That's estimated by the formula:

Square root of $(p(1-p)/g)$

For baseball, $p = .500$ (since the average team must be .500), and $g = 162$. So the standard deviation of luck works out to about 0.039 (6.36 games per season).

So standard deviation (performance) = 0.070, and standard deviation (luck) = 0.039. Square those numbers to get variance (performance) and variance (luck). Then, if luck is independent of talent, we have:

variance (performance) = variance (talent) + variance (luck)

That means variance (talent) equals 0.058 squared, so standard deviation (talent) = 0.058.

Now, find the number of games for which the SD(luck) equals SD(talent), or 0.058. It turns out that's about 74 games, because the square root of $(p(1-p))/74$ is approximately equal to 0.058.

That number, 74, is your "answer." So, now, any time you want to regress a team's record to the mean, take 74 games of .500 ball (37-37), and add them to the actual performance. The result is your best estimate of the team's talent.

For instance, suppose your team goes 100-62. What's its expected talent? Adjust the record to 137-99. That gives an estimated talent of .581, or 94-68.

Or, suppose your team starts 2-6. Adjust it to 39-43. That's an estimated talent of .476, or 77-85.

Here is Phil's original blog post:

sabermetricresearch. blogspot.com/2011/08/ tango-method-of-regres- sion-to-mean-kind.html

- Dave Studenmund

The Odds Ratio

So let's say we've got a batter and a pitcher. Let's also say that we've regressed their stats to the mean, so that we have the best feel we can have for the "true talent" of these two players. And let's say that our best guess is that the batter is a .310 batter and the pitcher is a .240 pitcher (that is, batters hit .240 off him) in a league in which the overall batting average is .260.

What's the expected outcome of this matchup? .288.

How do I know? Well, I don't, really. But I've calculated it by using something called the Odds Ratio.

hitters' peak talent estimates do not coincide with their most productive seasons; for example, Bonds in 2003.

While Bonds had more productive seasons at other points in his dominant stretch in the early-to-mid-2000s, keep in mind that his season results are a combination of both his talent level in those seasons and variation in how far above or below his talent level he performs. What this model is saying is that Bonds was extremely talented throughout his run of dominance, and that it is more likely that the spikes in produc- tivity in the years surrounding 2003 were variation of his performance around his talent level than it was that his talent level rose sharply, dipped momentarily in 2003, and then jumped back up in 2004.

Rather, our best guess from the data is not that Bonds' talent peaked in 2001, when he was still on the rise from his previous seasons. Nor is our best guess that his talent peaked in 2004, when his production was on the verge of becoming simply great rather than historic. Our best guess is that Bonds' talent rose and then declined in a somewhat steady manner, and that the time we are most confident Bonds was at his best was in 2003, when he was a few years removed from his less historic numbers and everything he was doing for a several-year period was virtu- ally unparalleled.

Likewise, there are great single seasons that don't necessarily imply similarly great talent, even just for that season. While we are trying to pinpoint a player's talent level within a given season rather than measure his production over several years, we still can't take one anomalous season at face value. It is, of course, possible that some players really did reach high talent levels for a very brief period of time (such as a single season, or even part of a season), but it is more likely that a player with a big spike in production was simply playing well over his talent level than that his talent level rapidly shot up or down. Unfortunately, we cannot tell from a player's stats whether he is one of the few who truly did have an anoma- lous talent spike, so we instead make the best guess we can from the data.

Perhaps the most confounding issue with estimating a player's talent level is translating his numbers from one environment to another. The issue arises both in separating a hitter's performance from the influence of his home park and in accounting for changes in the league baseline from year to year. There are numerous ways to approach these transla- tions, all of which can lead to markedly different results when dealing with extreme cases.

Take, for example, Stan Spence. I have Spence peaking at 58 percent better than league average, which, despite including multi-year data and regression, is higher than either Baseball Reference or FanGraphs lists his best single-season OPS+ or wRC+. The park factors are culpable for the difference. In the mid-1940s, Griffith Stadium greatly suppressed hitters' component rates, especially home runs, to a larger extent than was reflected in run scoring. For example, in 1943, the Senators and their opponents scored 652 runs in Washington's home games and 609 in their road games, but hit only 23 home runs at home compared to 72 on the road.

As a result, while I get an unregressed single-season peak for Spence in the low 150s using run-based park factors (as Baseball Reference and FanGraphs use), that number shoots up to the high 170s with my component park factors. Furthermore, the Odds Ratio method I am using produces a larger adjustment than the additive park factors used by FanGraphs (I'm not sure about B-R; OPS+ uses a more complicated park adjustment process that I haven't examined enough to compare). Where Spence truly falls hinges on how you interpret the effects of Griffith Stadium.

A similar issue arises with Joe Jackson's 1914 season, in which I have him peaking despite his best years clearly being focused in the span from 1911-1913. Between 1912 and 1914, the American League batting average plummeted from .265 to .248. Such a dramatic change, coupled with the lack of strikeout data prior to 1913, make for a monumental task in trying to estimate how Jackson's .395 average in 1912 plays on the 1914 scale.

The resulting peak for Jackson in 1914 is not an indication that any of his talents improved in 1914, but rather that Jackson's immense batting average skill displayed in the earlier part of the decade was more valuable in the 1914 AL environment. Similarly, Jackson's top contemporaries—Ty Cobb, Tris Speaker, and Eddie Collins—also peaked in the 1914 AL. However, I strongly suspect this is a case of the Odds Ratio adjustment being ill-equipped for this specific translation rather than a real effect. As a result, the 1914 peaks are all probably a bit higher than they should be. Unfortunately, the sensitivity of extreme environmental translations is an issue beyond the scope of this article, and which has no clear answer. I have left these numbers untouched in the listed rankings, but if you ignore 1914, Jackson's peak falls at 164 in 1911 (though his 1912 estimate might actually be higher once you consider the likelihood that the translation from 1914 to 1912 is suppressing that estimate).

Beyond these translation issues, we still have some uncertainty inherent in our estimates. We can never fully separate the random variation of a player's performance from his talent level, and two players with the same talent estimate might in reality have had different levels of talent. While we can say from their numbers that we think Bonds peaked higher

The Odds Ratio is a formula to use whenever you want to find out the outcome between two percentages facing each other. Batting average is just one example. Another is figuring out what happens when a .450 team plays a .600 team. There are lots of potential uses of the Odds Ratio in baseball.

Here's the math: First, turn all your percentages into odds, so that .260 is .26/.74, .310 is .31/.69 and .240 is .24/.76. Let's call those A, B and C, respectively.

Then apply the following math: C*B/A. In other words, the pitcher's odds times (the batter's odds divided by the league average odds). In this case, the answer is 0.404.

This answer is expressed as odds, so you turn it back into batting average through this formula: (0.404/(1+0.404)). Or .288.

You can read more about the Odds Ratio at:

http://www.insidethe-book.com/ee/index.php/site/comments/the_odds_ratio_method/

- Dave Studenmund

The Bayesian method used here assumes a Beta prior, and the distribution of possible talent levels for each component follows a Beta Distribution with parameters $kp+s$ and $k(1-p)+n-s$, where k is the regression constant for that component, p is the population mean, s is the weighted number of observed successes for the player, and n is the weighted number of observed opportunities for the player. For a more detailed mathematical description, see my article, "Regression to the Mean and Beta Distributions" on 3-DBaseball.net.

- Adam Dorhauer

than Ruth, or that his performance implies a higher talent level, we can't be 100 percent certain. In fact, if we took 100 players who performed exactly like Bonds, and another 100 who performed exactly like Ruth, it's a near-certainty that some of the Ruth-like players would be better hitters than some of the Bonds-like players.

We can estimate how certain we are that Bonds was actually better than Ruth, assuming we've properly weighted and interpreted their numbers. The method of regression we use to estimate each player's talent level from his production is a shortcut for the more comprehensive Bayesian method. By using the Bayesian method, we can derive not only estimates of each player's skill in each component, but also full distributions of their possible skill levels. Using these distributions and assuming that each of the seven components is independent of the others, we can estimate the odds that one player was really better than another.

This was done using a simulation of 100,000 pairs of Ruth-like and Bonds-like players (hypothetical players with identical numbers and talent estimates to Ruth and Bonds) which randomly selected talent levels from their full distributions. In the sim, the Bonds-like player was better than the Ruth-like player 70 percent of the time, so the model suggests about a 70 percent likelihood that Bonds in 2003 was in fact a better hitter, relative to his league, than Ruth in 1921. Even with a seven-point difference in estimated wRC+ talent, there is still about a 30 percent chance that their true rankings are reversed.

We can run the same comparison for any pair of hitters. Hornsby's stats, for example, imply only a 54 percent chance that his peak was better than Williams'. Any pair of hitters so close in estimated talent is close to a toss-up in terms of ordinal ranking.

We can also run comparisons to see who the best hitters were in a given year. For example, in 1961, MVP runner-up Mickey Mantle comes out ahead of Maris 95 percent of the time. The 1998 season isn't even that close, with Sammy Sosa coming out ahead of McGwire just eight times in 100,000 simulations. (Bonds was closer, with an eight percent chance of being better than Mac that year.) Even if we assume Sosa's talent changed so drastically in 1998 that his more pedestrian '96 and '97 seasons tell us nothing about his talent level in 1998 (his 1998 talent estimate jumps from 137 to 150 if we give zero weight to those seasons), McGwire still comes out ahead 99 percent of the time.

Going back to the Musial/DiMaggio comparison, we can see that Musial has a 13-point advantage over DiMaggio in estimated peak wRC+ talent. Even that big an edge leaves about a 10 percent chance DiMaggio was better, so it is conceivable, if not all that likely, that the two were equals as hitters. The numbers certainly make a stronger case for Musial's bat; however, the case for DiMaggio doesn't require that he be a better hitter than Musial.

While DiMaggio could hit with anyone this side of Frank Robinson, he could also field better than most of the players ahead of him on the list. Without wading into the quagmire of trying to estimate defensive talent, we can still play around with some ballpark adjustments for defense. Ten points of wRC+ is worth roughly seven runs per 600 PA, so the difference between Musial's and DiMaggio's bats is about 10 runs over a full season. Given that the positional difference (center field vs. corner outfield) covers the majority of that, it's not hard to envision DiMaggio surpassing Musial in overall peak talent.

In fact, if you take an elite view of DiMaggio's defense, he stacks up pretty well with all but a handful of players listed. He may not make up much ground on Mays or Mantle, but sluggers like McGwire and Thomas are well within his range. In dealing with such an elusive measure as instantaneous talent, DiMaggio, along with several others, at least falls within the uncertainty of all but a few players in baseball history, and possibly every one of his contemporaries. No Mays or Bonds, to be sure, but he creeps into the conversation the same way Musial does on a career scale.

There is nothing in the numbers that precludes an argument for DiMaggio as one of the best to have played the game. At the very least, it's clear that watching him was something special. His rare combination of elite offense and highly-regarded defense may not have translated to a career to rival the Pantheon, but that does not deny his greatness.

In a game so rich in numbers, it is easy to dismiss that which is not readily quantified and to see the numbers as absolutes, as if they speak some infallible truth. But we give the numbers too little credit: They are complex tools to explore innumerable questions and untangle unknowable things. When the question is difficult, the numbers don't stop with the simplest answers.

When I nodded back at my grandpa's contention, I hadn't the heart to question him, but I couldn't agree. The numbers were far simpler than the question could ever allow. Now, digging deeper, the numbers peel away another layer of baseball history, exposing at the center another dozen names I'd never before considered, my grandpa's hero among them. It was not that the numbers defied my grandpa's answer; I was simply too caught up in the numbers I already knew to notice.

Ah, but, as Bob Dylan said of his own pseudo-certainty, "I was so much older then, I'm younger than that now."

The Greatest Batters in History at their Peak
Numbers 11-100

Rank	Year	Player	wRC+
11	1969	Willie McCovey	176
12	1950	Stan Musial	176
13	2010	Albert Pujols	174
14	1973	Willie Stargell	174
15	1934	Jimmie Foxx	173
16	1963	Willie Mays	172
17	1955	Eddie Mathews	171
18	1972	Dick Allen	171
19	1923	Harry Heilmann	171
20	1914	Eddie Collins	170
21	1926	Goose Goslin	169
22	1939	Johnny Mize	169
23	2001	Jason Giambi	169
24	1914	Joe Jackson	168
25	1996	Gary Sheffield	167
26	1966	Frank Robinson	167
27	1949	Ralph Kiner	167
28	1969	Harmon Killebrew	166
29	2002	Manny Ramirez	166
30	1996	Jeff Bagwell	166
31	1903	Nap Lajoie	165
32	1929	Al Simmons	165
33	1925	Jack Fournier	163
34	1935	Arky Vaughan	163
35	1963	Hank Aaron	163
36	1939	Joe DiMaggio	163
37	1974	Joe Morgan	163
38	1928	Hack Wilson	162
39	1969	Frank Howard	162
40	1907	Honus Wagner	162
41	1924	Edd Roush	161
42	1982	Mike Schmidt	161
43	1943	Charlie Keller	161
44	1994	Albert Belle	161
45	1981	George Brett	160
46	1921	George Sisler	160

Rank	Year	Player	wRC+
47	1997	Edgar Martinez	160
48	1967	Jimmy Wynn	160
49	2006	David Ortiz	159
50	1996	Mike Piazza	159
51	1955	Duke Snider	159
52	1985	Pedro Guerrero	159
53	1926	Paul Waner	159
54	1938	Hank Greenberg	159
55	2002	Jim Thome	158
56	1946	Stan Spence	158
57	1924	Bubbles Hargrave	158
58	1968	Carl Yastrzemski	157
59	2000	Sammy Sosa	157
60	2000	Chipper Jones	157
61	1969	Roberto Clemente	157
62	2000	Brian Giles	156
63	1932	Chuck Klein	156
64	1914	Frank Baker	156
65	1946	Jeff Heath	155
66	1938	Mel Ott	155
67	1973	John Mayberry	154
68	1994	Ken Griffey	154
69	1977	George Foster	154
70	2000	Carlos Delgado	154
71	1915	Gavvy Cravath	154
72	1987	Darryl Strawberry	154
73	1946	Roy Cullenbine	154
74	2007	Alex Rodriguez	153
75	1961	Roger Maris	153
76	1990	Fred McGriff	153
77	1990	Rickey Henderson	153
78	1970	Rico Carty	153
79	1939	Dolph Camilli	153
80	1987	Jack Clark	152
81	1990	Jose Canseco	152
82	1922	Ken Williams	152
83	2010	Miguel Cabrera	152
84	1991	Kevin Mitchell	151

Rank	Year	Player	wRC+
85	2006	Travis Hafner	151
86	1972	Ron Blomberg	151
87	1977	Reggie Smith	151
88	1981	Eddie Murray	151
89	1950	Sid Gordon	151
90	1929	Earl Averill	151
91	1933	Wally Berger	151
92	1963	Orlando Cepeda	151
93	1925	Rube Bressler	151
94	1966	Ron Santo	151
95	1981	Dave Winfield	151
96	1999	Larry Walker	151
97	1925	Kiki Cuyler	151
98	1979	Oscar Gamble	150
99	2003	Todd Helton	150
100	2000	Vladimir Guerrero	150

Down with Other People's Players

by Matt Swartz

In 1991, Naughty by Nature released the chart-topping single, "O.P.P." declaring that they were "Down with O.P.P." As they explained, "O is for Other, P is for People's. The Last P, well, that's not that simple." In this article, I will look at the case where the last "P" is for "Players," and ask when signing or trading for a player belonging to another team is wise.

When a team attempts to trade a player, it must have more information on him than the potential buyer. Similarly, when a player reaches free agency, his former club must have more knowledge about him than potential new teams. How could it not? It has employed him and worked with him daily.

But does this extra information matter? Does another team's extra knowledge about a player affect the market? Should GMs think twice before signing a free agent from another team? Should they wonder why the other team is so willing to trade that highly ranked prospect?

Yes, a thousand times, yes. Here's how we know.

Free Agents

Teams that sign their own players to free agent contracts get better deals than those who sign free agents from other teams.

I began by looking at free agent contracts lasting at least two years, and comparing the performance of players who were re-signed by their clubs with that of players who were newly signed (which I will subsequently call "OPP" or "Other People's Players"). Multi-year deals are particularly useful to look at, because these players were typically strong enough to be regular contributors, and because one-year deals are often non-guaranteed deals or deals with options that affect their true value significantly.

Free agent deals shine light on how much value teams place on these players, since teams put an actual dollar amount on their willingness to pay for them. Another useful property of multi-year deals is that any private information a player's former team may have been able to gather on his expected aging trajectory would show up in its willingness to pay as well, since many bidding wars for free agents end when one team decides not to add an extra year to its offer. Teams' beliefs about both current talent level and future talent level affect the offers a player's former team and potential

Collectively, teams who signed players from other teams to deals of two-to-four years did poorly, but some teams were particularly suckered in by lemons.

Nobody signed more OPP to new deals than the Giants, who spent $130.55 million to generate just 9.3 WAR in this sample. These deals included two-year deals to Rich Aurilia, Jeremy Affeldt, Edgar Renteria, Mark Sweeney, Steve Kline and Ray Durham, and three-year deals for Omar Vizquel, Armando Benitez, Dave Roberts, Randy Winn, Matt Morris and Bengie Molina. The only players who managed to significantly out-produce their contracts were Winn with 9.0 WAR for $23.25 million and Vizquel with 6.4 WAR with $12.25 million. The biggest disasters were to Renteria, Roberts, Morris and Durham.

new team will offer. When a player's former employer stops bidding, does that tell us something?

Using data on all 196 of the mutli-year contracts that ended after the 2007 through 2010 seasons, I gathered the total salary and the total production according to WAR as listed on Baseball Reference.com (commonly referred to as "rWAR") of players in both the group of re-signed players (RSP) and the group of newly signed players (OPP).

Throughout this section, I will examine how much money teams paid for each Win Above Replacement. This approach allows us to put all players on the same scale and, since teams essentially pay for wins when they sign free agents, this can be considered the ultimate way to judge a contract. We'll call the difference between WAR costs for OPP compared to WAR costs for RSP the "OPP Premium."

I found that teams pay 39 percent more for Other People's Players than for their own players. This was true across all contract lengths, as you can see in this table:

Millions of Dollars per WAR

Type	N	RSP	OPP	Diff
All	196	$4.9	$6.8	39%
Two Year	95	$8.8	$12.7	44%
Three-Year	59	$4.2	$13.5	221%
Four-Year	24	$5.1	$5.6	10%
Five-Year+	18	$3.9	$5.1	31%

Don't be too concerned with the differences between contract lengths. With sample sizes this small, we could be seeing random differences. On the other hand, longer deals may have smaller OPP Premiums because of the overall price—for example, the Expos were not going to re-sign Vladimir Guerrero, no matter how much their inside look made them covet him. The bottom line is that, across all contract lengths, teams paid more for Other People's Players than for their own. A lot more. The OPP Premium is large.

The ages of the RSP and OPP groups were not significantly different, by the way.

This is especially true of pitchers.

While the evidence appears strong in the tables above, it is important to break down these deals further into hitters and pitchers (and into starting and relief pitchers) to see if the OPP Premium is larger for hitters or pitchers, and what that can tell us about the cause of this trend.

Millions of Dollars per WAR

	N	RSP	OPP	Diff
All	196	$4.9	$6.8	39%
Hitters	104	$4.7	$5.5	17%
Starting Pitchers	44	$5.5	$10.5	93%
Relief Pitchers	46	$4.5	$10.8	139%

While teams pay more for OPP in both cases, this chart shows just how badly teams have cost themselves while dabbling in other people's pitchers. The OPP Premium for hitters is 17 percent, while it is 93 percent for starting pitchers and 139 percent for relief pitchers. Given that teams may have more inside information about health and aging for pitchers (who wear down more easily and suddenly than hitters) it is not surprising that pitchers show a larger OPP bias.

I also looked at two-year deals only, and found that hitters actually had a larger OPP Premium than pitchers. In particular, there was only a nine percent difference between re-signed and newly signed starting pitchers. This is likely a sample size issue, but it could be that pitchers sometimes trick new teams into giving them third years that they do not deserve, but when they are unable to get any teams to bite on a three-year deal, they are otherwise similar in production.

Three-year deals for starting pitchers resulted in the highest OPP Premium. There were 10 three-year deals that enticed starting pitchers to change teams, and eight of them were disasters. Going over the details of these deals may prove insightful.

Eric Milton produced -1.3 WAR during 2005-07 in a three-year deal with the Reds for $25.5 million. He was not the only pitcher who was below replacement level in a three-year deal. The Giants allowed the Dodgers to sign Jason Schmidt for 2007-09, and he made only 10 total starts in L.A. His total WAR was -0.6 despite earning $47 million.

Matt Morris produced -1.3 WAR for $27 million, too. Adam Eaton had -1.6 WAR in a disastrous three-year, $24.51 million deal with the Phillies, from which he was released after two years. He proceeded to play below replacement level in the last year of his deal with the Orioles and Rockies, still on the Phillies' dime. Those are four of the 10 deals given to starting pitchers for three years, totaling $124 million spent without one of them peeking above replacement level.

Of the other six deals with new teams that went to players who managed replacement level performance, four still went badly. Jon Lieber

The Giants weren't the only team with lemons on their hands. The Orioles signed eight OPP and spent $109.5 million to get just 11.7 WAR, including three simultaneous three-year deals for 2007 to 2009 for relievers Jamie Walker, Chad Bradford and Danys Baez on whom they spent $41.5 million for 3.8 WAR. The Royals spent $80.35 million for a total of only 0.7 WAR, staying short with two-year deals, but still not propelling the team forward.

The Dodgers had just 16.3 WAR to show for the $170.3 million they spent on OPP, but 12.7 WAR came from a four-year deal given to Derek Lowe. Otherwise, they went for some of the most famous lemons—deals given to Andruw Jones and Jason Schmidt. Meanwhile, the Phillies got only 2.2 WAR for the $93.81 million they spent, throwing two-year deals away at aging hitters like Geoff Jenkins, Pedro Feliz, Abraham Nunez and Wes Helms, while getting tricked into three-year deals for pitchers Tom Gordon, Jon Lieber and Adam Eaton.

had only 3.2 WAR for $21 million with the Phillies, Miguel Batista had just 0.3 WAR for $25 million with the Mariners, Jaret Wright mustered 0.6 WAR for $21 million for the Yankees, and Esteban Loaiza had 0.6 WAR for $21.38 million with the A's.

Jason Marquis was okay but not amazing in a three-year deal with the Cubs, in which he earned $21 million for 5.1 WAR. The one good deal among these 10 was one given to A.J. Burnett, in which he produced 7.6 WAR for $31 million in a three-year deal, and then left town after declining his two-year player option.

On the other hand, there were 10 three-year extensions, and only three of them went badly, while the rest went either well or very well.

Roy Halladay provided the most production of the bunch, generating 20.5 WAR for $40 million. Javier Vazquez managed 8.0 WAR for $34.5 million, Livan Hernandez had 5.9 WAR at a cost of $21 million, Kelvim Escobar produced 5.2 WAR for $28.5 million, Freddy Garcia had 7.2 WAR for $27 million, and Josh Beckett had 6.5 WAR for $30 million.

On the other hand, Odalis Perez's $33.75 million bought only 1.1 WAR, Jake Westbrook produced 1.4 WAR for $33 million, and Vicente Padilla got paid $33.75 million for just 1.1 WAR. However, the frequency of terrible deals was far lower in the group of re-signed players.

Taking all of these deals together, it's obvious that something is going on. Re-signed players are signing for fewer dollars per win than newly signed players by a large margin, and this holds especially true for pitchers. Figuring out the reason why is the next step.

Previous team's competitiveness does not the affect OPP Premium.

Suppose you are a general manager and you find yourself negotiating with one of these Other People's Players. All the tables above should warn you about why the player's old team is not putting up a fight. After all, if the hypothesis is that teams re-sign only the players who are smart bets to maintain their production and health, maybe you should be trying to figure out why the player is being let go.

For that reason, I hypothesized that you might learn something by trying to find other reasons why the player's old team isn't putting up much of a fight. Maybe we're talking about a small-market team or a rebuilding team that just isn't interested in getting the last few good years out of a guy on the wrong side of 30? If so, then we would expect that teams that finished under .500 the previous season would let their players go more often even if they thought they were healthy.

My guess was that the OPP bias would be larger for players on teams who finished over .500 last year, but I was wrong. Players on teams below .500

actually were among the best if they re-signed, while the worst deals went to signing other people's players who were on .500-plus teams the year before.

Millions of Dollars per WAR

	N	RPP	OPP
Below .500	57	4.6	10.9
Above .500	121	5.8	8.4

(Note: For this table, I excluded all deals longer than four years, since previous season performance of previous teams had little to do with expectations of competitiveness five years down the line.)

Players give hometown discounts, but not large enough discounts to explain the OPP Premium.

Another possibility for the cause of this OPP bias is the so-called "hometown discount." Certainly this will not apply to all players. Regarding his upcoming negotiations on his contract after the 2012 season, Brandon Phillips told a *Cincinnati Enquirer* reporter, "There's no homeboy hookup. That ain't going to work. I want to be paid what I'm worth." However, in other cases, there may be a "homeboy hookup." Instead of other teams misjudging OPP, perhaps players are choosing to sign for less with their own teams.

Naturally, players who do this will be unlikely to wait around for free agency if they are willing to give their clubs a bargain anyway, so I separated re-signings into those made before the season ended and those made afterward, so that I could compare re-signings and OPP signings of players who reached free agency.

There are often very large bargains provided by players willing to sign early, but even among players who reach free agency, there is still a staggering 35 percent OPP bias, albeit smaller than the overall 65 percent OPP bias of two-to-four year deals. OPP still cost more per win than re-signed players who reach free agency for two-year, three-year, and four-year deals.

Millions of Dollars per WAR

	N	Cost
Re-signed early	41	4.6
Re-signed off-season	43	6.6
OPP	94	8.9

(Note: For this table, I excluded all deals longer than four years as well, since all but one extension over four years was signed in advance.)

The Marlins and Braves each let eight players depart on two-to-four-year deals. The Braves' ex-players earned $153.4 million for 8.8 WAR, including disappointments avoided by not re-signing Jaret Wright and Andruw Jones, and not getting stuck on relievers like Kyle Farnsworth and Danys Baez. While they may not have been known for being stingy because they expecting their players to fall apart, the Marlins who left town managed just 22.3 WAR for the $167.4 WAR they earned.

The Phillies and Yankees both spent a lot of money, but each of them let four lemons go as well. The Phillies' lemons (Billy Wagner, Eric Milton, Pat Burrell, David Dellucci) produced 3.9 WAR for $96 million for other clubs, and Yankees' flops produced 3.7 WAR for $74.5 million, including Jon Lieber and Tom Gordon who signed with the Phillies, Luis Vizcaino and Gary Sheffield. (They refused to entrust Sheffield with a three-year deal when he demanded an extension, and instead succumbed to his demand to be traded and extended, making him a pseudo-free agent.)

Not to be outdone, the D-backs let five players (Miguel Batista, Adam Dunn, Juan Cruz, Craig Counsell, Richie Sexson) earn a total of $107 million elsewhere, combining for only 9.0 WAR.

Of course, it remains possible that players who reach free agency and re-sign may be using the bidding process to get a better deal from their original team, but still may be giving a discount. I was able to get a handful of employees of player agencies to give me some not-for-attribution answers on this topic, so I asked two questions:

1) How often do players who reach free agency and re-sign have a better offer on the table from a new team?

2) When such a player gives a bargain, how much does he leave on the table?

The answers from different people varied wildly. Some people said that this almost never happens, while others said that it happens quite frequently. One even suggested that it was common for a player to pick a new team in a location he preferred. Cliff Lee in December 2010 actually signed with the Phillies, whom he had played for in 2009, for less money than he was offered by Texas, where he finished 2010. Other players choose to live in their original hometown.

One source said hometown discounts occur with about 20-25 percent of players who re-sign, and that it tends to be a deal that is one year shorter and/or $1 million less per season. With that in mind, I re-visited OPP signings on three-year and four-year deals and approximated how these players' deals would have looked if you removed their (often disappointing) last seasons, and reduced their contracts by one year and $1 million per year.

The three-year deals averaging $15.2 million per win turned into two-year deals averaging $9.0 million per win. The four-year deals averaging $5.6 million per win turned into three-year deals averaging $5.0 million per win. These numbers are even better than the $10.5 million per win spent on re-signed players who signed two-year deals with their previous teams after the season ended, and the $5.2 million per win spent on re-signed players who reached three-year agreements after the season ended. However, when incorporating the fact that this does not seem to happen more than 25 percent of the time, the re-signings of players who reached free agency were still much better deals than OPP signings.

Overall, it appears that the hometown discount is real and nontrivial. Sources say it matters a lot, and early re-signings suggest that it is consequential when it does happen. However, the magnitude is unlikely to explain away the enormous OPP Premium.

A Quick Summary

Combining everything that we have learned from the contracts studied above, we can be confident of several things:

- The OPP Premium exists: Teams pay 39 percent more for the same production from other teams' free agents.

- The OPP Premium is particularly strong for pitchers: Teams pay 93 percent more for starters and 139 percent more for relievers, but only 17 percent more for hitters.

- Part of the reason for the OPP premium is probably the hometown discount that players are willing to give to their teams, but this can explain only a fraction of the OPP Premium.

- The rest of the effect probably has to do with the fact that teams know their own players better, since it is larger for pitchers (for whom private information is likely to be more important), and larger for two- and three-year deals (which virtually all original teams can afford if they think they have good reason to expect the player will be good) than for longer deals.

Contracts are only part of the story, so let's take a better look at what an outsider might expect a player to produce from the numbers alone. Do teams know more about their own players than a savvy projection system would know?

Re-signed hitters do not beat projections any better than newly signed hitters.

I asked Brian Cartwright for his multi-year Oliver projections from previous seasons so that I could compare projections and actual performance for the re-signed players and newly signed players in this study. Once again, I excluded deals longer than four years, since projections are difficult for that time frame, and a few other projections for players were unavailable for various reasons.

Weighting everything by plate appearances, I combined the 90 contracts given to hitters into overall wOBAs and Oliver-projected wOBAs and found little difference based on whether a player re-signed. Even though hitters who signed with new teams received a 17 percent premium in dollars per win ($5.5 million versus $4.7 million), they did not differ significantly in how they performed relative to their Oliver projections.

Re-signed hitters beat their projections by 1.5 points and OPP hitters beat them by 2.9 points, which is well within what we would expect from random variation. The apparent contradiction between the 17 percent

---

Top Five Prospects

Only a few top five prospects were traded, but those who were failed to produce as much as top five prospects whose teams would not let them go.

Delmon Young was the only No. 1 prospect traded (he also was ranked No. 3 in 2004, 2005 and 2007 as well as No. 1 in 2006), and his career has yet to flourish. He was still seen as very promising at the time of his trade, which is why the Twins were willing to part with Matt Garza and Jason Bartlett in the six-player deal headlined by Young.

He already had some question marks on his record, particularly with respect to his makeup. He had flipped a bat at an umpire in a Triple-A game, but the Twins said at the time of the trade that they felt this was one unique blemish on an otherwise solid record. Issues or not, his actual performance has been far below that of the other 17 prospects that topped the *Baseball America* rankings between 1990 and 2007. These 17 guys averaged 33.1 WAR in contrast with the -0.1 WAR Young had through 2010.

Paul Konerko was the only No. 2 prospect traded, and he actually had 25.6 WAR through 2010. He and Dennys Reyes were traded for reliever Jeff Shaw, who managed just 4.3 WAR over three and a half seasons with the Dodgers after the trade.

Ruben Rivera was a No. 3 prospect, but he was traded within two years of his ranking and produced only 5.4 WAR in his career. Edwin Jackson was ranked No. 4 with the Dodgers in 2004, but was traded in January of 2006. Through 2010, he only had 7.6 WAR. Bruce Chen was also a No. 4 prospect who did not reach the type, producing 6.0 WAR through 2010.

OPP Premium and the negligible wOBA difference may be random statistical variation or a hometown discount, or it might just be that a few teams would have benefited from using Oliver instead of their own projection systems.

Of course, performance is only part of the puzzle; staying healthy is the other issue. For that reason, I looked at Oliver's projected plate appearances for hitters and their actual PA during these deals. Actual PA were about 80 short of projections for re-signed players and 77 short for newly signed players.

Thus, we can conclude that in terms of both performance and playing time, there is little difference among hitters who signed with new teams versus hitters who re-signed with their previous teams in their abilities to beat their Oliver projections.

Re-signed pitchers beat their projections, while newly signed pitchers fall short of their own.

I looked at projected ERA vs. actual ERA for pitchers who re-signed and pitchers who signed with new teams to see if teams could predict their own pitchers' future performances better than other teams. The OPP Premium of 93 percent for starters and 139 percent for relievers certainly suggests this is true, but looking at how a projection system would predict future pitching performance was also illuminating. Teams were decidedly better at picking which pitchers they wanted to keep around.

Pitchers who signed with new teams fell short of their projections by seven points (4.23 expected, 4.30 actual), while pitchers who re-signed beat their projections by eight points (4.16 expected, 4.08 actual). The OPP bias for pitchers probably does have to do with teams knowing their own pitchers' likely future performances better than a projection system could.

Does the same fact hold true for pitcher health? Do teams know their own pitchers' likely future health better than other teams in the league? These answers seem less clear. Overall, the difference is similar, with pitchers throwing 28 fewer innings than projected if they re-signed with their old clubs, and 22 fewer innings than projected with new clubs. The difference between WAR for other people's pitchers and re-signed pitchers has more to do with beating expected performance than health.

Pitching is very different from hitting, because the injury risk is much higher and because pitchers' performances decline more rapidly than hitters'. If you listed the best hitters in the league a few years ago and did so again today, you would probably have two lists that look pretty similar. However, if you did the same with pitchers, your list from today would not look much like your list from a few years ago at all. We come up with theories like Defense Independent Pitching Statistics to try to get better at understanding pitching, but drop-offs in performance seem unexpected and sudden for many pitchers. However, it seems that these drop-offs are not so unexpected for the people who work with these hurlers every day.

Interestingly, it was not injuries that seemed to be the secret that private information revealed, because innings pitched were similarly short of expectations for re-signed pitchers as newly signed pitchers. However, this may be that newly signed pitchers should have been rested more and were less forthcoming about injuries, so these two factors are more intertwined than they might seem.

Trades and Lemons

Free agency is not the only way players change teams. Often, they are traded too. If the reason for the OPP Premium is that teams know their own players better and choose to let them leave town, then players who are traded should also be similarly unproductive upon leaving town. GMs will sell high on players likely to decline quickly, or on prospects who have holes in their swings or flaws in their deliveries that coaches who watch them every day are able to notice.

We would expect that players who are traded will underperform projections more than players who stay on the same team. Guess what. This is exactly what happens.

Everyday players and starting pitchers both fall short of projections more often after being traded.

Dozens and dozens of small trades every year involve players who do not reach the big leagues, and they are often poorly documented. In an effort to study only major trades in a systematic way, I focused only on players who had 500 plate appearance in the previous season and pitchers who had 160 innings pitched in the previous season. While this will remove relievers, it also will remove any insignificant trades. I also restricted my study only to players traded during the offseason to avoid the issue of midseason projections.

There were 40 hitters with 500 PA and 32 pitchers with 160 IP who were traded during the offseasons before 2005-2010. Of course, looking at how these players did compared to their projections will tell only part of the story, and a test group is required. Fortunately, I had Oliver projec-

There were also a bunch of No. 5 prospects who had various levels of success in their careers: Brad Penny (20.2 WAR), Sandy Alomar Jr. (13.2), Carlos Pena (13.1), Brian Hunter (7.0), and Joel Guzman (-0.5). Collectively these No. 5 prospects averaged 10.6 WAR, as compared with 13.6 WAR produced by the 13 No. 5 prospects who stayed put.

- Matt Swartz

tions available for all players who had 500 PA or 160 IP the previous year to use as a control group.

Remember that we had somewhat ambiguous findings about hitters when studying free agency. On one hand, there was a 17 percent OPP Premium; on the other hand, there was no real difference in projections between re-signed and newly signed pitchers. So, do teams know their own hitters better or not? Looking at hitters who were traded should push us in one direction or the other.

Overall, the 892 players who got 500 PA or more beat their Oliver projections for wOBA by a solid eight points and their PA projections by 60. However, the 40 hitters who were traded fell short of their projected wOBAs by two points and 38 PA. This means that knowing that a player was traded should lower your expectation for his performance by 10 points of wOBA and 98 PA.

	All w/ 500 PA	All traded w/ 500 PA
Actual wOBA	.351	.336
Oliver wOBA	.343	.338
Actual PA	616	527
Oliver PA	556	565

We know that pitchers already had a hefty OPP Premium—re-signed players produced about twice as much per dollar as OPP. Not only that, a pitcher had a .15 higher ERA (relative to his projection) if he signed with a new team than if he re-signed. Unsurprisingly, pitchers also showed a large difference in performance if they were traded. Traded pitchers fell .22 short of their Oliver projected ERA, despite the control group beating projected ERA by .14.

Innings showed an even larger difference. Traded pitchers fell 31 innings short of their projections, while the control group exceeded projections by 27 IP. Although there was no discernable difference in IP for free agents based on whether they were re-signed, traded pitchers did throw significantly fewer innings than untraded pitchers (relative to their projections).

Teams probably were able to detect injury risks that would not be observable to an outside projection system and send those players away in advance. The large difference in both ERA and IP shows again how much knowing your own pitchers can play an important role in OPP bias—simply the knowledge that a pitcher was traded should lower your expectation for his performance by .38 of ERA and 58 IP.

	All w/ 160 IP	All traded w/ 160 IP
Actual ERA	4.08	4.48
Oliver ERA	4.22	4.26
Actual IP	198	157
Oliver IP	171	188

This is very strong evidence that teams know their own players—hitters and pitchers—better than even reasonable forecast systems do. Caveat emptor.

Highly ranked prospects who are traded are more likely to be busts than the highly ranked prospects that teams retain.

Full-time regulars and established starting pitchers may be lemons whom their owners try to trade away, but what about prospects? Are elite prospects more likely to be traded if there is a flaw in their game that only their own teams have discovered?

To answer this, I gathered *Baseball America's* Top 20 Prospects from every offseason between 1990 and 2007, totaling 360 seemingly elite prospects. I found 50 who were traded within two seasons of their elite ranking and 27 who were traded within one season of their elite ranking. Then I gathered all career WAR through 2010 (which naturally abbreviated more recent prospects' careers more than those from previous seasons), and compared the distribution of career WAR among traded and untraded prospects.

Prospects who were traded within two seasons of their ranking were not much more likely to be lower ranked—they averaged a rank of 11.1 as compared with untraded prospects' rank of 10.4. However, the average WAR of traded prospects was just 7.5, and untraded prospects averaged a WAR of 17.1.

Some of this was undoubtedly due to very strong performance by a handful of top prospects, but even the median WAR for the traded group was less than that of the untraded group by a margin of 5.4 to 9.9. Overall, the biggest difference was the number of elite prospects who managed 15 WAR, which 42 percent of untraded prospects were able to do, but only 18 percent of traded prospects did.

	Traded	Untraded
Count	50	310
Rank Average	11.1	10.4
Average WAR	7.5	17.4
Median WAR	5.4	9.9
% Prospects with >5 WAR	54%	64%
% Prospects with >10 WAR	38%	49%
% Prospects with >15 WAR	18%	42%
% Prospects with >20 WAR	14%	33%

I also looked at only the 27 players traded within one year of their elite ranking, since two lackluster years in a row might have encouraged a team to make a change-of-scenery trade, but this would be especially unlikely for players who were traded while their ranking was no more than one season old. Therefore, this could potentially be a more appropriate test if not for the smaller sample size of traded players.

These players still were far less likely to have great careers if they were traded, but the frequency of traded and untraded players who failed to produce 10 WAR was very similar. However, while half of each group of players reached 10 WAR, 31 percent of untraded players reached 20 WAR as compared with 22 percent of traded players.

I also ran tests on more specific subsets of prospects, looking at those ranked 1-5, 6-10, 11-15, and 16-20 separately. Each untraded group had a higher average WAR than traded prospects, whether "traded" was defined as being traded within two years or within one year.

Regardless of the test we run, prospects who are traded are less likely to pan out than similarly ranked prospects who teams do not let go. Teams are better able to tell which of their own minor leaguers are going to succeed than other teams' scouts, who see them less frequency.

Other People's Players and where to go from here

So we've seen solid evidence that teams know their own players (and particularly pitchers) better than other teams and outside forecast systems do. We have seen evidence that teams pay about 39 percent more for the same production when signing Other People's Players than when re-signing their own players. Hitters cost 17 percent more per win if they signed elsewhere, while starting pitchers cost 93 percent more, and relief pitchers cost 139 percent more.

We have seen that pitchers fall short of their projected ERAs upon leaving town, while they exceed their projected ERAs when their old teams retain them. We have seen that traded pitchers fall short of projections by an even larger margin than free agent pitchers do upon leaving their team, and that even traded hitters fail to beat projections as much as untraded hitters do. Traded prospects even succeed less frequently than similarly ranked prospects who are not traded. Across the board, there is evidence that teams know their own players better, and this is reflected in their decision-making.

Finding such an extreme effect is surprising for a researcher, and there are a few things to do when you find it. First, check your data. Believe me: I have. Second, splice your data into smaller subsets to see if outliers are driving the results, or if the results hold for only certain players. Outliers were not a factor, but putting the data into smaller subsets did allow us to learn that pitchers do seem to be a bigger piece of the OPP Premium puzzle than hitters. Third, we need to wonder if teams already know this is going on.

So let's do a thought experiment. Suppose that all teams were aware that players were under-producing on a production per dollar basis upon signing elsewhere. What could they do about it? If the answer is hometown discounts, then there would be nothing teams could do and these discrepancies in production per dollar would continue. However, the difference in performance among traded players rules this out, as does the fact that players who reached free agency before re-signing still produced far less than players who signed early. If changing teams caused a player to perform worse than if he stayed put, then the OPP Premium may continue being large, since players could not tell their teams that they needed to pay up to retain them. Their teams would just counter by saying that other teams won't pay as much for inferior production, so they might as well take the same money to stay in town and be happy to be able to play better.

However, suppose players are usually willing to leave town, that leaving town is not the cause of inferior performance, and that the OPP Premium is only symptomatic of teams knowing which players to keep. Agents could then begin to demand higher salaries from hometown teams when they are willing to re-sign players. Similarly, agents would no longer be able to coerce higher salaries from other teams. Those teams would know that if they won the auction for a player's services, there was probably a disappointing reason why. Even if teams know they are getting less than it seems for other people's players and are willing to spend more because of limited supply, agents will capitalize on this and extract more from hometown teams, rather than let hometown teams sign them for less than the market will bear if they wait.

If teams were aware of this looming inferior production, knew that it wasn't caused by leaving town, and players were willing to switch teams, than the market would have adjusted already. The prices would have risen for re-signed players and fallen for newly signed players. As this information becomes more widespread, this may be exactly what happens.

What will happen to trades if teams start to realize they have been getting less than they thought? Nothing may happen. They were already trading away less than their trading partners thought too, so now they will probably just realize that they are both trading away less than it seems to outsiders.

The effect of widespread statistical analysis in the game of baseball is that it has become less useful in this regard. Billy Beane was able to rob other teams blind when he was the only one appropriately valuing certain skills, but after the league adjusted and started paying players with high OBP according to their true values, scouts became more important. In the effort to discern why a player is being let go, scouting becomes more important as well. Teams seem to know much more about their own players than other teams do, but better scouts can close that gap.

However, even great scouts may not be able to learn what other scouts know about their own players. The safest bet is to develop your own players and keep them when they seem likely to maintain or improve their performance. When teams do need external help, they should fill holes with the reservation and suspicion derived from the knowledge that if a player is available, there is probably a reason.

People Will Most Definitely Come

by Max Marchi

Between Aug. 11 and 14, 2011, the Potomac Nationals hosted a four-game series against the Myrtle Beach Pelicans. The Carolina League (Single-A-advanced) contests drew crowds of 1,681, 8,619, 2,902 and 1,806 people.

Less than a week earlier, the Hagerstown Suns had lured 6,758 fans on Aug. 9, against the Greensboro Grasshoppers (South Atlantic League, Single-A). The next day, a mere 704 showed up even though the Suns shared the battlefield with the same opponent.

At the end of the month, a few steps above in the minor league ladder, the Syracuse Chiefs of the Triple-A International League atracted 5,516 and 9,678 spectators in consecutive games featuring the Rochester Red Wings.

Finally, going into September, in the Double-A Eastern League, 3,187, 3,450, 3,357 and 8,637 individuals crossed the turnstiles to attend four consecutive match-ups between the visiting Portland Sea Dogs and the Harrisburg Senators.

The four home teams of these series share a common trait: They all belong to the Washington Nationals organization. The four games that drew over 6,000 people stand head-and-shoulders above the other contests of their respective series. They also share a common attribute: They featured Stephen Strasburg pitching his way back to the major leagues after Tommy John surgery.

You won't notice a huge attendance bump indicating Strasburg's return to The Show, as the Nationals sold 25,518, 29,092 and 21,638 tickets from Sept. 5 through 8 against the Dodgers. Strasburg was on the hill in the second game, which drew the most of the three, but not by a lot. However, when you consider that it was a rainy Tuesday night game (the action was suspended for half an hour) and it outdrew the Labor Day contest by 3,500 people, you might suspect the comeback kid sold his share of tickets.

One year earlier, on his much anticipated big league debut, Strasburg had notched 14 strikeouts in front of 40,315 people on a Tuesday night. Were all those fans in the stands for what basically was nothing more than a Quadruple-A game with the Pirates? The answer was revealed in the remaining games in the series: Games Two and Three brought 40,643 fans to Nationals Park—combined.

Fun with Other Numbers

Normally, only round-number accomplishments get celebrations. What about career totals that match a year, e.g. the year they happened or the player's birth year? Pete Rose recorded hit 1,973 in 1973, but anyone over 2,011 hits will have lined up the year and the hit total once. Along that line, here are some birth year-statistic match-ups.

Many players get close with putouts or assists, but the lists you'd get aren't of notable players.

The closest birth year-career hits match is Larry Doyle, who was born in 1886 and tallied 1,887 hits, followed by Jay Bell (1,963 and 1,965, respectively). Pitcher strikeouts is a tougher list to match up, but you can make a good rotation from the closest ones (+ meaning more strikeouts than the birth year):

Livan Hernandez ? (He ended 2011 with 1,928 whiffs... maybe he'll get it.)

Kenny Rogers +4

Al Leiter +9

Mickey Welch -9

Bobby Witt -9

Kid Nichols +12

Danny Darwin -13

Even in trivia land Danny Darwin is the spot starter.

The Nationals brass capitalized on every occasion Strasburg took the mound last season. Washington managed his minor league rehabilitation so that he always pitched at home; that's why he pitched in Triple-A before appearing in a Double-A game. The Washington front office also went all the way to increase its own gate receipts, scheduling the young pitcher mostly for home games even when he was back on the major league roster, stretching his rest periods to fit within the plan.

It's very difficult to estimate the number of people who go to a ballgame because a particular pitcher is starting. Among the 29,000 at Nationals Park on Sept. 6, there certainly were a number of regulars, as well as some who like to catch a game on Tuesdays. Who knows how many people, formerly living in Los Angeles and relocated to the D.C. area, were in attendance just to watch their beloved Dodgers? And how many more stayed home because of the rain?

This article is a hunt for those pitchers who, no matter what kind of value they produced on the field, put people in the stands and helped pad owners'—and possibly opposing owners'—pockets. The next section describes the efforts made to isolate the impact of the starting pitchers from whatever else can influence attendance figures. After that, the results will be reported, along with commentary on the top ticket-sellers.

Data: Sources, Quality, Issues

Most of the data used for this article come from Retrosheet gamelogs. The gamelogs are summaries of every major league game played all the way back to the 19th century, providing a tremendous amount of information. I included the following data elements from the gamelogs for analysis:

- Date and time of the game (day or night)
- Whether the contest was part of a doubleheader
- The starting pitchers
- The number of people in the stands

Attendance data are missing for several games before World War II, and they often appear to be estimates based on original sources. This article, then, will focus on seasons from 1947.

Stadium capacities come from The Seamheads.com Park Factors database.

Weather data come from the National Climatic Data Center website. Daily data come from historical weather stations that have records for the entire period. Those stations can be, for some locations, very distant from the ballpark.

The alternate approach would have been to gather hourly (or even more frequent) measurements from websites like WeatherUnderground, being careful in selecting the stations closest to the ballparks. However, data with finer granularity go back only to the late '70s at best, and the stations have a pretty wide range of trustworthiness and data completeness.

The Framework

Multilevel linear models (a generalization of linear regression models) were built to evaluate the simultaneous effect of several factors on attendance. A separate model was developed for every season from 1947 to 2010; the reason for this will be clear in the sections that follow. The expected attendance (the figure predicted by the model) of each game was compared to the actual one, and the difference was credited to the starting pitchers.

So, what factors had the biggest impact on attendance?

Team-Related Factors

Several elements related to the two teams on the field can make a difference in the number of tickets sold.

The home team has its fan base, though attendance varies with the club performance on the field. For example, a game played in Detroit in 2003, when the Tigers were on their way to a 119-loss season (and coming off a 106-loss season), drew 35 percent fewer people than the average game. Four years later, coming off their 2006 American League pennant, their attendance was 27 percent bigger than the average team's.

The visiting team also contributes to ticket sales—the Yankees, for example, are constantly one of the clubs with the highest attendance figures on the road. This also varies with time and performance on the field: When the Blue Jays came to town back in 1993 (on their way to repeating their World Series triumph) teams could expect a 10 percent rise in attendance; these days a 10 percent drop is more likely.

Since a different model has been created for each season, the differences in performance by both the home and the visiting team are taken into account. Building a single model containing six-and-a-half decades of data would have required finding a way to measure the effect that winning has on attendance, which may be very different from team to team and throughout baseball history.

Separate seasonal models also ensure another difficult-to-measure effect is somewhat removed: Teams build new ballparks (or even relocate) and this has an impact on attendance, different in intensity and duration from team to team.

Willie Stargell struck out 1,936 times, four fewer than his birth year. Don Robinson pitched 1.1 more innings than his birth year, Preacher Roe and Rick Mahler 1.2 fewer.

So if you've been bored with milestones, birth year-stat correlations are fun to follow. Ten or so players could get to 2,012 hits next year, although only seven seem likely. A similar number of pitchers could pass the threshold for innings and strike-outs. If round-number achievements are made-up times to celebrate, then why not make up your own achievements?

- Brandon Isleib

Baseball and the Interstate System go together like apples and pie, which is fortunate given their combined roster spots in Americana. The 1985 World Series is sometimes called the I-70 Series for the road linking the two teams; in the late '90s it was thought the Rangers and Astros might produce an I-45 Series. But who are each interstate's all-time players? To research this, I laid down a few guidelines:

1) Each player needs to have played in the days of the Interstate Era (sorry, George Davis); and

2) Each player needs to have played in at least three discrete locations along an Interstate for at least 50 games per location (eliminating players who hopped around the same city in the former and Manny Ramirez's White Sox stint in the latter).

Requiring three cities narrowed the search to 10 interstates. I'm looking at both games played for teams along the Interstate and percentage of career played for those teams.

In 1969 Major League Baseball introduced divisions. Since then, match-ups featuring teams in the same division have attracted around seven percent more people. In 1997, interleague play made its debut. Though generally speaking interleague games have brought more people to the ballparks, especially in the first years, the games that most increase the selling of tickets are those featuring teams located in the same area. Those contests have regularly drawn an extra 20 to 30 percent of fans over the years.

Calendar-Related Factors

The mere fact of *when* a game is played has a great bearing on the number of people that will show up.

The day of the week plays a role, with Sundays being most favorable. Also, workers are more likely to have a chance to catch a night game than one played under the sunshine during the week .

National holidays, as well as Opening Day, are good bets for sellouts. As you can see from the table below, the percentage of extra tickets sold on those occasions has diminished in recent years. It's not that people do not appreciate Opening Day or a Fourth of July at the ballpark anymore. It's that the overall average attendance has steadily grown in the last years while stadium capacities have shrunk from around 50,000 from the late '60s to the '80s to fewer than 45,000 in recent years, thus limiting the ceiling for tickets sales on special days.

Decade	Opening Day	Holiday
1950s	+227%	+153%
1960s	+245%	+87%
1970s	+194%	+28%
1980s	+170%	+22%
1990s	+124%	+8%
2000s	+101%	+10%

There is a final-home-game-of-the-season effect as well, of an 11 percent magnitude throughout baseball history.

The month also has an impact. July and August generally bring more fans to the stands, while September crowds are likely to be influenced by the tightness of playoff races. For example, on Sept. 1, 1985, the National League West had the top two teams separated by six games in the standings, and that was the largest gap in baseball at the time. That year, September attendance was more than 50 percent higher than April attendance. Three years later, with only the American League East still close at the beginning of the final month, the average September crowd was nearly 30 percent smaller than the average April crowd.

Obviously, September has a different meaning for a team in the race, thus an interaction term between month and home team is in the models. In fact, not every ballpark went deserted in September, 1988. The Tigers and Red Sox started the month separated by one game atop the AL East and the interaction term recognizes an improvement in attracting people for both teams during the race.

Weather

The limits of the weather data used for this article have already been mentioned.

The dichotomous "rain" variable introduced in the models reflects the fact that some precipitation was recorded during the day by the weather station linked to the ballpark. The fact that some water dropped possibly miles and hours away from the game location and time isn't certainly a strong indicator of fans behavior. However a small rain effect (a three to five percent reduction in attendance) was detected by the models.

No effect was found for cold and hot days.

Factors Not Considered

Every model is a simplification of reality and the ones created for this article are no exception. Thus not every single factor that can possibly affect attendance has been taken into account.

Rivalries did not get any special treatment. This is likely a negligible problem for recent Red Sox - Yankees games, especially at Fenway where the stadium is packed no matter who the opponent is. Games featuring the Mets and the Braves probably attracted some extra fans in the '90s because of their duels at the top of the National League East during that period. Unfortunately, it's not easy to precisely define rivalries because, except for a few notable exceptions, they exist for a limited time.

Promotions are another reason for increased gate receipts. In his *Diamond Dollars* book, Vince Gennaro estimated that the giveaway of Brian Roberts' bobblehead was responsible for roughly 16,000 extra tickets sold in one 2006 game in Baltimore.

Promotions are not an exclusive practice of recent years. The late Bill Veeck was renowned across baseball for his original ideas to bring people to the park. The infamous Disco Demolition Night held in 1979 brought a forfeited game and damage to Comiskey Park, but also nearly

I-5: Ruppert Jones by one game over percentage leader Dave Hansen (1,141 to 1,140). Bobby Valentine played at least 62 games for each team on I-5.

I-10: Luis Gonzalez for games and percentage. Steve Finley played at least 58 games for each team on I-10.

I-35: Ron Mahay. With only the Rangers, Royals, and Twins along I-35, Mahay is the only qualified player.

I-70: Moe Drabowsky is the only qualified player and played at least 76 games for all four teams of his era, including both Kansas City entries.

I-75: Surprisingly they're both active: Alex Gonzalez for games and Omar Infante for percentage. Infante has spent his entire career along I-75.

I-76: I'm cheating a little due to I-76 being in two parts, but Charlie Hayes wins both sections over Jose Mesa.

48,000 fans in a time when crowds in the South Side were usually of the 15-20,000 magnitude.

Retrieving information on promotions, especially going back in time, would have proven a prohibitive task, so they have not been included in the modeling.

Approaching milestones are also an important source of attendance variability. When Barry Bonds had Hank Aaron's home run record in sight, the Giants regularly outperformed the crowds estimated by the model—which does not include an "approaching milestone" predictor. The effect, which obviously had its peak on the day the record was broken, did not immediately dissipate, continuing until the end of the homestand—a byproduct of presales and devotees wanting to show their appreciation for the new home run king.

A plethora of other factors that can increase or decrease stadium attendance are not included in the models for this article, from a return of a former idol in a new uniform to local holidays like Patriot's Day in Boston.

And then there are the starting pitchers.

Results

Adjusted R-squared is a statistical coefficient measuring the proportion of variability accounted for by the model; in other words, it is one (albeit not the ultimate) way to evaluate how good the model is. Generally, it ranges from zero, meaning the factors used in the model explain nothing about how the dependent variable (attendance in our case) fluctuates, to one, meaning that the predictors used in the model thoroughly explain the variance of the dependent variable.

For models built for this article, using the predictors outlined in the previous sections, the adjusted R-squared values range from a healthy 0.76 up to 0.90. For every season, the average absolute difference between the estimated and actual attendance has also been calculated: the values span from around 3,000 to 6,000.

Both the adjusted R-squared and the average difference figures seem to indicate better performance for models pertaining to recent years. This is probably due to the already mentioned simultaneous increase of average attendance and decrease in stadium capacity, which results in a lower variability in ticket sales.

For each game played from 1947 to 2010 the difference between the actual attendance and that predicted by the model has fully been attributed to the starting pitchers (while acknowledging that part of the difference is certainly due to omitted factors—see previous section—and randomness). When the predicted attendance exceeded the ballpark capacity, it has been lowered to the reported maximum number of people the stadium can contain.

The extra attendance (either a positive or negative number) has been split between the home and visiting starters using a With-Or-Without-You approach; i.e., evaluating how the home starter fared at home with other opponents and how the visiting starter fared on the road with other opponents.

Two tables are presented as results. One reports the top 20 in career extra tickets sold, the other the greatest gate attractions in each considered season (it's at the end of the article). The great majority of names in either list pass the sniff test, another important, albeit not formal, indication of the good performance of the models.

The final part of this article will consist of brief focuses on some of the best careers and seasons.

Career Ticket Sellers: You Just Have to be Great

The Top 20 Attendance Draws

Pitcher	Total	Seasons*	Season Average
Nolan Ryan	641,000	26	24,654
Sandy Koufax	573,000	14	40,929
Tom Seaver	562,000	20	28,100
Vida Blue	493,000	15	32,867
Roger Clemens	488,000	24	20,333
Phil Niekro	452,000	21	21,524
Randy Johnson	414,000	21	19,714
Fernando Valenzuela	393,000	15	26,200
Bob Feller	372,000	10	37,200
Warren Spahn	337,000	23	14,652
Fergie Jenkins	334,000	18	18,556
Dwight Gooden	328,000	15	21,867
Gaylord Perry	327,000	21	15,571
Whitey Ford	327,000	18	18,167
Dennis Martinez	322,000	21	15,333
Juan Marichal	313,000	18	17,389
Mark Fidrych	301,000	3	100,333
Jim Palmer	286,000	17	16,824
Greg Maddux	273,000	22	12,409
Rick Reuschel	267,000	17	15,706

Seasons from 1947 to 2010 with at least 5 games started both at home and on the road

I-80: Omar Vizquel for games. For all Dave Kingman's traveling, 97 percent of it was on I-80, but Bobby Murcer spent his entire career along it.

I-90: Vizquel again; the James W. Shocknessy Ohio Turnpike is good for something after all. Reggie Jefferson spent all but five games of his career on I-90.

I-94: The weirdest one. It was Henry Blanco for games entering 2011, but LaTroy Hawkins passed him. Mark Salas is the percentage leader.

I-95: There were and are so many more teams to help someone get on this list that it's odd for Jackie Jensen to top the games list. He spent his entire career with three I-95 teams, as did Don Lock.

And although it doesn't meet our criteria, I-87/ Autoroute 15, connecting New York and Montreal, is held by Tim Foli for games and Dale Murray for percentage. That record seems safe.

- Brandon Isleib

There is not much to say about the top career crowd drawers; with few exceptions, they were the top men in the business.

As impressive as many of his playing statistics, Sandy Koufax's over half-a-million extra fans placed him second despite having played half the seasons played by leader Nolan Ryan.

Bob Feller's numbers in the table starts from year 1947, but his career began way back in 1936, when he was a teenager. Running the models on the less reliable data of the late '30s and early '40s indicates Rapid Robert was already attracting a couple of extra thousands fans per game from 1939 to 1941, when he left for four years of military service.

People went to see Nolan Ryan throughout his career, putting him in first place as the pitcher selling the most tickets after World War II. He also topped four seasons, from 1989 to 1991 and 1993—the year he announced, during spring training, that he was about to play his last season. The summer became a farewell tour for the Ryan Express, as people filled the stands to pay tribute to the retiring star. More than 7,500 extra fans showed up for the average Ryan road start in his final year.

A full list of year-by-year leaders in this analysis will appear at the end of the article, but here are a few highlights of individual seasons:

Stephen Strasburg was the biggest gate attraction of 2010, thanks to the media hype and his brilliant performance on the field. Strasburg drew an extra 55,700 people in just 12 starts. But it wasn't the first time a rookie phenom made the owners rich.

After throwing 17 innings in 1980, Fernando Valenzuela made his first full major league campaign one to remember, walking away with the Cy Young and Rookie of the Year Awards. Fans packed Dodger Stadium and the other venues where he appeared, to the tune of over 3,000 extra seats per game—85,600 in all.

From 1984 through 1987, fans responded to Dwight Gooden, especially at Shea Stadium in his first year. The Doc continued to dominate NL batters, and gate receipts soared when he was scheduled to start both at home and on the road for the next three seasons. During those four seasons, Gooden averaged an extra 61,125 attendees per season.

Both Gooden's and Valenzuela's fortunes went up and down, but both managed to last more than 15 years in the majors.

The two (arguably) best seasons ever in attendance boosting, on the other hand, came from two youngsters who had but one bright spot under the sun.

David Clyde was selected first overall in the 1973 draft and went straight from high school to The Show. Rangers owner Bob Short hoped the 18-year-old pitcher, known across the nation for having gone 18-0 with just three earned runs in 148 innings in his final high school season, could fill some of the empty seats in Arlington. In fact, the franchise freshly relocated from the nation's capital to Texas often had trouble cracking 10,000 tickets sold.

The owner's plot worked perfectly from the beginning, as a sellout crowd (the first in Arlington) of 35,698 came to witness Clyde's debut. At the end of the season his on-field numbers weren't impressive (4-8, 5.01 ERA), but his summer was among the best in crowd drawing, especially at home. Short made sure he was mostly employed in games at Arlington Stadium. Overall, Clyde drew an extra 87,000 fans in just 18 starts.

The rush to get him to the big leagues so quickly probably cost Clyde his career, as he soon developed arm troubles and managed to stay in baseball Olympus for five forgettable seasons.

The greatest season ever in putting people in the stands had a similarly sad ending. Mark Fidrych made the Tigers roster without much fanfare on the last day of spring training in 1976. The proof that not much was expected from him in his first year is the number of people witnessing his first start, a 2-1 two-hit complete game win over Cleveland: Fewer than 15,000 attended that Saturday afternoon game in May.

But after a 2-0 loss in Boston and consecutive 11-inning complete game victories against Milwaukee and Texas, people started to come in droves to Tiger Stadium to watch The Bird pitch.

Then, after a nationally televised Yankees-Tigers game showed his brilliance and characteristic demeanor on the mound to the entire nation, fans started to fill ballparks whenever he was pitching on the road as well. Owners of the other teams were expressly asking the Tigers to adjust their scheduled turns in the rotation to make sure the youngster—who talked to the ball and went all the way to the outfield in mid-inning to shake hands with his teammates after a good play—was to start a game in their ballpark.

Once, Fidrych had to skip a road start against the Angels due to a minor ailment. To avoid the disappointment of Californian fans who had come just to watch him pitch, The Bird was put into a giant, purposely built cage, where he signed thousands of autographs for the eager crowd.

According to the model used for this article, Mark Fidrych alone put 200,000 extra people in the stands in 1976. Only Vida Blue's 1971 (an extra 160,600 people in 10 more starts) comes close to Fidrych's record.

The following year, Fidrych tore knee cartilage while shagging fly balls in spring training. He was so eager to get back playing the game he loved

On July 29, the Indians, Pirates and White Sox were above .500 and within three games of first place. The Indians had contended all year, while the Pirates had spent six weeks in contention. All three ended the season below .500.

July 29 was the last day meeting the above-.500 and three-games-out criteria for both the Pirates and White Sox; for the Sox, it was their only day. The Indians stayed in it until Aug. 19, then ended at 80-82. Despite their late contention, their final line gives no indication that they mattered for much of the season.

Before 2011, how many teams were above .500 and within three games of first place on July 29 or later while ending the season below .500?

that he probably caused the arm troubles that plagued him for the rest of his short career. Though injuries prevented Fidrych from silencing major league hitters as he had in his first year, people continued to swarm to ballparks when he was pitching in 1977: In eight home starts he averaged 10,000 more people than expected.

The Japanese Attack

When agent Don Nomura was showcasing his client Hideo Nomo to major league teams in the strike-prolonged 1994 offseason, he promised potential employers that, other than recording strong numbers on the mound, his protégé was going to sell many tickets in his starts.

He was not lying, as the first Japanese pitcher to cross the Pacific Ocean in 30 years was the main gate attraction in his first two seasons in the States (70,800 extra fans that first year).

A decade later, when the much hyped Daisuke Matsuzaka made the same jump, he also emerged as the top ticket seller in the majors with 48,600 extra fans in the seats, despite playing his home games in a ballpark that leaves little room for attendance improvement.

Should the Hokkaido Nippon Ham Fighters make ace Yu Darvish available through the posting system in one of the next couple of seasons, the American front office guys will certainly consider the box office effect of a young Japanese phenom when bidding for his services.

Satchel's Corner

When talking about pitchers, one must always make sure to reserve a special place for Leroy Robert Paige, and this article is no exception.

Satchel Paige spent more than 20 years of his career barnstorming across the United States and the Caribbean. He usually pitched two or three innings per outing at most, because his name was on top of the bill in another city for the next day (or even later in the same day), and obviously people wanted to see the legendary pitcher in action.

In 1948, Paige was given a chance to play as a 42-year-old rookie in the majors by Cleveland Indians owner Bill Veeck. Since Veeck was the man of the many wacky promotions, Satch's call-up was viewed by many as a publicity stunt. However, he went 6-1 (with a 2.48 ERA) down the stretch, helping the Indians capture the pennant in a very tight race, culminating in a tie-breaking playoff game against the Red Sox.

You won't see Satchel Paige's name in the best seasons table because a cut-off of at least five games started both at home and on the road was imposed to avoid odd results due to tiny matching samples in the With-Or-Without-You process.

But Ol' Satch deserves an exception, so I re-ran the 1948 model with a lower threshold to make room for him. In seven starts, the old rookie was responsible for a combined 56,600 extra people in the stands, a feat even more remarkable when you consider he played on the same team with the attendance-boosting king of the era, Mr. Bob Feller.

References, Resources and Acknowledgements

The inspiration for this project came to me as I read the news about Fidrych passing away a couple of years ago, so this is a statistician's tribute to The Bird.

That occurred at the same time I was taken on board here at The Hardball Times. Big thanks go to Dave Studenmund, who drafted me, and David Gassko, the scout who suggested I was a prospect. Moreover, as soon as I declared my intentions to write on this topic, Gassko kindly sent me a draft paper of his own on the same subject which never was published.

Game-related information used here was obtained free of charge from and is copyrighted by Retrosheet. Interested parties may contact Retrosheet at "www.retrosheet.org".

OK, that's the proper citation, as required. But I believe it's not enough. Hey Retrosheet guys! The job you do is fabulous. We can never thank you enough for the comprehensive and superb quality data you provide us. Thank you, thank you, thank you! You guys rock.

A big thank you also goes to Kevin Johnson, who makes his tremendous work freely available as the Seamheads.com Parkfactors Database at Seamheads website. And to Brian Cartwright, who provided the necessary data to include 2011 line data.

This and other works I recently published are deeply indebted to Tom Tango and his WOWY approach, which he outlined in the 2008 edition of this Annual.

Finally, there is another group of guys who really rock. All the analyses I perform for the articles that end up published on The Hardball Times website and on the Annuals would be infinitely harder to perform without the work of the R Development Core Team and all the great minds creating additional packages for the free statistical software R. As goes for the Retrosheet people, my gratitude for them goes way beyond the suggested citation, which is reported below anyway.

R Development Core Team (2008). R: A language and environment for statistical computing. R Foundation for Statistical Computing, Vienna, Austria. ISBN 3-900051-07-0, URL http://www.R-project.org.

The 1915 Giants, 1986 Orioles, 1987 Angels and 2006 Diamondbacks made the list but ended in last place. The Angels were in contention on Aug. 31 with a 66-66 record but ended at 75-87. The Orioles ended earlier but were more impressive, hanging in the division on Aug. 5 with a 59-47 record but going 14-42 the rest of the way.

So fans in Chicago, Cleveland and Pittsburgh might be discouraged in their teams' late slumps, but historically they're far from alone. That's at least something, yes?

- Brandon Isleib

Top Attendance Draws by Year

Year	Pitcher	Starts	Total	At Home	On the Road
1947	Bob Feller	37	101,800	2,700	2,800
1948	Bob Feller	38	51,200	1,500	1,200
1949	Bob Feller	28	49,900	2,200	1,400
1950	Sheldon Jones	26	55,800	2,400	1,900
1951	Bob Feller	32	66,600	2,700	1,400
1952	Sid Hudson	24	34,700	300	2,600
1953	Whitey Ford	30	45,700	2,400	500
1954	Eddie Lopat	23	48,600	2,100	2,100
1955	Mike Garcia	31	31,500	800	1,300
1956	Bob Lemon	35	32,000	800	1,000
1957	Tom Sturdivant	28	15,800	1,200	100
1958	Taylor Phillips	27	34,000	1,800	600
1959	Lew Burdette	39	47,200	700	1,800
1960	Herb Score	22	37,600	3,400	300
1961	Sandy Koufax	35	40,000	1,800	400
1962	Whitey Ford	37	42,800	300	1,900
1963	Sandy Koufax	40	50,200	1,900	800
1964	Sandy Koufax	28	56,600	1,300	2,700
1965	Sandy Koufax	41	105,100	2,500	2,700
1966	Sandy Koufax	41	108,800	1,800	3,600
1967	Denny McLain	37	40,700	1,600	700
1968	Luis Tiant	32	58,800	1,700	2,000
1969	Phil Niekro	35	52,500	2,200	700
1970	Larry Dierker	36	46,000	500	2,000
1971	Vida Blue	39	160,600	4,400	3,800
1972	Steve Carlton	40	69,300	3,200	300
1973	David Clyde	18	87,000	6,200	2,100
1974	Randy Jones	34	59,100	1,900	1,600
1975	Catfish Hunter	39	61,200	1,200	1,900
1976	Mark Fidrych	29	200,000	8,800	3,800
1977	Jim Palmer	39	68,500	2,100	1,500
1978	Vida Blue	34	44,800	1,300	1,400
1979	Tom Seaver	32	44,800	900	2,000
1980	John Candelaria	34	52,300	2,800	300
1981	Fernando Valenzuela	25	85,600	3,300	3,500
1982	Fernando Valenzuela	37	70,300	2,000	1,800

Year	Pitcher	Starts	Total	At Home	On the Road
1983	Tom Seaver	34	74,200	4,000	-100
1984	Dwight Gooden	31	53,300	3,100	300
1985	Dwight Gooden	35	68,500	2,100	1,800
1986	Dwight Gooden	33	77,900	1,800	2,900
1987	Dwight Gooden	25	44,800	1,800	1,700
1988	Roger Clemens	35	37,500	1,000	1,100
1989	Nolan Ryan	32	61,000	2,300	1,400
1990	Nolan Ryan	30	96,800	3,400	3,000
1991	Nolan Ryan	27	41,800	2,000	300
1992	Charles Nagy	33	59,200	2,200	1,300
1993	Nolan Ryan	13	67,400	3,100	7,700
1994	John Burkett	25	37,700	1,900	1,000
1995	Hideo Nomo	28	70,800	2,900	2,200
1996	Hideo Nomo	33	41,100	2,100	200
1997	Ken Hill	31	41,100	300	2,200
1998	Kevin Brown	35	47,300	2,100	600
1999	Brian Boehringer	11	48,600	8,100	100
2000	Jon Lieber	35	30,500	500	1,200
2001	Freddy Garcia	34	45,200	800	1,900
2002	Tim Hudson	34	55,000	2,800	200
2003	Brett Myers	32	37,100	1,900	400
2004	Roger Clemens	33	47,700	1,600	1,300
2005	Pedro Martinez	31	40,300	1,900	700
2006	Dontrelle Willis	34	30,800	1,200	600
2007	Daisuke Matsuzaka	32	48,600	1,400	1,600
2008	Ben Sheets	31	37,900	2,000	700
2009	Roy Halladay	32	42,200	1,500	1,100
2010	Stephen Strasburg	12	55,700	3,600	6,000

Simple Fielding Runs Estimates

by Michael A. Humphreys

Forget all the complex data and math. A very accurate estimate of the value a fielder brings to his team consists of nothing more than simple arithmetic. All you need are the fielder's plays made and the number of ground balls and non-ground balls hit by opponent right- and left-handed batters while he was in field that year—all of which is publicly available at the Retrosheet website (retrosheet.org).

This approach is in the spirit of Colin Wyers' new defensive runs estimates for *Baseball Prospectus*, except the resulting "linear weights" formulas—if you want to call them that, they're so simple—are fully disclosed here.

The formulas are derived from the first application of Defensive Regression Analysis ("DRA") methodologies to Retrosheet's open-source play-by-play data for 1989-99 and 2003-10. DRA was introduced in general terms on the Internet in 2003 and is fully disclosed in my book, *Wizardry: Baseball's All-Time Greatest Fielders Revealed* (Oxford University Press 2011).

Why We Need Open-Source Defensive Runs Estimates

Defensive runs are essentially just plays made minus the estimated number of plays a league-average fielder would have made playing that position for that team ("expected plays"). This results in positive or negative "net plays," which are multiplied by the number of runs saved per successful play. This is usually about 0.8 runs (the sum of the value of the out created (about 0.27 runs) and the hit prevented (about 0.53 on average)). Since the number of successful plays each player makes is known, the whole business of estimating defensive runs comes down to estimating expected plays.

The most direct method is based on batted-ball data, which is different from play-by-play data. Play-by-play data tracks which players were on the field and the plays they made, plate appearance by plate appearance. For example, "right-handed pitcher X pitched to left-handed batter Y who hit a ball caught by center fielder Z." Batted-ball data goes beyond that to track certain key characteristics of each batted ball in order to estimate the probability of that batted ball being converted into an out.

The most important batted-ball characteristics are trajectory (ground ball, line drive, fly ball, or pop up) and location (the zone in which a ball hit in the air landed or was fielded on some sort of grid superimposed on the field, or the slice of the infield in which a ground ball was hit). In the

DRA Rankings: The Best Fielders at Catcher

1. Ivan Rodriguez
2. Bob Boone
3. Steve Yeager
4. Bill Bergen
5. Jack Warner
6. Lou Criger
7. Brad Ausmus
8. Jim Sundberg
9. Del Crandall
10. Gary Carter

- From *Wizardry: Baseball's All-time Greatest Fielders Revealed*

example just given, the batted ball data might be "fly ball hit to the zone denoted as left-left center, deep."

Based on single-season samples of over ten thousand batted balls fielded by all fielders (or even larger multi-year samples), probabilities can be assigned to each category of batted ball, defined by trajectory and location. The number of expected plays for a fielder would be the sum of the out probabilities per batted ball for all batted balls hit in areas of the field assigned to his position while he was in the field. There are more sophisticated calculation methods, but this gets to the gist of the idea.

Although defensive runs estimates based on batted-ball data are the most conceptually simple, most direct, and theoretically most accurate, the data are proprietary. Furthermore, some articles and blog posts have been written, starting with an article I contributed to *The Hardball Times* in 2007, regarding the degree to which batted-ball data may be subject to measurement error and systematic bias, as inferred from published defensive runs estimates based on the proprietary underlying data. I'll talk more about this later in the article.

The solution to this challenge is a system called FIELDf/x, which will begin collecting batted ball data this upcoming season (see last year's *Hardball Times Annual* for an in-depth review of this system). In theory, FIELDf/x will eliminate these measurement errors by having four video cameras in each ballpark that will record the exact speed, complete trajectory, and precise landing point of every batted ball. No human judgment or guesswork will be involved. In addition, the cameras will record the movements of the players. This fielder data may permit the separate quantification of each of the components of fielding performance that go into overall effectiveness measured by defensive runs: positioning, first step, speed, path to the ball, and so forth. Approximately 2.5 million data records will be generated per game.

This unimaginably rich and precise data will be made available to all major league teams but, according to Tom Tippett, Director, Baseball Information Systems for the Red Sox, it is unlikely you or I will ever see it, even at a price. And I doubt there even will be published defensive runs estimates based on this data. So we will likely never see defensive runs estimates based on the "perfect" FIELDf/x data.

In the meantime, the only defensive runs estimates based on batted-ball data available on-line (at FanGraphs.com)—John Dewan's "Defensive Runs Saved" (DRS) and Mitchel Lichtman's "Ultimate Zone Rating" (UZR)—may be susceptible to measurement error and/or bias. Furthermore, both systems are based on proprietary data. I don't know about you, but I'd like a good open-source alternative.

As an alternative to batted-ball data, analysts (including Tom Tippett, Charles Saeger and Bill James) have for quite some time tried to estimate expected plays per position. Typically, they start with the league-average number of plays per season and adjust for a particular team based on publicly available team statistics—mainly controlled by the team's pitchers—that would impact expected plays at each position. These "global" factors include estimates of groundball versus flyball pitching and relative levels of opponent batter handedness. Calculations of net plays based on these adjusted estimates of expected plays have been called Adjusted Range Factors, as they adjust "plain" Range Factor, which simply counts gross plays per nine innings.

DRA is somewhat like Adjusted Range Factor, but DRA also...

- estimates runs per net play,
- provides a general and unique framework for organizing all the calculations,
- minimizes bias in estimating the impact of groundball and flyball pitching for seasons in which we do not have exact counts of ground balls and fly balls, and
- minimizes the extent to which the quality of team fielding biases an individual fielder's rating.

DRA also estimates pitching runs, which, combined with defensive runs estimates for fielders, provide an estimate of team runs allowed. DRA estimates of team runs allowed are nearly as accurate as the many models of team runs scored, such as Pete Palmer's Linear Weights.

In the effort to get *Wizardry* done on time, I did not utilize all of the Retrosheet data currently available, particularly the 1989-99 and 2003-10 data that provide exact counts of ground balls and fly balls. Here we'll use the DRA approach to identify which of the many factors more recently recorded can help us estimate expected plays.

A Complex Methodology Yielding a Simple Result

We can easily guess the kind of factors that would tend to increase or decrease expected plays for fielders at various positions. Clearly, the more total balls in play, the more plays everywhere in the field. The more batted balls that are ground balls, the more chances in the infield; the more batted balls that are fly balls, the more chances in the outfield. The more ground balls hit by right-handed batters, the more chances at short and third. The more fly balls hit by left-handed batters, the more chances

Pitching Runs Saved

I have also taken the DRA techniques and applied them to pitching performance. Using the most current Retrosheet data, I found something that most everyone has acknowledged by now: You can tell a lot about a pitcher by just his strikeout and walk rates.

It's not that other things, such as home runs allowed, wild pitches and groundball rate, aren't important. It's that strikeout rate is closely correlated with those variables.

So, a quick and dirty way to estimate a pitcher's runs saved (above or below the league average) is the following formula:

$$(SO - 2*BB)/3$$

Note that this formula only works for contemporary pitchers. As the ratio of strikeouts to walks has changed over time, the relationship between those two events and other events has changed too.

- Michael Humphreys

DRA Rankings: The Best Fielders at First Base

1. Keith Hernandez
2. Fred Tenney
3. Albert Pujols
4. John Olerud
5. Todd Helton
6. George Scott
7. Pete O'Brien
8. Vic Power
9. Buddy Hassett
10. Hank Greenberg

- From *Wizardry: Baseball's All-time Greatest Fielders Revealed*

in left field. (Yes, batters pull ground outs, but most of their fly outs are recorded in the opposite field.)

But what about pitcher-handedness? And what about batters with unusual batter-out distributions, like Ryan Howard, for whom teams put on a version of the famous "Williams shift?" If there is a runner at first, how much does this reduce expected plays at first (because the first baseman has to stay close to the bag) or at second and short (because middle infielders have to shade toward second base for stolen base attempts and perhaps also play at double play depth)? Most importantly, how much do these factors impact plays made, independent of the impact of the other factors?

I am sure there are many approaches to this problem, but one relatively simple one is the DRA method. Here's the technical explanation:

First, you start with a "centered" variable of plays made by each team each season, that is, gross plays above or below the league average rate ("preliminary net plays"). Note that this treats average net plays across all teams as zero. For infielders, plays made are ground outs, including assists from fielding a batted ball and unassisted groundball putouts often made at first and occasionally as second. For outfielders, plays made are putouts.

Then you regress preliminary net plays at a position onto other variables centered at zero that you expect would help explain variance in preliminary net plays (but not attributable to fielding skill; let's call these "explanatory variables"). The regression results tell you which factors are significant and how significant they are in estimating expected plays at that position.

When you apply those factors to a team's statistics, you get an estimate of expected plays for that team at that position that is above or below zero. When you subtract such "expected plays above or below average" from the preliminary net plays made by the team, you get total net plays for the team, which we consider the result of fielding skill.

Obviously, team balls in play above or below the league average, or net balls in play, would be one explanatory variable. For this purpose, balls in play exclude sacrifice bunts, because fielding a sacrifice bunt (that is, *not* getting the lead runner) rarely reflects fielder value. Whether the first baseman or third baseman fields a sacrifice bunt attempt without getting the batter or lead runner out is less a matter of the skill of the fielder than which way the batter aims the bunt and how eager the pitcher is to field bunts. (See, we're starting to simplify things already.)

What about the number of batted balls that are ground balls? If we simply used total team ground balls above or below the league average rate, that number would reflect both the total number of balls in play, which we've just already taken into account, as well as the relative number that were ground balls. If we want to isolate the groundball factor versus the total-balls-in-play factor, we need to do something.

DRA simply calculates team ground balls above or below the league average rate, given the team's total balls in play. Note that the negative of this number is the relative number of "air" balls (including fly balls, line drives, etc.). The "how many X above or below the league rate, given X" arithmetic is simple and will be the same for all the rest of the explanatory variables (denoted by the term "net").

Well, what about batter-handedness? This time we have to do two calculations, one for ground balls and the other for air balls. We calculate team ground balls hit by opponent left-handed batters above or below the league average rate, given total ground balls. Then we calculate net team air balls hit by opponent left-handed batters, given total air balls. Note that in each case that a *negative* number would simply mean "extra" ground/air balls hit by opponent *right*-handed batters.

To measure the impact of pitcher-handedness (beyond the effect of facing more opposite-handed batters), we do four calculations. First calculate net ground balls allowed by left-handed pitchers given total groundballs hit by left-handed batters and right-handed batters. Then calculate net air balls allowed by left-handed pitchers given total air balls hit by left-handed batters and right-handed batters.

Finally, to measure the impact of having a runner at first on ground-ball plays, we calculate net runners on first when a ground ball is hit, given total ground balls. (I also sliced this up by batter and pitcher handedness, but none of the variables was significant.) We'll hold off for the moment on the adjustment for batters with unusual batted-ball distributions.

Results for First Basemen

When we regress net team ground balls fielded and converted into outs by first basemen, including the times the first baseman touches the bag himself or tosses to the pitcher covering the bag (ground outs by first basemen, or "GO3"), onto all our centered variables above, we get the following result:

Footnote:

The specific formula for net ground balls (and all other "net" formulas), is:

Team GB – league GB * (team BIP / league BIP); i.e., the team variable minus the league variable multiplied by the team's percentage of league "opportunities" relevant to the variable.

- Michael Humphreys

DRA Rankings: The Best Fielders at Second Base

1. Joe Gordon
2. Bill Mazeroski
3. Glenn Hubbard
4. Bobby Grich
5. Rennie Stennett
6. Willie Randolph
7. Lou Whitaker
8. Pokey Reese
9. Frank White
10. Mark Lemke

- From *Wizardry: Base-ball's All-time Greatest Fielders Revealed*

Vs. League Average	Coefficients	P-value
Intercept	0.00	1.00
Net Balls in Play (BIP)	0.04	0.00
Net Ground balls (GB), given BIP	0.09	0.00
Net GB from Lefty Batters (LB), given GB	0.16	0.00
Net GB allowed by Lefty Pitchers (LP), given LB GB	-0.07	0.21
Net GB from Righty Batters (RB) off LP, given RB GB	-0.01	0.70
Net runners on first when a GB is hit, given total GB	-0.06	0.03

Note: P-value is the measure of a statistic's significance. A p-value under 0.05 is typically considered significant.

The chart above indicates that for each extra ball in play, expected GO3 goes up by 0.04. So if a team has 100 more balls in play during a season than the league-average team, expected GO3 goes up by 4. Each extra ground ball, given total balls in play, increases expected GO3 by 0.09. So 100 extra ground balls, given total balls in play, increases expected GO3 by 9.

For each extra ground ball hit by a left-handed batter, given total ground balls, expected GO3 go up by 0.16. This makes sense, because left-handed batters pull ground balls. If the team has minus 100 grounders hit by a left-handed batter, that means that the team had 100 more ground balls hit by opponent right-handed batters, which would reduce expected plays by first baseman by 16. All of these estimates are statistically significant, given the p-value.

However, pitcher-handedness given batter-handedness is not statistically significant (p-values are far above 0.05). Each extra runner on first, given total ground balls, reduces GO3.

Now let's re-do the regression looking at just the statistically significant variables, but also calculate the standard deviation of the impact of each variable on expected GO3, to assess the practical significance of each one. The standard deviation of impact is simply the regression coefficient multiplied by the standard deviation of the explanatory variable.

	Coefficients	P-value	StDev of Variable	StDev of Impact
Intercept	0.00	1.00		
Net Balls in Play	0.04	0.00	135	6
Net Ground balls (GB), given BIP	0.09	0.00	93	8
Net GB from Lefty Batters (LB), given GB	0.16	0.00	90	15
Net runners on first when a GB is hit, given total GB	-0.06	0.03	32	-2

DRA Rankings: The Best Fielders at Shortstop

1. Mark Belanger
2. Rey Sanchez
3. Ozzie Smith
4. Joe Tinker
5. Art Fletcher
6. Jose Valentin
7. Ozzie Guillen
8. Roy McMillan
9. Phil Rizzuto
10. Luke Appling

- From *Wizardry: Baseball's All-time Greatest Fielders Revealed*

Batter-handedness is the most important fact; the standard deviation by which it increases or decreases expected GO3 is 15 plays. But the standard deviation in impact of having a runner on first is only two plays. This suggests that over the course of a season, the variation in the number of runners at first base when a ground ball is hit has an extremely modest impact on expected GO3. Even a two-standard deviation impact would be only four plays, or three runs.

Furthermore, there is some chance the average effect is actually closer to zero. That's because we're implicitly assuming that extra runners at first cause first basemen to make fewer plays. But it is also true that extra runners at first are caused *by* first basemen making fewer plays—in other words, by allowing more singles.

I have no doubt that whenever a ground ball is hit toward the first base side with a runner on first, the probability of the first baseman fielding that ground ball is lower than if there were no runner at first. The point, however, is that over the course of a season there is not enough variation from team to team in the number of runners at first, when a ground ball is hit, for this effect to be material or reliable even to a small extent. Since even the strongest supporters of batted-ball data systems believe you really need two seasons of data to get a good read on a player, why complicate the model with a factor that "dies out" in one year?

Other Infield Results

Exactly the same analysis applies to ground balls successfully fielded by second basemen and shortstops; the presence of a runner at first has a slightly lower and also statistically insignificant impact on expected plays. All that matters are total balls in play, the relative number that are ground balls, and the relative number of ground balls that are hit by right- and left-handed batters. Pitcher handedness does not matter.

DRA Rankings: The Best Fielders at Third Base

1. Brooks Robinson
2. Buddy Bell
3. Mike Schmidt
4. Jimmy Collins
5. Clete Boyer
6. Scott Rolen
7. Graig Nettles
8. Tim Wallach
9. Tommy Leach
10. Terry Pendleton

- From *Wizardry: Base- ball's All-time Greatest Fielders Revealed*

Third base is a little tricky. The standard deviation seasonal "impact" of having extra/fewer runners on first when a ground ball is hit was −4/+4 plays at third if batter handedness is ignored. However, having more left-handed opponent batters at the plate more than cancels out this effect, which means that having more right-opponent batters hitting ground balls with a runner on first has an impact.

I was surprised by this at first, but the result now seems obvious to me. With a runner on first, the chance of a bunt goes up. Third basemen are expected to charge the plate for bunts more than first basemen. But the bunt might not happen. The chance of a right-handed batter pulling a very hard hit ground ball past the third baseman must go up if the third baseman is charging in. Still, including both factors explains less than two percent of the variance in plays at third base. (Technically, it increases the adjusted r-squared by less than two percent.) It just doesn't matter.

Outfield Results

Results in the outfield were generally consistent with results in the infield. The key determinant of expected plays in the outfield is simply the number of air balls hit by right- and left-handed batters. Not surprisingly, batter handedness is irrelevant in center field, but oddly enough, pitcher-handedness has a slight impact.

Basically, if the pitcher and the batter are both right-handed or both left-handed, expected plays in center field go down, though the results have borderline statistical significance, and the standard deviation in impact over the course of a season is only two or three runs.

I wondered how this could be. Then Colin Wyers reported that Matt Thomas' photogrammetry data indicated that center fielders shift to get a better view of the ball coming off the bat. If the pitcher and the batter are both right-handed or both left-handed, the pitcher probably blocks the center fielder's view of the batter slightly more. Anyway, it's nothing to get too excited about, because adding these factors to the model explains less than one percent of the variance in preliminary net plays.

Williams Shifts

More and more teams are putting on extreme infield shifts for certain batters, usually left-handed batters who, if they hit a ground ball, tend to pull it sharply. Ryan Howard is a prime example. (Incidentally, Howard sprays his fly balls and home runs all around the field.) Does the tendency of opponent batters to have idiosyncratic batted ball distributions—independent of batter-handedness, which we've already taken into account—significantly impact expected plays at each position, particularly in the infield?

This involves some heavier-duty database calculations, though the concept is pretty simple. First, you have to calculate for every batter his career ground outs per infield position as a percentage of his total ground balls hit, and his career air outs per outfield position as a percentage of his total air balls hit. Track the handedness of the batter, and do separate calculations if he is a switch-hitter.

Second, each time a batter comes to the plate against a given team and hits a ground ball, apply his ground out percentage to each infield position, as a form of expected outs for that team, given total ground balls hit by batters with the same batter-handedness. Do the same for air balls.

Third, sum up the expected ground outs and air outs at each position separately for opponent left- and right-handed batters for that team and season. The sum of all the teams' expected outs that year is the league distribution of expected outs, given ground balls and air balls hit by left- and right-handed batters.

Fourth, calculate the team's expected outs at each position, above or below the league rate, just as we've done before. For example, calculate the team's expected ground outs at third hit by opponent right-handed batters, above or below the league average rate, given the team's total ground balls hit by opponent right-handed batters.

Result? The standard deviation in team expected plays at each position based on opponent career out distribution was less than three at every position, resulting in an impact of only plus or minus two runs per season. The most extreme impact at any position in the entire sample of over 500 teams was eight runs at third base. Furthermore, if you included these variables in a regression analysis, they often did not have statistical significance, though usually the coefficient was approximately 1.0, as you would expect it to be.

A Simple, Open-source Defensive Runs Formula

It appears that, as a practical matter, the only variables with statistical and practical significance over the course of a season are total balls in play, the relative number that were ground balls or air balls, and the relative number of such ground balls and air balls that were hit by opponent right- and left-handed batters.

Pitcher handedness is irrelevant. The presence of runners at first base is practically irrelevant. Batter tendencies to have unusual batted-ball

Footnote:

Note that the run weights on this page are higher than the weights in *Wizardry*. As explained in *Wizardry*, the estimators of relative groundball versus airball pitching have a bias that causes the run weights to be understated. Since we have exact groundball and air ball counts here, this understatement is eliminated.

- Michael Humphreys

distributions (after taking into account whether they are right- or left-handed and whether they are hitting the ball on the ground or in the air, which is already taken into account) simply do not have a material impact over the course of a season.

On the one hand, it might seem disappointing that all that data manipulation yielded so little in the way of improved estimates of expected plays. On the other hand, since we can reasonably conclude that the only thing that matters for infielders is the total number of ground balls by batter hand, relative to the league, and for outfielders, the total number of air balls by batter hand, relative to the league, we can dispense with regression analysis to determine a fielder's plays above or below average, and just use simple arithmetic.

An infielder's net plays are simply the sum of his net plays against right- and left-handed batters relative to the league-average fielder that year at that position, given the number of ground balls hit by right- and left-handed batters while the infielder was playing relative to the league average rate. The calculation is done separately by batter hand and you take the sum. The same applies in the outfield. (Because I had the data handy and found the interesting interaction between pitcher- and batter-handedness, I did this type of calculation in center for each of the four combinations of pitcher- and batter-handedness.)

When I did input these net play estimates and ran a global DRA regression including pitching variables, I obtained run weights for each fielding play ranging from 0.74 runs per shortstop ground out to 0.88 runs per left field air out. These were within the expected range of values for the out created and hit prevented (singles at shortstop and some combination of singles and doubles in the outfield). For all intents and purposes, you could just multiply the net plays calculated in the prior paragraph by 0.8 runs to arrive at a player's defensive runs.

Time Tames the Somewhat Wild Results

Based on the regression analyses at each position, our three variables (balls in play, ground vs. air balls and batter-handedness) explain approximately half of the total variance in team plays at each position. In other words, the "adjusted r-squared" at each position was approximately 50 percent. However, the unexplained variance results in a standard deviation in ostensible "skill" plays per season per team of about 23 per position (18 at first base).

That's a little high. Almost 10 years ago, Tom Tippett wrote an article about defense (I can no longer find it on the Internet) in which he reported that batted ball data indicated that the best fielders, such as

Scott Rolen at third, consistently recorded, year after year, about 30 plays above average, while the worst fielders were about 30 plays below average. Assuming they are the typical two-standard deviation outliers, the standard deviation in ostensible skill plays should be about 15, or about 12 runs.

However, if you look at a complete sample of players from 2008 to 2010 who played the equivalent of something close to two full seasons or more at one position, based on having been in the field for at least 8,000 balls in play (the average per team has typically been about 4,400 per season) the standard deviation in their defensive runs per 4,100 balls in play, the equivalent of 151 games (a typical number of defensive games for a top fielder), approaches 12 runs:

Position	Standard Deviation in Team Runs	Number of Players with >8000 Balls in Play	Average Number of the 4400 Balls in Play 'Years'	Runs per 4400 Balls in Plan	Runs per 4100 Balls in Play
1B	15	18	2.4	15	14
2B	17	13	2.4	12	11
3B	17	14	2.2	14	13
SS	17	17	2.2	14	13
LF/RF	19	18	2.3	15	14
CF	21	14	2.2	14	13

Okay, we've got this comically simple system, and though it can give extreme values per player after one season, after two it settles down to something reasonable. Still, it's not based on batted ball data and so is presumptively less accurate.

Is There "Range Bias" in Batted Ball Data?

As far as I know, my 2007 *Hardball Times* article was one of the first to report any potential problem with batted ball data. That article focused mainly on the surprisingly large inconsistencies in defensive runs estimates for outfielders when an identical calculation methodology was applied to batted-ball data from different suppliers. However, my thinking at the time was that the coding errors were random, so if you combined results using two data sets, you'd get a good estimate.

In 2009, Shane Jensen, a professor of statistics at the University of Pennsylvania, published an article in *The Annals of Applied Statistics* showing how he applied Bayesian statistical techniques to batted-ball

DRA Rankings: The Best Fielders in Center Field

1. Andruw Jones
2. Willie Mays
3. Tris Speaker
4. Paul Blair
5. Gary Pettis
6. Richie Ashburn
7. Devon White
8. Mike Cameron
9. Willie Davis
10. Dom DiMaggio

- From *Wizardry: Baseball's All-time Greatest Fielders Revealed*

DRA Rankings: The Best Fielders in Right Field

1. Roberto Clemente
2. Jesse Barfield
3. Harry Hooper
4. Hank Aaron
5. Ichiro Suzuki
6. Brian Jordan
7. Sammy Sosa
8. Al Kaline
9. Reggie Sanders
10. David Justice

- From *Wizardry: Baseball's All-time Greatest Fielders Revealed*

data in order to estimate "true" fielder value. The Bayesian techniques are way beyond the scope of this article. But what struck me most were the first graphs presented: contour plots of the distribution of batted balls.

The charts showed that total batted balls, not just batted balls that were caught, were clustered around each of the standard fielding positions. I emailed Shane and met with his co-author Ken Shirley to confirm that someone hadn't mistakenly substituted the chart of caught batted balls for the chart of total batted balls. They both confirmed that, indeed, total batted balls were coded as being clustered near the fielders.

Batters don't aim their hits toward each of the standard fielding positions. It appears that stringers coding location data, regardless of who they work for, may be "anchoring" their estimates by reference to the position of the fielder.

One possible indirect result of this anchoring effect is that if a fielder catches the ball, the coders may tend to locate the ball close to the fielder's position, while if the fielder does not catch the ball, the coder will tend to code the ball as having been farther away.

If you think about it a little bit, that would mean that a rangy fielder's great plays would tend to be coded as close to his position, and a non-rangy fielder's hits allowed would tend to be coded as having been difficult to reach. Any such "range bias," as Colin Wyers has called it, would systematically pull defensive runs estimates toward the mean.

Does range bias actually exist? Since I don't have the data, I can't say for sure. But one way to investigate it is to compare our new DRA defensive runs estimates with defensive runs estimates that use batted-ball data.

Results

Below are the results for fielders who have been consistently recognized for their fielding prowess over the past eight years. The three systems I'm going to present are "simple DRA," as described in this article, UZR and Plus/Minus, which is the "range" portion of Defensive Runs Saved. Plus/Minus is labeled "rPM" on the FanGraphs site, so we'll use that label here.

Here are the results, showing total runs saved from 2002 to 2010:

		UZR	rPM	DRA
Second Base	Orlando Hudson	14	104	145
	Aaron Hill	23	56	83
Third Base	Scott Rolen	85	89	108
	Adrian Beltre	101	129	77
Shortstop	Adam Everett	74	107	102
	Jack Wilson	31	91	91
Centerfield	Andruw Jones	88	71	76
	Carlos Beltran	13	42	96
Left Field	Carl Crawford	110	72	162
Right Field	Ichiro Suzuki	76	72	66
	Average Total	**61**	**83**	**101**
	Per 151 games	**10**	**14**	**17**

All three systems rate these fielders highly. In virtually all cases, the DRA findings are larger than those from UZR and rPM. Is this evidence of a range bias in the batted-ball data, pulling the best fielders toward the mean, or are there other systemic reasons for these differences? We can't say for sure, and further research is obviously called for.

Next Steps

The primary limitation of this new version of DRA is that it does produce occasional single-season results that simply cannot reflect skill and must reflect unusual batted-ball distributions in that given year for that player. Reporting two-year averages instead would generally reflect "reality," but all other baseball statistics are reported on a single-season basis, so fans will want single-season DRA. At this point, the best approach might very well be to discount (or "regress") the single-season DRA result for purposes of evaluating the player's overall value that season, but also to report the un-regressed number right next to it and to use the un-regressed numbers for longer-term or career evaluation. This is probably how all these fielding systems should be presented.

The ideal method for regressing single-season ratings would involve some very complicated Bayesian techniques. However, something much simpler would be more transparent to fans and probably not that much less accurate. My current guess would be something like the fraction of a given year's DRA for a full-time player that predicts the following year's DRA (if the player also plays full-time), based on an ordinary regression analyses performed over multiple paired seasons of full-time players at

Footnote:

Baseball Prospectus seems to be regressing Colin Wyer's new defensive runs for single season estimates, but does not report un-regressed results. Regressing every season to the league average is inappropriate for consistently good or bad hitters.

It makes a difference. For example, *Baseball Prospectus* reports approximately +60 runs for Adam Everett during his career; the simple version of DRA (which does not include double play runs) credits Everett with approximately +100 defensive runs. And Derek Jeter? BPro charges him approximately -250 defensive runs; the simple version of DRA charges him approximately -350 runs. Yes, you read that right.

- Michael Humphreys

each of the positions. My guess would be that the result would be about 0.5, thus indicating each defensive runs estimate should be discounted by half for purposes of single-season reporting. But now that this version of DRA is open source, perhaps one of you will find the best way to figure it out.

What Ground Balls Can Tell Us about Fly Balls

by Brian Cartwright

Fly balls are not all the same. This seems obvious, but consider how often we say they are:

- We assign all pitchers the same Batting Average on Balls in Play (BABIP), or we adjust it by looking at ALL flyballs.

- We use the same BABIP in FIP; the same home run percentage in xFIP

- When we regress batter and pitcher projections, we regress them to the same BABIP

- We give all line drives and fly balls the same hit rates in defensive metrics.

What I will show is that knowing a batter's or pitcher's groundball rate can tell us something extra about their fly balls, such as hit and home run rates.

Major League Baseball Advanced Media's (MLBAM) Gameday web application is a widely used source for real time play-by-play data of all games in the major leagues as well as their affiliated minor leagues. Gameday defines balls in the air to the outfield as either line drives or fly balls. Pop ups are scored only for infield flies, and ground balls are those that touch the ground before reaching an infielder.

To further analyze the properties of these batted balls, Sportvision has graciously provided me with HITf/x data from April, May and June of 2009. Using video from cameras installed for PITCHf/x data collection, HITf/x measures the horizontal angle, vertical angle and batted ball speed of the ball as it comes off the bat. For this article, I will be focusing on the vertical angles of the batted balls.

On the following page is a graph of the distribution of batted balls (as defined by Gameday), by vertical (up or down) angle.

The batted balls follow a natural pattern. Grounders come off the bat at a negative angle (downward) while line drives and fly balls have a positive angle. Line drives are centered on the most common vertical angle, about 15 degrees, but in a narrow band. They are also centered on the angles

Carlton Fisk played in the greatest World Series ever. Red Sox versus Reds. Hit one of the most famous home runs ever in Game Six. This 12th-inning blast was made possible by a game-tying home run by Bernie Carbo, who was an ex-Red. As Carbo was rounding the bases, he yelled over to his ex-teammate Pete Rose, "Don't you wish you were this strong?"

Rose was a good hitter, but he didn't have much power. He also killed Bart Giamatti. Not literally, but the stress of the Rose investigation probably led to the commissioner-poet's fatal heart attack. Giamatti's son Paul became an actor. He appeared in *Sideways* along with Thomas Haden Church. So did Bart, incidentally. A Giamatti family photo that included him was in the movie. Tony Shaloub appeared with Church in *Wings* where he played a cabbie. Shaloub would later go on to star in *Monk*. Bitty Schram played his assistant. She appeared in *A League of Their Own* along with folks like Madonna and Tom Hanks. Hanks was in *Saving Private Ryan* along with Tom Sizemore. Sizemore portrayed Rose in a made-for-ESPN movie.

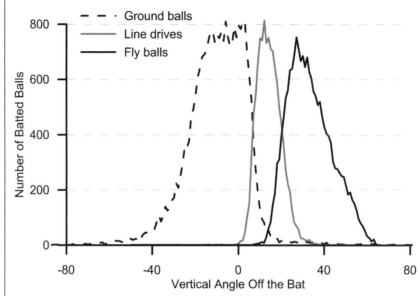

which are most likely to result in hits. This may be the result of some bias, however, as balls that become hits may be more likely to be scored as line drives.

There is also a sizable overlap of line drives and fly balls. At 20 degrees, half the balls are scored as line drives, half as fly balls. Much of the difference may be in how hard the ball was hit (which is not shown here), but there are also subjective and perceptive differences.

In 2009, I wrote an article at FanGraphs that introduced park factors for line drives, showing a plus or minus 20 percent range of line drives scored per batted balls. This was a measure of how many balls were scored as line drives, not how many were actually line drives.

Colin Wyers then did a series of articles at The Hardball Times looking for reasons why the perceptions of line drives might differ from park to park, including the height of the press box above the playing field.

While 70-80 percent of line drives are hits, regardless of the vertical angle, and almost all pop ups are outs, fly balls show a marked difference in outcome as their vertical angles change. While the lower half of fly balls have a hit rate as high as 50 percent and home run rates up to 20 percent, the higher half has virtually no home runs and a hit rate under 10 percent. These balls are basically pop ups to the outfield, high fly balls easily fielded.

With the fuzzy overlap of line drives and fly balls, and the widely different expected values of each, let's ignore the classifications and take a look at all batted balls in the HITf/x sample, along with the total

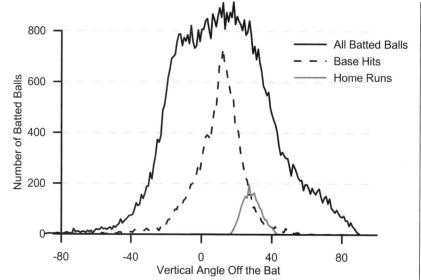

number of base hits (those in play) and over the fence home runs. In the graph above, the bottom axis is still the vertical angle of the ball off the bat.

This graph makes sense, right? Balls that come off the bat at a slightly elevated angle—but not too much—are most likely to be hits and home runs. The difference between the two is how hard they are hit—not the angle off the bat—and we don't have those data here.

Now for the big question: These are the distributions of all batted balls for all players, but how do they vary by different types of players?

To get at this next level of analysis, I grouped pitchers into three types: groundball pitchers (15 percent of pitchers with the highest groundball rates), flyball pitchers (15 percent of pitchers with the lowest groundball rates) and average pitchers (everyone else).

Look at the graph on the next page. You can see that the curves shift to the left. A high groundball pitcher gets more ground balls by getting a lower vertical angle on all balls, not just ground balls.

As the groundball rate increases and the average vertical angle decreases, infield pop ups become outfield fly balls, fly balls become line drives, and line drives become ground balls. Pop ups per balls in the air drop 66 percent, while line drives increase 61 percent.

This changes the expected hit rate of those air balls, as the high groundball pitchers get 50 percent fewer easy flies, while only 10 percent fewer low-angle flies and 10 percent more line drives, leading to a 38 percent increase in the hit rate for balls in the air to the outfield.

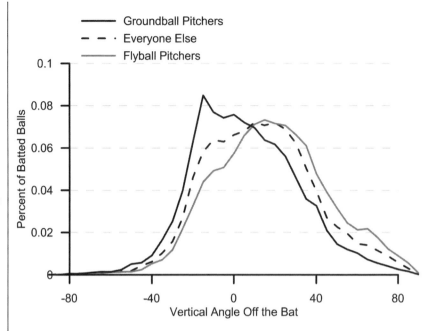

To illustrate the point, here are pitchers' hit rates on all outfield air balls (line drives and outfield flies), broken out by the groundball rate of the pitchers:

GB Rate Group	Balls Contacted	Vertical Launch Angle	OF Airball Hit Rate	Overall BABIP
30%	17,813	21.1	34%	.266
35%	70,925	19.5	37%	.284
40%	200,824	17.4	39%	.294
45%	259,398	14.2	41%	.300
50%	208,559	11.8	42%	.303
55%	103,421	9.3	44%	.302
60%	44,399	5.5	46%	.301
65%	19,316	--	47%	.291

The bottom line: Due to the lower vertical angle of all balls of the pitches from groundball pitchers, balls hit in the air are more likely to be hits. This is the result of two things: air balls off groundball pitchers are more likely to be line drives, and balls categorized as "outfield flies" are more likely to be hits. All because of the lower vertical angle.

Many "true talent" systems, including all projection systems, regress a player's past performance to some mean in order to derive the most accurate projection possible. Many systems take a pitcher's BABIP performance and add about 1,000 more balls in play—at the league-average BABIP rate—to fully "regress" the pitcher's stats and project his future BABIP performance.

The question to consider here is: For batting average on balls in play for pitchers, what mean should their stats be regressed to?

Our analysis shows that we can expect almost 40 points of difference in expected BABIP by measuring the pitcher's groundball rate, yielding a more customized regression. And, along those lines, recent work by Harry Pavlidis at The Hardball Times and Derek Carty at Baseball Prospectus showed that groundball rates for pitchers need only be regressed with about 100 "average" balls in play in order to project a pitcher's future groundball rate.

So I ran two different projections. In the first one, I followed the typical regression of 1,000 balls in play to determine future BABIP. In the second, I applied the groundball regression rate with just 100 balls in play and then assumed the pitcher's BABIP would regress to the average BABIP observed for the groundball rate.

Both projections achieved the same root mean square error, at all sample size levels. In other words, I achieved as good an outcome estimating future BABIP with only the groundball rate as I did knowing past BABIP. We will be able to obtain more accurate forecasts by regressing past BABIP to the BABIP implied by a pitcher's groundball rate. This is the process I plan to use for THT Forecasts, our own projection system.

This also has implications for defensive metrics. Outfielders are often rated by comparing their observed-to-expected catch rates. Because of the overlap of line drives and fly balls, and the subjectivity of how they are scored, if an expected catch rate is determined in part by the number of line drives and fly balls hit to an outfielder, that rate could be subject to wide variation.

Balls would be moved from the 82 percent out rate (for fly balls) to 27 percent out rate (line drives) catch buckets, when those balls might have actually had a 50 percent expectation of being caught. When the outfielder is trying to make the catch, he's concerned most with hang time, which is determined by the vertical launch angle, batted ball speed and back spin.

Back spin is not available from HITf/x, but having looked at the batted ball speed allowed by each pitcher at each vertical angle in the HITf/x data, I found a range of only four mph (plus or minus two) for pitchers,

A-Rod played with Junior early in his career when both were with Seattle. Then Tom Hicks lured him to Texas with his filthy, filthy lucre. Hicks had purchased the team from a group that included George W. Bush. Bush's dad played first base for a Yale team that made it to the first College World Series. He was one of those rare cats who bat right, throw left, and vote center-right. Another Eli (or Bulldog) on that squad was Frank Quinn. Quinn pitched for a couple of years for the Red Sox and was a teammate of Ted Williams. Williams played until 1960 and was really the only reason to watch the Red Sox in his later days. Bobby Thomson was a Red Sock in Ted's final year. But he is more famous for being a Giant in Willie Mays' rookie year.

Mays went to Fairfield High School in suburban Birmingham, Ala. One of his teachers was Angeline Rice. Her daughter was Condi Rice, who went on to become W's national security advisor and secretary of state. Now, when W owned the Rangers, they got rid of a young Sammy Sosa. There are only three degrees of baseball separation between Sosa and Mays, and a few ways to do it. Sosa was a Cub with the peripatetic Mike Morgan, who was once a Blue Jay with Randy Moffitt, who was a Giant for the early '70s Red Juice Giants. Moffitt, incidentally, was the second-best athlete in his family. His sister was Billie Jean King. You can also go Mays to Juan Marichal to Carlton Fisk (1974 Red Sox) to Sosa (1990 White Sox). But my favorite path might be through two knuckleballers. Hoyt Wilhelm was a New York Giants teammate of Mays and an L.A. Dodgers teammate of Charlie Hough. Hough and Sosa later played together.

Griffey, incidentally, played with his dad. His dad was part of the Big Red Machine along with Foster. Foster started out as a Giant, but Bobby Bonds made him expendable.

Griffey was from Donora, Pa. So were Stan Musial and Joe Montana. Montana made the first of many legendary come-backs in his career when he came off the bench and led Notre Dame over North Carolina. The date was Oct. 11, 1975.

- Jon Daly

compared to range of 10 (plus or minus five) for batters. Thus, I believe a weighted mean of the groundball rates of the pitchers an outfielder plays behind would be a less volatile method of determining each player's expected catch rate.

It's been nearly a decade since Voros McCracken introduced "Defense Independent Pitching" (DIPS), which states that pitchers have little influence over the batting average on their balls hit into play. This finding is reflected in stats such as FIP and xFIP—earned run average estimators which assume no differences between pitchers in BABIP.

There are skeptics who keep looking for ways to measure and explain differences in the hit rates allowed by pitchers, leading to work such as Matt Lentzer counting pitches on the edge of the strike zone or Josh Weinstock looking for soft contact on change-ups. I believe those and others are factors, and I will be doing more of my own research on the subject, but groundball rate, as a proxy for vertical launch angle, may be the most persistent and meaningful way that pitchers, as well as batters, control the hit rate on their balls in play.

Resources:

HITf/x for April to June 2009, provided for this article by Sportvision

Gameday play by play, published by Major League Baseball Advanced Media

Separating the Pitching from the Fielding

by John Dewan

Who were the best pitching staffs in baseball in 2011? The standard answer is: In the American League the Los Angeles Angels led with a 3.57 team ERA, with the Tampa Bay Rays a point behind at 3.58; in the National League the Philadelphia Phillies were at the top with a 3.02 ERA, while the San Francisco Giants weren't too far behind at 3.20.

But that's not really just pitching. When you look at a team ERA, it's about how well the pitchers pitched, but it's also about how well the defenders defended. Last year in the *Hardball Times Baseball Annual* we came up with a technique to factor out the defense. This gave us a fielding-independent pitching stat called Pitching Runs Allowed, or just Pitching Runs.

Here's the shocker: The best pitching staff in the American League in 2011 was . . . cough, cough . . . The New York Yankees!

Are you kidding me? This blows me away. At the beginning of the year I was taunting our die-hard Yankees fan in the Baseball Info Solutions office, Rob Burckhard, about how bad the Yankees pitching was looking. Rob wasn't too optimistic about it either, but he was confident that the offense would easily carry the day. For pitching, it was CC Sabathia and Mariano Rivera, and that's it. Phil Hughes was a maybe at best. A.J. Burnett was more than questionable. And Ivan Nova was an unknown commodity. The Yanks were planning to see if they could work in a couple of old has-beens named Freddy Garcia and Bartolo Colon.

Sabathia (19-8, 3.00 ERA) and Rivera (1.91, 44 saves) did their usual thing during the year. But the next two hopefuls, Hughes and Burnett, turned in 5.79 and 5.15 ERAs, respectively. So then, how did the Yankees do it? How did they have the fewest Pitching Runs in the American League? It had to be mirrors, I'm thinking. But it was the Retreads and The Rookie who came through in the rotation. Garcia and Colon posted 3.62 and 4.00 ERAs, respectively, in 51 starts between them, while Nova is a Rookie of the Year candidate with his 16-4 record and 3.70 ERA. In the bullpen, Mariano received massive assistance from David Robertson with a 1.08 ERA in 70 games. Overall, the bullpen ERA of 3.12 was the best in the American League.

Using the Pitching Runs technique, we showed that it was the Chicago White Sox who had the best pitching staff in the American League in 2010. In 2011 they fared well again, coming in third. Pitching Runs uses Team Runs Saved (as presented in the following pages for all teams) to remove the

Fun with Other Numbers

On Sept. 18, Jose Mijares, Alex Burnett, Vinnie Pestano and Vinnie Pestano again walked in a run in an Indians-Twins game that also featured six errors. How rare is it for pitchers to force in that many runs in a game?

To my surprise, in the DH era the ignoble four-peat has happened 32 times. Most of them have occurred in the Wild Card era. Before Sept. 18, the last time was just two weeks before, as Tyler Chatwood, Jerome Williams and Fernando Rodney combined to walk in four Twins on Sept. 2. No one pitcher's been responsible for all four, though several have walked in three, ranging from starters (Randy Johnson on May 1, 1992) to relievers (Mike Munoz on April 7, 1993) to neither (Manny Alexander on April 19, 1996).

The Indians-Twins game was nearly unique in having each team walk in two runs, forming a two-game club with the Sept. 20, 2008 contest between the Giants and Dodgers. Rookie Hiroki Kuroda and veteran Chan Ho Park (Park's only two years older, surprisingly enough) walked in two Giants, and Jack Taschner walked in two Dodgers.

defensive component out of team runs allowed. In short, Pitching Runs are the number of runs the team would have allowed with an average defense.

The best defensive team in the American League in 2011 was the Tampa Bay Rays. Their defense saved them 77 runs. Overall, the team allowed 614 runs. If they had fielded an average defense (0 runs saved), they would have allowed 77 more runs. For 2011, Tampa Bay had 691 Pitching Runs (614 plus 77). The Yankees had 642 Pitching Runs (657 Runs Allowed plus -15 Runs Saved).

Thus, in our opinion, the top pitching staffs in the American League during 2011 were:

Team	Runs Allowed	Runs Saved	Pitching Runs
New York	657	-15	642
Oakland	679	-9	670
Chicago	706	-18	688
Seattle	675	15	690
Tampa Bay	614	77	691
Los Angeles	633	59	692
Detroit	711	-18	693

The Rays and the Angels allowed the fewest runs in the AL. They had formidable defenses, finishing No. 1 and No. 2 in all of baseball in Defensive Runs Saved. The Yankees had a slightly below-average defense and, as a result, rise to the top on the Pitching Runs list.

The Seattle Mariners are fourth on this list, which reminds us of park effects. The Mariners' pitching is good, but their park also helped save a lot of runs. As did Tropicana Field for Tampa Bay.

Over in the National League, the Philadelphia Phillies lapped the field. And then some. Their defense in 2011 was, shall we say, not so good. It cost the team 32 runs. The pitchers were overwhelmingly good. They only allowed 497 Pitching Runs. The next best team was San Francisco, way behind at 604. Here are the best NL pitching staffs of 2011:

Team	Runs Allowed	Runs Saved	Pitching Runs
Philadelphia	529	-32	497
San Francisco	578	26	604

Team	Runs Allowed	Runs Saved	Pitching Runs
Los Angeles	612	6	618
Atlanta	605	24	629
San Diego	611	36	647
Milwaukee	638	19	657
Washington	643	33	676
St. Louis	692	-13	679

Defensive Projections

One of the things that Baseball Info Solutions did for its team clients before the 2011 season was to provide Defensive Projections. We can only give you a taste of this here. We will go into more detail about this in *The Fielding Bible—Volume III*, which comes out in Spring, 2012.

There have been some doubts as to whether Defensive Runs Saved, or other fielding metrics, can be projected. The short answer is, yes they can. In March of 2011 we developed defensive projections for every player on every team in baseball who looked like they would play in the majors last season. We estimated innings in the field by position for every player as best we could. We then projected Runs Saved for each player at each position, totaled them up for each team, and provided both individual and team projections to our clients.

Some of the results weren't too good. We projected the Mariners to finish with 69 runs saved as a team, but due to a variety of reasons, they came in with only -5. We projected the Orioles to have six runs saved, but Mark Reynolds almost single-handedly destroyed that by costing the team 39 runs with his defense (if that's what you call it) at first base and third base, leading to a team total of -59 Runs Saved.

However, quite a few of our projections came out quite well. The Kansas City Royals defense cost them 107 runs in 2010. We projected a huge improvement of 99 runs to only eight runs lost. They improved by 86 runs and finished with -21. We projected the Padres to drop off a bit from 67 Runs Saved in 2010 to 25 in 2011. They came in at 30.

All in all, the correlation coefficient between actual and projected team totals of Defensive Runs for 2011 was .39. We're happy with that for our first attempt at doing defensive projections and expect to do better in the future.

Quick note: You probably didn't notice, but Kansas City's 2010 team Runs Saved figure shown in the following pages is -88, not -107. Some

Two other notable games: the record-setter, and Manny Alexander's wild ride.

Five of the 32 games had five bases-loaded walks. But on May 7, 1992, the White Sox topped them all by walking in six Red Sox runs—and winning 7-6. Charlie Hough's knuckleball was dancing, so much so that he walked five straight batters with two outs in the first inning. Time for the long reliever, which would have been fine except that it was a young and still very wild Wilson Alvarez, who walked in a fourth straight run. In the second, Alvarez got to one out and a runner on third when he walked Ellis Burks—and then walked three more batters to force in two runs. (Burks scored in the first as well and was pulled early, leaving him a line of two runs in zero at-bats.)

But the White Sox were facing Matt Young, and by the end of the third inning the game was tied at 6. The Pale Hose scored a late run to win possibly the ugliest game on record.

As for Alexander, he was pitching because the game was already a blowout (it was a 1996 Orioles-Rangers game; of course it was). But Alexander also recorded two outs, giving him a season ERA+ of 11 to go with his OPS+ of -37. For his IP (0.2) and plate appearance (73) thresholds, his combined score of -26 is the worst by far, beating Mike Torrez's 1983 (13 from 83 ERA+/-70 OPS+) and Charlie McCullough's 1890 (15 from 79/-64). I'd add some snark but I don't need to. -26. He was actually as bad as games feel like when four runs are walked in. And that takes some doing.

- Brandon Isleib

of the other numbers mentioned here also do not match. For our team clients, we provide a more sophisticated version of Defensive Runs Saved. We'll unveil this system for the public in the next *Fielding Bible*.

Description of the Team Defensive Charts

Defensive Runs Saved (Runs Saved, for short) is the analytical metric introduced in *The Fielding Bible—Volume II*. The Runs Saved value indicates how many runs a player saved or hurt his team in the field compared to the average player at his position. A player near zero Runs Saved is about average; a positive number of runs saved indicates above-average defense; below-average fielders post negative Runs Saved totals.

On the following pages, we break down each team's defense by Runs Saved at each position to isolate their strengths and weaknesses for the last three years. For example, in 2011 the best outfield in baseball was the Los Angeles Angels. They had 38 runs saved with two former Gold Glove center fielders playing left and right field (Vernon Wells and Torii Hunter) and the amazing Peter Bourjos in center. The worst defensive position in all of baseball was the aforementioned Baltimore Orioles at third base, where Mark Reynolds botched many, many batted balls, leading to -37 team runs for the Oriole third base unit as a whole.

Comparing 2010 to 2011 we find that, out of the 30 teams in baseball, 14 teams improved their defense in 2011 and 16 teams got worse. The 14 teams that improved had an average of 37 more runs saved over the previous year. Those teams increased their win total by an average of 2.8 wins per team. The 16 teams with a falloff in defense in 2011 fell off by an average of 39 runs, and fell off by 2.5 wins per team. Defense matters.

Team Defense

2011 Defensive Runs Saved by Position and Team

Team	Pitcher	Catcher	First Base	Second Base	Third Base	Shortstop	Left Field	Center Field	Right Field	Total
Tampa Bay Rays	-2	1	2	21	11	20	15	-2	11	77
Los Angeles Angels	-6	0	9	8	10	0	5	23	10	59
Cincinnati Reds	12	-1	3	7	10	13	14	-3	-1	54
Texas Rangers	1	-1	-9	14	10	13	6	9	2	45
San Diego Padres	8	-2	11	-9	12	-6	0	10	12	36
Arizona Diamondbacks	10	7	-4	2	-4	1	9	6	6	33
Washington Nationals	-3	3	-6	3	0	1	14	13	8	33
San Francisco Giants	1	7	10	-14	27	3	6	1	-15	26
Atlanta Braves	1	-1	0	-11	3	12	10	-5	15	24
Toronto Blue Jays	3	-2	-6	12	27	9	-9	-12	-1	21
Milwaukee Brewers	7	-6	1	8	-2	-5	-7	20	3	19
Colorado Rockies	20	10	-4	-4	0	13	-8	-7	-3	17
Seattle Mariners	1	-3	-6	14	1	16	-6	-5	3	15
Cleveland Indians	11	2	-7	-8	8	-5	9	-5	3	8
Los Angeles Dodgers	6	-1	2	-13	8	-8	1	4	7	6
Kansas City Royals	0	4	-18	-2	-5	4	8	2	10	3
Boston Red Sox	-15	0	6	12	-8	-6	1	6	0	-4
Oakland Athletics	-5	0	0	4	-17	-2	5	-5	11	-9
Florida Marlins	2	-3	3	-3	-10	-16	1	1	15	-10
St Louis Cardinals	11	-7	0	-1	-4	-19	1	4	2	-13
Houston Astros	-6	-1	8	-13	-23	9	10	-7	9	-14
New York Yankees	-8	1	2	6	5	-31	22	-15	3	-15
Pittsburgh Pirates	-1	-3	-5	-6	1	-2	4	5	-11	-18
Detroit Tigers	-9	-1	-4	-9	-8	-2	3	21	-9	-18
Chicago White Sox	-7	-3	-12	0	-3	8	-2	-5	6	-18
Minnesota Twins	11	-1	7	-12	-13	-27	-1	11	-2	-27
Philadelphia Phillies	-7	-8	-11	0	12	0	-15	4	-7	-32
New York Mets	5	-8	13	-16	-7	-13	-4	1	-7	-36
Chicago Cubs	-6	-1	4	-6	-17	-15	-3	-4	11	-37
Baltimore Orioles	4	13	-4	-4	-37	6	-6	-13	-4	-45

Team Defense
2010 Defensive Runs Saved by Position and Team

Team	Pitcher	Catcher	First Base	Second Base	Third Base	Shortstop	Left Field	Center Field	Right Field	Total
Oakland Athletics	16	3	19	10	10	4	-5	1	16	74
St Louis Cardinals	11	11	0	-4	0	24	10	-1	10	61
San Francisco Giants	-2	7	7	1	5	-5	21	6	14	54
Minnesota Twins	2	6	3	16	10	11	-4	10	0	54
San Diego Padres	10	1	0	5	21	2	0	14	0	53
Cleveland Indians	19	-3	5	12	9	-12	14	-8	13	49
Toronto Blue Jays	5	-2	11	16	4	13	2	-6	3	46
Tampa Bay Rays	-13	-5	0	29	10	9	11	-7	8	42
Seattle Mariners	-2	1	-1	-12	12	8	3	17	11	37
Atlanta Braves	4	0	-9	7	8	26	-3	-7	9	35
Cincinnati Reds	0	-4	0	1	0	-2	5	10	23	33
New York Mets	10	-1	16	-3	-7	-2	2	5	12	32
Colorado Rockies	8	11	0	-1	-6	28	8	-3	-15	30
Arizona Diamondbacks	-13	-6	2	3	0	-2	16	9	13	22
Detroit Tigers	-18	-4	-2	3	1	2	15	27	-6	18
Philadelphia Phillies	9	5	-17	16	-8	9	-7	7	4	18
Washington Nationals	-2	-1	-8	-9	31	-7	2	1	3	10
Texas Rangers	-11	-6	2	4	-16	0	4	13	10	0
New York Yankees	-5	-10	-4	7	-1	-10	9	8	6	0
Baltimore Orioles	3	2	-3	-9	-9	1	11	3	-1	-2
Los Angeles Angels	0	-7	10	-14	11	-5	-7	14	-5	-3
Houston Astros	-1	5	6	-9	-17	-18	-13	15	12	-20
Los Angeles Dodgers	4	2	0	-2	12	0	-6	-19	-12	-21
Chicago Cubs	-2	-5	6	-10	-11	-3	-4	7	0	-22
Florida Marlins	-9	1	-4	-12	-11	-18	-1	2	29	-23
Chicago White Sox	4	6	-19	-5	-32	17	5	8	-14	-30
Milwaukee Brewers	-7	-5	-12	-10	-9	0	-2	12	-5	-38
Boston Red Sox	-13	-8	7	1	12	-14	-17	-15	-9	-56
Pittsburgh Pirates	2	-4	-6	-17	-13	-26	4	-20	-1	-81
Kansas City Royals	1	-4	-4	-12	-24	-20	-8	-4	-13	-88

Team Defense
2009 Defensive Runs Saved by Position and Team

Team	Pitcher	Catcher	First Base	Second Base	Third Base	Shortstop	Left Field	Center Field	Right Field	Total
Seattle Mariners	12	12	1	6	27	-6	8	36	14	110
Los Angeles Angels	-1	-3	10	14	28	-4	23	-1	-1	65
Tampa Bay Rays	-11	-4	-11	13	15	5	26	-1	25	57
Toronto Blue Jays	6	6	-1	22	11	14	-4	-10	8	52
Cincinnati Reds	12	1	-3	-3	-3	10	17	14	7	52
Texas Rangers	2	3	-8	20	-16	18	5	5	13	42
Detroit Tigers	-3	2	-2	5	8	4	13	15	-5	37
Arizona Diamondbacks	-5	3	-13	13	-4	9	15	4	12	34
San Francisco Giants	8	-4	11	-4	-6	-8	12	6	19	34
Pittsburgh Pirates	4	0	-1	-9	0	16	12	0	9	31
St Louis Cardinals	11	5	12	-8	-8	14	-5	4	6	31
Los Angeles Dodgers	0	5	3	8	15	5	-5	-3	2	30
New York Mets	13	-1	13	-12	-11	-6	5	11	8	20
Chicago Cubs	3	7	3	0	-4	2	-2	-1	8	16
Philadelphia Phillies	-5	2	-1	14	7	-5	-2	-6	12	16
Colorado Rockies	5	-2	-2	2	2	13	15	-10	-11	12
Atlanta Braves	4	2	7	-11	2	19	-11	-10	6	8
Washington Nationals	8	-1	-19	0	21	-3	-3	10	-6	7
New York Yankees	4	-7	1	6	-13	2	-1	3	7	2
San Diego Padres	5	2	12	-20	1	-14	0	17	-4	-1
Houston Astros	3	2	-2	-4	-12	-15	-3	10	19	-2
Cleveland Indians	-4	-9	5	2	-7	4	-7	-1	13	-4
Chicago White Sox	16	0	-4	1	-11	2	-8	5	-10	-9
Baltimore Orioles	7	-8	-12	-5	-5	14	0	-2	-3	-14
Oakland Athletics	1	2	-8	-10	-7	-32	19	12	8	-15
Milwaukee Brewers	-10	-7	-1	20	-8	2	-13	0	-5	-22
Florida Marlins	-12	-4	-8	-7	-5	4	-18	4	18	-28
Minnesota Twins	-4	-5	2	-22	9	-24	-1	17	-5	-33
Boston Red Sox	-17	-8	10	11	-18	-19	-2	-11	2	-52
Kansas City Royals	4	-5	-2	-13	-12	-17	6	-2	-21	-62

Statistics and Such

Quirky Baseball Stats

Here are some baseball stats you don't see every day. In the past, *The Hardball Times Annual* has included many, many baseball stats and graphs, ranging from standard stuff like batting average and ERA to the more esoteric stuff, like batted ball profiles.

We've come to realize that you can get the standard stuff anywhere. It's in the paper, on the Internet—it's especially in our "companion" publication, the *Bill James Handbook*. Actually, the Handbook has some pretty interesting nonstandard stats, too. So buy it, put it on your reading table or desk next to the *Hardball Times Annual*, and you'll have plenty of baseball to read during the offseason.

We've decided to just give you just some weird, esoteric stuff here: five stats for each player who played in the majors last year (well, mostly—a minimum of 10 at-bats or innings pitched was required to make these pages). We think our stats combine to tell a pretty interesting story about each player.

For instance, here are the top batters in Base Runs for the Atlanta Braves:

Batter	PA	BR	WAR	WPA	CL_WPA
Dan Uggla	672	86	2.5	0.9	3.0
Freddie Freeman	635	84	1.0	2.1	2.0
Brian McCann	527	72	3.7	1.2	0.6
Chipper Jones	512	69	2.1	3.0	1.2
Martin Prado	590	58	1.6	0.6	-1.5

Plate Appearances are listed first, to give you a sense of how much each player played. The next column is "BR," which stands for Base Runs. Base Runs is a model that estimates how many runs each batter contributed to his team. The scale is very similar to runs scored or RBI, so when you see that Dan Uggla contributed 86 Base Runs, you know that was pretty good but not quite as good as "100 RBI" territory. Base Runs are adjusted for ballpark effects.

An aside about run estimation systems: There are two fundamental types of systems used to estimate how many runs a batter contributed to his team. One type that has become popular on the leading baseball statistics websites, such as Baseball Reference and FanGraphs, can be called the the "linear weights" type. In linear weights, a batter's run environment provides context to his stats to determine how much each single, double, home run, etc. is worth (their "weights"). There are several methods for deriving the weights, but we won't get into that. This approach is used for a number of

Fun with Other Numbers

John Franco pitched 1,119 major league games and started none of them. This record isn't even close to being threatened, as only 36 pitchers have managed even half of it. Francisco Cordero is the closest active player... almost 400 games away.

But Franco was a starter the majority of his minor league career. Trevor Hoffman, third on the major league list, started 12 games in the minors, although one was a rehab start in 2009. Jeff Reardon didn't stay long in the minors, but he went 17-4 for Jackson in 1978.

So the "purest" reliever stands at eighth on the major league list: Steve Reed. Reed's professional career consisted of 261 minor league games and 883 major league ones; he started none of them. Having never been a major prospect (he was 23 when he entered pro ball) and being a submariner, he didn't have the upside for starting; he had the upside of a non-prospect reliever. To make this list, that's the type of pitcher you need to be: one with clear situational uses but insufficient prospect status to let any manager think of you as a starter. This is the same story as Dan Quisenberry except that Quisenberry started a game for Waterloo in 1975.

stats you see (including some in this book), such as wOBA (available at FanGraphs) or Adjusted Batting Runs (available at Baseball Reference).

The other type of run system is the "model" type, in which a player's batting stats are combined into a formula that estimates how many runs the player contributed. Bill James' Runs Created is one such system. The commonly used OPS (on-base plus slugging percentage) is essentially a model system, too, though it really acts like a broken linear weights system.

Those of us who create these THT Annual stats have a fondness for "model" systems. There are two reasons for this. One is that models give you a sense of how the elements come together, if you will. If a player walks more, then he's also on base more often for a home run. Models capture the way runners move around the bases; linear weights just kind of sums them up. Nothing wrong with that; I'm just sayin'.

The other reason is that there are many ways to produce the weights behind a linear weights system, and there's no guarantee that a certain set of weights is "correct" (whatever that might mean, exactly). Most of the time there's not enough difference to worry about it, but every once in a while it might matter.

A last thing: Linear weights systems tend to rate a player above/below average, while "model" systems tend to rate a player from 0 runs and up. We prefer the latter.

Our run estimation model of choice is Base Runs, created by David Smyth many years ago. The basic framework for Base Runs is...

$$A*B/(B+C)+D$$

...where A is baserunners, B is base advancements, C is outs and D is home runs. That middle part of the equation $(B/(B+C))$ is basically a "base advancement" ratio that can be adjusted for a specific league, team or park.

In other words, the Base Runs model says that runs are scored by getting on base, advancing runners and hitting home runs. Makes sense, right?

We take the model one step further and we calculate how many runs a league-average team would have scored **without** that specific batter on the team. The difference is his Base Runs. (We do this because players are only part of a run environment—they aren't a team in and of themselves. So you generally shouldn't apply the Base Runs formula directly to a batter's stats—you should first place him in an environment and then take him out to see what the difference is. Follow?)

In the end, it all kind of comes together, because Base Runs is one of the models that people use to determine Linear Weights.

I highly recommend Colin Wyers' article in the *Hardball Times Annual 2009* for more information about run estimators.

Anyway, the next batter stat is WAR, which stands for Wins Above Replacement. WAR has taken the baseball analytic world by storm and you can find it at both FanGraphs and Baseball Reference. The figure we use here is from our buddies at FanGraphs.

WAR estimates the number of wins a player contributed to his team, based on his batting and fielding stats. It also factors in the position he played because it's harder to find people who can play shortstop in the majors than people who can play first base (as an example). It then compares that player to a theoretical "replacement" player, someone sitting on the end of the bench or perhaps playing down in Triple-A.

A lot of people are confused by the idea of replacement level, but it's really nothing new. Bill James talked about replacement level back in his *1982 Abstract*. It's a critical baseline because it factors in both playing time and the relative "supply" of major league ballplayers at different levels of performance.

You can learn something by comparing Base Runs and WAR, keeping in mind that WAR includes fielding and position. For instance, Dan Uggla and Freddie Freeman produced about the same number of Base Runs, but Uggla is 1.5 WAR ahead of him in our stats. This is primarily because Uggla plays second base, a premium position, while Freeman plays first. The third player on the list, Brian McCann, rates even more highly in WAR because he catches. Good catchers are hard to find, and he's a darn good one.

WPA and CL_WPA are both described in the article "In All Probability" earlier in this here book. In short, these are "story stats." WPA captures the impact a player had on his team's chances of winning a game, play by play. It's based on average running scoring assumptions by both teams.

CL_WPA takes WPA one step futher by factoring in the importance of each game on that team's chances for the postseason. If a game is near the end of the season and the team is in the pennant race, it will have a higher rating in the stat.

They're included here because they help tell the story of how this team and its players did during the year. Both stats are based on "real time," which means that late-season games are ranked more highly than early-season games in a pennant race. Both games count the same in the standings, but the tension is "palpable" at the end of the year.

Freeman, for instance, outranks Uggla in WPA by about two to one (technically that means he contributed four wins above an average player

Sorted by major league games, the top five pitchers who never started a game:

1. Steve Reed, 883 (261 in minors)

2. Jesse Crain, 443 (126)

3. Dave Heaverlo, 356 (138)

4. Mike Venafro, 307 (424)

5. Joakim Soria, 298 (50)

Many pitchers made rehab starts while their careers were in full swing—Gregg Olson and Stan Belinda, e.g.—taking them off this list. Several, like Quisenberry, started a game or two on their way to the majors. Joe Boever started three games in Triple-A in his final season, leaving him ineligible for the record he then held.

And...

By ERA+, Greg Swindell was below-average his first two seasons, above-average four of his next five (1988-1992), below-average the next four (1993-1996), above-average the next five (1997-2001), and below-average his final season. How many players have come close to this yo-yo performance?

Danny MacFayden had a very similar career arc, although he was right-handed, always a starter, and caught his second wind from playing for Bill McKechnie rather than going to the bullpen. Dennis Martinez had a major lull mid-career, but he found success again as a starter, distinguishing him from Swindell. Ray Sadecki kinda fits, but he wasn't as good as Swindell overall.

To my surprise, the best fit appears to be Darren Oliver. Not that I remembered it this way, but Oliver was above-average from 1993 to 1999, save for a disastrous 1998. He then posted ugly ERAs as a starter through 2004. After a year off, he returned as a reliever and has been consistently above-average.

Swindell and Oliver aren't on each other's lists for similarity scores, but their seasons read in order tell the same story, a story that ordinarily can be written only by lefties in the modern era. Sometimes players are done, but occasionally they come back as important pieces long after the public thinks they're toast.

Absolutely none of this explains David Weathers, however. The righty Weathers posted a below-average ERA+ his first nine seasons (1991-99), then posted an above-average one his final 10 seasons (2000-09). Did something click? Was Y2K's only known effect to make David Weathers better? The world may never know.

- Brandon Isleib

while Uggla contributed two—a win is .5 in WPA talk), partly due to one or two big ninth-inning hits. But Uggla outranks him in CL_WPA primarily because of a home run he hit in that critical final game of the season—the one that the Braves eventually lost.

You might call Base Runs and WAR "value stats" and WPA and CL_WPA "story stats." We think they combine to uniquely lay out an interesting statistical picture of each batter.

Okay, let's move onto pitchers.

Pitcher	IP	LI	WAR	WPA	CL_WPA
Tim Hudson	215.0	0.93	3.7	1.0	1.3
Eric O'Flaherty	73.2	1.55	1.6	2.5	4.3
Jair Jurrjens	152.0	1.03	1.5	1.6	1.9
Jonny Venters	88.0	1.79	1.7	4.3	5.9
Brandon Beachy	141.2	1.01	2.8	0.3	0.6
Craig Kimbrel	77.0	1.89	3.2	1.5	-1.6

This is actually an easier set of numbers to describe, because we've gone over most of them already. The list starts with IP, or Innings Pitched, so you can see how much each pitcher pitched. The next stat is the average Leverage Index ("LI") of each pitcher. This is also described in the Probability article, but the key point is that starting pitchers will usually have an LI around 1.0, but good relievers will have higher numbers. The best-used relievers will have an LI approaching 2.0. This stat allows you to see how each pitcher was used by the manager.

And then you've got WAR (the FanGraphs version), WPA and CL_WPA. As an example, Jonny Venters scores very well in WPA and CL_WPA because, as a key setup man, he pitched (and pitched well) in many high-leverage situations. What's more, he pitched well for the Braves down the stretch and in that last game of the season, so his CL_WPA goes up to 5.9. Closer Craig Kimbrel, who gave up the tying run on Sept. 28, has a negative CL_WPA number.

These are the stats you'll find on the next 30 pages, one page per team. You'll also be able to download spreadsheets of stats from our THT Annual page, created just for purchasers of the Annual. Go to http://www.hardballtimes.com/THT2012Annual/ (mind those capital letters) and type in the username "tht12" and the password "andrus".

Enjoy!

Arizona Diamondbacks

Batter	PA	BR	WAR	WPA	CL_WPA
Justin Upton	674	104	6.4	2.7	5.0
Chris Young	659	79	4.6	2.6	2.5
Miguel Montero	553	70	4.3	1.1	1.6
Ryan Roberts	555	68	3.6	2.8	3.0
Gerardo Parra	493	60	2.8	0.8	0.7
Kelly Johnson	481	52	1.4	0.5	0.5
Stephen Drew	354	37	1.9	-0.2	-1.0
Willie Bloomquist	381	35	0.3	-0.8	-0.8
Paul Goldschmidt	177	24	0.6	0.7	1.5
Juan Miranda	202	22	0.1	0.1	-0.2
Aaron Hill	142	20	1.6	0.3	0.2
Xavier Nady	223	19	-0.2	0.2	0.3
Henry Blanco	112	16	1.2	-0.3	-0.7
Sean Burroughs	115	9	0.0	-0.8	-1.1
Collin Cowgill	100	8	0.3	-0.3	-0.6
Lyle Overbay	49	7	0.2	1.5	0.9
Daniel Hudson	79	6	1.1	0.2	0.5
Russell Branyan	69	6	-0.1	-0.9	-0.7
Melvin Mora	135	6	-0.5	-1.4	-1.5
Geoff Blum	55	5	0.3	-0.2	-0.0
Brandon Allen	37	5	0.3	0.3	0.5
Wily Mo Pena	46	5	-0.0	0.3	0.4
Zach Duke	23	4	0.5	-0.0	-0.0
John McDonald	63	2	-0.0	-0.5	-0.3
Cody Ransom	37	2	-0.0	-0.0	0.0
Joe Saunders	67	2	0.3	-0.5	-0.3
Ian Kennedy	75	1	0.3	-0.9	-1.2
Barry Enright	15	1	0.2	-0.2	-0.2
Josh Collmenter	47	1	0.0	-0.5	-0.5
Micah Owings	19	1	0.1	-0.4	-0.5
Josh Wilson	10	1	0.0	-0.2	-0.2
Wade Miley	16	0	0.0	-0.3	-0.2
Armando Galar-raga	16	-1	-0.3	-0.4	-0.3

Pitcher	IP	LI	WAR	WPA	CL_WPA
Ian Kennedy	222.0	1.07	5.0	4.6	5.3
Daniel Hudson	222.0	0.98	4.9	1.0	1.1
Joe Saunders	212.0	0.95	1.0	1.4	1.7
Josh Collmenter	154.1	0.89	2.2	1.8	1.6
J.J. Putz	58.0	2.05	1.7	3.5	3.1
David Hernandez	69.1	1.62	1.3	1.6	2.2
Micah Owings	63.0	0.84	0.1	0.1	0.7
Zach Duke	76.2	0.56	0.8	-0.6	-1.1
Joe Paterson	34.0	0.97	0.3	-0.0	-0.5
Bryan Shaw	28.1	0.81	0.2	0.6	0.6
Wade Miley	40.0	0.99	0.1	-0.0	0.2
Brad Ziegler	20.2	0.71	0.4	0.8	0.7
Esmerling Vasquez	30.1	1.07	0.0	-0.3	-0.1
Sam Demel	25.2	1.04	-0.4	-0.8	-0.9
Armando Galar-raga	42.2	1.00	-0.8	-1.3	-1.1
Aaron Heilman	35.1	0.66	-0.3	-0.4	-0.3
Barry Enright	37.2	0.83	-0.6	-1.5	-1.6
Alberto Castillo	11.2	0.77	0.0	-0.1	-0.1
Juan Gutierrez	18.1	0.73	0.0	-0.4	-0.5
Jason Marquis	11.1	0.89	-0.2	-0.7	-1.6

Atlanta Braves

Batter	PA	BR	WAR	WPA	CL_WPA
Dan Uggla	672	86	2.5	0.9	3.0
Freddie Freeman	635	84	1.0	2.1	2.0
Brian McCann	527	72	3.7	1.2	0.6
Chipper Jones	512	69	2.1	3.0	1.2
Martin Prado	590	58	1.6	0.6	-1.5
Jason Heyward	456	52	2.2	0.1	-0.2
Alex Gonzalez	593	52	1.1	-1.4	-1.9
Nate McLouth	321	33	0.2	0.2	0.2
Eric Hinske	264	29	0.9	-0.5	-0.9
Michael Bourn	249	27	1.2	-0.2	1.0
David Ross	171	21	1.3	1.0	1.2
Jordan Schafer	220	21	0.6	0.6	1.0
Brooks Conrad	122	14	0.6	0.4	-0.1
Jose Constanza	119	14	0.8	0.2	0.6
Joe Mather	83	6	-0.4	-0.1	-0.2
Derek Lowe	65	4	0.6	0.0	-0.1
Matt Young	52	3	-0.1	-0.8	-0.9
Matt Diaz	37	2	-0.1	-0.3	-0.2
Wilkin Ramirez	30	2	-0.2	-0.2	-0.4
Diory Hernandez	35	2	-0.2	0.3	0.4
Jack Wilson	45	2	-0.2	-0.2	-1.6
Mike Minor	32	1	0.1	-0.4	-0.2
Julio Lugo	48	1	-0.4	-0.4	-0.8
Tim Hudson	80	1	0.2	-0.7	-1.2
Randall Delgado	11	-1	-0.1	-0.3	-0.4
Brandon Hicks	22	-1	-0.4	-0.1	-0.2
Brandon Beachy	50	-2	-0.2	-0.9	-0.9
Jair Jurrjens	55	-2	-0.1	-0.9	-1.1
Tommy Hanson	45	-3	-0.3	-1.2	-1.5

Pitcher	IP	LI	WAR	WPA	CL_WPA
Tim Hudson	215.0	0.93	3.7	1.0	1.3
Eric O'Flaherty	73.2	1.55	1.6	2.5	4.3
Jair Jurrjens	152.0	1.03	1.5	1.6	1.9
Jonny Venters	88.0	1.79	1.7	4.3	5.9
Brandon Beachy	141.2	1.01	2.8	0.3	0.6
Craig Kimbrel	77.0	1.89	3.2	1.5	-1.6
Tommy Hanson	130.0	0.95	1.8	-0.3	-0.5
Derek Lowe	187.0	0.96	2.5	-3.1	-4.5
Cristhian Martinez	77.2	0.65	0.2	0.5	2.1
Mike Minor	82.2	1.08	1.4	0.3	0.4
Scott Linebrink	54.1	0.97	-0.2	-1.0	-3.4
George Sherrill	36.0	1.04	0.5	0.4	0.3
Randall Delgado	35.0	1.04	-0.1	0.2	0.4
Anthony Varvaro	24.0	0.86	-0.0	-0.2	1.1
Scott Proctor	29.1	1.04	-0.8	-0.9	-1.4
Arodys Vizcaino	17.1	1.12	0.1	0.2	0.3
Julio Teheran	19.2	0.75	-0.2	-0.1	-0.2
Cory Gearrin	18.1	1.17	0.4	-0.4	-0.4
Jairo Asencio	10.1	0.42	-0.0	-0.8	-0.7

Baltimore Orioles

Batter	PA	BR	WAR	WPA	CL_WPA
Nick Markakis	716	87	2.2	-0.1	-0.6
Mark Reynolds	620	84	0.3	0.2	0.0
Adam Jones	618	79	2.9	0.6	1.0
J.J. Hardy	567	76	4.8	0.0	0.3
Matt Wieters	551	69	4.3	-0.1	-0.0
Vladimir Guerrero	590	63	-0.0	-1.1	0.0
Robert Andino	511	50	1.8	-0.9	-1.5
Nolan Reimold	305	40	1.5	1.4	0.5
Derrek Lee	364	38	0.5	-1.4	-1.4
Luke Scott	236	26	-0.1	-0.8	-0.6
Brian Roberts	178	15	0.2	-0.2	-0.1
Chris Davis	129	14	-0.3	-0.1	-0.0
Felix Pie	175	12	-2.1	0.2	0.2
Matt Angle	95	9	-0.1	0.4	-0.0
Ryan Adams	96	8	-0.3	-0.5	-0.2
Jake Fox	67	7	-0.1	0.3	-0.5
Blake Davis	65	7	0.0	-0.2	0.0
Craig Tatum	96	3	-0.1	-0.4	0.0
Brandon Snyder	17	2	0.0	0.2	0.2
Cesar Izturis	33	1	0.1	-0.3	-0.3
Josh Bell	65	1	-0.6	-0.8	-0.0
Pedro Florimon	10	0	-0.1	0.0	0.0
Kyle Hudson	29	-1	-0.4	-0.2	0.0

Pitcher	IP	LI	WAR	WPA	CL_WPA
Jeremy Guthrie	208.0	0.90	2.1	-0.5	-0.2
Jim Johnson	91.0	1.53	1.6	2.7	1.0
Zach Britton	154.1	0.98	2.5	-1.0	0.4
Koji Uehara	47.0	1.19	1.1	1.9	1.0
Jake Arrieta	119.1	0.93	0.2	-1.1	0.2
Alfredo Simon	115.2	0.91	1.1	-1.1	-0.0
Brad Bergesen	101.0	0.67	0.3	-1.8	-1.1
Chris Jakubauskas	72.1	0.56	0.0	-0.5	-0.0
Kevin Gregg	59.2	1.75	-0.3	-0.2	0.2
Tommy Hunter	69.1	0.94	0.6	-1.1	0.0
Pedro Strop	12.1	1.91	0.5	0.8	0.0
Chris Tillman	62.0	0.99	1.0	-0.8	-0.4
Mike Gonzalez	46.1	0.74	0.1	0.2	-0.6
Troy Patton	30.0	0.72	0.5	0.4	0.0
Jason Berken	47.0	0.78	-0.5	-1.4	-0.9
Jeremy Accardo	37.2	1.10	-0.2	-0.7	-0.5
Willie Eyre	18.1	0.97	0.1	0.1	0.0
Jo-Jo Reyes	30.2	0.85	-0.2	-0.2	0.0
Brian Matusz	49.2	0.96	-1.0	-3.0	-0.5
Clay Rapada	16.1	0.77	0.0	0.6	0.1
Josh Rupe	14.1	0.14	-0.3	-0.1	-0.1
Mark Hendrickson	11.0	0.54	-0.0	-0.0	0.0
Mitch Atkins	10.2	1.10	-0.3	-0.3	0.0

Boston Red Sox

Batter	PA	BR	WAR	WPA	CL_WPA
Jacoby Ellsbury	732	123	9.4	5.7	7.9
Adrian Gonzalez	715	115	6.6	3.3	4.5
Dustin Pedroia	731	108	8.0	1.8	4.9
David Ortiz	605	97	4.2	1.4	-1.2
Kevin Youkilis	517	71	3.7	1.1	2.0
Carl Crawford	539	57	0.2	-2.6	-4.2
Marco Scutaro	445	54	2.9	-1.7	-0.6
Jarrod Saltalamacchia	386	44	2.5	-1.3	-2.7
Josh Reddick	278	35	1.9	-0.6	-0.7
Jed Lowrie	341	33	0.3	-1.3	-1.2
Jason Varitek	250	28	0.5	-1.1	-0.3
J.D. Drew	286	24	-0.3	-1.4	-2.4
Darnell McDonald	175	18	0.2	-0.1	0.7
Mike Aviles	107	13	0.3	-0.0	-1.0
Drew Sutton	60	8	0.4	0.0	-0.3
Ryan Lavarnway	43	5	0.1	-0.2	-1.8
Mike Cameron	105	5	-0.9	-0.9	-0.9
Yamaico Navarro	40	4	0.0	-0.3	-0.2
Conor Jackson	22	1	-0.2	-0.3	-0.4

Pitcher	IP	LI	WAR	WPA	CL_WPA
Josh Beckett	193.0	1.01	4.3	3.9	2.7
Jon Lester	191.2	0.98	3.7	1.8	2.0
Alfredo Aceves	114.0	0.95	1.0	2.2	5.0
Jonathan Papelbon	64.1	1.69	3.0	3.5	-2.2
John Lackey	160.0	0.97	1.5	-2.0	-2.6
Tim Wakefield	154.2	0.85	0.8	-2.6	-3.2
Clay Buchholz	82.2	1.10	1.1	1.1	1.3
Daniel Bard	73.0	1.69	1.8	1.7	3.0
Matt Albers	64.2	0.93	0.5	-0.1	0.5
Dan Wheeler	49.1	0.44	0.4	-0.0	0.0
Andrew Miller	65.0	0.96	0.2	-1.0	-0.6
Scott Atchison	30.1	0.31	0.5	0.3	0.8
Franklin Morales	32.1	0.94	0.2	0.9	1.9
Erik Bedard	38.0	0.98	0.9	-0.3	-1.8
Daisuke Matsuzaka	37.1	0.97	0.2	-0.4	-0.4
Michael Bowden	20.0	0.17	-0.0	0.1	0.1
Kyle Weiland	24.2	0.90	-0.3	-1.3	-2.1
Bobby Jenks	15.2	1.47	0.1	-0.5	-0.2
Felix Doubront	10.1	0.40	-0.1	-0.0	0.3

Chicago Cubs

Batter	PA	BR	WAR	WPA	CL_WPA
Aramis Ramirez	626	91	3.6	3.9	-0.0
Starlin Castro	715	85	3.4	0.1	0.1
Carlos Pena	606	82	2.6	3.0	0.5
Alfonso Soriano	508	59	1.3	1.3	-0.0
Darwin Barney	571	51	2.2	0.6	0.4
Geovany Soto	474	51	2.1	-0.3	-0.1
Marlon Byrd	482	50	2.0	-1.8	-0.3
Kosuke Fukudome	345	39	-0.1	0.1	0.4
Reed Johnson	266	35	1.2	0.2	0.9
Blake DeWitt	243	25	0.2	-1.1	-0.0
Jeff Baker	212	19	-0.1	-0.4	0.5
Tony Campana	155	16	1.5	0.4	0.1
Tyler Colvin	222	12	-1.0	-0.3	-0.3
Bryan LaHair	69	10	0.3	0.8	0.0
Koyie Hill	153	9	-0.4	-1.5	-0.5
Carlos Zambrano	48	7	1.0	-0.1	-0.1
Lou Montanez	57	5	-0.1	0.2	0.1
DJ LeMahieu	62	3	-0.1	-0.3	-0.1
Casey Coleman	29	1	0.1	-0.4	-0.1
Randy Wells	50	-0	0.0	-0.8	-0.1
Welington Castillo	13	-0	-0.1	-0.1	-0.1
Doug Davis	13	-1	-0.1	-0.3	-0.1
Rodrigo Lopez	33	-1	-0.1	-0.6	-0.0
Matt Garza	71	-2	-0.1	-1.4	-0.5
Ryan Dempster	70	-2	-0.3	-1.5	-0.4

Pitcher	IP	LI	WAR	WPA	CL_WPA
Matt Garza	198.0	1.03	5.0	0.5	-0.5
Ryan Dempster	202.1	0.99	2.8	-0.9	-1.4
Sean Marshall	75.2	1.63	2.8	1.7	0.7
Carlos Zambrano	145.2	0.98	0.9	-0.5	-0.1
Jeff Samardzija	88.0	1.01	0.6	0.5	0.4
Randy Wells	135.1	1.03	0.1	-2.4	-0.2
Carlos Marmol	74.0	2.04	0.8	-1.0	-0.1
Rodrigo Lopez	97.2	1.00	-0.3	-1.3	-0.3
Kerry Wood	51.0	1.74	0.5	-1.0	-0.7
James Russell	67.2	0.79	-0.2	-1.0	-1.0
Casey Coleman	84.1	1.07	0.6	-1.9	-0.8
John Grabow	62.1	0.59	-0.5	-0.5	0.1
Ramon Ortiz	33.1	0.51	-0.1	0.0	-0.0
Marcos Mateo	23.0	0.70	0.2	-0.2	-0.4
Doug Davis	45.2	1.10	0.7	-1.1	-0.5
Andrew Cashner	10.2	0.68	0.1	0.3	0.1
Justin Berg	12.0	0.31	-0.1	-0.1	-0.0

Chicago White Sox

Batter	PA	BR	WAR	WPA	CL_ WPA
Paul Konerko	639	98	3.1	2.6	2.0
Alexei Ramirez	684	74	4.9	-0.2	-0.2
Carlos Quentin	483	69	2.6	2.7	1.9
Juan Pierre	711	66	-0.4	-0.5	-0.6
A.J. Pierzynski	500	52	1.7	-0.3	0.3
Gordon Beckham	557	50	1.1	-1.3	-1.0
Alex Rios	570	43	-0.7	-3.4	-2.5
Brent Morel	444	40	0.5	-1.2	-1.3
Adam Dunn	496	37	-2.9	-2.2	-1.7
Brent Lillibridge	216	31	1.3	-0.5	-0.8
Alejandro De Aza	171	29	2.8	2.0	0.9
Tyler Flowers	129	14	0.7	-0.5	-0.4
Omar Vizquel	182	13	-0.5	-0.9	-0.5
Dayan Viciedo	113	10	0.2	-0.5	0.1
Ramon Castro	75	10	0.4	-0.0	-0.1
Mark Teahen	130	9	-0.4	-1.1	-0.7
Donny Lucy	11	1	-0.0	-0.1	-0.1
Dallas McPherson	15	-0	-0.2	-0.1	-0.1

Pitcher	IP	LI	WAR	WPA	CL_ WPA
Mark Buehrle	205.1	0.97	3.4	1.6	1.3
Gavin Floyd	193.2	0.92	3.6	-0.3	-0.3
Philip Humber	163.0	0.97	3.5	1.1	0.7
John Danks	170.1	1.02	3.2	0.0	0.5
Edwin Jackson	121.2	0.97	3.1	0.9	0.8
Chris Sale	71.0	1.55	1.4	3.5	2.5
Jesse Crain	65.1	1.76	0.9	1.6	1.4
Jake Peavy	111.2	1.07	2.9	-1.2	-1.6
Sergio Santos	63.1	1.77	1.6	0.2	0.3
Will Ohman	53.1	0.58	0.2	-0.2	-0.2
Matt Thornton	59.2	1.48	1.6	-1.7	-1.7
Zach Stewart	50.2	0.93	0.4	-0.9	-0.4
Dylan Axelrod	18.2	0.97	0.4	0.2	0.0
Jeff Gray	13.1	0.24	0.0	0.1	0.1
Jason Frasor	17.2	0.99	-0.1	-0.3	-0.2
Tony Pena	20.1	0.48	0.1	-0.9	-0.9
Josh Kinney	17.2	0.12	0.2	0.0	0.0
Brian Bruney	19.2	0.54	-0.2	0.0	-0.0

Cincinnati Reds

Batter	PA	BR	WAR	WPA	CL_WPA
Joey Votto	719	116	6.9	6.7	5.8
Jay Bruce	664	89	3.3	1.0	1.0
Brandon Phillips	675	88	6.0	1.5	-0.4
Drew Stubbs	681	76	2.6	-1.7	-1.2
Chris Heisey	308	42	1.6	-0.4	-0.7
Ramon Hernandez	328	40	2.0	0.1	0.9
Ryan Hanigan	304	33	1.8	0.6	0.6
Jonny Gomes	265	32	1.1	-0.3	-0.3
Miguel Cairo	276	31	1.9	-0.0	0.3
Edgar Renteria	333	30	0.9	-0.0	-0.3
Scott Rolen	269	27	1.3	-0.5	-0.4
Paul Janish	366	20	-0.4	-2.2	-1.8
Fred Lewis	210	18	0.2	-0.0	0.1
Yonder Alonso	98	17	0.6	0.9	0.1
Todd Frazier	121	14	0.7	0.2	-0.1
Juan Francisco	97	11	0.2	0.2	-0.4
Dave Sappelt	118	9	0.3	-0.4	-0.1
Dontrelle Willis	34	6	0.9	-0.0	0.0
Zack Cozart	38	5	0.7	0.1	0.1
Devin Mesoraco	53	4	-0.1	-0.4	-0.0
Homer Bailey	45	3	0.4	-0.1	-0.2
Chris Valaika	27	3	0.3	-0.1	-0.1
Mike Leake	66	1	0.5	-0.6	-0.3
Jeremy Hermida	18	0	-0.2	-0.2	-0.3
Sam LeCure	11	0	0.1	-0.0	0.0
Travis Wood	35	-1	-0.1	-0.6	-0.6
Edinson Volquez	34	-1	-0.0	-0.4	-0.2
Bronson Arroyo	66	-1	-0.0	-1.4	-0.9
Johnny Cueto	56	-2	-0.2	-0.8	-0.6

Pitcher	IP	LI	WAR	WPA	CL_WPA
Johnny Cueto	156.0	1.17	2.8	2.0	1.9
Mike Leake	167.2	0.94	1.5	-0.4	-0.6
Bronson Arroyo	199.0	0.93	-1.3	-0.8	-1.2
Homer Bailey	132.0	0.95	1.5	-1.0	-0.6
Francisco Cordero	69.2	2.07	0.1	2.0	-0.1
Travis Wood	106.0	0.95	1.1	-0.6	-0.9
Sam LeCure	77.2	0.82	0.5	0.9	0.8
Nick Masset	70.1	1.32	0.6	-2.7	-0.9
Edinson Volquez	108.2	1.00	-0.3	-2.0	-2.3
Bill Bray	48.1	1.26	0.7	0.6	0.5
Logan Ondrusek	61.1	1.30	-0.2	-0.0	0.5
Jose Arredondo	53.0	1.10	-0.1	0.1	-0.2
Aroldis Chapman	50.0	1.42	0.6	2.1	1.2
Dontrelle Willis	75.2	1.18	0.8	-0.7	0.2
Carlos Fisher	24.0	0.91	-0.1	-0.4	-0.6
Jeremy Horst	15.1	0.34	-0.1	-0.1	-0.1
Jordan Smith	20.0	0.73	-0.2	-0.3	-0.3
Matt Maloney	18.2	0.41	-0.4	-0.7	-0.2

Cleveland Indians

Batter	PA	BR	WAR	WPA	CL_WPA
Asdrubal Cabrera	667	92	3.6	1.3	1.7
Carlos Santana	658	91	3.8	0.3	-0.5
Michael Brantley	496	54	1.4	0.5	0.2
Travis Hafner	368	51	1.3	2.7	2.4
Matt LaPorta	385	45	-0.8	-0.7	-1.6
Shin-Soo Choo	358	43	1.4	-0.2	-0.1
Jack Hannahan	366	42	2.4	1.1	0.9
Shelley Duncan	247	34	0.9	0.6	-0.5
Grady Sizemore	295	33	0.2	-1.9	-2.0
Orlando Cabrera	344	27	-0.6	-1.1	-1.5
Lonnie Chisenhall	223	25	0.7	0.4	-0.5
Kosuke Fukudome	258	24	-0.1	-0.8	-0.2
Jason Kipnis	150	24	0.8	-0.3	-0.6
Lou Marson	272	22	0.9	-1.6	-1.5
Ezequiel Carrera	226	19	0.3	0.1	0.6
Jason Donald	143	18	0.5	-0.4	-0.6
Travis Buck	160	14	-0.0	-0.1	-0.2
Austin Kearns	174	13	-0.8	-1.1	-1.4
Jim Thome	82	13	0.5	-0.1	-0.2
Cord Phelps	80	4	-0.9	-0.5	-0.4
Adam Everett	67	4	-0.4	-0.4	-0.6
Trevor Crowe	32	3	0.1	-0.3	-0.0
Luis Valbuena	44	3	-0.3	-0.4	-1.0
Jerad Head	25	0	-0.3	-0.1	-0.1

Pitcher	IP	LI	WAR	WPA	CL_WPA
Justin Masterson	216.0	1.06	4.9	1.9	3.5
Josh Tomlin	165.1	0.91	1.8	0.5	0.6
Fausto Carmona	188.2	0.97	1.5	-2.5	-2.2
Vinnie Pestano	62.0	1.57	1.5	1.9	1.9
Joe Smith	67.0	1.05	1.2	0.8	1.2
Carlos Carrasco	124.2	0.99	1.4	-0.7	-0.9
Tony Sipp	62.1	1.32	-0.1	0.7	1.6
Chris Perez	59.2	2.15	0.1	1.8	1.2
Rafael Perez	63.0	1.02	0.8	0.9	1.3
Chad Durbin	68.1	0.70	-0.3	0.3	1.0
Ubaldo Jimenez	65.1	0.97	1.0	-0.9	-1.5
Jeanmar Gomez	58.1	0.88	0.7	-0.2	-0.5
Frank Herrmann	56.1	0.40	0.0	0.4	0.7
Mitch Talbot	63.2	0.88	-0.1	-1.4	-1.8
David Huff	50.2	1.06	0.6	-0.3	-0.1
Alex White	15.0	1.16	-0.1	-0.1	-0.1
Nick Hagadone	11.0	0.38	0.1	0.1	0.0
Josh Judy	14.0	0.17	-0.3	-0.0	0.0
Zach McAllister	17.2	1.04	0.4	-0.2	-0.6
Justin Germano	12.2	0.27	-0.1	-0.4	-0.4

Colorado Rockies

Batter	PA	BR	WAR	WPA	CL_WPA
Troy Tulowitzki	606	88	6.3	2.4	1.0
Carlos Gonzalez	542	78	4.1	2.1	1.1
Seth Smith	533	69	1.9	0.9	1.4
Dexter Fowler	563	67	2.9	1.7	0.8
Todd Helton	491	65	2.6	1.9	1.4
Chris Iannetta	426	50	3.3	0.2	0.5
Ty Wigginton	446	47	0.3	-1.4	-0.5
Mark Ellis	286	28	1.4	-1.7	-0.0
Jason Giambi	152	25	1.3	0.8	0.4
Eric Young	229	23	-0.1	-0.4	-0.5
Jonathan Herrera	320	23	0.0	-0.8	-0.8
Chris Nelson	189	16	-0.6	-1.5	-0.8
Ryan Spilborghs	223	14	-1.1	-1.3	-0.8
Kevin Kouzmanoff	108	11	-0.0	-0.2	-0.0
Jordan Pacheco	88	8	-0.3	-0.3	0.0
Jose Lopez	129	7	-0.3	-1.2	-1.6
Charlie Blackmon	102	7	-0.7	-0.6	-0.6
Eliezer Alfonzo	79	6	0.1	-0.0	0.0
Jose Morales	71	6	-0.1	-0.3	-0.3
Wilin Rosario	57	6	0.2	-0.8	0.0
Ian Stewart	136	5	-0.6	-1.5	-1.3
Tommy Field	51	3	0.0	-0.0	0.0
Alfredo Amezaga	38	3	-0.1	-0.1	-0.1
Kevin Millwood	23	2	0.2	-0.4	-0.0
Matt Pagnozzi	25	2	0.0	-0.2	-0.2
Esmil Rogers	31	2	0.2	-0.3	-0.2
Jason Hammel	61	1	0.2	-0.5	-0.2
Jhoulys Chacin	68	1	0.2	-0.7	-0.8
Jorge de la Rosa	23	1	0.1	-0.2	-0.3
Cole Garner	10	1	-0.0	-0.1	-0.1
Juan Nicasio	23	0	-0.0	-0.2	-0.1
Greg Reynolds	12	-0	-0.1	-0.1	-0.1
Aaron Cook	35	-0	-0.0	-0.5	-0.1
Alex White	14	-0	-0.0	-0.4	-0.0
Ubaldo Jimenez	42	-0	-0.0	-0.5	-0.5
Clay Mortensen	15	-1	-0.1	-0.2	-0.3

Pitcher	IP	LI	WAR	WPA	CL_WPA
Jhoulys Chacin	194.0	0.88	2.5	1.1	1.3
Jason Hammel	170.1	1.01	1.0	-0.4	0.4
Ubaldo Jimenez	123.0	0.97	2.5	-0.9	-1.0
Rafael Betancourt	62.1	1.19	1.6	1.9	0.3
Matt Belisle	72.0	1.22	1.3	0.4	-0.2
Juan Nicasio	71.2	0.93	1.4	-0.2	-0.4
Jorge de la Rosa	59.0	1.07	1.4	0.4	0.4
Matt Lindstrom	54.0	1.38	0.8	0.5	1.4
Rex Brothers	40.2	1.17	0.8	0.5	0.0
Huston Street	58.1	1.75	0.5	1.2	1.3
Aaron Cook	97.0	0.92	1.0	-1.4	-0.4
Matt Reynolds	50.2	0.99	-0.1	0.3	0.9
Kevin Millwood	54.1	0.86	0.7	0.2	0.0
Clay Mortensen	58.1	0.73	-0.1	-0.8	-0.9
Esmil Rogers	83.0	1.03	-0.2	-1.2	-0.8
Edgmer Escalona	25.2	0.60	0.1	0.4	0.0
Greg Reynolds	32.0	0.59	-0.1	-0.0	0.1
Josh Roenicke	16.2	1.11	0.1	0.4	0.0
Franklin Morales	14.0	0.97	-0.1	-0.4	-0.5
Alex White	36.1	0.94	-0.7	-1.6	-0.0
Drew Pomeranz	18.1	0.87	0.6	0.2	0.0
Eric Stults	12.0	0.21	-0.3	-0.1	-0.0
Felipe Paulino	14.2	1.10	-0.1	-1.6	-2.2

Detroit Tigers

Batter	PA	BR	WAR	WPA	CL_WPA
Miguel Cabrera	688	127	7.3	7.3	6.4
Alex Avila	551	87	5.5	2.6	3.1
Victor Martinez	595	84	2.9	3.1	2.5
Jhonny Peralta	576	78	5.2	0.2	1.0
Austin Jackson	668	71	2.8	-0.4	0.5
Brennan Boesch	472	64	1.7	0.5	0.3
Ryan Raburn	418	48	1.2	-1.3	-1.7
Magglio Ordonez	357	31	-1.0	-1.0	-1.2
Ramon Santiago	294	30	1.4	-0.8	-1.1
Don Kelly	281	27	0.6	-0.7	-1.4
Andy Dirks	235	26	0.4	-1.3	-1.5
Wilson Betemit	133	21	0.5	0.6	0.7
Delmon Young	178	21	0.1	-0.5	0.1
Brandon Inge	303	19	-0.4	-0.7	-1.2
Casper Wells	125	16	0.9	-0.2	-0.1
Carlos Guillen	102	8	-0.1	-0.9	-2.3
Will Rhymes	99	8	-0.2	-0.3	-0.4
Scott Sizemore	74	6	0.1	-0.2	-0.2
Danny Worth	39	4	-0.1	-0.1	-0.1
Omir Santos	22	1	-0.1	-0.1	-0.1

Pitcher	IP	LI	WAR	WPA	CL_WPA
Justin Verlander	251.0	0.94	7.0	5.1	6.9
Max Scherzer	195.0	0.98	2.7	-0.0	0.7
Rick Porcello	182.0	1.01	2.7	-0.3	-1.2
Jose Valverde	72.1	1.76	1.0	4.2	5.0
Doug Fister	70.1	0.94	2.4	2.0	1.1
Brad Penny	181.2	1.00	0.8	-2.7	-2.7
Al Alburquerque	43.1	1.12	1.3	1.8	1.8
Joaquin Benoit	61.0	1.54	1.3	1.7	2.4
Phil Coke	108.2	1.06	2.0	-0.3	-0.3
Daniel Schlereth	49.0	0.74	-0.3	-0.3	0.0
Charlie Furbush	32.1	0.78	-0.1	-0.1	-0.4
Ryan Perry	37.0	0.87	0.2	0.6	0.5
Duane Below	29.0	0.99	0.2	-0.3	-0.4
David Pauley	19.2	0.67	-0.2	-0.6	-1.0
Brayan Villarreal	16.0	0.82	-0.2	-0.0	-0.1
David Purcey	18.2	0.69	-0.2	-0.5	-0.8
Adam Wilk	13.1	0.15	-0.1	-0.1	-0.1
Jacob Turner	12.2	1.05	-0.1	-0.4	-0.0
Brad Thomas	11.0	0.27	-0.0	-0.2	-0.2

Florida Marlins

Batter	PA	BR	WAR	WPA	CL_WPA
Mike Stanton	601	93	4.5	2.3	0.7
Gaby Sanchez	661	81	3.0	-0.7	1.0
Emilio Bonifacio	641	80	3.3	0.3	-0.6
Logan Morrison	525	69	1.0	1.0	1.2
Omar Infante	640	63	2.7	0.3	-0.6
John Buck	530	52	1.8	0.4	1.5
Greg Dobbs	439	44	0.5	0.6	1.7
Hanley Ramirez	385	43	1.3	0.6	-0.1
Bryan Petersen	241	29	1.7	0.4	-0.2
Chris Coghlan	298	28	-0.3	-0.8	-1.1
Mike Cameron	164	20	1.3	0.3	-0.1
Brett Hayes	144	15	0.6	-1.0	-0.2
Jose Lopez	113	12	0.1	-0.3	-0.2
Donnie Murphy	100	7	0.1	-0.2	-0.2
Wes Helms	124	7	-0.7	-0.9	-1.0
DeWayne Wise	72	5	0.2	-0.0	0.1
Matt Dominguez	48	4	-0.2	-0.3	0.0
Scott Cousins	58	2	-0.0	0.1	0.1
Chris Volstad	52	2	0.3	-0.5	-0.5
Javier Vazquez	67	1	0.4	-0.6	-0.4
Vinny Rottino	14	1	-0.1	0.2	0.0
John Baker	16	1	-0.1	-0.1	0.0
Alfredo Amezaga	49	0	-0.5	-0.7	-0.0
Josh Johnson	23	0	0.1	0.1	0.1
Anibal Sanchez	70	0	0.1	-1.0	-0.5
Brad Hand	20	-0	-0.0	-0.4	-0.2
Osvaldo Martinez	23	-1	-0.3	-0.3	-0.5
Ricky Nolasco	71	-1	0.0	-1.1	-0.4
Clay Hensley	17	-1	-0.1	-0.6	-0.1

Pitcher	IP	LI	WAR	WPA	CL_WPA
Anibal Sanchez	196.1	1.02	3.8	0.6	1.8
Javier Vazquez	192.2	0.93	3.2	-0.4	-3.3
Ricky Nolasco	206.0	1.01	3.5	-1.1	-0.7
Chris Volstad	165.2	1.03	1.3	-2.4	-2.3
Josh Johnson	60.1	1.03	1.7	1.4	1.8
Edward Mujica	76.0	1.23	1.0	0.2	0.5
Steve Cishek	54.2	0.87	1.0	0.6	0.1
Mike Dunn	63.0	1.12	-0.1	-1.3	-1.1
Leo Nunez	64.1	1.90	0.2	1.1	0.5
Burke Badenhop	63.2	0.74	0.9	-1.2	-0.4
Brian Sanches	61.2	0.48	-0.3	-0.5	-0.3
Ryan Webb	50.2	1.23	0.3	-0.3	-0.0
Brad Hand	60.0	0.96	-0.4	-0.9	-0.1
Clay Hensley	67.2	1.24	-0.1	-1.1	-1.1
Randy Choate	24.2	1.08	0.1	0.5	1.2
Jose Ceda	20.1	0.34	0.1	-0.2	-0.0
Alex Sanabia	11.0	0.87	0.0	-0.0	0.0
Chris Hatcher	10.1	0.37	-0.1	0.0	0.0

Houston Astros

Batter	PA	BR	WAR	WPA	CL_WPA
Carlos Lee	653	86	3.2	0.2	-0.3
Michael Bourn	473	65	3.0	1.3	0.1
Hunter Pence	432	63	2.1	2.3	0.7
Clint Barmes	495	53	3.1	-1.2	-0.4
Chris Johnson	405	41	-0.8	-0.5	-0.3
Brett Wallace	379	39	-0.2	0.0	0.4
Matt Downs	222	35	1.4	0.8	0.3
Jason Bourgeois	252	29	1.2	-0.6	0.2
J.D. Martinez	226	27	1.5	-0.3	0.0
Angel Sanchez	328	26	0.5	-0.3	-0.1
Brian Bogusevic	182	23	2.4	-0.2	0.1
Jose Altuve	234	22	0.3	-1.2	0.0
Jeff Keppinger	170	20	0.7	-0.2	-0.1
Jimmy Paredes	179	19	0.4	-0.1	0.0
Humberto Quintero	272	18	-0.0	-2.3	0.1
Bill Hall	158	13	-1.0	-0.7	-0.3
Jordan Schafer	118	12	0.1	0.1	0.0
J.R. Towles	165	11	-0.2	-0.6	-0.1
Jason Michaels	169	11	-0.5	-1.5	-0.2
J.B. Shuck	92	9	0.3	-0.8	0.0
Carlos Corporan	173	8	-0.6	-2.0	-0.0
J.A. Happ	53	2	0.5	-0.3	0.2
Wandy Rodriguez	67	2	0.2	-1.0	-0.2
Joe Inglett	27	1	-0.3	-0.4	-0.3
Brett Myers	71	1	0.3	-1.2	-0.2
Nelson Figueroa	10	0	0.1	-0.2	-0.1
Henry Sosa	18	0	0.1	-0.3	0.0
Jordan Lyles	29	0	0.1	-0.5	-0.0
Bud Norris	66	-0	0.0	-0.7	-0.0
Aneury Rodriguez	11	-1	-0.1	-0.3	-0.1

Pitcher	IP	LI	WAR	WPA	CL_WPA
Wandy Rodriguez	191.0	0.94	1.5	0.8	0.2
Brett Myers	216.0	0.90	1.5	-1.3	-0.1
Bud Norris	186.0	1.03	1.8	-0.4	-0.1
J.A. Happ	156.1	0.92	0.3	-2.0	-0.5
Mark Melancon	74.1	1.60	0.8	1.5	0.2
Wilton Lopez	71.0	1.14	0.5	-0.7	-0.2
Jordan Lyles	94.0	1.06	0.3	-1.8	-0.0
Fernando Rodriguez	52.1	1.20	-0.2	1.1	0.0
Aneury Rodriguez	85.1	0.60	-0.2	-1.5	-0.2
Henry Sosa	53.1	1.08	0.1	-0.6	0.0
Enerio Del Rosario	53.0	0.62	-0.3	0.0	-0.0
David Carpenter	27.2	1.28	-0.1	-0.8	0.0
Sergio Escalona	27.2	0.97	-0.0	-0.3	0.0
Wesley Wright	12.0	1.45	0.1	0.2	0.0
Jeff Fulchino	33.0	0.88	-0.3	-1.1	-0.3
Lucas Harrell	13.0	1.17	0.2	-0.1	0.0
Nelson Figueroa	29.0	0.91	0.0	-1.3	-1.0
Fernando Abad	19.2	1.11	-0.6	-1.7	-1.0
Jose Valdez	14.0	0.24	-0.1	0.2	0.1
Brandon Lyon	13.1	2.37	-0.7	-2.4	-1.6

Kansas City Royals

Batter	PA	BR	WAR	WPA	CL_WPA
Alex Gordon	690	110	6.9	3.5	0.6
Melky Cabrera	706	97	4.2	1.5	0.4
Billy Butler	673	92	1.8	0.7	-0.1
Jeff Francoeur	656	89	2.9	-0.5	0.0
Eric Hosmer	563	75	1.6	1.8	0.1
Alcides Escobar	598	53	2.2	-5.0	-3.2
Mike Moustakas	365	37	0.7	-1.3	-0.1
Chris Getz	429	36	1.0	-0.8	-0.2
Wilson Betemit	226	26	0.5	-0.1	0.1
Matt Treanor	230	23	0.9	0.7	0.3
Salvador Perez	158	22	1.4	0.5	-0.0
Brayan Pena	240	20	0.5	-1.9	-0.4
Mike Aviles	202	20	-0.0	-1.5	-1.1
Johnny Giavotella	187	17	-0.0	-0.9	0.0
Mitch Maier	113	12	0.7	-0.7	0.1
Kila Ka'aihue	96	8	-0.1	0.0	-0.0
Jarrod Dyson	53	6	0.3	0.1	0.2
Yamaico Navarro	26	3	0.1	0.2	0.0
Lorenzo Cain	23	2	0.1	-0.2	0.0
Manuel Pina	15	1	0.1	-0.3	-0.0

Pitcher	IP	LI	WAR	WPA	CL_WPA
Luke Hochevar	198.0	0.98	2.3	-0.3	-0.4
Bruce Chen	155.0	0.98	1.7	1.0	0.4
Jeff Francis	183.0	0.96	2.6	-1.8	-0.6
Greg Holland	60.0	1.41	2.0	3.1	0.5
Felipe Paulino	124.2	1.13	2.6	-0.8	0.1
Aaron Crow	62.0	1.72	0.3	-0.2	1.7
Louis Coleman	59.2	1.24	0.1	1.0	0.2
Danny Duffy	105.1	1.09	0.6	-1.7	-0.0
Tim Collins	67.0	1.01	0.0	0.5	0.4
Blake Wood	69.2	0.86	0.6	-1.3	-0.0
Joakim Soria	60.1	2.08	0.9	-0.5	-1.1
Everett Teaford	44.0	0.64	-0.1	0.5	0.3
Nathan Adcock	60.1	0.58	0.2	-0.6	0.1
Kyle Davies	61.1	0.91	0.7	-1.7	-1.4
Luis Mendoza	14.2	0.85	0.3	0.6	0.0
Sean O'Sullivan	58.1	1.00	-0.5	-1.7	-1.3
Jeremy Jeffress	15.1	1.09	0.0	-0.4	-0.5
Vin Mazzaro	28.1	0.76	-0.2	-0.4	-0.3

Los Angeles Angels of Anaheim

Batter	PA	BR	WAR	WPA	CL_WPA
Torii Hunter	649	79	2.5	1.4	1.1
Howie Kendrick	583	79	5.8	0.7	1.4
Erick Aybar	605	76	4.0	-0.1	-0.4
Peter Bourjos	552	73	4.3	-0.2	-0.8
Mark Trumbo	573	72	2.3	0.9	0.5
Bobby Abreu	585	71	0.4	3.7	4.2
Alberto Callaspo	536	65	3.6	0.4	0.0
Maicer Izturis	494	58	2.0	-0.1	0.4
Vernon Wells	529	53	0.3	-1.1	-1.4
Hank Conger	197	18	0.2	-0.2	-0.2
Mike Trout	135	15	0.8	0.3	0.4
Jeff Mathis	281	13	-1.0	-1.9	-2.3
Russell Branyan	77	9	0.0	-0.6	-0.6
Bobby Wilson	127	7	-0.0	-0.7	-1.0
Alexi Amarista	56	2	-0.7	-0.3	-0.2
Efren Navarro	12	1	0.0	-0.0	-0.0
Andrew Romine	18	0	-0.1	-0.1	-0.2
Reggie Willits	28	0	-0.3	-0.1	-0.1
Brandon Wood	15	-0	-0.2	-0.3	-0.3

Pitcher	IP	LI	WAR	WPA	CL_WPA
Jered Weaver	235.2	0.99	5.6	4.6	5.8
Dan Haren	238.1	0.99	6.4	3.7	4.5
Ervin Santana	228.2	1.09	3.2	0.2	0.5
Tyler Chatwood	142.0	0.96	0.5	-1.8	-2.5
Scott Downs	53.2	1.95	0.9	1.7	2.0
Joel Pineiro	145.2	0.95	1.3	-1.5	-2.3
Jordan Walden	60.1	2.51	1.7	0.5	1.2
Rich Thompson	54.0	0.66	0.6	-0.6	-0.9
Hisanori Takahashi	68.0	0.99	0.4	0.5	0.1
Bobby Cassevah	39.2	0.75	0.3	0.8	0.9
Jerome Williams	44.0	0.95	0.4	0.3	0.1
Trevor Bell	34.1	0.48	0.2	0.0	0.1
Fernando Rodney	32.0	1.67	-0.2	-2.0	-2.4
Francisco Rodri-guez	13.2	0.20	-0.1	0.0	0.0
Matt Palmer	15.2	1.04	0.4	-0.5	-0.4
Garrett Richards	14.0	0.64	-0.3	-0.5	-1.1
Michael Kohn	12.1	1.11	-0.9	-0.5	-0.7
Kevin Jepsen	13.0	1.82	-0.4	-0.8	-1.0

Los Angeles Dodgers

Batter	PA	BR	WAR	WPA	CL_WPA
Matt Kemp	689	130	8.7	6.4	2.7
Andre Ethier	551	73	2.9	0.9	1.4
James Loney	582	72	2.3	1.1	0.2
Jamey Carroll	510	58	2.2	-0.2	0.4
Aaron Miles	490	46	0.8	-0.2	-0.5
Rod Barajas	337	39	1.3	-0.7	-1.1
Tony Gwynn	340	36	1.6	0.8	0.6
Juan Rivera	246	30	0.8	1.6	0.0
Dee Gordon	233	27	0.6	0.1	-0.1
Jerry Sands	227	26	0.9	-0.0	-0.3
Casey Blake	239	25	1.1	-0.4	0.2
Juan Uribe	295	19	0.4	-2.1	-1.0
Dioner Navarro	202	16	-0.1	-1.0	-0.9
A.J. Ellis	103	13	0.7	-0.3	0.0
Justin Sellers	139	11	0.8	-0.4	-0.0
Rafael Furcal	152	10	-0.3	-0.5	-0.5
Trent Oeltjen	91	10	0.3	-0.3	-0.0
Jay Gibbons	62	6	-0.3	-0.4	-0.4
Marcus Thames	70	5	-0.3	-0.5	-0.2
Clayton Kershaw	86	4	0.8	-0.6	-0.3
Chad Billingsley	65	3	0.6	-0.5	-0.1
Russ Mitchell	58	3	-0.2	-0.2	0.0
Juan Castro	15	1	0.0	0.1	0.0
Tim Federowicz	16	1	0.1	0.1	-0.0
Ivan De Jesus	35	1	-0.5	-0.4	-0.3
Rubby De La Rosa	16	1	0.2	-0.2	0.0
Xavier Paul	11	1	-0.1	-0.1	-0.1
Nathan Eovaldi	12	-0	0.0	-0.2	-0.0
Hiroki Kuroda	71	-0	0.1	-0.9	-0.5
Dana Eveland	11	-0	-0.0	-0.2	-0.0
Jon Garland	16	-1	-0.1	-0.3	-0.3
Ted Lilly	63	-2	-0.2	-1.1	-0.6
Eugenio Velez	40	-2	-0.7	-0.3	-0.0

Pitcher	IP	LI	WAR	WPA	CL_WPA
Clayton Kershaw	233.1	1.00	6.8	3.5	0.6
Hiroki Kuroda	202.0	0.95	2.4	0.8	0.0
Ted Lilly	192.2	0.93	1.3	-0.9	-1.3
Chad Billingsley	188.0	1.03	2.1	-1.2	-0.5
Kenley Jansen	53.2	0.95	1.5	1.3	-0.1
Mike MacDougal	57.0	1.14	-0.0	1.6	0.2
Javy Guerra	46.2	1.37	0.4	1.2	0.4
Rubby De La Rosa	60.2	1.20	0.6	-0.2	-0.1
Matt Guerrier	66.1	1.22	0.4	-1.0	-0.6
Scott Elbert	33.1	0.81	0.5	0.6	0.1
Jon Garland	54.0	0.94	0.1	-0.4	-0.4
Blake Hawksworth	53.0	0.85	0.1	-1.7	-0.5
Josh Lindblom	29.2	0.84	0.6	0.5	0.0
Nathan Eovaldi	34.2	1.10	0.2	0.3	0.0
Dana Eveland	29.2	0.82	0.6	0.2	0.0
John Ely	12.2	0.59	-0.1	-0.2	-0.3
Ramon Troncoso	22.2	0.15	-0.2	-0.2	-0.1
Hong-Chih Kuo	27.0	0.77	-0.4	-0.8	0.0
Jonathan Broxton	12.2	1.69	-0.3	-0.7	-0.7
Lance Cormier	13.2	0.27	-0.3	-0.6	-0.5

Milwaukee Brewers

Batter	PA	BR	WAR	WPA	CL_WPA
Ryan Braun	629	123	7.8	6.3	5.6
Prince Fielder	692	120	5.5	7.5	7.7
Corey Hart	551	83	4.2	0.4	0.2
Rickie Weeks	515	74	3.7	1.5	2.1
Nyjer Morgan	429	54	4.0	2.0	2.7
Yuniesky Betancourt	584	52	0.5	-2.5	-1.7
Jonathan Lucroy	468	51	1.9	-0.4	0.0
Casey McGehee	600	49	0.3	-1.6	0.1
Carlos Gomez	258	29	2.0	0.1	-0.5
Mark Kotsay	255	28	0.2	1.0	1.6
Jerry Hairston	138	16	0.8	0.0	-0.4
George Kottaras	123	15	0.7	0.5	0.7
Craig Counsell	187	11	0.5	-1.0	-1.2
Josh Wilson	82	7	0.1	0.0	0.2
Yovani Gallardo	78	6	0.9	-0.3	-0.1
Shaun Marcum	76	3	0.6	-0.5	-0.5
Taylor Green	37	3	0.1	-0.3	-0.1
Brandon Boggs	22	3	0.1	0.0	-0.0
Zack Greinke	59	2	0.4	-0.3	-0.2
Chris Narveson	59	2	0.3	-0.5	-0.8
Randy Wolf	66	1	0.3	-0.6	-0.7
Felipe Lopez	51	1	-0.4	-0.4	-0.7
Marco Estrada	16	1	0.1	0.0	-0.0
Wil Nieves	54	0	-0.4	-0.9	-0.9
Mat Gamel	27	-0	-0.4	-0.3	-0.5
Erick Almonte	29	-0	-0.6	-1.0	-1.0

Pitcher	IP	LI	WAR	WPA	CL_WPA
Yovani Gallardo	207.1	0.99	3.1	0.7	-0.4
Shaun Marcum	200.2	0.98	2.7	1.5	1.1
Randy Wolf	212.1	1.05	1.4	1.2	2.2
Zack Greinke	171.2	0.94	3.9	0.6	0.3
Chris Narveson	161.2	0.96	1.5	0.1	0.1
John Axford	73.2	1.87	1.9	4.3	4.8
Marco Estrada	92.2	0.82	0.8	-1.2	-2.4
Kameron Loe	72.0	1.21	1.2	-1.4	-2.2
LaTroy Hawkins	48.1	1.00	0.7	1.5	2.1
Francisco Rodriguez	29.0	1.76	0.8	1.0	0.8
Takashi Saito	26.2	1.40	0.2	0.5	0.9
Sergio Mitre	33.0	0.62	-0.1	-0.2	-0.4
Tim Dillard	28.2	0.42	0.3	-0.0	-0.1
Frankie de la Cruz	13.0	0.20	0.1	-0.1	0.0
Mike McClendon	13.2	0.52	0.1	-0.2	-0.1
Brandon Kintzler	14.2	0.48	-0.0	-0.2	-0.3
Zach Braddock	17.1	0.63	-0.1	-0.8	-1.2
Sean Green	11.2	0.93	0.1	-0.5	-0.6

Minnesota Twins

Batter	PA	BR	WAR	WPA	CL_WPA
Michael Cuddyer	584	81	3.1	0.2	0.0
Danny Valencia	608	60	0.5	-1.7	-0.4
Jason Kubel	401	51	1.1	-0.0	0.6
Ben Revere	481	45	2.0	-0.6	-0.2
Alexi Casilla	365	41	1.4	-0.0	-0.5
Joe Mauer	333	38	1.8	1.1	0.4
Jim Thome	242	35	0.8	1.5	0.2
Denard Span	311	35	2.2	0.4	0.2
Trevor Plouffe	320	35	-0.6	0.2	0.0
Delmon Young	325	30	0.3	-1.0	-0.5
Luke Hughes	317	30	0.4	-1.8	-0.6
Justin Morneau	288	24	-0.3	-1.2	-0.8
Chris Parmelee	88	17	1.3	0.4	0.0
Rene Tosoni	189	17	-0.5	0.7	-0.1
Tsuyoshi Nishioka	240	14	-1.4	-0.3	-0.2
Matt Tolbert	226	13	-0.5	-0.9	-0.2
Jason Repko	144	11	0.0	-0.3	0.0
Drew Butera	254	9	-0.8	-1.8	-0.5
Brian Dinkelman	78	8	0.1	-0.6	-0.0
Joe Benson	74	6	-0.1	-0.7	0.0
Rene Rivera	114	3	-0.5	-0.9	-0.2
Scott Baker	5	1	0.1	-0.0	-0.0
Francisco Liriano	3	1	0.1	0.0	0.0
Steve Holm	18	0	-0.3	-0.2	-0.1
Nick Blackburn	2	-0	-0.0	-0.0	-0.0
Brian Duensing	4	-0	-0.0	-0.1	-0.0
Carl Pavano	6	-1	-0.1	-0.1	-0.0

Pitcher	IP	LI	WAR	WPA	CL_WPA
Scott Baker	134.2	0.95	2.7	1.6	0.7
Carl Pavano	222.0	1.02	2.9	-0.5	-0.5
Brian Duensing	161.2	0.91	1.7	-3.1	-0.6
Francisco Liriano	134.1	1.03	1.0	-0.9	-0.8
Nick Blackburn	148.1	1.06	0.7	-1.6	-0.7
Glen Perkins	61.2	1.43	1.7	0.0	0.4
Anthony Swarzak	102.0	0.78	1.0	-0.5	-0.1
Matt Capps	65.2	1.53	-0.4	-1.1	-0.1
Joe Nathan	44.2	1.45	0.0	0.5	0.1
Phil Dumatrait	41.1	0.74	-0.6	0.0	0.0
Alex Burnett	50.2	0.94	-0.1	-1.2	-0.6
Jose Mijares	49.0	0.82	-0.3	-0.2	0.1
Kevin Slowey	59.1	0.83	0.4	-1.9	-0.1
Scott Diamond	39.0	0.99	0.4	-0.3	-0.1
Liam Hendriks	23.1	0.93	0.3	-0.6	0.0
Lester Oliveros	13.1	0.39	0.1	0.1	-0.0
Jim Hoey	24.2	0.70	-0.4	-1.1	-0.2
Kyle Waldrop	11.0	0.70	-0.1	0.0	0.0
Chuck James	10.1	0.45	0.1	0.3	0.0
Dusty Hughes	12.2	0.37	-0.4	0.2	0.2

New York Mets

Batter	PA	BR	WAR	WPA	CL_WPA
Jose Reyes	586	97	6.2	1.9	1.4
Carlos Beltran	419	69	3.4	3.0	2.1
Angel Pagan	532	62	0.9	0.5	0.0
David Wright	447	61	1.9	1.8	1.1
Jason Bay	509	59	0.7	-0.1	-0.8
Daniel Murphy	423	56	3.2	0.5	0.1
Lucas Duda	347	52	0.9	2.3	0.3
Justin Turner	487	52	0.8	1.0	0.3
Ruben Tejada	376	41	1.8	0.9	-0.4
Josh Thole	386	39	1.0	-1.1	-0.7
Willie Harris	283	28	-0.3	-0.5	-0.6
Jason Pridie	236	26	0.8	-0.8	-0.4
Ike Davis	149	25	1.4	1.1	0.9
Ronny Paulino	248	22	0.3	-0.1	0.5
Nick Evans	194	21	0.7	-0.6	-0.2
Scott Hairston	145	19	0.3	0.5	0.3
Mike Baxter	40	5	0.3	0.1	0.0
Mike Nickeas	59	3	-0.1	-0.2	0.1
Fernando Martinez	23	3	-0.0	-0.1	-0.1
Val Pascucci	11	2	0.0	0.1	0.0
Josh Satin	27	1	-0.0	-0.1	-0.0
Chris Young	11	1	0.2	-0.0	-0.0
Brad Emaus	42	1	-0.1	-0.4	-0.4
Mike Pelfrey	63	0	0.2	-0.6	-0.4
Dillon Gee	58	-1	0.1	-1.1	-0.6
Chin-lung Hu	23	-1	-0.5	-0.4	-0.3
R.A. Dickey	69	-1	0.0	-1.1	-0.4
Jonathon Niese	60	-1	-0.0	-0.8	-0.5
Chris Capuano	62	-2	-0.2	-1.3	-0.5

Pitcher	IP	LI	WAR	WPA	CL_WPA
R.A. Dickey	208.2	1.04	2.5	-0.2	-0.8
Chris Capuano	186.0	0.95	1.6	-1.8	-0.7
Mike Pelfrey	193.2	0.98	0.7	-1.5	-0.7
Dillon Gee	160.2	1.05	0.2	-0.4	0.4
Jonathon Niese	157.1	0.99	2.7	-1.1	-0.4
Bobby Parnell	59.1	1.43	0.6	-2.9	-0.7
Francisco Rodriguez	42.2	1.84	0.6	1.1	0.6
Manny Acosta	47.0	1.22	0.1	1.2	0.1
Chris Young	24.0	1.06	0.1	0.7	0.6
Pedro Beato	67.0	0.92	-0.3	-0.2	0.2
Jason Isringhausen	46.2	1.90	-0.4	0.5	0.4
Miguel Batista	30.2	1.14	0.4	0.7	0.0
Ryota Igarashi	38.2	0.96	-0.0	0.2	-0.3
Tim Byrdak	37.2	1.06	0.4	-0.9	-0.2
Taylor Buchholz	26.0	0.89	-0.2	0.1	0.1
D.J. Carrasco	49.1	0.53	-0.5	-1.2	-0.6
Chris Schwinden	21.0	1.05	0.4	-0.3	-0.0
Dale Thayer	10.1	0.69	0.2	-0.7	-0.3
Josh Stinson	13.0	1.22	-0.1	-0.3	0.0

New York Yankees

Batter	PA	BR	WAR	WPA	CL_WPA
Curtis Granderson	691	114	7.0	2.9	3.5
Robinson Cano	681	103	5.6	3.0	2.0
Mark Teixeira	684	98	4.2	1.3	0.6
Nick Swisher	635	86	3.8	-0.1	0.5
Derek Jeter	607	72	2.3	0.5	-0.4
Brett Gardner	588	71	5.1	-1.1	-0.7
Alex Rodriguez	428	59	4.2	-0.1	-0.2
Russell Martin	476	53	3.1	0.4	0.5
Jorge Posada	387	39	-0.4	-1.3	-1.0
Eduardo Nunez	338	37	-0.6	-0.8	-0.2
Andruw Jones	222	33	1.4	0.0	-0.2
Eric Chavez	175	17	0.6	0.2	0.3
Francisco Cervelli	137	15	0.5	0.1	-0.1
Jesus Montero	69	12	0.6	0.4	-0.0
Chris Dickerson	55	6	0.3	-0.1	-0.2
Brandon Laird	25	1	-0.1	-0.3	-0.2
Greg Golson	12	1	-0.1	0.0	-0.0
Austin Romine	20	0	-0.1	-0.7	-0.0
Ramiro Pena	46	0	-0.9	-0.6	-0.3

Pitcher	IP	LI	WAR	WPA	CL_WPA
CC Sabathia	237.1	0.95	7.1	3.2	4.1
David Robertson	66.2	1.68	2.8	4.3	2.8
Ivan Nova	165.1	1.01	2.7	0.2	-0.3
Freddy Garcia	146.2	0.90	2.2	1.2	1.9
A.J. Burnett	190.1	1.02	1.5	-1.3	-1.1
Bartolo Colon	164.1	0.98	2.9	0.7	1.6
Mariano Rivera	61.1	2.19	2.4	3.5	2.7
Luis Ayala	56.0	0.81	0.2	0.1	-0.1
Cory Wade	39.2	0.94	0.4	0.8	0.9
Hector Noesi	56.1	0.83	0.3	0.2	1.0
Phil Hughes	74.2	0.94	0.7	-0.7	-0.6
Boone Logan	41.2	1.20	0.7	-0.1	0.2
Rafael Soriano	39.1	1.60	0.3	0.9	0.6
Joba Chamberlain	28.2	1.23	0.4	0.8	0.9
Lance Pendleton	14.0	0.11	-0.1	-0.0	-0.1
Aaron Laffey	10.2	0.79	0.1	0.3	-0.0
Brian Gordon	10.1	1.14	-0.2	-0.1	-0.2
Scott Proctor	11.0	1.40	-0.7	-0.9	-0.0

Oakland Athletics

Batter	PA	BR	WAR	WPA	CL_WPA
Josh Willingham	563	83	2.1	2.1	0.9
Coco Crisp	583	70	2.2	1.0	0.7
Hideki Matsui	585	65	0.3	-0.1	-0.8
Cliff Pennington	570	62	1.5	0.0	-0.6
Jemile Weeks	437	58	2.0	0.0	-0.2
David DeJesus	506	55	2.2	-1.8	-1.4
Kurt Suzuki	515	54	2.2	-3.0	-1.6
Scott Sizemore	355	47	1.8	1.9	0.3
Conor Jackson	368	36	0.2	-1.4	-0.7
Ryan Sweeney	299	31	0.1	-0.3	0.5
Daric Barton	280	23	-0.3	0.2	0.3
Mark Ellis	233	16	-0.0	-1.6	-1.5
Brandon Allen	158	15	-0.2	-1.0	0.0
Kevin Kouzmanoff	149	14	0.2	-0.5	-0.4
Andy LaRoche	104	9	-0.4	-0.6	-0.7
Eric Sogard	74	5	0.0	-0.5	0.0
Landon Powell	122	5	-0.2	-1.1	-0.7
Michael Taylor	35	3	-0.3	0.1	0.0
Anthony Recker	21	2	0.1	-0.1	-0.0
Jai Miller	12	2	0.0	0.1	0.0
Adam Rosales	68	0	-1.0	-0.9	-0.2
Chris Carter	46	-0	-0.6	-0.6	-0.1

Pitcher	IP	LI	WAR	WPA	CL_WPA
Gio Gonzalez	202.0	1.00	3.5	1.7	1.1
Trevor Cahill	207.2	1.01	2.5	-0.4	1.0
Brandon McCarthy	170.2	0.94	4.7	0.3	-0.7
Guillermo Moscoso	128.0	0.96	1.3	-0.6	-0.1
Grant Balfour	62.0	1.33	0.4	1.8	0.6
Brett Anderson	83.1	1.13	1.1	0.2	0.2
Rich Harden	82.2	0.94	0.4	-0.8	0.0
Craig Breslow	59.1	0.78	0.4	-0.9	-0.8
Josh Outman	58.1	1.08	0.8	-0.0	0.2
Brian Fuentes	58.1	1.48	0.1	-1.0	-1.7
Tyson Ross	36.0	1.22	0.8	0.8	0.9
Andrew Bailey	41.2	1.86	0.9	0.7	0.0
Brad Ziegler	37.2	1.01	0.8	0.3	0.5
Fautino De Los Santos	33.1	0.77	0.3	-0.5	0.0
Joey Devine	23.0	1.13	0.4	0.4	0.4
Jerry Blevins	28.1	0.44	0.2	0.4	0.0
Bobby Cramer	8.1	0.30	0.1	-0.3	-0.3
Dallas Braden	18.0	0.93	0.3	0.1	0.1
Michael Wuertz	33.2	0.86	-0.5	-0.3	0.1
David Purcey	12.2	0.39	0.1	0.0	0.0
Graham Godfrey	25.0	0.85	0.2	-0.2	-0.1
Trystan Magnuson	14.2	0.10	-0.1	-0.1	-0.0

Philadelphia Phillies

Batter	PA	BR	WAR	WPA	CL_WPA
Ryan Howard	644	90	1.6	5.1	4.2
Shane Victorino	586	89	5.9	3.4	3.0
Jimmy Rollins	631	76	3.8	-0.0	0.3
Raul Ibanez	575	61	-1.3	-0.6	-1.0
Chase Utley	454	60	3.9	1.5	1.1
Carlos Ruiz	472	55	2.8	0.6	0.5
Placido Polanco	523	50	2.8	-1.1	-1.0
John Mayberry	296	44	2.5	1.9	0.6
Hunter Pence	236	39	2.6	0.8	0.0
Ben Francisco	293	31	-0.1	0.0	0.1
Domonic Brown	210	24	-0.0	-0.3	-0.4
Wilson Valdez	300	22	-0.0	-0.2	-0.9
Michael Martinez	234	16	-0.4	0.2	0.1
Ross Gload	118	9	-0.3	-0.1	0.2
Brian Schneider	139	7	-0.9	-0.8	-0.4
Pete Orr	104	7	-0.2	-0.1	0.3
Dane Sardinha	43	5	0.2	0.1	0.1
Cliff Lee	82	4	0.7	-0.2	0.0
Vance Worley	48	2	0.4	-0.4	-0.2
Kyle Kendrick	31	1	0.3	-0.3	-0.2
Cole Hamels	75	1	0.3	-0.9	-0.9
Joe Blanton	12	0	-0.1	-0.1	-0.0
Roy Oswalt	49	-0	-0.1	-0.5	-0.6
Roy Halladay	92	-1	-0.1	-1.4	-1.7
John Bowker	13	-1	-0.3	-0.4	0.0

Pitcher	IP	LI	WAR	WPA	CL_WPA
Roy Halladay	233.2	1.11	8.2	3.8	2.9
Cliff Lee	232.2	0.95	6.7	3.6	1.8
Cole Hamels	216.0	0.97	4.9	3.4	3.4
Vance Worley	131.2	1.02	2.5	1.2	1.4
Roy Oswalt	139.0	0.99	2.5	-0.4	-0.2
Kyle Kendrick	114.2	0.88	0.2	-0.8	-0.7
Ryan Madson	60.2	1.92	1.7	2.3	1.7
Antonio Bastardo	58.0	1.22	0.7	2.4	2.5
Michael Stutes	62.0	1.09	0.0	0.8	0.9
David Herndon	57.0	1.06	-0.6	-0.4	-0.1
Brad Lidge	19.1	1.49	0.3	0.3	0.0
Joe Blanton	41.1	0.96	0.6	-0.6	-0.9
Danys Baez	36.0	0.70	-0.4	-0.3	-0.3
J.C. Romero	16.1	0.81	-0.0	-0.5	-0.8
Jose Contreras	14.0	1.32	0.2	0.6	0.8
Michael Schwimer	14.1	1.31	-0.0	-0.6	0.0

Pittsburgh Pirates

Batter	PA	BR	WAR	WPA	CL_WPA
Andrew McCutchen	678	98	5.7	2.7	2.0
Neil Walker	662	77	3.0	1.5	1.9
Garrett Jones	478	59	0.9	1.8	0.5
Jose Tabata	382	43	1.0	-0.5	-0.8
Ronny Cedeno	454	37	1.4	-2.2	-1.3
Lyle Overbay	391	35	-0.8	-0.5	-0.9
Ryan Doumit	236	33	1.8	1.5	0.6
Alex Presley	231	33	1.2	0.7	0.2
Xavier Paul	251	24	-0.1	0.2	-0.1
Brandon Wood	257	22	0.3	-0.9	-0.0
Derrek Lee	113	21	0.9	0.9	0.3
Matt Diaz	231	19	-0.1	-0.7	-0.4
Josh Harrison	204	18	0.9	0.4	0.8
Pedro Alvarez	262	17	-0.8	-1.8	-1.6
Michael McKenry	201	15	0.1	-0.6	-0.6
Chris Snyder	119	15	0.7	0.2	0.1
Ryan Ludwick	133	13	-0.4	-0.2	-0.1
Chase D'Arnaud	151	10	-0.2	-0.9	-0.9
Jason Jaramillo	45	5	0.1	0.3	0.1
Steve Pearce	105	5	-0.7	-1.1	-1.1
Pedro Ciriaco	34	4	0.2	-0.0	-0.0
Eric Fryer	29	2	0.3	-0.2	-0.2
Ross Ohlendorf	15	1	0.2	0.1	-0.0
John Bowker	19	1	-0.1	0.1	0.1
Josh Rodriguez	14	0	-0.1	-0.2	-0.2
Brad Lincoln	14	0	0.0	-0.2	-0.0
Jeff Karstens	58	-0	-0.0	-0.7	-0.5
Dusty Brown	30	-0	-0.3	-0.6	-0.5
Paul Maholm	53	-1	0.0	-0.8	-0.7
Kevin Correia	55	-1	-0.1	-0.4	-0.2
Charlie Morton	64	-1	-0.1	-0.9	-0.5
James McDonald	63	-2	-0.0	-0.9	-0.6

Pitcher	IP	LI	WAR	WPA	CL_WPA
Jeff Karstens	162.1	1.02	1.0	-0.5	0.7
James McDonald	171.0	1.13	0.4	-1.1	-0.4
Paul Maholm	162.1	0.93	2.1	0.0	0.2
Charlie Morton	171.2	1.09	2.2	-0.3	-0.8
Joel Hanrahan	68.2	1.94	2.0	2.1	3.5
Kevin Correia	154.0	0.96	0.0	-1.7	-1.6
Daniel Mc-Cutchen	84.2	0.84	-0.3	0.9	1.6
Jose Veras	71.0	1.37	0.5	0.1	0.5
Chris Resop	69.2	1.23	0.3	-0.5	0.4
Jason Grilli	32.2	1.57	0.4	2.0	0.9
Tony Watson	41.0	1.06	-0.4	0.5	0.2
Brad Lincoln	47.2	0.91	0.4	-0.5	0.1
Chris Leroux	25.0	1.05	0.6	-0.1	-0.3
Daniel Moskos	24.1	0.63	0.2	-0.6	-0.6
Evan Meek	20.2	0.84	0.1	-1.0	-1.1
Joe Beimel	25.1	0.86	-0.7	0.2	0.8
Brian Burres	14.0	0.71	-0.2	-0.1	0.0
Ross Ohlendorf	38.2	1.07	-0.6	-2.0	-0.5
Jared Hughes	11.0	0.57	0.1	-0.0	0.0
Jeff Locke	16.2	1.03	-0.3	-0.6	0.0
Mike Crotta	10.2	1.07	-0.2	-0.6	-0.6

San Diego Padres

Batter	PA	BR	WAR	WPA	CL_WPA
Cameron Maybin	568	75	4.7	1.3	0.8
Chase Headley	439	62	2.7	1.4	0.1
Jason Bartlett	618	57	1.8	-1.0	-0.3
Will Venable	411	54	1.8	1.0	0.3
Orlando Hudson	454	54	1.8	1.4	0.6
Nick Hundley	308	47	3.3	0.0	-0.3
Ryan Ludwick	425	46	0.7	-0.8	-0.4
Jesus Guzman	271	44	2.3	1.9	0.0
Chris Denorfia	340	40	1.5	-0.2	-0.1
Kyle Blanks	190	23	1.1	-0.6	-0.0
Brad Hawpe	216	21	0.4	-0.7	-0.9
Alberto Gonzalez	267	17	-0.2	-1.6	-0.7
Rob Johnson	199	15	-0.1	-1.1	-0.4
Logan Forsythe	169	13	0.4	-0.8	-0.2
Anthony Rizzo	153	11	-0.4	-0.6	0.0
Aaron Cunningham	101	10	0.3	-0.1	0.0
Eric Patterson	104	10	-0.1	-0.1	-0.1
Jorge Cantu	155	8	-0.7	-2.2	-1.3
Jeremy Hermida	48	7	0.6	0.0	0.0
Luis Martinez	68	7	0.1	0.3	0.0
Kyle Phillips	85	6	0.1	-1.0	-0.2
Andy Parrino	55	4	0.4	0.0	0.0
James Darnell	52	4	-0.2	-0.2	-0.0
Wade LeBlanc	26	3	0.4	0.0	-0.0
Blake Tekotte	40	3	-0.3	-0.2	-0.0
Cory Luebke	36	2	0.4	-0.4	-0.2
Dustin Moseley	36	0	0.1	-0.6	-0.2
Tim Stauffer	63	-0	0.2	-0.7	-0.2
Clayton Richard	32	-0	0.0	-0.6	-0.4
Mat Latos	63	-2	0.0	-0.9	-0.2
Aaron Harang	62	-2	-0.2	-1.2	-0.3

Pitcher	IP	LI	WAR	WPA	CL_WPA
Mat Latos	194.1	1.06	3.2	-0.1	-0.8
Tim Stauffer	185.2	1.01	1.0	0.1	0.2
Aaron Harang	170.2	1.00	0.6	0.6	0.5
Cory Luebke	139.2	0.81	2.4	-0.4	-0.2
Mike Adams	48.0	1.48	1.3	1.8	0.9
Dustin Moseley	120.0	0.92	0.7	-1.3	-0.4
Ernesto Frieri	63.0	0.69	0.3	-0.0	0.0
Anthony Bass	48.1	0.67	-0.2	1.2	0.1
Heath Bell	62.2	2.11	0.5	1.6	0.8
Clayton Richard	99.2	0.85	0.3	-1.0	-0.8
Chad Qualls	74.1	1.39	-0.3	-0.8	-0.1
Wade LeBlanc	79.2	0.98	0.5	-0.9	-0.1
Luke Gregerson	55.2	1.38	0.2	-0.8	0.1
Josh Spence	29.2	1.00	-0.1	-0.0	0.1
Pat Neshek	24.2	0.48	-0.7	-0.8	-0.5
Erik Hamren	12.1	0.50	-0.4	-0.0	0.0
Joe Thatcher	10.0	0.62	-0.1	-0.1	0.0
Evan Scribner	14.0	0.11	0.0	-0.1	-0.0

San Francisco Giants

Batter	PA	BR	WAR	WPA	CL_WPA
Pablo Sandoval	466	74	5.5	3.7	4.2
Aubrey Huff	579	58	-0.6	-0.1	-0.2
Cody Ross	461	54	0.9	0.6	0.7
Nate Schierholtz	362	45	1.4	3.4	4.8
Andres Torres	398	40	2.1	-0.4	-0.7
Aaron Rowand	351	29	0.7	-0.9	-2.2
Freddy Sanchez	261	29	1.0	1.6	2.2
Carlos Beltran	179	28	1.2	0.7	0.4
Pat Burrell	219	28	0.5	0.1	0.5
Mike Fontenot	252	27	1.0	-0.5	-1.5
Brandon Belt	209	24	0.7	0.5	0.8
Miguel Tejada	343	24	0.0	-0.9	-1.7
Buster Posey	185	23	1.6	-0.1	-0.1
Jeff Keppinger	230	19	-0.3	0.2	0.6
Brandon Crawford	220	16	0.5	-0.5	-0.7
Eli Whiteside	236	16	0.1	-1.3	-1.7
Chris Stewart	183	14	0.9	-1.0	-1.7
Mark DeRosa	97	8	0.1	0.3	-0.1
Brett Pill	53	8	0.5	0.3	0.1
Manny Burriss	152	8	-0.6	0.4	0.6
Orlando Cabrera	133	7	-0.6	-0.3	-0.6
Justin Christian	51	5	-0.0	0.2	0.0
Hector Sanchez	34	3	0.0	0.0	0.4
Ryan Vogelsong	61	3	0.6	-0.3	-0.6
Conor Gillaspie	21	3	0.1	-0.2	-0.2
Jonathan Sanchez	31	2	0.3	-0.1	-0.1
Darren Ford	16	2	0.3	-0.2	-0.0
Madison Bumgarner	75	2	0.4	-0.8	-1.0
Matt Cain	78	1	0.3	-0.4	-0.4
Bill Hall	41	1	-0.6	-0.4	-0.7
Guillermo Mota	10	-0	0.0	-0.2	-0.2
Barry Zito	14	-1	-0.1	-0.3	-0.4
Tim Lincecum	72	-2	-0.1	-1.2	-1.6

Pitcher	IP	LI	WAR	WPA	CL_WPA
Tim Lincecum	217.0	1.05	4.4	1.0	1.2
Matt Cain	221.2	1.07	5.2	0.1	-0.8
Madison Bumgarner	204.2	1.01	5.5	-0.1	-0.5
Ryan Vogelsong	179.2	0.99	2.4	1.2	1.7
Sergio Romo	48.0	1.43	2.2	1.6	2.1
Santiago Casilla	51.2	1.02	0.6	0.7	1.2
Ramon Ramirez	68.2	0.86	0.9	0.3	-0.7
Jonathan Sanchez	101.1	1.07	0.6	-2.1	-3.1
Guillermo Mota	80.1	0.69	0.0	-0.0	0.2
Jeremy Affeldt	61.2	1.10	0.2	0.2	0.6
Javier Lopez	53.0	1.48	0.7	2.0	2.7
Brian Wilson	55.0	2.24	0.6	0.3	-0.1
Barry Zito	53.2	0.69	-0.4	-1.1	-1.1
Dan Runzler	27.1	0.82	0.3	-0.1	-0.4
Eric Surkamp	26.2	1.16	0.0	-0.4	0.2
Steve Edlefsen	11.1	0.44	-0.3	-0.2	0.2

Seattle Mariners

Batter	PA	BR	WAR	WPA	CL_WPA
Ichiro Suzuki	721	73	0.2	-1.5	-0.8
Justin Smoak	489	58	0.5	1.4	0.9
Dustin Ackley	376	52	2.7	1.0	1.0
Brendan Ryan	494	49	2.6	-0.9	-0.4
Miguel Olivo	507	48	0.9	-1.5	-0.2
Mike Carp	313	42	0.5	0.6	-0.4
Adam Kennedy	409	39	0.1	-1.1	-0.2
Jack Cust	270	30	-0.1	-0.2	0.2
Franklin Gutierrez	344	23	1.1	-1.2	-1.1
Kyle Seager	201	22	0.5	-0.6	-0.2
Chone Figgins	313	16	-1.2	-2.5	-2.3
Jack Wilson	187	15	0.2	0.2	0.0
Casper Wells	116	15	0.6	0.1	-0.0
Carlos Peguero	155	14	-0.3	0.3	0.5
Luis Rodriguez	139	14	-0.2	0.7	0.3
Milton Bradley	115	13	-0.6	-0.2	-0.3
Trayvon Robinson	155	13	-0.9	0.0	-0.0
Greg Halman	91	8	-0.4	-0.6	-0.1
Josh Bard	86	7	-0.0	0.0	0.1
Wily Mo Pena	74	7	-0.1	-0.5	-0.0
Ryan Langerhans	64	7	-0.7	-0.2	-0.3
Michael Saunders	179	7	-0.5	-2.1	-1.6
Alex Liddi	44	7	0.3	0.3	0.0
Chris Gimenez	70	6	0.2	-0.2	-0.2
Mike Wilson	28	0	-0.4	-0.2	-0.2

Pitcher	IP	LI	WAR	WPA	CL_WPA
Felix Hernandez	233.2	1.05	5.5	0.8	0.9
Michael Pineda	171.0	0.96	3.4	0.3	1.2
Jason Vargas	201.0	0.97	2.4	-0.3	0.4
Doug Fister	146.0	0.94	3.2	0.0	-0.1
Erik Bedard	91.1	0.96	1.5	-0.1	0.3
David Pauley	54.1	1.12	0.6	0.2	-0.0
Blake Beavan	97.0	0.90	0.7	-0.6	0.2
Jamey Wright	68.1	1.13	-0.1	-0.5	-0.9
Brandon League	61.1	1.88	1.4	0.3	0.1
Aaron Laffey	42.2	0.86	-0.6	-0.3	0.3
Tom Wilhelmsen	32.2	0.46	0.3	0.3	-0.0
Charlie Furbush	53.0	0.93	0.0	-1.7	-0.0
Jeff Gray	35.0	0.80	-0.2	-0.3	0.0
Chris Ray	32.2	0.81	0.2	-0.7	-0.7
Josh Lueke	32.2	0.39	0.3	-0.6	-0.3
Chance Ruffin	14.0	0.48	-0.1	0.2	0.0
Anthony Vasquez	29.1	0.81	-1.1	-1.6	0.0
Dan Cortes	10.2	0.84	-0.1	-0.6	-0.0
Shawn Kelley	12.2	0.41	0.2	0.2	0.0

St. Louis Cardinals

Batter	PA	BR	WAR	WPA	CL_WPA
Albert Pujols	651	104	5.1	4.3	6.1
Lance Berkman	587	103	5.0	5.4	7.2
Matt Holliday	516	83	5.0	2.8	4.8
Yadier Molina	518	68	4.1	2.4	3.4
Jon Jay	503	62	2.8	-0.6	-1.8
Colby Rasmus	386	48	1.3	-0.3	-1.0
David Freese	363	46	2.7	0.5	1.7
Ryan Theriot	483	44	0.7	-0.7	-1.9
Skip Schumaker	400	40	0.6	0.2	0.6
Daniel Descalso	375	38	0.5	1.5	1.9
Allen Craig	219	38	2.6	1.1	2.5
Rafael Furcal	217	26	0.9	0.3	-0.0
Nick Punto	166	22	1.8	0.8	1.1
Tyler Greene	121	12	0.1	-0.8	-1.3
Gerald Laird	108	10	0.1	0.1	0.7
Tony Cruz	72	7	0.3	0.1	0.3
Mark Hamilton	51	3	-0.1	-0.1	-0.1
Edwin Jackson	30	2	0.4	-0.4	-0.5
Peter Kozma	22	2	0.1	-0.2	-0.2
Kyle Lohse	70	2	0.3	-0.5	-0.6
Chris Carpenter	82	1	0.4	-1.0	-1.1
Corey Patterson	56	1	-0.3	-0.5	-0.0
Jake Westbrook	60	1	0.3	-0.4	-0.9
Matt Carpenter	19	1	-0.1	-0.3	-0.5
Andrew Brown	22	0	-0.1	0.0	0.0
Kyle McClellan	41	0	0.1	-0.4	-0.7
Jaime Garcia	68	-1	-0.0	-0.6	-0.8

Pitcher	IP	LI	WAR	WPA	CL_WPA
Chris Carpenter	237.1	1.06	5.0	1.1	2.6
Kyle Lohse	188.1	1.02	2.5	0.2	-0.4
Jaime Garcia	194.2	1.01	3.6	-0.5	-1.9
Jake Westbrook	183.1	1.07	1.1	-1.6	-2.6
Fernando Salas	75.0	1.61	1.0	0.8	1.1
Kyle McClellan	141.2	1.02	-0.6	-0.4	-1.5
Jason Motte	68.0	1.35	1.5	1.3	0.8
Edwin Jackson	78.0	1.10	0.7	-0.2	-1.7
Eduardo Sanchez	30.0	1.53	0.4	0.7	1.1
Mitchell Boggs	60.2	0.73	0.3	-1.0	-1.3
Lance Lynn	34.2	1.45	0.6	1.1	2.1
Octavio Dotel	24.2	1.11	0.9	0.2	-1.1
Marc Rzepczynski	22.2	1.04	0.4	-0.4	-0.7
Miguel Batista	29.1	1.34	-0.5	0.1	-0.0
Trever Miller	15.2	1.23	-0.3	-0.8	-1.2
Brandon Dickson	8.1	0.56	-0.1	-0.1	-0.1
Ryan Franklin	27.2	0.94	-1.2	-2.8	-2.8
Brian Tallet	13.0	0.86	-0.5	-0.6	-0.7

Tampa Bay Rays

Batter	PA	BR	WAR	WPA	CL_WPA
Ben Zobrist	674	103	6.6	1.6	2.3
Evan Longoria	574	90	6.1	3.9	9.2
B.J. Upton	640	86	4.1	1.2	3.8
Johnny Damon	647	86	1.5	2.5	1.1
Matt Joyce	522	80	3.8	2.2	3.6
Casey Kotchman	563	79	2.8	1.4	-0.4
Sean Rodriguez	436	47	2.3	-0.4	-0.9
Desmond Jennings	287	45	2.4	2.4	-1.4
Sam Fuld	346	39	1.9	0.2	-0.5
John Jaso	273	26	0.5	-0.6	-0.9
Kelly Shoppach	253	22	1.1	-1.7	-2.0
Elliot Johnson	181	14	0.5	-0.6	-0.3
Justin Ruggiano	111	12	0.4	-0.3	-0.5
Reid Brignac	264	11	-1.1	-2.2	-2.8
Felipe Lopez	102	7	-0.3	-1.0	-1.0
Robinson Chirinos	60	5	-0.1	-0.0	-0.2
Brandon Guyer	43	3	0.4	-0.3	0.2
Dan Johnson	91	2	-0.8	-0.3	3.6
Jose Lobaton	39	1	-0.2	-0.5	-1.0
Manny Ramirez	17	-1	-0.3	-0.2	-0.2

Pitcher	IP	LI	WAR	WPA	CL_WPA
James Shields	249.1	0.95	4.9	3.7	4.2
David Price	224.1	0.94	4.7	-0.5	-4.6
Jeremy Hellickson	189.0	0.84	1.4	1.4	0.4
Wade Davis	184.0	0.99	0.9	-1.6	-1.5
Jeff Niemann	135.1	0.88	1.5	0.5	1.1
Kyle Farnsworth	57.2	1.48	0.9	0.9	2.2
Joel Peralta	67.2	1.31	0.8	1.4	1.2
Alex Cobb	52.1	0.93	0.9	0.2	0.5
Juan Cruz	48.2	0.80	0.0	0.5	1.0
Brandon Gomes	37.0	0.70	0.2	0.2	0.9
Cesar Ramos	43.2	0.63	-0.2	-0.3	-0.7
Adam Russell	32.2	0.47	-0.3	-0.9	-1.0
Jake McGee	28.0	0.72	-0.2	-0.6	2.2
Andy Sonnanstine	35.2	0.58	-0.8	-0.9	-1.2
J.P. Howell	30.2	1.19	-0.5	-1.5	-2.1
Matt Moore	9.1	1.02	0.4	0.3	0.5

Texas Rangers

Batter	PA	BR	WAR	WPA	CL_WPA
Ian Kinsler	723	103	7.7	1.4	2.0
Michael Young	689	96	3.8	2.6	3.1
Mike Napoli	432	82	5.6	1.8	2.0
Josh Hamilton	538	81	4.2	4.6	7.0
Adrian Beltre	525	80	5.7	1.4	0.9
Nelson Cruz	513	71	1.6	0.1	0.9
Elvis Andrus	665	70	4.5	-0.3	0.2
Mitch Moreland	512	56	0.4	-0.3	-1.3
David Murphy	440	48	1.1	-1.6	-1.8
Yorvit Torrealba	419	42	1.1	-2.3	-3.0
Endy Chavez	274	31	1.5	-0.9	-1.4
Craig Gentry	153	19	1.8	-0.0	0.1
Julio Borbon	98	9	0.0	-0.2	-0.3
Chris Davis	81	8	-0.1	-0.2	-0.3
Andres Blanco	82	6	-0.3	-0.2	-0.5
Esteban German	13	3	0.3	0.3	0.0
Taylor Teagarden	36	3	0.2	-0.2	-0.2
Matt Treanor	12	-1	-0.2	-0.2	-0.2
Omar Quintanilla	23	-1	-0.3	-0.4	-0.5

Pitcher	IP	LI	WAR	WPA	CL_WPA
C.J. Wilson	223.1	0.96	5.9	2.8	4.0
Matt Harrison	185.2	0.98	4.2	2.3	2.6
Derek Holland	198.0	0.86	3.6	1.1	2.1
Colby Lewis	200.1	0.87	2.3	0.6	0.8
Alexi Ogando	169.0	0.95	3.6	2.2	2.6
Neftali Feliz	62.1	1.60	1.0	1.0	1.1
Darren Oliver	51.0	1.46	1.3	-0.2	0.1
Mike Adams	25.2	1.03	0.5	-0.1	0.2
Yoshinori Tateyama	44.0	0.63	0.2	0.7	0.7
Mark Lowe	45.0	0.92	0.3	0.8	1.1
Scott Feldman	32.0	0.51	0.3	0.2	0.4
Dave Bush	37.1	0.60	0.1	-0.5	-0.7
Koji Uehara	18.0	1.07	0.1	0.4	0.0
Arthur Rhodes	24.1	1.11	-0.4	-0.6	-1.0
Tommy Hunter	15.1	0.94	0.2	-0.2	-0.4
Brett Tomko	17.2	0.83	-0.2	-0.0	-0.0
Michael Kirkman	27.1	0.61	-0.2	0.1	0.0
Darren O'Day	16.2	0.62	-0.4	-0.4	-0.5

Toronto Blue Jays

Batter	PA	BR	WAR	WPA	CL_WPA
Jose Bautista	655	130	8.3	7.9	4.3
Yunel Escobar	590	76	4.3	2.0	1.5
Edwin Encarnacion	530	69	1.5	-1.0	-1.2
Adam Lind	542	63	0.5	-0.1	0.5
J.P. Arencibia	486	56	1.5	-2.0	-1.3
Eric Thames	394	50	0.9	-0.5	0.1
Aaron Hill	429	34	-0.8	-2.3	-1.6
Rajai Davis	338	33	-0.2	-1.4	-1.3
Corey Patterson	341	33	0.3	-0.9	-0.7
Brett Lawrie	171	32	2.7	1.8	0.1
Juan Rivera	275	26	-0.1	-1.5	-1.3
Jose Molina	191	24	1.3	0.4	0.4
Mike McCoy	228	19	0.3	-0.7	-0.3
Kelly Johnson	132	18	0.8	0.5	0.0
Travis Snider	202	17	0.3	-0.9	-0.4
John McDonald	182	16	0.6	-0.7	-0.8
Jayson Nix	151	11	0.2	-1.0	-1.0
David Cooper	81	8	-0.1	0.2	-0.0
Colby Rasmus	140	8	-0.5	-0.8	0.0
Adam Loewen	37	3	-0.2	0.5	0.0
Mark Teahen	47	3	-0.0	0.2	-0.0
DeWayne Wise	32	2	-0.2	-0.4	-0.0
Chris Woodward	10	-1	-0.2	-0.2	-0.1

Pitcher	IP	LI	WAR	WPA	CL_WPA
Ricky Romero	225.0	0.98	2.9	3.8	1.8
Brandon Morrow	179.1	0.92	3.4	-0.4	0.3
Carlos Villanueva	107.0	0.95	1.1	0.2	0.5
Brett Cecil	123.2	0.90	0.4	-1.4	-0.8
Casey Janssen	55.2	0.96	1.3	2.1	0.9
Henderson Alvarez	63.2	0.87	1.0	0.1	-0.0
Jesse Litsch	75.0	0.92	0.7	0.1	-0.4
Jo-Jo Reyes	110.0	0.94	0.9	-2.0	-1.5
Frank Francisco	50.2	1.48	0.5	0.4	-1.4
Jason Frasor	42.1	1.26	0.4	1.1	0.6
Shawn Camp	66.1	1.05	0.4	0.1	0.3
Luis Perez	65.0	0.86	0.0	-0.4	0.7
Kyle Drabek	78.2	1.02	-0.2	-1.1	-1.0
Marc Rzepczynski	39.1	1.30	0.5	0.2	0.1
Jon Rauch	52.0	1.46	-0.6	-0.4	0.0
Joel Carreno	15.2	0.35	0.2	0.3	0.0
Octavio Dotel	29.1	0.88	-0.1	1.1	0.8
Dustin McGowan	21.0	0.79	-0.1	-0.4	0.0
Zach Stewart	16.2	1.00	0.2	-0.1	-0.0
Brad Mills	18.1	0.98	-0.1	-0.7	-0.0

Washington Nationals

Batter	PA	BR	WAR	WPA	CL_WPA
Michael Morse	575	94	3.4	3.9	0.9
Danny Espinosa	658	80	3.5	1.6	1.6
Jayson Werth	649	76	2.5	-0.3	-0.9
Ian Desmond	639	61	1.4	-0.7	-1.1
Ryan Zimmerman	440	57	2.5	1.2	-0.1
Wilson Ramos	435	51	3.1	-1.1	-0.3
Laynce Nix	351	44	0.6	1.4	1.3
Rick Ankiel	415	41	1.4	0.6	0.3
Roger Bernadina	337	35	0.8	-0.0	0.1
Jerry Hairston	238	27	0.4	-0.4	-0.2
Adam LaRoche	177	13	-0.2	-0.7	-0.6
Alex Cora	172	12	0.2	-0.2	-0.0
Jonny Gomes	107	11	0.4	0.3	0.0
Ivan Rodriguez	137	10	0.4	-0.7	-0.4
Chris Marrero	117	8	-0.7	-1.0	0.0
Jesus Flores	91	6	-0.1	-1.1	-0.2
Brian Bixler	94	5	-0.2	-0.4	0.2
Matt Stairs	74	3	-0.6	-1.3	-0.9
Jordan Zimmer-mann	56	2	0.5	-0.5	-0.2
Livan Hernandez	61	2	0.3	-0.2	-0.2
Steve Lombardozzi	32	1	-0.2	0.0	0.0
Jason Marquis	45	1	0.2	-0.4	-0.2
Tom Milone	10	1	0.2	-0.1	0.0
Tom Gorzelanny	33	-0	0.0	-0.5	-0.4
John Lannan	65	-0	0.0	-0.5	-0.3
Ross Detwiler	22	-1	-0.1	-0.3	-0.0
Chien-Ming Wang	20	-1	-0.1	-0.4	-0.0

Pitcher	IP	LI	WAR	WPA	CL_WPA
Jordan Zimmer-mann	161.1	1.04	3.4	1.0	0.2
Tyler Clippard	88.1	1.52	1.2	5.0	2.3
John Lannan	184.2	1.11	1.3	-1.2	-0.5
Livan Hernandez	175.1	0.92	1.9	-1.1	-0.3
Drew Storen	75.1	1.82	0.9	2.6	1.5
Jason Marquis	120.2	1.10	1.6	0.2	0.0
Tom Gorzelanny	105.0	1.03	0.7	-0.4	-0.4
Ross Detwiler	66.0	0.98	0.4	0.7	0.1
Henry Rodriguez	65.2	1.02	0.6	-0.8	-0.3
Todd Coffey	59.2	0.93	0.5	0.3	-0.1
Sean Burnett	56.2	1.38	-0.4	-1.4	-1.6
Stephen Strasburg	24.0	0.87	1.1	0.6	0.0
Chien-Ming Wang	62.1	0.91	0.2	-0.3	-0.1
Ryan Mattheus	32.0	0.90	-0.1	-0.0	0.1
Craig Stammen	10.1	1.54	0.4	0.2	-0.2
Brad Peacock	12.0	1.34	0.1	0.3	0.0
Collin Balester	35.2	0.67	-0.3	-1.3	-0.3
Cole Kimball	14.0	0.78	0.0	0.2	0.1
Tom Milone	26.0	1.19	0.4	0.2	0.0
Yunesky Maya	32.2	0.83	0.1	-0.3	-0.2
Doug Slaten	16.1	0.89	-0.3	-1.6	-0.9
Brian Broderick	12.1	0.42	0.0	-0.4	-0.3

Glossary

BABIP: Batting Average on Balls in Play. This is a measure of the number of batted balls that safely fall in for hits (not including home runs). The exact formula we use is (H-HR)/(AB-K-HR+SF).

BB/9: Walks allowed per nine innings

BR: Base Runs, a run contribution formula created by David Smyth, which quantifies the number of runs contributed by a batter. The fundamental formula for Base Runs is (baserunners * scoring rate) + home runs. Note that our Base Runs are adjusted for park effects.

Champ LI: Championship Leverage Index, the importance of a game in terms of its impact on the team's chance of making the postseason. Please refer to the article "In All Probability" for more information.

CL_WPA: In-game WPA (see below) multiplied by Champ LI to capture the relative importance of each individual game.

DER: Defense Efficiency Ratio. The percent of times a batted ball is turned into an out by the team's fielders, not including home runs. The exact formula we use is (BFP-H-K-BB-HBP-0.6*E)/(BFP-HR-K-BB-HBP). This is similar to BABIP, but from the defensive team's perspective.

ERA+: ERA measured against the league average and adjusted for ballpark factors. An ERA+ over 100 is better than average, less than 100 is below average.

FIP: Fielding Independent Pitching, a measure of all those things for which a pitcher is specifically responsible. The formula is (HR*13+(BB+HBP)*3-K*2)/IP, plus a league-specific factor (usually around 3.2) to round out the number to an equivalent ERA number. FIP helps you understand how well a pitcher pitched, regardless of how well his fielders fielded. FIP was invented by Tom M. Tango.

K/9: Strikeouts per nine innings

LI: Leverage Index. Invented by Tom M. Tango, LI measures the criticality of a play or plate appearance. It is based on the range of potential WPA outcomes of a play, compared to all other plays. 1.0 is an average Index.

OPS: On Base plus Slugging Percentage, a crude but quick measure of a batter's true contribution to his team's offense. See wOBA for a better approach.

OPS+: OPS measured against the league average, and adjusted for ballpark factors. An OPS+ over 100 is better than average, less than 100 is below average.

Pythagorean Formula: A formula for converting a team's Run Differential into a projected win-loss record. The formula is RS^2/(RS^2+RA^2). Teams' actual win-loss records tend to mirror their Pythagorean records, and variances usually can be attributed to luck.

You can improve the accuracy of the Pythagorean formula by using a different exponent (the 2 in the formula). In particular, a sabermetrician named US Patriot discovered that the best exponent can be calculated this way: (RS/G+RA/G)^.285, where RS/G is Runs Scored per Game and RA/G is Runs Allowed per Game. This is called the PythagoPat formula.

Slash Line: Everyone once in a while, one of our writers may refer to a batter's "slash line." He means something like this: .287/.345/.443. The numbers between those slashes are the batter's batting average, on-base average and slugging percentage.

UZR: A fielding system invented by Mitchel Lichtman, similar to John Dewan's Defensive Runs Saved system. Both systems calculate a fielder's range by comparing his plays made in various "vectors" across the baseball diamond to the major league average rate of plays made in those vectors. Both systems also look at other factors such as the effectiveness of outfield throwing, handling bunts and turning double plays.

WAR: Wins Above Replacement. A "win stat" that calculates the number of wins a player contributed to his team above a certain replacement level. WAR is calculated at FanGraphs and Baseball Reference. Though the two implementations vary a bit, they share a common framework that includes a "linear weights" approach to runs created, advanced fielding metrics, leverage for relievers and replacement levels that vary by position. The methodology was established over time at the *Book Blog* (www.insidethebook.com).

wOBA: Introduced in *The Book: Playing the Percentages in Baseball,* by Tom Tango and friends, this is a "linear weight" offensive rating system that is similar to OPS, except that it's better and is set to the scale of on-base percentage.

WPA: Win Probability Added. A system in which each player is given credit toward helping his team win, based on play-by-play data and the impact each specific play has on the team's probability of winning. Read "In All Probability" for more details.

wRC+: Like OPS+ and ERA+, wRC+ is scaled so that 100 is average and a higher number is positive. The "RC" stands for Runs Created, but it's not Bill James' Runs Created. It's a "linear weights" version derived from wOBA.

xFIP: Expected Fielding Independent Pitching. This is an experimental stat that adjusts FIP and "normalizes" the home run component according to the number of fly balls a pitcher allowed.

Who Was That?

Lucas Apostoleris is a baseball fan, aspiring musician and undergraduate student born and raised in New England. His affinity for the New York Yankees often prohibits him from wearing t-shirts of his favorite team into restaurants.

Richard Barbieri has contributed to five Hardball Times Annuals and written more than 200 articles for The Hardball Times website. This almost justifies the huge amount of baseball-related books, memorabilia and clothing he owns. But not quite.

A graduate of Michigan State University, **Brian Borawski** is a CPA who owns his own small business consulting practice as well as other business ventures. A lifelong Tigers fan, Brian writes about his favorite team at Tigerblog (www.tigerblog.net) and he's a member of SABR's Business of Baseball committee.

Craig Calcaterra is the Blogger-in-Chief for HardballTalk at NBC Sports.com. He used to think that gig wouldn't last long, but he's got those suckers at NBC so fooled that now they even put him on TV from time to time. I know, right? Craig lives in a fortified compound in New Albany, Ohio with his daughter Mookie and his son Carlo.

Brian Cartwright started reading Bill James more than 30 years ago while spending his summers as the statistician and head scorer for the host league of the All-American Amateur Baseball Association in Johnstown, Pa. In recent years, he's expanded that early research into his Oliver projection system, which became The Hardball Times Forecasts. For the past 25 years he has worked as a photogrammetrist, compiling digital map products from 3D aerial photography, most recently specializing in creating airport obstruction charts to FAA requirements.

Jon Daly lives with his lovely wife in Manchester, Conn. He is working with former outfielder Milton Bradley on a board game called Toto Recall. It involves trying to get from one musical act to Toto in the fewest moves. Jon last dipped Skoal over five years ago, but misses seeing players with huge gobs of Red Man in their cheeks. He is not a fan of the DH, but is less of a fan of windbreakers on baserunners. Lastly, Jon Daly didn't think it was over when the Germans bombed Pearl Harbor.

John Dewan is the owner of Baseball Info Solutions and a long-time partner with Bill James in the development and publication of baseball statistics.

Joe Distelheim is a recovering newspaperman and the Hardball Times' style and grammar scold. He is an unreconstructed Cubs fan who is sure the Theo Epstein era will produce a World Series contender. He also was optimistic about the Wid Matthews era.

Adam Dorhauer grew up a third-generation Cardinal fan in Missouri. He now lives in Arizona where he occasionally blogs about mathematics and baseball at 3-DBaseball.net.

A Duquesne University graduate, **David Golebiewski** is a freelance writer for BaseballAnalytics.org, FanGraphs, *The Pittsburgh Sports Report* and *Pop City*. His work has also appeared on ESPN.com, Yahoo.com and Rotoworld. David's first baseball memory is slow-as-molasses Sid Bream sliding into home to beat the Pirates in Game seven the 1992 NLCS, though he'd like to have that erased, Men In Black style, if you happen to know where he can find Will Smith and Tommy Lee Jones.

Carolina Bolado Hale is a legal writer by day and a THT copy editor by night. She roots for her hometown Marlins, despite living in New York City with her Mets fan husband. When not watching baseball, she spends her time swimming, cooking, and weaving her little blue bicycle in and out of traffic in Manhattan.

Sam Hendrickson is a junior in Cornell University's College of Arts and Sciences majoring in Statistical Science. He joined The Hardball Times' staff in the summer of 2011, and he continues to work for THT while away at school. As a native of the San Francisco Bay Area, he has been a passionate Oakland A's fan since his childhood.

James Holzhauer recently finished his tour of duty in Las Vegas. He now spends his weekdays traveling the globe in search of thrilling adventures and delicious diet sodas.

Michael A. Humphreys is a licensed attorney at Ernst & Young LLP providing U.S. tax advice regarding cross-border financial transactions. He is also the author of *Wizardry: Baseball's All-Time Greatest Fielders Revealed* (Oxford University Press 2011), which *The Wall Street Journal* proclaimed "the book of the season," and "a representation of the future of statistical sabermetrics."

Brandon Isleib would buy this Annual even if he weren't in it. He is a lawyer with columns on multiple topics and is wrapping up his sixth album and his first book. He is an expert at making his bio sound more impressive than it is.

Frank Jackson was born in Philadelphia in 1950 and was weaned on baseball at Connie Mack Stadium. He now calls Dallas home and has shifted his allegiance to the Texas Rangers but also follows the Grand

Prairie Air Hogs and the Dallas Baptist University Patriots. He has published previous baseball articles in *National Pastime* and *Elysian Fields Quarterly*.

Chris Jaffe is a double threat: history nerd and baseball stat nerd. His book, *Evaluating Baseball's Manager, 1876-2008* won *The Sporting News*-SABR Baseball Research Award for outstanding baseball research.

Brad Johnson is a baseball addict and a statistics junkie who currently resides in Atlanta, Georgia. He played four seasons of injury-plagued baseball at Macalester College from 2006-2009 and has since made the transition to a purely off-the-field existence. Baseball has and always will be the unifying principle of his life.

Mat Kovach lives in Northeast Ohio and proudly owns and wears his bright red 1977 Duane Kuiper jersey. His lifetime curiosity about the spitball started when he read Gaylord Perry's masterpiece, *The Spitter and Me*. To better research the unsanitary wet one, Mat has learned the physics behind a pitched baseball and now probably holds the largest collection of "suspected pitches" of any PITCHf/x enthusiast. To answer the question most asked of him, 'Yes, it still is in the game."

Max Marchi first donned a baseball uniform before he could steadily walk. He watches ballgames daily (sometimes nightly, since he lives in Europe) on MLB.tv and is constantly immersed in baseball data. For all the above he has to thank (or blame) his father, Leo.

Jack Marshall is president of ProEthics, a Virginia-based ethics training and consulting firm. He is a lawyer, speaker, writer and professional ethicist who specializes in training attorneys, business executives and government officials. His ethics commentary blog *Ethics Alarms* (http://www.ethicsalarms.com) explores ethical issues in all aspects of the culture, including sports and whenever possible, baseball, his lifelong passion.

Jeff Moore is the founder of MLBProspectWatch.com and is a former college baseball player and current college baseball coach. Despite being a resident of Baltimore, MD and living within walking distance of Camden Yards, he remains a devout Phillies fan. Jeff's work deals primarily with prospect development, news and rankings.

When **Rob Neyer** isn't sleeping or running, he's writing for *Baseball Nation*.

Harry Pavlidis is a software and web consultant and a partner in Complete Game Consulting. The New Jersey native and Syracuse grad has lived in Chicago, with a Cub obsession, since 1993.

That list might not strike you as out of place, but it is. Outside World War II and 2011, there's never been a decade's worth of World Series-winning managers in the jobs where they won them, and World War II was aided by Joe McCarthy's having won four in a row. The peacetime record for unbroken champion managers is seven, first established in 1926 while 1920s Tris Speaker still managed the Indians, and tied in 1938, 1955, 2004, and 2010. Three other years—1938, 1955 and 2004—are about Yankees managers, making 2010-2011 far more unusual, as Francona is the only repeat winner of the group. Even without McKeon, 2004-2011 would have been a peacetime record.

So obviously it couldn't last. It would have been nice if Guillen and Francona could have kept things together until after the World Series for the sake of this sidebar. After all, I would have done it for them.

- Brandon Isleib

Though this is **Greg Simons'** first time contributing to *The Hardball Times Annual*, he has been writing and editing baseball articles since 1999. An avid Cardinals fan who has lived in "enemy territory" around the country his entire life, he was pleasantly surprised—okay, stunned—by how the 2011 season worked out for St. Louis.

Dave Studenmund learned how to swim in Otsego Lake. See if you can spot the baseball connection.

Matt Swartz is an economist, who finished his Ph.D. at UPenn in 2009. His recent work can be found at FanGraphs, The Hardball Times, and MLB Trade Rumors. He lives in Philadelphia with his wife, Laura.

Steve Treder has been a writer for The Hardball Times since its founding in 2004. He's also been a frequent presenter/contributor to other forums, such as the SABR national convention, the NINE Spring Training Conference, and the Cooperstown Symposium. He roots for the Giants from his home in Sanata Clara, California.

TUCK's toons—commenting on sports, pop culture, politics, and life's other necessities—have appeared at or on or in an array of websites, publications, and other venues for the last 20-mumblemumble years. Having just completed his fourth full season at The Hardball Times, this is his fifth *THT Annual*.

David Wade and his family live in Lexington, KY. He holds a B.A. in History from the University of Kentucky and has contributed to the Hardball Times website since 2010, covering the American League West and providing analysis of rules and players, as well as examining baseball history.

Josh Weinstock is a student at Emory University, studying psychology and computer science. He roots for the Yankees and only feels slightly evil about it.